D0204120

MEN OF BRONZE

In 2007, a Greek helmet of gilded bronze was recovered from Haifa Bay, Israel, during commercial dredging operations. Following conservation by the Israel Antiquities Authority, the helmet emerged as a remarkable example of the type of closed "Corinthian" helmet traditionally associated with Greek hoplites. The helmet had been shaped by a master craftsman from a lost-wax bronze casting less than 2 mm thick, with a riveted nose guard 11 mm thick to provide extra protection to the warrior's face. A glittering coat of gilding covered the exterior, some of which still remains to testify to the wealth and elite status of the helmet's original owner. Rich decoration had been applied with chasing hammers and punches: two snakes curling above the eye-holes; a palmette or peacock's tail on the forehead; and heraldic lions on the cheek-pieces. Such elaborate decoration is rare on Corinthian helmets, though more common in the Archaic period than in the fifth and fourth centuries BC. This spectacular piece of early Greek metalworking is now on display at Israel's National Maritime Museum in Haifa, which overlooks the waters where the helmet lay hidden for some 2600 years. Photo by Warhaftig Venezian Photographers for the Maritime Museum of Haifa. Text description courtesy of Israel Antiquities Authority and Jacob Sharvit.

MEN OF BRONZE

Hoplite Warfare in Ancient Greece

EDITED BY DONALD KAGAN AND GREGORY F. VIGGIANO

PRINCETON UNIVERSITY PRESS PRINCETON AND OXFORD

Published by Princeton University Press, 41 William Street,
Princeton, New Jersey 08540
In the United Kingdom: Princeton University Press, 6 Oxford Street,
Woodstock, Oxfordshire OX20 1TW

press.princeton.edu

Jacket Photograph: Haifa Bay helmet. Photo by Warhaftig Venezian
Photographers for the Maritime Museum of Haifa. Courtesy of
Israel Antiquities Authority and Jacob Sharvit.

Library of Congress Cataloging-in-Publication Data

Men of bronze : hoplite warfare in ancient Greece / edited by Donald Kagan and Gregory F. Viggiano.
pages cm

"The papers published in this volume resulted from a conference on early Greek hoplite warfare held at Yale University in April 2008."

Includes bibliographical references and index.

ISBN 978-0-691-14301-9 (hardcover : alk. paper) 1. Military art and science—Greece—History—To 1500—Congresses. 2. Soldiers—Greece—History—To 1500—Congresses. 3. Greece—History, Military—To 146 B.C.—Congresses. 4. Weapons, Ancient—Greece—Congresses. 5. Armor, Ancient—Greece—Congresses. I. Kagan, Donald, author, editor of compilation. II. Viggiano, Gregory, author, editor of compilation.

U33.M46 2013
355.4'738—dc23

2012047892

British Library Cataloging-in-Publication Data is available

This book has been composed in Garamond Premier Pro

Printed on acid-free paper. ∞

Printed in the United States of America

10 9 8 7 6 5 4 3

CONTENTS

LIST OF FIGURES *vii*

PREFACE *ix*
DONALD KAGAN AND GREGORY F. VIGGIANO

INTRODUCTION *xi*
DONALD KAGAN AND GREGORY F. VIGGIANO

CHAPTER 1 The Hoplite Debate *1*
DONALD KAGAN AND GREGORY F. VIGGIANO

CHAPTER 2 The Arms, Armor, and Iconography of Early Greek Hoplite Warfare *57*
GREGORY F. VIGGIANO AND HANS VAN WEES

CHAPTER 3 Hoplitai/Politai: Refighting Ancient Battles *74*
PAUL CARTLEDGE

CHAPTER 4 Setting the Frame Chronologically *85*
ANTHONY SNODGRASS

CHAPTER 5 Early Greek Infantry Fighting in a Mediterranean Context *95*
KURT A. RAAFLAUB

CHAPTER 6 The Hoplite Revolution and the Rise of the Polis *112*
GREGORY F. VIGGIANO

CHAPTER 7 Hoplite Hell: How Hoplites Fought *134*
PETER KRENTZ

CHAPTER 8 Large Weapons, Small Greeks: The Practical Limitations of Hoplite Weapons and Equipment *157*
ADAM SCHWARTZ

CHAPTER 9 Not Patriots, Not Farmers, Not Amateurs: Greek Soldiers of Fortune and the Origins of Hoplite Warfare *176*
JOHN R. HALE

CHAPTER 10 Can We See the "Hoplite Revolution" on the Ground? Archaeological Landscapes, Material Culture, and Social Status in Early Greece *194*
LIN FOXHALL

CHAPTER 11 Farmers and Hoplites: Models of Historical Development *222*
HANS VAN WEES

CHAPTER 12 The Hoplite Narrative *256*
VICTOR DAVIS HANSON

LIST OF CONTRIBUTORS *277*

INDEX *279*

LIST OF FIGURES

FRONTIS Hoplite helmet *ii*

FIGURE F-1 Map of Ancient Greece *xxiv–xxv*

FIGURE 2-1 Rhodian plate, c. 600 BC *58*

FIGURE 2-2 Line drawings illustrating the use of the hoplite shield *60–61*

FIGURE 2-3 Classical hoplite equipment, Attic tombstone, late fifth century BC *62*

FIGURE 2-4 Protocorinthian aryballos from Lechaion, c. 690 BC *63*

FIGURE 2-5 Protocorinthian aryballos from Perachora, c. 675 BC *64*

FIGURE 2-6 Battle frieze from the Berlin aryballos, Middle Protocorinthian aryballos, c. 650 BC *65*

FIGURE 2-7 Battle frieze from the Macmillan aryballos, Middle Protocorinthian, c. 650 BC *66*

FIGURE 2-8 Chigi vase, Middle Protocorinthian olpe from Veii, c. 640 BC *67*

FIGURE 2-9 Alabastron from Corinth, c. 625 BC *69*

FIGURE 2-10 Middle Corinthian krater, c. 600–575 BC *69*

FIGURE 2-11 Battle in the Highlands of Papua New Guinea *71*

FIGURE 9-1 Amathus bowl *183*

FIGURE 10-1 Keos Survey: numbers of sherds that can be dated to a single century *198*

FIGURE 10-2 Thespiai, southern approaches, Geometric-Archaic sites *203*

FIGURE 10-3 Thespiai, southern approaches, Classical-Hellenistic sites *205*

FIGURE 10-4 Keos Survey, Protogeometric-Geometric sites *206*

FIGURE 10-5 Keos Survey, Archaic-Classical sites *206*

FIGURE 10-6 Methana, Early Iron Age and Archaic sites 208–9

FIGURE 10-7 Methana, Classical sites *210*

FIGURE 10-8 Berbati-Limnes Survey, Geometric-Archaic find spots *211*

FIGURE 10-9 Berbati-Limnes Survey, Classical-Hellenistic find spots *213*

PREFACE

DONALD KAGAN AND GREGORY F. VIGGIANO

The papers published in this volume resulted from a conference on early Greek hoplite warfare held at Yale University in April 2008. The idea for the conference grew out of a spirited debate that took place following a panel presentation at the American Philological Association's annual meeting at San Diego in January 2007, "New Perspectives on Ancient Warfare." From the audience, Gregory Viggiano argued in favor of the theses of Victor Davis Hanson's *The Western Way of War* and *The Other Greeks* against the positions of Peter Krentz and Hans van Wees. These scholars later agreed to continue the debate in a formal setting. Viggiano then discussed with Donald Kagan the unique possibility of having the world's leading scholars on the subject air out their differences face-to-face at Yale. Further discussions with Paul Cartledge helped bring about the Yale conference. The conference panels debated a variety of issues surrounding the hoplite orthodoxy and the attempts to revise it: (1) questions concerning the origins of the tactics and weapons employed by the Greek hoplite (heavily-armed infantryman), fighting in massed formation on behalf of his autonomous city-state (polis); (2) questions about the political, economic, and social significance of the new mode of fighting; and (3) questions regarding the impact hoplite warfare had on Greek culture in general. All these issues have in recent years been at the center of one of the liveliest and most important controversies in the fields of classical studies, ancient political history, and ancient military history.

We want to thank everyone who contributed to the success of the Yale conference, which was held at the Hall of Graduate Studies on the Yale campus. Our first concern in putting together an international workshop was making sure that the scholars would be willing to come and debate, so we are grateful to all the participants for sharing our enthusiasm for the idea. We were very fortunate to have Susan Hennigan's superb assistance in arranging the travel and stays of the participants, and in taking care of all the logistics (meals, programs, audiovisual equipment, etc.) for the event. One scholar remarked that everyone got along so well because there was so much good food to eat. The panel sessions were well attended by faculty, undergraduate and graduate students from Yale, as well as faculty from Sacred Heart University, especially the Department of History. A number of scholars and graduate students from universities as far away as the West Coast came to attend the sessions, in addition to people from the New Haven community. Therefore, we owe special thanks to International Security Studies (ISS) at Yale, as well as the Yale Classics Department; for without their kind generosity there would not have been any conference. We make special mention of Ted Bromund of ISS and his dedication to the project, and the support of Professor Christina Kraus, the chair of Yale Classics. Rob Tempio of Princeton University Press has given invaluable support and inspiration at every stage in the production of this volume.

INTRODUCTION

DONALD KAGAN AND GREGORY F. VIGGIANO

The study of ancient Greek warfare begins with what scholars might infer about fighting techniques from the archaeological remains of the late Bronze Age (1600–1100 BC). It appears that, similarly to the situation in the contemporary Near East, the war chariot was the main offensive arm of the king's military. But during the chaos that attended the collapse of Bronze Age civilization, infantry seems to have become capable of breaking the charges of the palace's chariot forces. The ensuing period from the eleventh to the eighth century, which scholars often call the Dark Age,[1] is notable to the military historian for the introduction of iron weapons. However, to the ancient Greeks themselves this was the Age of Heroes, and the bard Homer was its most famous witness.

At its most basic level, the hoplite orthodoxy argues that critical changes took place in Greek warfare around 700 BC that had fundamental importance for the rise of the polis. Prior to that "revolution" in arms, armor, and tactics, the aristocrats dominated in war. They fought at long range with missiles and in close combat as individual "heroic" champions with swords. The main equipment they used included the short throwing spear, an open-face helmet, a round single-grip shield, and a sword. Since these heroic figures bore the brunt of battle in the protection of their communities, it followed that they had a monopoly on political power as well. The semidivine heroes of the *Iliad* give the most brilliant expression of the fighting style and ethos of this period. For example, there are the famous duels between the champions Menelaus and Paris, Hector and Ajax, and Achilles and Hector above all. Hector learned to be valiant always and fight far out in front of the others. Achilles was taught always to be the best and to be preeminent among men in order to win his own godlike glory. The consensus placed Homer in the second half of the eighth century and claimed that the *Iliad* provided an idealistic depiction of warfare before the polis.

But warfare changed with the introduction of the double-grip hoplite shield and the tight formation of the phalanx at the beginning of the seventh century. In the new fighting style the warrior substituted for his pair of throwing spears a single heavy thrusting spear. The new shield, which was much wider, heavier, and more difficult to wield than a single-grip model, only made sense in close ranks, where one soldier sought cover for his vulnerable right-hand side behind the redundant half of the shield of the neighbor on his right. Therefore, soldiers arranged themselves in orderly rows with about three feet between them and in columns about (usually) eight men deep. The phalanx required many more men and much greater cohesion than the open-order combat of the Dark Age. It was essential for each soldier to keep his assigned place in the formation in order to provide cover for his neighbor and to make it possible for his side to break through the opposing ranks of the enemy.

Whereas in the Dark Age the common soldiers fought as an unorganized, open, and fluid mass subordinate to the elite, the hoplites played a decisive role in the phalanx. Unlike the heroes in Homer's epics who strive for individual honor, the hoplites in the martial poet Tyrtaeus' elegies must hold their ground in the phalanx to win glory for the polis. The phalanx was unique in ancient warfare in that each soldier was a citizen of his polis and provided his own arms to fight in its defense. The hoplites comprised a middling stratum,[2] wealthy enough to afford their own panoply, but lacking the divine ancestry and large landholdings of the elite aristocrats. On the other hand, the newfound military importance of the hoplite put him in a position to demand greater political power from the aristocrat who now fought at his side and in an identical fashion. In some poleis, the hoplites supported an aristocrat as a tyrant to overthrow his oppressive peers. The hoplite revolution brought an end to narrow aristocracies and paved the way for the creation of democracy. The American Philological Association panel and discussion showed how closely the hoplite orthodoxy has become associated with the work of Victor Davis Hanson over the past two decades.[3] Notwithstanding the undeniable influence that Hanson's *Western Way of War* and *The Other Greeks* have exercised in the field, the grand hoplite narrative has in fact taken shape over the course of more than 150 years.[4]

George Grote in the 1846–1856 edition of his famous twelve-volume *History of Greece* gave the first full expression of what was to become the hoplite orthodoxy. His narrative of the rise of the polis includes all the hallmarks of the later narrative. A revolution in military tactics occurred at the same time as the political change in Greece from monarchies to republics. During this period the numbers and importance of the middling farmers rose for manning the ranks of the phalanx. At the same time, the Greeks transformed their political institutions from heroic kingdoms to narrow oligarchies in which eligibility for high office was based on a claim to divine or heroic descent. Grote considered the *Iliad* useless for historical accuracy, but a reliable witness of Greek warfare and society in the ninth century. The champions of Homer had enjoyed armor and fighting skills far superior to those of the common soldier in both long-range and close combat. During the eighth and seventh centuries, on the other hand, the phalanx became the driving force behind the political and cultural as well as the military developments in Greece. The hoplite, having an assigned place and duty in battle, transformed what had been an unorganized and ineffective mass into a disciplined group striving for a common victory.

The discipline of the phalanx, Grote points out, trained citizen soldiers to understand their civil and social rights and duties by making the polis their primary source of obligation. The common citizen did not acquire much political power at first. But the intellectual revolution that accompanied the emergence of the first oligarchies had trained the Greek mind not to accept a subordinate role in the polis. A second revolution took place in the seventh century when in some poleis the hoplites supported a tyrant to break the power of the exclusive aristocracies. The age of tyrants marked the rise of the citizens of middling property, who might back a despot for a limited time. However, by the seventh century there was universal hatred for the idea of permanent hereditary rule, which worked against the principles of the polis. For Grote, the hoplite citizen soldier as an autonomous middling farmer effected the major political and social changes in the early polis. Hoplites, in whose mind the idea of equality was instilled through training for the phalanx, determined the direction of Sparta as well; but the Spartans avoided tyranny and had a subject population to work their fields. Athens, on the other hand, may have remained an oligarchy after Solon, but he gave the middling farmers enough power to oppose the aristocrats.

The field of scientific archaeology has made some of the most significant contributions to the hoplite question in the twentieth century. For example, Wolfgang Helbig in 1909 used the earliest datable finds of hoplite arms and equipment to determine when the Greeks first adopted the phalanx. The appearance of the phalanx in art, the Protocorinthian Chigi vase in particular, gave the basis for Martin Nilsson's 1929 classic statement of the hoplite orthodoxy.[5] Lorimer in 1947 became the first English scholar to employ the monuments, vase painting above all, to date the origins of the phalanx. Grote had had to rely on Homer's epics alone to discuss early Greek warfare and the rise of the polis. Scholars could now use actual finds not only to be more precise in their arguments. They could also provide the framework for more nuanced arguments and disagreements. Nilsson, for instance, thought that the martial elegies of Tyrtaeus were inconclusive for proving the existence of the phalanx in the seventh century, since the poet mentions foremost fighters (*promachoi*), reminiscent of Homer's champions. However, the round shields of the figures depicted in art and of the lead figurines dedicated at the temple of Artemis Orthia in Sparta seemed to leave no doubt.[6] The phalanx may have taken time to develop; perhaps the transition lasted until the period of the Chigi vase in the mid-seventh century. But the census classes of Solon showed that the principle of having citizens provide their own arms to defend the polis in return for political privileges was well established by the early sixth century. Therefore, Nilsson reasoned that the practice must have begun much earlier.

For Lorimer, the single structural change involving the replacement of the round shield slung on a telamon marked the end of the long-range fighting of the eighth century.[7] The substitution of the single central handgrip for a central armband of metal (*porpax*), through which the hoplite thrust his forearm up to the elbow, and a handgrip (*antilabe*), which he grasped with his left hand, just inside the rim of the shield, created a shield suited for only one form of combat. Whereas the single-grip shield had been easy to maneuver, the double-grip shield restricted the hoplite to the close confines of the phalanx, which afforded him maximum protection as long as the entire formation stood firm. The new formation led the soldier to substitute the throwing spears of the Homeric hero for a single heavy thrusting spear as well. Lorimer dated this momentous change to about 675 BC. She argued that artists in Corinth and Athens at the time depicted hoplite equipment and the tight formations that characterized the phalanx. In addition, there were the lead figurines of the warriors in hoplite armor from Sparta to confirm the date. Lorimer accounted for the anomalies of the lyric poets by positing that they drew on epic diction and that the extant poems contained interpolations.

Like Grote, both Nilsson and Lorimer had connected the early Greek tyrants with the emergence of the hoplite middle class. A seminal study in 1956 by Andrewes, moreover, applied to the tyrants Aristotle's theory on how political systems in Greece changed from aristocracies to democracies. The most important element was military strength. The early poleis relied on cavalry to defend the state, which only the wealthy could afford. The next stage involved the middling farmers possessing enough wealth to provide their own hoplite arms. The final stage of democracy and naval supremacy gave political power to those who rowed the ships, the landless poor. Prior to that, however, Andrewes argued that hoplite revolutions played a crucial role in transferring power from narrow aristocracies to a much broader class of citizens. Aristotle himself does not say that the hoplites backed the tyrants in their struggles against their peers, but Andrewes found it impossible that no connection existed. He details the rise of the tyrants from Cypselus to Peisistratus. To compete with its neighbors and stave off civil war, polis after polis adopted the phalanx and yielded power to the citizens that manned its ranks. The hoplites drove the tyrants from power and created broad oligarchies in their place.

The seminal work of Snodgrass in the 1960s began the first sustained attack on the hoplite orthodoxy, which has continued to the present. He concluded from his study of arms and armor, much of which was unknown to previous scholars, that the adoption of hoplite equipment was a "long drawn out, piecemeal process," and that the double-grip shield did *not* imply the phalanx. Furthermore, the fully developed phalanx did not appear until after 650 BC—too late to play a role in the Greek tyrants' rise to power and the other revolutionary changes associated with the emergence of the polis. In fact, the aristocrats filled the first phalanxes, and it was only with prodding that the middling farmers joined them; hoplite *equipment* had been adopted by aristocratic warriors before the later development of hoplite *tactics*. The demands of the mature phalanx with its denser formations forced the elite in time to recruit reluctant commoners to help fill its ranks.

In response to Snodgrass's thesis of gradual phalanx development, Cartledge proposed some nuances to the sudden-change theory. He emphasized above all the nature of the double-grip shield and its severe limitations for the *un*organized tactics of prehoplite warfare. The shield's design indicates that the Greeks created it with a new style of fighting in mind, and that a change in tactics toward organized, hand-to-hand fighting had already been taking place. Frontal protection became valued over mobility and protection in the flank and rear. On the other hand, Cartledge finds the visual and literary evidence too insecure to ground an argument. Instead, the whole gamut of economic, social, and political changes during the last half of the eighth and first half of the seventh century explains the broad revolutionary effects that the phalanx had on the polis. Relative overpopulation and land hunger placed a premium on arable land and forced the aristocrats to relinquish their military dominance. Success in war now depended on fielding the greatest possible number of men for a battle. Yet the number of farmers wealthy enough to equip themselves still represented less than one-half of the state's citizen population. Between 675 and 650 all the major poleis had adopted the phalanx to secure and to defend the maximum possible amount of land.

There has been a tendency over the last thirty years to try to dismantle just about every aspect of the hoplite orthodoxy through the gradualist position. On the one hand, some gradualists maintain that the hoplite reform came early in the seventh century. But they deny that the hoplite class could have had the confidence and experience necessary to bring about revolutionary political and social change. A great deal of the revisionism, however, has challenged the very idea that any significant reform took place in infantry tactics in the archaic period. Krentz has argued not only that hoplite warfare went through a long period of transition before reaching the classic formation described by Thucydides. He contends that throughout its history hoplite battle involved much looser deployments of troops and emphasized the hand-to-hand combat of individual fighters and small groups in the front rank. Hoplites did not seek to maintain the cohesion of their line, while breaking apart the phalanx of the enemy. The warriors kept much greater spacing between themselves and their neighbors than the traditional narrative imagines. Krentz has also challenged the notion that the two-handled hoplite shield was much less maneuverable than the single-grip model.

In this spirit, an important 1989 paper by Cawkwell explains that the orthodox model for how hoplites fought in the phalanx is far too rigid. Troops may have advanced into battle in tight formation, but in actual combat they would have required more room to fight. The phalanx must have been flexible for hoplites to employ the type of fighting skills the sources such as Xenophon and Plato mention that they developed in training and used in battle. The iconography also indicates open-order fighting and more variety in style and technique than some of the literary sources suggest.

One of the most thoroughgoing critiques of the hoplite orthodoxy has come from van Wees. He argues for a third position among the gradualists and sudden-change theorists. For him the hoplite phalanx had much less cohesion and evolved over a much longer period of time than the two to three generations for which most gradualists allow. There was no great change in tactics from the eighth to the seventh century, and, in as far as Homer can be taken as an historical witness, the fighting in the *Iliad* bears a striking resemblance to the picture one may reconstruct for the early phalanx. Perhaps mass combat, and not massed hoplite warfare per se, undermined the power of the aristocracy and initiated political and social change.

The theses in *The Western Way of War* and *The Other Greeks* reassert the tradition of the grand hoplite narrative. In *The Western Way of War* Hanson provides from the ancient sources the most graphic account available of what the experience of battle might have been like in the phalanx. He finds unconvincing the attempts to prove that the fighting was fluid, and that individual skirmishing took place instead of collective pushing. His argument stresses the cumbersomeness and sheer weight of hoplite equipment, especially the helmet and the shield. Mass infantry fighting in some less rigid form probably existed before the complete adoption of the panoply. But it is inconceivable that men fought in hoplite equipment in *any* formation apart from the phalanx. The battles were brief and depended on the shock collision of heavy infantry with the aim of breaking apart the enemy phalanx or shoving it off the battlefield. The idea was to limit the killing through a decisive contest, so that the farmer-citizen-soldiers could return to their fields with minimal disruption to their way of life. Conflicts became highly ritualized pitched battles fought over farmland. The main elements included the tight deployment of troops, an accumulation of shields, and the charge across a level field, the crashing together of opposing lines, the push and collapse, and the rout. Hoplite warfare remained virtually unchanged for more than two centuries, from its start until the fifth century.

Two remarkable features set Hanson's account of the hoplite apart from that of his predecessors. First is the idea that the preference of Western armies for decisive battle began with the archaic Greek phalanx. Second, he identifies intensive farming as the main element that shaped the character and values of the middling group that provided its own arms to fight for the polis. These *georgoi* in turn shaped the ideals, institutions, and culture that gave rise to the polis. Unlike any prior civilization, the culture of the Greek polis combined citizen militias with the rule of law. That involved having a broad middle class of independent small landowners that met in assemblies where the votes of these nonelite determined laws, and foreign and domestic policy. These smallholders gained in status as population growth in the ninth and eighth centuries forced an agricultural revolution. Labor- intensive farming of marginal lands came to replace the Dark Age pastoral economy. This required a growth in private landownership, which motivated *georgoi* to assume the risks involved in cultivating land that was unproductive using traditional farming techniques. These farmers created the ritual of hoplite warfare to decide disputes in a manner that did not contradict their agrarian agenda. The *georgoi* and their agrarian ideology became the driving force behind the hoplite revolution during the early seventh century.

Scholars in the past decade have heavily criticized the hoplite orthodoxy in general and Hanson's model of it in particular. For example, some gradualists have lowered the date for the introduction of the phalanx to well into the fifth century. They claim that the equipment hoplites wore was much lighter and that the warriors were more mobile than the traditional narrative contends. In addition, revisionists have challenged the idea that opposing phalanxes maintained rigid formations and crashed into one another in the opening stages of battle. They have attempted to refute the notion of collective pushing. Another form of revisionism has used Homer's *Iliad* to argue that a protophalanx existed in the eighth century, hence lessening the significance of the adoption of hoplite arms and armor in the seventh. According to this thinking, there was no hoplite reform, let alone revolution, to effect changes in the political and social structures of the polis. Van Wees, in his examination of the iconography and the elegies of Tyrtaeus, sees much continuity in the fluid style of the protophalanx and early hoplite warfare. Therefore, the hoplites did not suddenly emerge in the seventh century to support the tyrants and break the backs of the aristocracy. In fact, the warfare and the politics of the Greek state remained very much an elite affair until the fifth century. And when change occurred, the hoplites had little to do with bringing it about. Foxhall has employed survey archaeology, moreover, to deny that a substantial middle stratum of farmers living on the land even existed as early as the orthodoxy believes. She has suggested that the countryside remained largely devoid of settlement far into the sixth century in most places, while the best lands were farmed from nucleated settlements, with little evidence for intensive agricultural practices or the cultivation of marginal lands.

The idea for the Yale conference was to bring together the leading scholars from both the orthodox and the revisionist' schools of thought to examine the current state of the field, which is at a crucial turning point. A number of outcomes were possible. First, everyone could have agreed that in fact the traditional hoplite narrative was correct and that there was no need to rewrite the textbooks. Second, the revisionists might have convinced the orthodox that their model had fatal flaws. In that case, we all might have either conceded that we could know little or nothing about the rise of the Greek state and culture, or at least that the early hoplites had nothing to do with it. Or we could have agreed that what we thought we knew was wrong, but an alternative theory could better explain the major movements of the formative period in classical Greece. Third, a great synthesis might have combined key elements of the traditional model with new insights to produce a higher truth. Despite the recognition of much common ground among the participants, none of those things happened at the conference. Instead of working toward a consensus, each side sharpened its position in response to the latest research. The keynote speaker, Paul Cartledge, set up the framework for the debate that took place. Panels were arranged in pairs of scholars to discuss essential aspects of the orthodoxy in light of recent attempts to revise it. In the first panel, Kurt Raaflaub and Gregory Viggiano considered whether or not a hoplite revolution transformed the Greek world in the seventh century. In the second, Peter Krentz and Adam Schwartz presented opposing views about the significance of hoplite arms and weapons and how hoplites fought in archaic Greece. In the third, Anthony Snodgrass responded to current theories on early Greek warfare, and John Hale considered the role of Greek mercenaries in the seventh and sixth centuries. In the fourth panel, Hans van Wees critiqued *The Other Greeks* and argued that an agrarian revolution did occur but centuries later than Hanson envisions. For his part, Victor Davis Hanson explained why the orthodoxy is still orthodox. The conference concluded on the third day with a roundtable discussion, which covered topics debated over the three-day event. The chapters in this volume represent the rewritten drafts of the papers presented at Yale, though they often contain the original spirit in which they were delivered.

Paul Cartledge notes and welcomes the shift in the study of ancient Greek warfare over the past thirty years from the "narrowly technical" toward sociopolitical issues and approaches. The study is no longer an abstract exercise in military history, but a "totalizing history of war and society." He reveals how his own views on the subject have and have not changed since his first major publication in the field. Cartledge also sets the stage for all the essays that follow by examining several key issues. What were the causally related variables or factors that link the evolution of the hoplite phenomenon to the rise of the polis? Do the notorious source(s) problems prevent us from understanding them? What tipped mass fighting over into phalanx fighting? Was there a hoplite "ideology"? Did Aristotle get it right when he posited a connection between warfare and political development in Greece? In light of the nature of the sources, Cartledge emphasizes the strength of a theoretical approach to the inextricable link between warfare and politics in the Greek state.

Anthony Snodgrass lays out the chronological framework for the history of hoplite warfare. He discusses the impact the studies of Homeric warfare have had on the orthodoxy since the groundbreaking work of Latacz. Indeed there was a "hoplite reform" despite the contention of many scholars that fighting in the *Iliad* and hoplite fighting are one and the same. He considers the problems posed by the evidence of iconography and archaeology, especially the dedications of actual armor in the sanctuaries at Olympia and Delphi, and the various philological and historical approaches that scholars have applied to the literary sources. Snodgrass also notes the potential significance that Nagy's evolutionary model for the creation of the Homeric epics has when historians use the poems to understand archaic warfare and its relation to the polis. He reaffirms his gradualist position on the hoplite reform, while he underscores the often overlooked common ground among scholars involved in the debate. The persistence of the hoplite in the Hellenistic period defies any simple reading of the phenomenon.

Most of the paper Kurt Raaflaub gave at Yale on the nature of mass fighting in the *Iliad* has already been published, but we are happy to include in this volume his ideas on early Greek infantry fighting in a Mediterranean context. Raaflaub sees the emergence of hoplite warfare as part of a long interactive process associated with the rise of the polis. The polis, its institutions and political thought, evolved from the eighth to the fifth century along with its military practices. Despite intense interaction with the states of the Near East, the Greeks of the eighth and seventh centuries developed the phalanx independent of Oriental influence. Raaflaub examines Assyrian and Persian armies, arms, and armor as well as formation and tactics to determine that there is no prior model for the equipment and style of Greek infantry. Having no Near Eastern example, the Greeks must have invented the double-grip shield for use in the already existing phalanx for which the hoplite was always intended. Therefore, Raaflaub rejects van Wees's picture of Homeric and early hoplite fighting as open-order combat by many small and loosely organized bands of warriors. On the other hand, he is a "gradualist" in that he believes that the phalanx developed over too long a period of time and in conjunction with too many other factors to bring about a "revolution" in warfare or society.

Gregory Viggiano contests the idea that any argument put forth in recent years is reason to push down the traditional date for the origin of the polis or to reject the hoplite orthodoxy. He states the basic elements of the theory that have their beginnings in Aristotle's *Politics*, and then tests their merit against revisionist claims. Viggiano finds unconvincing the notion that the Greeks would have invented equipment such as the double-grip shield and Corinthian helmet for a purpose that contradicted their design. The change in fighting style and tactics provides the best explanation for the transformation in Greek values from the epic poetry of Homer to the martial elegies of Tyrtaeus, as well as the rise of the early tyrants. Viggiano contests the recent claims that the evidence of survey archaeology has disproved the existence of a substantial class of middling farmers in the late eighth and seventh centuries. He argues that, despite gaps in the evidence, a clear picture of how the polis emerged can be made without omitting or contradicting any of the evidence from the literary sources, archaeology, and inscriptions.

Peter Krentz takes aim at *The Western Way of War*'s highly influential and popular conception of how hoplites fought. He critiques the orthodox view—especially the version of Hanson—concerning the actual weight of the hoplite panoply, which he argues was far lighter than the traditional estimate of about seventy pounds. Krentz proposes a different interpretation of the various stages of hoplite battle, such as the hoplite charge into battle. In his view, the evidence supports neither the picture of a mass collision between armies nor the concept of a mass pushing of troops or the account of the *othismos* as a rugby scrum. Revisionists such as van Wees deny that hoplites fought in tight formation until the phalanx of the fifth century. But instead Krentz contends that the phalanx did not consist exclusively of hoplites before Marathon. He suggests, however, that even in the fifth century hoplites never actually fought in a cohesive formation.

Adam Schwartz places the equipment of the hoplite in a very different light than Krentz. The defining elements of the hoplite were the spear and, above all, the double-grip shield. Other items of the panoply were subject to much change and innovation over the centuries, but the shield and spear remained essentially unaltered throughout the entire hoplite era. Schwartz reasons that the Greeks maintained the shield's original design—circular, concave, and about one meter in diameter—because it was preeminently suited for a specific purpose, fighting in tight formation in a phalanx. He gives a detailed analysis of the Etruscan Bomarzo shield, one of the few hoplite type shields to survive more or less intact from antiquity; and he assesses a number of key sources bearing out the burden and cumbersomeness of the hoplite shield, to conclude that its weight, shape, and sheer size in terms of surface area made the shield particularly unwieldy. Schwartz's discussion of comparable body shields used until recently by the riot squad of the Danish police adds a new dimension to the debate over tactics and the handling of shields in combat. He also points out that skeletal remains from Greek antiquity demonstrate that hoplites were significantly smaller in relation to their equipment than modern Western men, which has consequences for the tacit assumption that they are fully comparable.

John Hale disagrees with the two main theories proposed for the context within which hoplite warfare emerged. For Hale neither the leisured class of aristocrats who vied for high social and political status within the polis nor the middling citizen soldiers who defended their farmland provide the origins of archaic Greek arms and tactics. Instead he suggests looking for the first hoplites fighting as mercenaries in the service of Eastern monarchs in areas such as Syria, Egypt, and Babylon. These soldiers of fortune fought in search of gain and glory, not to defend a civic ideology or ethos. Hale finds evidence for his thesis in lyric poetry and in inscriptions, pottery, and the remains of hoplite armor discovered outside Greece. He calls mercenary service the "Main Event" of Greek military history in the seventh century, in contrast to the sporadic battles between poleis. The nearest historical parallel to the soldiers of fortune of the archaic period are the Viking armies of the ninth and tenth centuries AD. The

Greek raiders and mercenaries not only fought for hard-won riches but also created new communities around the Mediterranean world.

A major part of the debate regarding the rise of the polis turns on whether scholars believe a substantial class of small middling farmers emerged by the late eighth century. Perhaps more than any other scholar, Hanson has emphasized the rise of small independent farmers, who could afford hoplite arms and thereby serve in the phalanx and demand a greater share of political power. On the other hand, van Wees places the evolution of the phalanx and the emergence of the "middling" farmer-hoplite in the late sixth century; before that date, he argues, only members of the wealthy elite served as hoplites, and they fought alongside less well-off light infantry in open and fluid battle order. A recent approach to this question has been the study of the Greek landscape through archaeological survey, a technique that has been developing over the past thirty years. We invited Lin Foxhall to consider what site survey might reveal about the appearance of a new class of small farmers in archaic Greece. Foxhall gives a brief history of the discipline and explains the strengths and limitations of using its findings for historical analysis. Her study of eight survey projects across Greece, including Boeotia, the Argolid, Laconia, and Pylos, focuses on data for the Geometric through the Hellenistic periods. She suggests that the archaeology tells us a different story than the historical record of citizens, soldiers, and property owners. The survey data show the rise of a densely populated countryside of small-scale farmers neither in the eighth century nor, universally, in the sixth century.

Hans van Wees critiques the grand narrative of *The Other Greeks* and argues that it is wrong in important respects. Hanson presents the social and economic changes in the eighth century that took place with the rise of the independent yeoman farmer and his culture of agrarianism as the driving force behind the political and military history of Greece. But van Wees believes that something like the rise of small farmers occurred about two centuries later than Hanson relates. However, from the middle of the eighth century there was a class of elite leisured landowners that did not work the land themselves but supervised the toil of a large lower class of hired laborers and slaves. This era of gentlemen farmers who comprised the top 15–20 percent of society and competed with each other for status lasted for about two centuries. When the yeomen farmers emerged after the mid-sixth century, they joined the leisure class in the hoplite militia. Van Wees doubts that the small farmers brought about a revolution when they joined the phalanx, but, if they did effect political changes, it was in conjunction with the rise of the trireme rowers.

Victor Hanson defends the orthodoxy in light of the various attempts to revise it over the past twenty years, especially those of Krentz and van Wees. He points out the inherent difficulties in studying the origins and nature of hoplite battle since there are few prose accounts of set battles before Marathon. For example, the material the scholar must use includes Homer and lyric poetry, which makes it difficult to distinguish realistic portrayal from metaphorical expression. On the other hand, scenes painted on vases are hard to date and make it nearly impossible to depict a phalanx in proper perspective. Nevertheless, over the last two centuries of classical scholarship the "grand hoplite narrative" has emerged in most histories of Greece. Hanson suggests that the success of the orthodoxy is due to the fact that it best reflects the evidence for phalanx fighting and the larger social, economic, and political role of the hoplite. He responds to the recent attacks on the view that hoplites formed a distinct middle class, the claims that hoplites fought in an open and fluid formation, and that the phalanx was a late development. In addition, he examines the debate over the weight of hoplite equipment and key elements of the traditional battle narrative such as the attack on the run, the shock collision, and the role of mass and density in deciding hoplite contests.

The editors of this volume do not expect the following essays to end the debate over hoplite arms, tactics, and their relationship to the rise of the polis and the larger issues of Greek culture. On the contrary, the idea behind the conference was to determine how well the orthodoxy holds up in light of recent research and criticism. Second, we wanted to challenge revisionists to clarify their position with a view to offering a coherent paradigm as a more plausible alternative, if possible. In that respect, the objective is to initiate a debate that should result in either a restatement of the traditional narrative or nothing short of rewriting the history of the early Greek polis.

Notes

1. The term Dark Age has itself become controversial, and some scholars prefer Early Iron Age instead.

2. The phrase "middle stratum" is perhaps preferable to the word "class" as in "middle class," which has unfortunate anachronistic connotations. Nonetheless, "middle" or "middling" class is used frequently and need not cause difficulty as long as the ancient context is understood.

3. See the preface.

4. The following is a brief sketch of the history of the hoplite orthodoxy. Chapter 1 contains a much more extensive and detailed treatment of the issues debated in this volume; chapter 2 gives a discussion of the iconography.

5. Helbig in 1911 was the first historian to show and discuss the Chigi vase in connection with the phalanx.

6. Subsequent work has indicated that the lead figurines do not date to the eighth century, or even the earlier seventh century (although Nilsson and Lorimer did not know that). Boardman down-dated the complex stratigraphy of the site in 1963 (J. Boardman, 1963, "Artemis Orthia and Chronology," *BSA* 58:1–7), and this down-dating is generally accepted. Critically, he notes that none of the lead figurines of warriors is earlier than the middle of the seventh century (Boardman 1963:7). The hoplite warriors appear in Lead I, II, and III, some found below, but most found above the sand level (probably representing a major flood on the site) dated by Boardman to 570/560 BCE (A. Wace, 1929, The lead figurines, pp. 249–84 in R. M. Dawkins, "The Sanctuary of Artemis Orthia," *JHS* Suppl. 5, London). This means that the vast majority of the "hoplite" figurines are probably to be dated to the sixth century BCE. Also scholars using these warriors as early evidence for hoplites should note that there are also archers (e.g., Dawkins 1929: pl. CLXXXIII.16, 17) and light armed soldiers (e.g., Dawkins 1929: pl. CLXXXIII.18, 26) among the leads, even as early as Lead I, and continuing through the whole sequence.

7. NB Sylvia Benton, 1953, *BSA* 48:340, pointed out that certain blazons on the front of a shield had to be shown one way and only one way—the right way—up, which implied an unalterable grip on the shield.

MEN OF BRONZE

Greece and Western Asia Minor
Macedon
Mt. Olympus
Aegean Sea
Ionian Gulf
Thessaly
Thermopylae Pass
Euboea
Chalcis
Eretria
Aetolia
Delphi
Boeotia
Thebes
Athens
Megara
Sicyon
Corinth
Peloponnese
Argos
Olympia
Arcadia
Messenia
Sparta
Pylos
Laconia
Mediterranean Sea
battle sites
miles 0 50 100 150
kilometers 0 50 100 150

Thessaly
Thermopylae Pass
Euboea
Thrace
Leuctra (371 BC)
Chalcis
Lelantine Plain
Eretria
Aetolia
Delphi
Thebes
Coronea (447 and 394 BC)
Boeotia
Plataea (479 BC)
Megara
Athens
Sicyon
Nemea (394 BC)
Corinth
Peloponnese
Argos
Sepeia (494 BC)
Olympia
Mantinea
(418 and 362 BC)
Hysiae (669 BC)
Marathon
(490 BC)
Arcadia
Delium
(424 BC)
Tegea (560 BC)
Tanagra (457 BC)
Messenia
Sparta
Pylos
Laconia
Sphacteria (425 BC)
Lesbos
Aegean Sea
Samos
Miletus
Caria
Delos
Naxos
Lycia
Rhodes
Crete
Mediterranean Sea

CHAPTER 1

The Hoplite Debate

DONALD KAGAN AND GREGORY F. VIGGIANO

The study of war has not only interested military historians from the ancient world to the modern day; many scholars have held that the way in which societies organize for and fight war lies at the foundation of civilization itself. Cultural historian Lewis Mumford has remarked:

> War was not a mere residue of more common primitive forms of aggression.... In all its typical aspects, its discipline, its drill, its handling of large masses of men as units, in its destructive assaults en masse, in its heroic sacrifices, its final destructions, exterminations, seizures, enslavements, war was rather the special invention of civilization: its ultimate drama.[1]

For generations scholars have examined the relationship between how the Greeks fought and their social, political, and cultural development. The Greeks themselves considered war both part of the nature of human society and terrible. "Peace," Plato said, "is merely a name; in truth an undeclared war always exists by nature among all city-states."[2] The poet Pindar (F 15) called battle "a sweet thing to him who does not know it, but to him who has made trial of it, it is a thing of fear." For Thucydides war was "a violent schoolmaster."[3] Aristotle, in his *Politics* (1297b16–28), on the other hand, provided the first known theory to connect the evolution of the political institutions of the polis with the rise of heavy infantry. Modern historians of ancient Greece in turn have developed a grand narrative. This "orthodoxy" explains the rise of the early polis in terms of a dramatic change or "revolution" in arms, armor, and tactics; the military revolution became a driving force behind the emergence of the characteristic political and social structures of the Greek state. A central part of the thesis is that the change in fighting style was directly related to recent innovations in arms and armor. Second, the phalanx depended on the weight and the cohesion of heavily armed men who employed "shock" tactics in brief but decisive battles. Third, it has been critical to identify the greatest number of hoplites with a middling group within the polis, which had the wealth to provide its own arms. Fourth, this middling group transformed Greek values.

By the mid-nineteenth century, scholars had already recognized the basic elements of what was to become the hoplite orthodoxy. For example, George Grote, in his famous twelve-volume *History of Greece*, made a sharp distinction between heroic and historical Greece, and the emergence of the hoplite warrior marked the point of departure for the beginning of the age of history. "The mode of fighting among the Homeric heroes is not less different from the historical times, than the material of which their arms were composed." He described the essentials of the ancient Greek phalanx:

> The Hoplites, or heavy-armed infantry of historical Greece, maintained a close order and well-dressed line, charging the enemy with their spears protended at even distance, and coming thus to close conflict without breaking their rank: there were special troops, bowmen, slingers, etc. armed with missiles, but the hoplite had no weapon to employ in this manner.[4]

Grote compared the close-in approach of the hoplites with the long-range fighting style of the legendary figures of Homer:

> The heroes of the *Iliad* and *Odyssey*, on the contrary, habitually employ the spear as a missile, which they launch with tremendous force: each of them is mounted in his war-chariot, drawn by two horses, . . . advancing in his chariot at full speed, in front of his own soldiers, he hurls his spear against the enemy: sometimes, indeed, he will fight on foot, and hand to hand, but the chariot is near to receive him if he chooses, or to ensure his retreat. The mass of the Greeks and Trojans, coming forward to the charge, without any regular step or evenly-maintained line, make their attack in the same way by hurling their spears.[5]

The champions of Homer enjoy several advantages over the common soldier: "Every man is protected by shield, helmet, breastplate, and greaves: but the armor of the chiefs is greatly superior to that of the common men, while they themselves are both stronger and more expert in the use of their weapons." The weapons used included a long sword, a short dagger, and two throwing spears, which on occasion could be employed as a thrusting weapon. The few bowmen are rare exceptions to the equipment and tactics described above.

The loose battle array of the *Iliad* contrasts sharply with the inflexible ranks that attacked the Persian king at Plataea or Cunaxa, and "illustrates forcibly the general difference between heroic and historical Greece. While in the former, a few splendid figures stand forward, in prominent relief, the remainder being a mere unorganized and ineffective mass, —in the latter, these units have been combined into a system, in which every man, officer and soldier, has his assigned place and duty, and the victory, when gained is the joint work of all." With the introduction of the phalanx, the difference in the role of the individual and the military effectiveness of the group is remarkable: "preeminent individual prowess is indeed materially abridged, if not wholly excluded, —no man can do more than maintain his station in the line: but on the other hand, the grand purposes, aggressive or defensive, for which alone arms are taken up, become more assured and easy, and long-sighted combinations of the general are rendered for the first time practicable when he has a disciplined body of men to obey him."[6]

Grote derives his picture of how the classical phalanx engaged the enemy from Thucydides' account of the battle of Mantinea:

> It was the natural tendency of all Grecian armies, when coming into conflict, to march not exactly forward, but somewhat aslant to the right. The soldiers on the extreme right of both armies set the example of such inclination, in order to avoid exposing their own unshielded side; while for the same reason every man along the line took care to keep close to the shield of his right hand neighbor. We see from hence that, with equal numbers, the right was not merely the post of honor, but also of comparative safety. So it proved on the present occasion, even the Lacedaemonian discipline being noway exempt from this cause of disturbance. Though the Lacedaemonian front, from their superior numbers, was more extended than that of the enemy, still their right files did not think themselves safe without slanting still farther to the right, and thus outflanked greatly the Athenians on the opposite left wing; while on the opposite side the Mantineans who formed the right wing, from the same disposition to keep the left shoulder forward, outflanked, though not in so great a degree, the Skiritae and Brasideians on the Lacedaemonian left.[7]

From its start, the proto-orthodoxy posited a close link between military, political, and cultural developments in archaic Greece. Grote details the political revolution—the substitution of one or more temporary and accountable magistrates in the place of the Homeric king—that accompanied the emergence of the hoplite phalanx.

> It was always an oligarchy which arose on the defeasance of the heroic kingdom: the age of the democratical movement was yet far distant, and the condition of the people—the general body of freemen—was not immediately altered, either for better or worse, by the revolution; the small number of privileged persons, among whom the kingly attributes were distributed and put in rotation, being those nearest in rank to the king himself, perhaps members of the same large gens with him, pretending to a common divine or heroic descent.[8]

The composition of Homer's epics and the celebration of the first Olympiad were essential for dating the revolution. Consistent with Herodotus, who placed Homer four hundred years before his own time, Grote assigned the composition of the Homeric *Iliad* and *Odyssey* to the second half of the ninth century—the poems having reached their final form before the first Olympiad of 776 BC.[9] His method for dating the poems reflects the great debate surrounding the Homeric Question in the nineteenth century. He argues against Wolf and Lachmann's contention that the epics represented an amalgamation of many distinct poems brought about by Peisistratus in the middle of the sixth century in Athens. Lachmann, for instance, identified sixteen separate songs in the first twenty-two books of the *Iliad*. Grote, on the other hand, contends that, far from producing an original poem, Peisistratus simply enhanced the solemnity of the Great Panathenaic festival by selecting, among the divergences of rhapsodes in different parts of Greece, "that order of text which intelligent men could approve as a return to the pure and pristine *Iliad*."[10] For Grote, the poems have no historical value, because they contain no verifiable evidence. However, since Homer reflects the contemporary society of the ninth century, the *Iliad* and *Odyssey* have immense value for assessing the achievements of the Greeks in the eighth and seventh centuries. Civil society makes a transition similar to that of the military: "we pass from Herakles, Theseus, Jason, Achilles, to Solon, Pythagoras, and Perikles—from 'the shepherd of his people,' (to use the phrase in which Homer depicts the good side of the heroic king,) to the legislator who introduces, and the statesman who maintains, a preconcerted system by which willing citizens consent to bind themselves."[11]

There was for Grote a parallel between the individual who knows his place in the hoplite phalanx and the citizen who understands his predetermined rights and duties in the social order according to established principles. The result is that even without commanding individual talent, "the whole community is so trained as to be able to maintain its course under inferior leaders."[12] Grote had no doubt about the significance of these developments: "the military organization of the Grecian republic is an element of the greatest importance in respect to the conspicuous part they have played in human affairs,— their superiority in this respect being hardly less striking than it is in many others."[13] In the historical period following the first Olympiad, the emergence of hoplite warfare had dramatic implications for many of the major cities in Greece, especially Argos, Sparta, Corinth, Sicyon, Megara, and eventually Athens.

Grote envisioned the political transformation in the Greek world from the heroic kingdoms to the poleis taking place through two revolutions. The first involved the intellectual revolution[14] that accompanied the transition from the world of legend to the development of history.[15] This upheaval resulted in the emergence of oligarchies out of the divine kingships, and demonstrated to Grote the progressive character of the Greek mind and all its superiority over the "stationary and unimproving" Oriental mind.[16] The abolition of kingship came about through natural change and without violence. For example, sometimes the royal lineage died out or, after the death of the king, the king's son became acknowledged as archon only, or he gave way to a prytanis chosen from the aristocrats. These primitive oligarchies were common throughout Greek cities and colonies of the seventh century, and they represent an advance on heroic government. The primary characteristic of the heroic age had been "the omnipotence of private force, tempered and guided by family sympathies, and the practical nullity of that collective sovereign afterwards called *The City*,—who in historical Greece becomes the central and paramount source of obligation."[17] Grote describes the rise of the poleis: "Though they [the poleis] had little immediate tendency to benefit the mass of the freemen, yet when we compare them with the antecedent heroic government, they indicate an important advance,—the first adoption of a deliberate and preconceived system in the management of public affairs." The polis invented the concept of citizenship, the rule of law, and the accountability of elected magistrates.

> [The poleis] exhibit the first evidences of new and important political ideas in the Greek mind,—the separation of legislative and executive powers; the former vested in a collective body, not merely deliberating but finally deciding,—while the latter is confided to temporary individual magistrates, responsible to that body at the end of their period in office. We are first introduced to a community of citizens, according to the definition of Aristotle,—men qualified, and thinking themselves qualified, to take turns in command and obedience: the collective sovereign, called The City, is thus constituted.[18]

The second revolution took place when the usurpers Grote calls Despots subverted the first oligarchies. This period, which contemporary scholars refer to as the age of tyrants, involved "the gradual rise of the small proprietors and town-artisans" and "was marked by the substitution of heavy-armed infantry in place of cavalry."[19]

Cities such as Corinth, Sicyon, and Megara required the figure of the despot, backed by the hoplites, to bring about decisive political change.[20] This period occurred during the progress of the seventh and sixth centuries, with the expansion of wealth, power, and population. Grote distinguishes these early despots from those of later periods by their use of armed force. Notwithstanding the benefits tyrannies brought to their respective poleis, the age of the despots worked against the principles of the City: "this rooted antipathy to a permanent hereditary ruler stood apart as a sentiment almost unanimous."[21] The hoplites enabled the tyrant to overthrow the narrow oligarchies of the seventh century in many cities. These figures made possible the transition to broader oligarchies and later to democracies; but the tyrant's success could only be temporary.[22]

> The people by their armed aid had enabled him [the despot] to overthrow the existing rulers . . . but they acquired no political rights and no increased securities for themselves.[23] . . . The rise of these despots on the ruins of the previous oligarchies was, in appearance, a return to the principles of the heroic age,—the restoration of a government of personal will in place of that systematic arrangement known as the City. But the Greek mind had so far outgrown those early principles, that no new government founded thereupon could meet with willing acquiescence, except under some temporary excitement.[24]

The military force in the early days had been in the hands of the great landowners in the form of cavalry; these include the primitive oligarchical militia in seventh- and sixth-century Chalkis and Eretria on Euboea.[25] But such states lacked the egalitarian ethos and the rule of law that Grote associates with heavy infantry. He remarks on the Thessalians, "Breeding the finest horses in Greece, they were distinguished for their excellence as cavalry; but their infantry is little noticed, nor do the Thessalian cities seem to have possessed that congregation of free and tolerably equal citizens, each master of his own arms, out of whom the ranks of the hoplites were constituted." On the other hand the rise of the polis saw the emergence of the independent farmer.

> As a general rule, every Greek city-community included in its population, independent of bought slaves, the three elements above noticed,—considerable

> land proprietors with rustic dependents, small self-working proprietors, and town-artisans,—the three elements being found everywhere in different proportions. But the progress of Greece, from the seventh century B.C. downwards, tended continually to elevate the comparative importance of the two latter, while in those early days the ascendency of the former was at its maximum, and altered only to decline.

The development of a new class of middling farmers led to the transformation of the political and social relations in the Greek world. "All the changes which we are able to trace in the Grecian communities tended to break up the close and exclusive oligarchies with which our first historical knowledge commences, and to conduct them either to oligarchies rather more open, embracing all men of a certain amount of property, or else to democracies. But the transition in both cases was usually attained through the interlude of the despot."[26]

At Sparta, the transition to oligarchy came about through the reforms of Lycurgus. Grote attributed the superiority of the Spartan state to the superiority it obtained in warfare by the period 600–547. The arms of the Spartans did not differ from those of other Greek hoplites so much as the superior discipline that Lycurgus had instituted in the ninth century.[27] "Her military force was at that time superior to that of any of the rest, in a degree much greater than it afterwards came to be; Athens in particular was far short of the height which she afterwards reached."[28] Their perfect training, individual and collective in the face of the discontent of its subject population, the perioikoi and helots, set the Spartans apart from the other Greeks.[29] "It is in this universal schooling, training, and drilling, imposed alike upon boys and men, youths and virgins, rich and poor, that the distinctive attribute of Sparta is to be sought, —not in her laws or political constitution." This emphasis is on the military reform. "Lykurgus (or the individual to whom this system is owing, whoever he was) is the founder of a warlike brotherhood rather than the lawgiver of a political community."[30]

Grote denied that the Lykurgean system included a redistribution of land on principles of exact or approximate equality, and provisions for maintaining the number of distinct and equal lots. Instead, he attributes the egalitarian ethos of Sparta to, among other things, the training of its hoplites. "The Lykurgean discipline tended forcibly to suggest to men's minds the *idea* of equality among the citizens."[31] The connection of fighting tactics to the transformation of Greek values has been crucial to the hoplite narrative; in particular, the substitution of the Homeric goal of the individual striving for preeminence by the stress on warriors playing an equal role in battle.

In Athens, the essential powers of the state remained in the hands of the oligarchy after the reforms of Solon, "but the oligarchy which he established was very different from the unmitigated oligarchy which he found, so teeming with oppression and so destitute of redress."[32] Solon did not seek to overthrow the aristocrats but simply to check their power, and "it was he who first gave to the citizens of middling property and to the general mass, a *locus standi* against the eupatrids."[33] The hoplites broke the monopoly on political power that the aristocracy of birth had held.

The position of Grote on the transition from monarchy to oligarchy in the eighth century prefigures the hoplite orthodoxy of the twentieth century. He argued for a causal link between the emergence of the hoplite warrior of middling status and the rise of the Greek polis, and established the relevance of the Homeric Question for both ideas. Grote also made the connection between the early tyrants and the new form of heavy infantry. Furthermore, the concepts of citizenship and equality have their source in the new tactics as well.

In his book *Thucydides and the History of His Age*, published in 1911, Grundy discussed the Greek art of war in the fifth century in the light of the main historical sources of the period. For example, Herodotus (7.9) has the Persian general Mardonius explain the nature of hoplite warfare in a quip to the king Xerxes: "The Greeks are accustomed to wage wars in the most senseless way due to their ignorance and foolishness. When they have declared war against each other, they look for the fairest and most level ground, and then go there and fight, so that the victors depart with heavy casualties; I won't even begin to speak about the losers, for they are completely wiped out." These remarks indicate that the Greeks confined their battles to the flat alluvial plains of the country. In another passage, Herodotus (5.49) suggests both the Greek view of Persian warfare and how the Persians themselves fought; here Aristagoras, in his attempt to obtain help from Athens in the Ionian revolt, observed, "The Persians use neither the shield nor spear, and can be easily conquered." Aristagoras' comments suggest that light-armed troops played an insignificant role in classical Greek warfare. In fact, the success or failure of the hoplite force determined the fate of the battle.

The reliance on heavy infantry led Grundy to two paradoxes in the Greek art of war. First, whereas hoplites must fight on level ground, about four-fifths of the territory of Greece is mountainous and rugged. If one excludes the broad plains of Thessaly and Boeotia, the proportion of arable soil is even smaller. Grundy saw the issue complicated by the fact that the weight of the hoplite panoply was "very great." "Even a single Greek hoplite would have found himself in great difficulties on such ground. As for a body of hoplites, its position would have been hopeless. Its efficiency was absolutely dependent upon the maintenance of a peculiarly close and precise formation, such as it could not possibly have maintained for an advance of even ten yards over such ground as this." So, why did the Greeks choose a form of warfare ill suited for their country? Second, the strength of the natural positions of the country allowed states of all sizes to build nearly impregnable fortresses. Yet the Greek army was remarkably incapable of attacking such places. This was true of Sparta above all—a polis that dominated neighbors whose towns had an unassailable acropolis. How could the Greek state fail to advance the art of siege warfare against walled towns? And how could an enemy be confident that the citizens of the polis he invaded would march out to fight him in the alluvial plains, the only type of ground suited for hoplite tactics?

The answers to both questions are related. The system of fighting used until the last third of the fifth century could assume that invaded peoples would not retreat behind the absolute safety and security of their walls and defenses. This was a matter of pride and necessity. Of course the enemy could not operate upon the rugged land that made up most of the territory they had invaded, nor could they capture by assault the impregnable sites. But, since just 22 percent of the land was cultivable, the destruction of cereals, vines, and olive trees could bring disaster.[34] "The fruit and cereal crops must be saved at all costs, either by facing the enemy in the field or by prompt submission to his demands. The only other alternative was safety in the present, and starvation, or something like it in the near future."[35] The invaded polis had no choice but to place in the field hoplite against hoplite, because light-armed troops were useless under these circumstances. A negative example proves the rule. When Archidamus led the Peloponnesian army into Attica at the beginning of the Great War, the Spartans were certain that the Athenians had only two choices. They must either fight outside the walls and be destroyed, or have their fields devastated and be forced to surrender. The entire operation would take at most three years to succeed. Pericles' decision to refuse battle and to allow the ravaging of the crops, trees, and vines not only marked a radical departure from the traditional system of fighting. The strategy, for which the Athenians heavily criticized Pericles in their humiliation at not engaging the enemy in a showdown battle, altered the evolution of the art of war in Greece.

What was this traditional way of fighting? In addition to the battle narratives in the historians of the fifth century, Grundy's classic description of the nature of hoplite battle drew on the recent finds of weapons and armor. The pieces of equipment he examined, the helmet in particular, had impressed him with how heavy they were.[36] This influenced the way in which Grundy understood close fighting in the phalanx. "The hoplite force relied on two qualities, solidity and weight. The men were placed very close together in the ranks, and that tendency which Thucydides notices for each man to shelter his right side under the shield of the man next to him would promote the closeness of the order in the phalanx. The aim was to present to the enemy an unbroken line of shields and breastplates."[37]

Besides the importance of maintaining a close order of men, the phalanx depended for its effectiveness on the sheer weight and thrust it could bring to bear in its initial collision with the enemy. Here Grundy saw an analogy with a scrimmage in the Rugby game of football.

> Under ordinary circumstances the hoplite force advanced into battle in a compact mass, probably at the slow step, breaking, it may be, into a run in the last few yards of advance. When it came into contact with the enemy, it relied in the first instance on shock tactics, that is to say, on the weight put into the first onset and developed in the subsequent thrust. The principle was very much the same as that followed by the forwards in a scrimmage at the Rugby game of football.[38]

The depth of the phalanx contributed to its overall weight and thrust. Thucydides (5.68) suggests that the ranks were usually eight men deep, but much deeper phalanxes were possible. For example, the Athenians at Delium used a phalanx eight men deep; however, the Thebans were in ranks twenty-five shields deep. In their first engagement at Syracuse (6.67), each of the two bodies of Athenian troops had a depth of eight ranks, whereas the Syracusans drew up sixteen rows of men. The idea in any event was to overwhelm and drive the enemy phalanx back or to break it apart.

On the other hand, a general might hesitate to stack his troops deeper than usual because he would fear that the enemy might outflank him. For instance, the fear of a flank attack caused the Athenians to extend their front at Marathon so as to equal that of the Persians, even though this meant having a depth of just a few rows in the center (6.111). At Mantinea, Agis took precautions against the Mantineans outflanking his left wing. "One thing is evident. The hoplite phalanx was regarded as peculiarly vulnerable on either flank. The first care of a general seems to have been to make his front at least equal in length to that of the enemy."[39] For this reason it seems that the Greek generals of the fifth century avoided using the flank attack as an offensive strategy of their own. Should a general detach a body of hoplites from the rest of the line to attack the flank of the enemy, he might expose the flanks of his own army. "The general theory governing the fighting of large armies seems to have been that the most effective way of defeating an enemy was to roll up his line from one or both wings, not by attack in flank, but by defeating one, or, if possible, both of the opposing wings."[40] Therefore, Greek tactics throughout the fifth century demanded that armies place their most efficient elements on the wings. The Spartans were especially adept at using their best troops on the right, with the intent of rolling up the enemy's line from left to right. "The idea . . . seems to have been that the best troops should be on the right, with the intent to roll up the enemy's line from left to right; but inasmuch as the enemy would be pretty certain to attempt the same design, the second best troops were placed on the left in order to prevent him from being successful in this manoeuvre."[41]

In addition to the nonemployment of a flank attack, Grundy found it remarkable that Greek generals at the time did not use a reserve force in battle. The only exception Thucydides mentions is when Nicias retained half his hoplite army for such use in the first engagement at Syracuse. Grundy explains, "It is probable that the theory prevailed that it was all-important to put as much weight as possible into the first charge: that it was on the effect of this that the battle was decided; and therefore that it was necessary to throw into it the weight of the whole available force."[42] This idea could motivate a general to run the risk of exposing his flanks by overloading one of his wings. At Leuctra, for example, the brilliant Theban general Epaminondas stacked his top fighters fifty deep on his own left; having defeated the best troops on the right wing of the enemy, he more easily rolled up the rest of the line.

Grundy emphasizes the overall simplicity of hoplite tactics throughout the fifth century, conditioned as they were by "the nature of the country and the circumstances of the population." "In point of fact the hoplite phalanx was of such a nature," Grundy reasons, "that any great elaboration of tactical design in its evolution was practically impossible. Manoeuvres which a less heavily-armed soldier could have carried out would have been impossible for them."[43] Grundy attributes the nature of hoplite tactics not only to the geography of Greece; he points out that the Greek infantryman was a citizen above all, neither a mercenary nor a professional soldier.

Poverty explains in part why the Greek states did not employ mercenary forces. In addition, the democratic idea that those who profit from the existence of the state should serve it in their persons traces its origins to the time when the army was the political assembly. "The fifth-century democrat converted the idea. Aforetime a man had been a citizen because he was a soldier; now he was a soldier because he was a citizen."[44] The fact that most citizens were farmers affected their attitudes toward war.

> Such armies are not adapted for prolonged continuous service. Hence Greek wars tended to be short and sharp, and . . . decisive. Thucydides ascribes their brevity to lack of capital. That no doubt has something to do with it. But the dislike of the agriculturalist to be called away from home during a season of harvest, which inasmuch as it included the gathering of the produce of cereals, vines, and olives, extended throughout the greater part of the campaigning season, had a great deal more to do with it; and the fact . . . that a state when invaded, had either by submission or battle, to bring matters to a prompt decision, was most of all responsible for this feature of Greek warfare.[45]

The use of farmer-citizen-soldiers in the armies of the poleis discouraged the employment of mercenaries. But the situation changed throughout the course of the twenty-seven years of the Great War. The periods of activity were longer and the service more exacting than any prior experience of Greek citizen armies.

> Year after year the cultivator was called from his land, and the trader from his business, at the very season at which his presence was most needed, if the land and the business were not to go to ruin. It was naturally suggested to the mind of the Greek that it was better to support the burden of paying someone to take your place in the field rather than be robbed altogether of the means of supporting yourself.[46]

Thus, the idea of employing mercenary troops took root and grew rapidly during the last third of the fifth century. A direct impetus to employing professional soldiers on land came from an experience early in the war. The Athenians operating in Chalcidice learned to appreciate "the fact that light-armed could be employed effectively against hoplites, and, generally speaking, that a hoplite force by itself was not by any means invincible or invaluable on ground and under circumstances which differed fundamentally from those which were characteristic of Greece."[47] In Aetolia, moreover, light-armed troops had inflicted a humiliating defeat on Athenian hoplites after they forced them to act on ground unsuited to their usual tactics and without the assistance of an efficient light-armed force. Indeed, Demosthenes' experience fighting in northwest Greece had so impressed him with the potential of lightly armed troops that he made use of them against the Spartans at Sphakteria.

Yet Athens still did not have any regularly organized light infantry at the time of the battle of Delium. The main role of light-armed fighters in the fifth century was to protect the flanks of advancing heavy infantry. In any event it was not until the fourth century, with the rising importance of light infantry, peltasts in particular, that Greek armies became much more professional. Grundy argues that it would have been very difficult to persuade a citizen soldier to lighten his defensive armor to attain greater freedom of movement. He would have been reluctant to give up the personal security afforded by his heavy armor, since he did not regard war as his trade. Besides, "the Greek soldier, like other soldiers, was tenacious of old ideas. Could he have put them off, he might have put off his armour. But he clung to the one, and so he clung to the other."[48]

It took fighting outside Greece to initiate developments in the use of efficient light-armed troops; experience with peoples such as the Thracians inspired the development of the more mobile and highly trained bodies of peltasts who served under commanders like Iphikrates in the early fourth century. But in the Great War itself, "the Greek had never discovered that there was a sort of mean between the extremes of his heavy-armed and light-armed troops, and sufficient offensive and defensive armour to cope successfully, or, at any rate, with a fair hope of success, with bodies of hoplite troops."[49] It was only in situations in which hoplites were caught on ground unsuited for their formation and tactics that light-armed troops decided a battle.

Cavalry also played a limited part in the wars of Greece. For the most part cavalry seems to have been of considerable value only if used in combination with heavy infantry. Horsemen could guard the flanks of an army and protect or harass scattered bands of foragers. But cavalry of the fifth century was not good enough to employ against a hoplite force in close formation; however, having cavalry provided distinct advantages over an enemy without it. For example, the Athenian cavalry at Mantinea helped them overcome the fierce resistance of the Corinthian hoplites. Grundy explains that the weakness of cavalry among the Greeks had a different set of causes than was the case with light infantry. Above all, the very poor pasturage of the greater part of Greece makes it especially unsuited for horse breeding.

> The Greeks could not develop the cavalry because they had not the horses. Apart from that, an effective cavalry force such as would be required against hoplites, is very expensive to maintain. Its existence is only possible under two conditions: abundance of good horses, and a numerous and hardy nobility of sufficient wealth to supply themselves with horses and the horseman's panoply.[50]

As a result only Thessaly and Boeotia developed effective cavalry. And despite the significance of their cavalry the Boeotians themselves considered the horseman inferior in importance to the hoplite. It was only under the military genius of Philip of Macedon and his son Alexander that a Greek state created a force of heavy cavalry from the nobility of the country. Alexander realized the possibility of using heavy cavalry as the striking force of his army, "while the phalanx, more heavily armed than ever, and consequently more immobile, should give solidarity and rigidity to the resisting power of the line of battle." On the other hand, Grundy points out the ultimate supremacy of the phalanx for the Greek art of war. "The effectiveness of the cavalry declined as its personnel became scattered over the whole of Western Asia, but the phalanx remained as the type of all that men thought best in the military art, until it was wiped out of existence by those soldiers who combined all the best fighting qualities of the hoplite and the peltasts, the Roman legionaries."[51]

The analysis of Grundy has heavily influenced discussions of the classical hoplite phalanx for the past century. Hoplite armies comprised farmer-citizen-soldiers. The strategy and tactics of the phalanx required little training, because it relied on heavy infantry and did not integrate efficient light-armed troops or cavalry. The Greeks emphasized the cohesion of their ranks in their massed charge into battle; solidity and weight were of paramount importance in the initial collision with the enemy; in order to break apart and put to rout the opposing phalanx, a general attempted to roll up the enemy line from left to right by deploying his best troops on the right wing. Significant changes in the art of war occurred during the course of the last third of the fifth century, but did not fully take shape until the generation after Thucydides wrote. Later scholars would apply Grundy's description of hoplite warfare to the fighting that took place two centuries before the battle of Marathon.

Since Grote first published his *History of Greece*, scholars have come to view the development of the phalanx as the driving force of a revolution not only in military tactics; they argue that the hoplite helped shape the political and social structures of the early polis as well as transform the cultural values of archaic Greece. The progress of modern scientific archaeology has been one of the key factors in advancing the idea. For example, at about the time Grundy was writing, Wolfgang Helbig in 1909 used datable finds of hoplite arms and equipment, above all the shield, to ask when the Greeks first adopted their characteristic style of close combat in the phalanx. In addition, Helbig provided the first analysis of the Chigi vase. It was Martin Nilsson, however, who first gave the classic statement of the hoplite orthodoxy in his seminal article of 1929.

The appearance of the phalanx in art, especially the Protocorinthian Chigi vase, provides the basis for Nilsson's thesis. The Chigi vase shows two lines of hoplite warriors attacking with raised spears, preceded by a flute player. The vase provides a lower limit for the introduction of mature hoplite tactics by the second half of the seventh century and a vivid contrast with Homeric warfare:

> In Homer, we find a completely different battle style. . . . The aristocrats have the role of champions, the battle finds its resolution in solo combats and the large mass of soldiers only provides a background, being given but little consideration. Even when the epic poets exaggerate the deeds and importance of single individuals for the sake of their aristocratic public, there remains an unbridgeable difference.[52]

Nilsson points out the difficulty in setting a higher date for the phalanx because of the problems involved in interpreting the poetry of Tyrtaeus. On the one hand, Wilamowitz[53] had argued that Tyrtaeus describes the large tower shield found in Homer, "cover with the wide belly of the shield your thighs and shins below and your chest and shoulders." On these grounds he rejected passages that mention the round hoplite shield and the phalanx as interpolations.[54] It was also problematic that the elegies mention the Homeric word for champions, *promachoi*. But Nilsson saw the possibility that this term had taken on a new meaning in the context of Tyrtaeus. And even if Tyrtaeus indicates that the Spartans had not yet adopted the phalanx by the Second Messenian War,[55] Nilsson cites the unambiguous shields that turned up in the then unpublished Spartan excavations of 1906–1910 and 1924–1927 discussed by Woodward:[56]

> I do not remember a single shield of the figure-8 type on any Geometric or archaic work of art. . . . In these periods the Spartan shield was essentially the round one. . . . I cannot believe that the countless lead figurines of soldiers would all have a round shield unless this was the normal type; and the only clay votive model of a shield, found in 1926, is also circular; I think we may regard the collective evidence as convincing against the figure-8 shield having been in use at Sparta in post-Mycenaean times.

Nilsson accepted that the evidence of Tyrtaeus was inconclusive. The passages in question may "refer to a time when the hoplite tactic was still in its state of development and that the tightly packed phalanx first began to supersede the champions gradually." In fact, a stage of transition seemed likely.[57]

> The hoplite tactic was introduced in the seventh century at the latest, or more rightly was finalized. Because, of course, it did not step into the world in one go, but first people gradually learned how to repel and to dash to the ground the impetuous attack of the champions using the close-serried ranks of hoplites, a transition, which, as an aside, we can with some good will infer from a few passages of Tyrtaios. Maybe it did not go so dramatically as long ago, when the knightly army of Charles the Bold was annihilated by the pikes of the Swiss, rather, the new tactic developed more gradually and proved its superiority.[58]

Yet the sheer numbers of the archaeological finds left no doubt that the tower shield had never been in use at Dorian Sparta. If anything, the apparent Homeric references to it must illustrate the poetic language that Tyrtaeus had inherited from the epic. Nilsson used Solon and the timocracy he set up in Athens to fix the introduction of the hoplite phalanx high in the seventh century. He saw the economic demand placed on the hoplite to provide his own panoply as the forerunner to the thinking behind Solon's census classes. "The principle of the demarcation of political rights and responsibilities according to wealth was so naturalized and well developed in the first years of the 6th century that Solon could employ it for a real timocracy in his division of classes."[59]

Nilsson could not imagine the Greek polis without the introduction of the phalanx. "The Greek polis in its distinctiveness is inconceivable without the hoplite army, where the solidarity, of which the polis availed itself, was manifestly inculcated in the citizens."[60] The phalanx made cavalry obsolete and caused a breakdown in the aristocratic state. Nilsson draws an analogy between the feudal knight and the Homeric champion. The invention of gunpowder destroyed the military effectiveness of the knight and transformed the values of the medieval world. Likewise, hoplite tactics introduced a change in mentality and made futile the heroes' drive for preeminence and individual glory.[61] Nilsson describes how the new military order signaled the downfall of the aristocracy and gave birth to the short-lived tyrannies. "One can imagine the course of events, so that the hoplites, with the economic boom, gradually becoming more and more powerful and fit for military service, initially together with the unpropertied mass, turned against the aristocracy and accepted the tyranny, since it supported their economic interests; but then, with growing importance and increasing political-confidence, strongly contributed to preparing the end of tyranny." The immediate benefactors of the fall of the tyrants, however, are not the poor. "Not the mass, but rather the middle class has raked in the profit. In the motherland—for this is the concern here—a fully developed democracy does not follow from the rule of the tyrants, but a more or less moderate one, which corresponds to the interests of the middle class." Nilsson extends his thinking even into the early years of the democracy. "We see this, for example, in Korinth and in Athens, where the so-called rule of the Areopagus lasted for about 20 years after the Persian war; it is little known, but it demonstrates the moderate way that we must necessarily attribute to a middle class fit for military service."[62] The work of Nilsson anticipates the recent debate about Tyrtaeus and the idea that the development of phalanx tactics may have been gradual. But for Nilsson, much like Grote, the rise of the polis was inconceivable without the emergence of the middling hoplites, their values, and their ability to demand political change.

The first expression of the hoplite orthodoxy in English was the classic article by Lorimer in 1947.[63] She dated the adoption of hoplite tactics and equipment in the most important poleis to the first half of the seventh century. The introduction of the new shield caused an immediate change in tactics.

> The momentous change from the essentially long-range fighting of the eighth century involved a single structural alteration in the round shield slung on a telamon which was in vogue, an alteration designed to make it afford the maximum of protection to troops in close formation so long as they stood firm; in the case of flight it became a mere encumbrance and was fairly likely to be thrown away. The change consisted in the substitution for the single central hand-grip previously in use of a central arm-band of metal (*porpax*), through which the bearer thrust his arm up to the elbow, and a hand-grip (*antilabe*), at the end of the horizontal diameter and just within the rim, which he grasped with his left hand.[64]

Lorimer described the range of motion of the new shield as "extremely restricted" compared with the single-grip shield, which "unless exceptionally large" was "easily manoeuvrable," and "could be used to cover practically any part of the owner's body. The hoplite shield gave complete protection only to the left side of the trunk, with consequences when the phalanx went into action which Thucydides has made familiar to everyone." She outlined the hoplite revolution, linking the arms, armor, and tactics together:

> Hoplite equipment is inseparably linked with the phalanx and its tactics, whose whole object was to supersede long-range fighting by a hand-to-hand encounter waged by an unbreakable line uniformly armed. The essence of the change consisted for attack, in the substitution of the single heavy thrusting-spears and, for defence, in the adoption of the *porpax* shield with its powerful inducement to keep the line and not turn tail. Greaves extended protection

> without being a serious encumbrance; the Corinthian helmet superseded, not quite universally, forms which might offer a hand-hold to an opponent in the now inevitable close-locked struggle. These items form a natural and logical combination, and they all appear on one of our earliest monuments, the Perachora aryballos.[65]

The finds of arms and armor made it possible to date the revolution. Mainland Greece made the transition to hoplite armor right after the enigmatic Lelantine War, to which its adoption is somehow related. The single-grip shield had been current in Attica in the late eighth century, but the Hymettus amphora demonstrated that hoplite equipment had superseded it before 675. This change coincided with the earliest established date in Athenian history, the beginning of the list of annual archons. "It would seem that the consummation of the political revolution and the reorganization of the army were approximately contemporary, as is natural enough." In Sparta, the lead figurines of warriors from the sanctuary of Artemis Orthia seemed to confirm her hypothesis. "That part of the series which runs concurrently with Laconian I pottery—i.e., from circa 700 to circa 635, in which they are pretty numerous—has almost without exception hoplite equipment so far as it can be checked."[66] Furthermore, in Corinth, the Protocorinthian aryballos from Perachora dated to the same period.

The famous Chigi vase offered the strongest case for the revolution in tactics (see fig. 2-8). This Protocorinthian olpe, or pitcher, of the finest period, which falls shortly after 650, "succeeds in depicting the hoplite phalanx going into action," and furnishes "an indubitable representation of hoplite forces . . . the earliest reliable evidence for the new armature."[67] Lorimer explains:

> Each side forms a hoplite phalanx, pure and unadulterated; every article of hoplite equipment is plainly represented and nothing alien to it, and the tactics—hand-to-hand fighting with the spear—are purely hoplite. Of the ranks on the point of engaging each man holds his spear above his head, nearly horizontal but with a slight downward tilt, poised ready, not for a throw, but for a thrust at the exposed throat of an opponent.[68]

Some of the essential points include the presence of hoplite equipment, the shield with the *porpax* and *antilabe*, the metal corselet and greaves, and the fighting style, close combat with a thrusting instead of a throwing spear. Both the equipment and fighting style mark off the hoplite from the previous Geometric warrior armed with a single-grip shield, leather corselet, no greaves, and a javelin. The flutist in his purple tunic is significant. For example, Thucydides mentions in his description of the battle of Mantinea (5.70) that the Spartans used a flute player to help maintain their formation as they marched into battle. But Lorimer denies that the warriors on the Chigi vase carry more than one spear; she claims that the five redundant spears above the men are either "ghost spears" or are meant to be thrown.

> As the number of the ghost spears and of the combatants are the same, the artist presumably intended to indicate that each man had a second spear in reserve, carried by his servant, but at the same time to suggest by the extra spears

> the presence of a larger body of troops than he could depict without marring the clarity of his composition, a device which is completely successful.[69]

The early and complete change in the foot soldier's equipment, which produced a revolution in tactics and political change in the polis, transformed Greek art in the seventh century as well. Yet the transformation in art was more gradual and reveals itself in stages from the Perachora aryballos to the Chigi olpe.

The transformation from Geometric art marks the rise of the individual, which one may see on the Perachora aryballos. "There too struggling to assert itself against it [the individual], was the consciousness, equally foreign to Geometric art, that the battle engaged was between two organized fronts, in which the individual was merged in the fighting force of his *polis*. On the Berlin aryballos and in the relevant zone of the Chigi olpe the heroic motive is wholly discarded in favour of an exaltation of contemporary life, perhaps the glorification of the hoplite class." Lorimer posits that the tyrants such as Cypselus found the most reliable support of their power in the hoplite class. "What exportable monument could be better fitted than the olpe to spread the impression of Corinthian military power in the highest circles abroad?"[70] The link with the tyrants places Lorimer in the tradition of Grote and Nilsson.

Like Grote, Lorimer saw the revolution in hoplite tactics and the related political changes as sudden and dramatic. They marked not only a change in warfare and political structures but also the rise of the individual and a transformation of the Homeric ethos. The key element is the substitution of the single- for the double-grip shield, which required a close formation. She placed her confidence in dating the changes to the representations in Greek vase painting, the Chigi vase above all.

The modern textbook description of how the early Greek state emerged in the wake of a hoplite revolution took shape in the decade following Lorimer's work. This is evident in the work of Adcock and Andrewes. For his part Adcock built on the earlier work of Grundy, as well as Lorimer; he connected the Greek art of war in the seventh century with the social and political culture of the early polis. "We can see, as Aristotle saw, that it [the art of war] is in part a cause, and in part an effect, of the political development of the city-state."[71] It is unclear how the art was attained, but the epic tradition showed the historical Greeks that war had become something far different from fighting in the heroic age. War for the polis in the seventh century "meant the uniting of the armed men of the community to fight shoulder to shoulder, with an orderly, integrated valour."[72] Adcock disregards those parts of Greece which were not poleis; they not only had different forms of political organization; they also had different ways of fighting. Absent are the clashes of heroes or aristocrats. Instead of striving for individual glory, the hoplite must identify his interests with those of the polis. "This [the characteristic political form of the Greeks and its characteristic method of waging war] was to place in the field as its one dominant arm a phalanx of hoplites. I use phalanx as a convenient word to describe a body of infantry drawn up in close order in several ranks which are also close together."[73] Adcock emphasizes the importance of the shield for hoplites: "the character and use of their shields were of the essence of their fighting in battle." The aim of battle was to achieve a decisive victory through a contest of heavy infantry.

> The effectiveness of the phalanx depends in part on skill in fighting by those in the front rank, and in part on the physical and moral support of the lines behind them. The two opposing phalanxes meet each other with clash of shield on shield and blow of spear against spear. Their momentum is increased by the impetus of the charge that precedes their meeting. If the first clash is not decisive by the superior weight and thrust of the one phalanx over the other, the fighting goes on. The later ranks supply fighters as those before them fall. At last one side gains the upper hand. Then the other phalanx breaks and takes to flight and the battle is won and lost.

Hoplite battles depend on the shock collision of heavy infantry, exclude light-armed and missile troops, follow certain "rules" of engagement, tend to be fought by farmers over farmland, and are limited in extent and decisive. "The normal battle between hoplite armies ends, after a severe clash and some fighting at close quarters, in the rout of one side or the other. Pursuit is limited; the victor remains in possession of the battlefield, as though that was what he was fighting to possess. The vanquished accepts defeat: he is given his dead to bury: the victor sets up a trophy to mark his success." This account of hoplite strategy and tactics and the "rules" for the seventh century recalls that of Grundy for the fifth.

> The recipe for victory is to have more *or* better, or more *and* better, hoplites than the opponent. Except for the successful exploitation of an advantage on the right wing—and this requires more tactical control than most generals could apply—the battle is a head-on collision all along the line. It would seem to follow that it is almost irrational to engage in battle unless the hoplite strength of the two sides approaches parity.[74]

Adcock lays out the simplicity and economy of the hoplite art of war. "It is hard to conceive of a method of warfare that, in peace, made a more limited call on the time and effort of most citizens of most communities." The ritual of hoplite warfare made it possible for those who could provide their own shields to fight on equal terms with the elite of the polis. "It did not suit the ideas of an early aristocracy to provide equipment for men who could not afford to provide it for themselves, or to train such men to fight on an equality with their betters."[75] In general, the economy of hoplite warfare served the needs of the middling farmers.

> Campaigns were brief. The armies, operating in the summer, wished to be home again for the harvest and the gathering of the grapes and olives. And one battle nearly always settled the business. The losses of a defeated army were almost invariably greater than those of the victors, even though pursuit, after the hard exertion of the combat, was not prolonged. . . . The battle was, as it were, a mass "duel,"[76] a trial of strength; and the verdict of the trial was accepted. It would have seemed to the Greeks of this age folly not to know

> you were beaten. . . . Nor did they wish to press matters to the arduous task of besieging the enemy city. And so states passed from war to peace as easily, or more easily, than from peace to war.[77]

This version of fighting in the archaic polis contains all the essential elements that make up the orthodoxy on hoplite strategy and tactics. Adcock's account applies to the two hundred years prior to the battle of Marathon much of what Grundy had said about the art of war in the fifth century.

In his 1956 landmark study, *The Greek Tyrants*, Andrewes emphasized the hoplite as a basic factor to explain "the age of tyrants" in Greece; he covers the period from the usurpation of Cypselus of Corinth in about 650 to the expulsion of the Peisistratids from Athens in 510. Andrewes builds on the idea of a hoplite revolution, which scholars had established during the previous century. The age of the tyrants marked the turning point in the political development of Greece, namely, the breakdown of the old political order of oppressive or inadequate aristocracies of the early seventh century; these regimes gave way before the establishment of more broadly based oligarchies. This change coincides with the introduction of new tactics in war. "At the beginning of the seventh century the Greeks changed their style of fighting and began to use the mass formation of heavy-armed infantry called hoplites. . . . The essential features of the change concern the type of shield, the use of the spear, and the training of a formation instead of individual fighters."[78]

The tactical and ideological underpinnings of the orthodoxy espoused by Andrewes are essentially the same since Grote more than a century earlier. The hoplite marked the transition from the javelin warrior who was lightly armed and fought at close quarters with a single-grip shield and sword. "The outstanding difference between the two systems is that hoplites can only fight in formation." The revolution in weapons and tactics, moreover, transformed Greek values and notions of *arete*. "Defensively it is clear from the nature of the shield just described that the hoplite's safety depends on the line holding fast. This is what produces the characteristic Greek conception of courage, the picture shown to us by Tyrtaeus and Plato of the good man who keeps his place and does not give ground."

Since Grundy the emphasis on the weight and awkwardness of the defensive armor had become a key part of the orthodoxy. "In the new hoplite style, defensive armour was much heavier." The fighter could hold the new double-grip shield more firmly, but could only cover his left side. Moreover, it was difficult to maneuver the shield to protect the right. "This was not necessary while the line stood fast, for a good half of every man's shield projected to the left of his elbow and covered the next man's right side. In flight such a shield was no protection at all, merely a burden, and if he ran away the hoplite was apt to throw it down." The use of weapons distinguishes the hoplite from the Dark Age warrior. "The spear was still the first weapon of offence, but no longer as a missile: instead, it was held firmly for a thrust, the favorite stroke being made with the spear held high and pointed downwards to attack the neck above the edge of the breastplate. If the spear failed, the hoplite took to his sword like the older type of fighter."[79]

The description in Andrewes of the main elements of hoplite battle and its contrast with the style of fighting in the heroic age recalls both Grundy and Grote. "Offensively the decisive factor is the weight of the combined charge of several ranks of hoplites with a view to breaking the enemy's line, and this kind of charge needed practice." Homer's depictions of individual duels owe something to the needs of heroic poetry. On the other hand, "real fighting of the pre-hoplite period tended to be like that, with the mass of the troops only lightly armed and the expert fighters attacking one another individually."[80]

Following Lorimer, Andrewes dates the revolution to the first quarter of the seventh century based on iconography. The painting of battle scenes on Greek vases does not begin until the late eighth century, and the images are often indeterminate. But the representations of the old style at the end of the eighth century contrast with the depictions of fighting between hoplite warriors on Corinthian and Attic vases before 675, and the series of lead figurines with hoplite armor from Sparta in about 700. The definitive example is the Chigi vase painted around 650: "Protocorinthian artists had mastered the difficult problem of making a picture which represents hoplites in formation . . . for purposes of dating, the first representations of even single hoplites is decisive, since the nature of hoplite equipment is such that it must from the first have been used in formation and cannot have been adopted piecemeal."[81]

Drawing inspiration from Aristotle, he connects the emergence of hoplite warfare with the rise of the middling citizens, broad-based political reforms, and the rise of the early Greek tyrants.

> The social and political basis for these two styles of fighting must be entirely different. The earlier, more individual method is the method of a military aristocracy, where the mass of the people is of little account and the brunt of the fighting is borne by a class of privileged experts: the hoplite method needs a broader basis, a greater number of trained fighters accustomed to acting as a team and not to showing off their individual prowess.

Andrewes identifies the hoplites as "a sort of middle class, including the more substantial farmers, for the equipment of Greek armies was not provided by the state, and the hoplites were just that income-group which could afford hoplite armour." He points out the political effect of the new tactics: "the middle class would start to claim its share of power in the state, breaking into the monopoly held by the aristocrats.[82]

In the *Politics*, Aristotle made similar observations: the early polis relied for its military strength on cavalry, which only the wealthy class could afford; therefore, the first constitutions after the monarchies were very narrow; but when the polis came to depend on the hoplite army, political power was spread more widely. Andrewes points out that the remarks about cavalry in early Greece cannot be verified but that this in itself does not invalidate what the philosopher says about how the introduction of hoplite tactics affected the early constitutions. Indeed, Andrewes connects the hoplites with tyranny, though Aristotle does not. "The tyrannies begin a generation or so after the introduction of hoplites, and it is hardly possible that there should be no connection between them."[83] "There is no direct proof that the earliest tyrants, Cypselus of Corinth and Orthagoras of Sicyon, relied on hoplite support," but, since Cypselus never needed a bodyguard, he must have been sure of the army.[84]

Sparta and Solonian Athens provide stronger evidence for the emergence of the hoplite class. At Sparta, membership in the sovereign assembly depended on service in the phalanx. "These soldier-citizens proudly called themselves the 'Equals' (*homoioi*), and while they held down a subject population many times their own number, they attempted to preserve a strict equality within their own body." That the new style of fighting produced an egalitarian ethos is one of the essential features of the hoplite narrative. In the case of Sparta, it enabled the polis to avoid revolution and to attain its renowned stability. "There was no tyranny at Sparta, and one important reason is that they gave the hoplites the vote and insisted on equality between them." A comparable crisis later arose in Athens.

Early in the sixth century Solon staved off civil war by breaking the absolute political power of the noble families called Eupatridae. He divided the Athenians into four classes with privileges based on farm income instead of birth. The lowest class had minimal powers, which included the right to vote in the assembly and at elections, and to sit in the court of appeal. But Solon restricted eligibility for high office to the two richest classes. "In between comes the third class called *zeugitai*, who were roughly the hoplites, indeed that seems to be the meaning of the name: they were admitted to minor political office." The hoplites may have brought about the crisis in Athens, but Solon in his moderation did not satisfy their interests. "The hoplites were the politically active element, the group who would have gained most land if there had been a revolution. Solon, as he boasts, contrived to keep the demos [*sc.* the hoplites and no one else] in order. In his constitutional settlement the principle [*sic*] gainers were the rich men outside the circle of the great Eupatrid families. The hoplites got only as much as Solon thought good for them, and it was not nearly as much as they wanted."[85] However, in the case of both Athens and Sparta, the polis had to come to terms with the emergence of the middling farmers to avoid revolution and tyranny.

Andrewes credits hoplites with transferring power from the narrow aristocracies to a much wider class throughout Greece during the age of the tyrannies and the succeeding regimes. "The detailed evidence sometimes confirms and nowhere contradicts the thesis that these were mainly hoplite revolutions, and the *a priori* likelihood is very great that the institution of the hoplite army would entail such a shift of political power." The reason was simple: other poleis had no choice. "In military development no state can afford to lag behind, and if one city adopted the new arms and tactics the rest must do so in self defence. From now on the defence of the state rested on the hoplites, and with the knowledge of this it is not surprising that they should gradually acquire confidence and begin to demand a share of political power."[86]

The hoplite orthodoxy attained its complete form with the thesis of Andrewes. Subsequent scholars have drawn out its implications in various ways, and the theory has strongly influenced the manner in which many textbooks present the rise of the polis. W. G. Forrest's 1966 *The Emergence of Greek Democracy, 800–400 BC* is one of the earliest and most prominent examples.[87] Forrest uses the hoplite orthodoxy to explain the breakdown of the aristocratic Greek state of 800 BC and the attainments of the polis, namely, the absolute acceptance of laws, including constitutions, by citizens with equal rights and equal duties to administer and maintain those laws.

The Western Way of War

Two of Victor Davis Hanson's books, *The Western Way of War* and *The Other Greeks*, have made perhaps the largest and most controversial contributions to the hoplite grand narrative in the past thirty years. In *The Western Way of War*, Hanson discusses the changes that occurred in Greek warfare after the Dark Age.[88] The era of mounted fighters who dismounted from either a chariot (i.e., in Homer) or a horse to throw javelins came to a close in the eighth century with the introduction of the heavily armored infantryman. No longer did warfare consist of aristocrats fighting duels with their social equals. Victory in battle now depended more and more on the common soldier who was armed with his own panoply and fought head-on with a round double-grip shield and thrusting spear in the tight formation that became the classical phalanx. In this way, Hanson's account belongs to the long tradition of the hoplite orthodoxy. In part, his conclusions about the nature of hoplite battle reassert the orthodoxy contrary to recent scholarship. "I should confess that recent attempts to prove some idea of widespread fluidity in the phalanx, to envision individual skirmishing rather than collective pushing, make no sense at all; the image is not based, it seems to me, on a fair reading of the ancient evidence."[89] Similarly to Grundy and Adcock, Hanson calls Greek hoplite warfare "decisive engagement as shock battle and frontal assault."[90]

Grundy had pointed out the necessity for citizen militias to confront invaders outside the walls of the acropolis to protect their precious crops in the alluvial plains. Adcock suggested that in early hoplite battles the Greeks were fighting for possession of the battlefield, the farmland. In a 1983 work, Hanson argued that the amount of damage an army could do to the crops, vines, and fruit-bearing trees of an enemy polis was limited.[91] Therefore, despite reports in the ancient historians of invaders "laying waste" the fields of their enemy, Hanson countered, "the rationale of Greek battle between heavy infantry of the classical period cannot be that it was preventative to agricultural catastrophe but, rather, we must consider that it arose as a provocation or reaction to the mere *threat* of farm attack."[92] Since actual long-term damage to agriculture was minimal, when the enemy entered a city-state's farms, "infantrymen marched out not to save their livelihoods nor even their ancestral homes, but rather for an *idea*: that no enemy march uncontested through the plains of Greece, that, in Themistocles' words, 'no man become inferior to, or give way, before another.'"[93] This provides the background for a hoplite battle. "Usually a quick response was considered necessary, in the form of heavily armed and armored farmers filing into a suitable small plain—the usual peacetime workplace of all involved—where brief but brutal battle resulted either in concessions granted to the army of invasion, or humiliating, forced retreat back home for the defeated."

Like earlier scholars, Hanson argues that the fundamental differences between massed infantry combat and the style of fighting that existed prior to it are in part linked with the rise of the polis. But Hanson goes further. The Greek city-states formed "the first consensual governments in the history of civilization that fielded soldiers who were independent and free property owners—militiamen, family farmers, and voters all in one." These facts help explain why the Greeks wanted to limit warfare to single, brief, shock encounters, as well as why they developed an ethos that such face-to-face killing at close range in "pure" hoplite battles was more "fair" and "noble" than other forms of combat.

> Not only did such men find it in their own economic and political interests to fight decisively—they had no wish to be absent from their farms on long campaigns and no desire to tax or spend to hire others to do so—but also spiritually such fighting reaffirmed the free farmers' preeminence in Hellenic culture at large. In Greek art, literature, and popular culture only the free landowning citizen—the hoplite—was willing and able to endure the spear carnage of phalanx warfare, and thus alone deserving of the honors and prestige of his polis at large.[94]

The remarkable integration of civic and military duties within the polis accounts for the success of the farmer-citizen-soldier model. "In most cases, men were arranged within the phalanx right next to lifelong friends or family members, and fought not only for the safety of their community and farmland but also for the respect of the men at their front, rear, and side." These small landholders and craftsmen might be called up for military service any summer after their eighteenth birthday until they turned sixty.[95] "We can be sure that the greater danger to any landholding infantryman was painful death on the battlefield, not slow starvation brought on through loss of his farm."[96]

The Western Way of War sets the mass confrontations of the Greeks apart from those of any previous ancient civilization.

> Egyptians, Hittites, Persians, or tribal forces from central and northern Europe were not by Greek standards heavily armed and armored. The bow, the javelin, and the sling were usually the preeminent offensive weapons of such forces. Horsemen and chariots were often the decisive contingents that ensured victory or defeat. Even those footsoldiers who charged each other did so in small groups and often through uncoordinated attacks. None were free citizens, who could vote—much less buy, own, or pass on private property. Herodotus felt that no other armies fought in the "absurd" way of the Greeks—heavily armored militiamen crashing together on flat plains during the long days of summer, each side after the initial collision seeking quite literally to push the other off the battlefield through a combination of spear thrusting and the shove of bodies.[97]

These battle traits of the Greeks established a distinctive Western way of war. "Firepower and heavy defensive armament—not merely the ability but also the desire to deliver fatal blows and then steadfastly to endure, without retreat, any counterresponse—have always been the trademark of Western armies."[98] The geography of most of the major city-states favored this type of warfare. The valleys of Argos, Athens, Corinth, Mantinea, Sparta, and Thebes were surrounded and divided by nearby mountain ranges. "Such small and rolling plains not only favored the culture of small farming, but also allowed heavy infantry to march unencumbered, and gave no natural shelter for the less armored; the nearby hills also protected the flanks of such ponderous infantry columns from the sweeps of flanking horsemen."[99]

However, the brutal but brief and limited hoplite battles, which served as "a glorious method of saving lives and confining conflict to an hour's heroics between armored infantry,"[100] did not dominate throughout the entire life of the polis. Following the Persian invasions of Greece in the early fifth century, the rise of sea power and the constant struggle between Sparta and Athens for hegemony and empire changed the nature of warfare. In addition to naval forces, Greek warfare started to make use of a variety of light-armed troops, skirmishers and missile troops by the fifth century. Hoplites themselves had begun to wear lighter body armor. Cavalry, artillery, and sieges became integral to campaigns that were waged over longer periods of time and in multiple theaters of operations. But the process that culminated in the phalanx of Philip II and Alexander did not take hold until the early fourth century. Instead, Hanson focuses on the seventh and sixth centuries when discussing the ideal of the middling farmer-citizen-soldier who voted to fight the wars of his polis. "For at least the two centuries between 700 and 500 B.C., and perhaps for much of the early fifth century as well, hoplite infantry battle determined the very nature of Greek warfare, and became the means to settle disputes—instantaneously, economically, and ethically."

Hanson's account differs from other treatments of the orthodoxy by concentrating not on strategy and tactics but on the combat experience of the average Greek soldier. Like Adcock, Hanson cites the nineteenth- and early twentieth-century Germans Köchly and Rüstow (1852), Droysen (1888), Delbrück (1920), and, especially, Kromayer and Veith (1928) for their expertise in Greek hoplite arms, drill, and deployment, and the strategic limitations of the generals.[101] But Hanson has more serious reservations about the approach of these scholars to Greek battle. Their handbooks, "exemplars of nineteenth-century scholarship at both its best and its worst, view conflict strategically, topographically, logistically, tactically—in the end, nonsensically and amorally." The analytical distance in their accounts of the battles marks their detachment from the subject.[102] Even later British scholars such as Tarn (1930), Griffith (1935), and Greenhalgh (1973) maintain to an extent "the previous obsession with deployment, drill, weapons and tactics."[103] On the other hand, Hanson praises the shift in focus accomplished by Kendrick Pritchett in his five-volume *The Greek State at War* (1971–1979). "For the first time Greek warfare was really seen in its proper function as a social institution, as commonplace and integral an activity to the Greeks as agriculture or religion: in Garlan's words, "'ancient war has a reality, a manner of being, a practice and a mode of behavior that are as wide as society itself.'"[104]

Inspired by John Keegan's *The Face of Battle*, *The Western Way of War* depicts in graphic detail what it must have been like for Greek infantrymen to fight in the typical hoplite battle.[105] Hanson shows the Greek fighter as "warrior, killer and victim." "I try to suggest what the *environment* of ancient Greek battle was, the atmosphere in which the individual struggled to kill and to avoid death, the sequence of events seen from within the phalanx. I ask the question, What was it like? at any given stage of the fighting."[106] "John Keegan . . . had demonstrated that a firsthand description need not be mere blood and guts, but could tell us much about the society that yielded such fighters—and indeed about the human condition itself."[107] Several of the areas Hanson covers have been the subjects of much recent debate, including the weight and awkwardness of hoplite armor and its impact on fighting style, and the nature of the collision and the pushing of the troops.

In keeping with the orthodox belief that hoplite arms and armor must have been created for the special needs of close fighting in tight formation, Hanson discusses the disadvantages of the panoply.

> Heavy, uncomfortable, unbearably hot, the panoply was especially poorly suited for the Mediterranean summer; it restricted even simple movement, and in general must have made life miserable for the men who were expected to wear it. Most modern estimates of the weight of hoplite equipment range from fifty to seventy pounds for the panoply of greaves, shield, breastplate, helmet, spear, and sword—an incredible burden for the ancient infantryman, who himself probably weighed no more than some 150 pounds.[108]

The gradual move toward lighter panoplies over the 250 years from the seventh to the fifth century seems to have been in response to the discomfort the hoplite experienced.

> The introduction of a so-called race in armor at the Olympic Games (520) and the final Greek charge at Marathon (490) may reflect a newfound mobility arising from a reduced panoply. Such activity would have been quite impossible for the original hoplites of the seventh century, whose limbs were virtually encased in bronze. In any case, it is clear that the hoplites of the fifth century never had any auxiliary protection for the arms, thighs, and ankles. Their helmets, body armor, and greaves all became sleeker, lighter, and at times disappeared altogether, again suggesting continual displeasure with the weight of the old equipment of their forefathers.[109]

Two items receive the most discussion from scholars since they are essential to the panoply: the double-grip shield and the "Corinthian" helmet. Hanson analyses the uses of the shield. "The advantage over the earlier ox-hide models of the Dark Age was the greater protection against standing spear and sword thrusts, allowing the warrior the chance to approach his enemy at much closer range." The double-grip system relieved the weight of the shield by distributing it over the entire arm, but had several drawbacks.

> Overall body movement was impaired [by this grip] as the left arm—for most men the more awkward and weaker one—had to be held rigidly, stuck out in front of the body waist high, elbow bent and the forearm straight and parallel to the ground, the hand tightly clenched to the grip. If the hoplite bent down or slipped, the lower rim of the shield would scrape the ground—a likely

> occurrence when its wearer was not much over five and a half feet in height. Balance was affected as well, and crouching or even bending over was difficult. Nor could the shield be easily handled once battle commenced. Because the entire arm was needed to maintain its great weight, the angle of deflection could be adjusted only with difficulty, and its shape suggests that it may have been designed largely for pushing ahead. The shield could not be brought over at any angle to protect a man's right side, and we hear of entire phalanxes caught helpless by a flank attack upon the extreme right, where the last file of hoplites had no protection at all for their unshielded sides.[110]

The Corinthian helmet was the most widely used headgear throughout Greece during the first two centuries of hoplite warfare. The orthodoxy contends that only a warrior fighting in a phalanx would wear equipment that imposed such restrictions on sight and hearing. "It would not be surprising if the simple formation and tactics of phalanx warfare—the massing into formation, charge, collision, and final push—grew, at least in part, out of the lack of direct communication between soldiers and their commander; dueling, skirmishing, hit-and-run attacks were out of the question with such headgear, and the isolation created by the helmet demanded that each individual seek close association with his peers."[111]

Following the initial charge across no-man's-land, the battlefield having become filled with blinding dust and deafening noise, actual battle would commence with the horrific shock of the two armies colliding . Hanson argues against those who deny this aspect of hoplite battle took place.

> Some have suggested that the initial clash of many infantry battles is at times not literally a collision, there being a last-second avoidance of a real impact between the two bodies, a mutually understood step back on each side. Keegan, for example, . . . has said that "large masses of soldiers do not smash into each other, either because one gives way at the critical moment, or because the attackers during the advance to combat lose their faint hearts and arrive at the point very much inferior to the mass they are attacking." (71) And yet a fair reading of the ancient accounts of hoplite battles suggests that in the case of the Greeks—and perhaps among the Greeks alone—the first charge of men usually smashed right into the enemy line: the key was to achieve an initial shock through collision which literally knocked the enemy back and allowed troops to pour in through the subsequent tears in the line. That is exactly what Arrian meant when he remarked that the idea of Greek battle was to force back the enemy during the initial charge. While in most cases such a crash was spontaneously transformed into a grinding, hand-to-hand struggle between two locked phalanxes, each striving to tear a gap in the battle line of the other, on occasion we do hear of an entire army demolished, simply rammed right off the battlefield in shambles because of the force of the initial crash of men on the move.[112]

Hanson proposes four reasons why a terrible collision of soldiers on the run took place within the first few seconds of ancient Greek battle. First, they had no choice.

The great depth of the phalanx with its eight ranks of men generated irresistible momentum during the charge. "If they hesitated or gave into any natural fear of physical collision, they would, nevertheless, be shoved onward—or else trampled by successive waves piling against their backs from the rear."[113] Second, the protection afforded by the "unusual and bowl-like shape" of the hoplite shield gave the soldier a sense of invulnerability, which encouraged him in the seconds before the collision. Third, there was also the possibility of missing "the barrier of an enemy shield or spear, that rather than hitting a wall of wood and/or flesh, a point of iron, a plate of bronze, they might be forced in *between* the small gaps of running soldiers—a chance that they might smash their way through arms and legs, and begin stabbing at the second or third rank of the enemy phalanx."[114] Finally, Hanson points out that the hoplite was probably not rational at this stage and was affected by a "group" mentality. "He and the other men may have been drinking together in the morning before battle and may not have been sober but, rather, functioning in these moments on 'automatic pilot.'"[115]

Perhaps the most controversial aspect of the orthodoxy in general and of Hanson's depiction of it in particular is the nature of the *othismos* or "push" of shields. Following the collision of the warriors and a period of close-in fighting with thrusting spears, and then with short swords after the spears had shattered, the orthodoxy maintains that a sort of pushing or shoving match ensued. The precise nature of this obscure tactic mentioned in the sources has eluded modern scholars.

> In most hoplite battles, it is true, the initial collision of men and subsequent hand-to-hand fighting soon gave way to the *othismos*, the "push" of shields, as one side eventually achieved a breakthrough, allowing its troops to force their way on into and through the enemy's phalanx. On occasion, we hear that neither side could open up the requisite tear, and thus both sides simply butchered each other right where they stood, the dead discovered with "all their wounds to the front." (Diodorus 15.55.2) In these rare cases, the soldiers in the rear could not push their way to victory, but were forced to step up a rank over the fallen corpses and take their own turn in the stand-up killing.... That the push of shields in a hoplite battle might not lead to a quick collapse soon after the crash is clear also from the second stage of fighting at Koroneia, where the Theban and Spartan phalanxes met head-on: "throwing up their shields against each other, they pushed, fought, killed, and died."[116]

The troops stationed in the rear of the phalanx played a critical role in applying steady pressure without breaking formation once the push began.

> The real importance of these men in the rear was simply to push those in front with their shields—in Asklepiodotos' words, "to exert pressure with their bodies." Of course, from the moment of impact they had been doing essentially just that, as they piled up behind their file leaders; increasingly, their pressure grew stronger or more desperate, since they were striving to force back the entire mass which was itself trying to press forward. It is surprising how

> many ancient authors saw the crucial phases of hoplite battle as "the push," where each side sought desperately to create the greater momentum through the superior "weight" or "mass."[117] . . . The ancients took it for granted that the deeper the column, the greater its thrusting power and momentum; . . . most phalanxes were generally described not as rows, or ranks, or spears, but rather as "shields" in depth, which may indicate that the main idea for the ranks in the middle and rear was to push ahead with their shields and bodies. On occasion hoplite battle could be summarized simply an *othismos aspidon*, "the push of shields." The goal was to break the deadlock in those precious few moments before exhaustion set in.[118]

Hanson discusses exactly how this mass pushing was accomplished as "each hoplite pressed with the center of his shield against the back of the man to his front, probably steadying his balance at times with his upright spear shaft as he leaned forward. The shaft in this way served as a staff of sorts—used to push off, it provided extra momentum as well as balance."[119] The construction of the hoplite shield figures directly into the nature of the pushing.

> From reconstructions of the hoplite shield, evidence of vase painting, and suggestions in Greek literature, we know that the lip of the top rim of the hollow Greek model was ideal for precisely that steady pushing; the hoplite supported the shield on his shoulder as he drove it against the backs of his friends ahead. That way the weight was distributed over the entire body rather than the left arm alone, while the shield's broad surface ensured that such pressure would be distributed evenly across the back of the man in front, neither tripping him nor forcing him off balance. Polybius simply declared that men push by "the weight of their bodies"; that same image of pushing is found again in many varieties of authors and can only confirm our belief that men in fact shoved everyone forward as they dug their bodies into the spacious dish of their own shield.[120]

Descriptions in the sources referring to "men who either were trampled down or literally suffocated as they stood" underline the tremendous force generated by this "mass of shields."[121] This critical phase in battle of the "push" ultimately gave way to a collapse, in which the warriors of one side succeeded in tearing open and breaking apart the other side's phalanx, and then pouring in through the gaps they had created. The fighting ended in a general rout of the enemy's surviving troops.

> Battle degenerated into a massive, pushing contest as rank after rank struggled to solidify and increase local advantages until the entire enemy's formation was destroyed. Yet, if the defeated could somehow maintain enough cohesion, a fighting withdrawal of sorts was possible. A great number died only when there was a sudden collapse, a collective loss of nerve, when the abrupt disruption of the phalanx sent men trampling each other in mad panic to the rear, either in small groups or, worse, individually to save themselves from spear thrusts in the back. Even when one side was swept suddenly off the battlefield,

> casualties in such a disaster remained low by modern standards. . . . Long drawn-out pursuit was also rare.[122]
>
> For more than three hundred years Greece thrived under such a structured system of conflict between amateurs, where the waste of defense expenditure in lives and lost work from agricultural produce was kept within "limits."[123]

The account of hoplite battle in *The Western Way of War* follows the basic sequence of the orthodoxy as laid out by Grundy and Adcock. On the other hand, Hanson provides by far the most ambitious, detailed, and vivid portrayal of the hoplite's experience of battle, incorporating a wide array of primary and comparative sources. As a result, *The Western Way of War* has become the most cited and popular, as well as the most controversial depiction of the modern orthodoxy.[124] In his next work, *The Other Greeks*, Hanson advanced the most far-reaching theory as to who these hoplites were. How and why did they emerge in the early polis to become the dominant force that shaped not only the fighting style but also the political forms, values, and culture of the Greeks?

The Other Greeks

Probably the most influential book written in the last two decades on the emergence of hoplite warfare and its relation to the rise of the Greek polis is Victor Davis Hanson's *The Other Greeks: the Family Farm and the Agrarian Roots of Western Civilization*. Hanson argues in the long tradition of the hoplite orthodoxy, but differs in remarkable ways from any of his predecessors. First, the idea that a new commercial economy underlies the hoplite phenomenon,[125] even of the moderate variety proposed by Forrest, is absent. For Hanson, "Greek fighting of the *polis should never be discussed outside the context of farming*."[126] In the thousand or so agrarian city-states outside Athens and Corinth, the craftsmen and traders were few in number and exerted limited influence. "The real political, social, economic, and military issues were over land, not arising from commercial rivalry among a purported large class of manufacturers and tradesmen."[127]

Second, scholars have often seen overseas colonization as simply an attempt to relieve population pressure at home or to further a new commercial economy. But Hanson thinks that starting in the eighth century an underlying change was taking place in the early polis. "Colonization of the eighth and seventh centuries did not alleviate the need for local agricultural change, but rather was a symptom that *such transformation was already occurring in Greece proper*."[128] He refers to the gradual *internal* colonization of marginal lands. In short, the increase in the population of the late Dark Age created pressures on land use, which inspired a revolution in agricultural technique that led to the birth of a new economic class, the independent middling farmer. Third, Hanson minimizes the significance of individual figures such as the Greek tyrants in creating the political revolution. "Although at some city-states tyrants at the head of a phalanx could bring about a dramatic end to old aristocracies . . . more often they simply were not needed. Farmers themselves, through their own agricultural expertise and agrarian ideology, had ensured their economic, political, and military superiority."[129]

Fourth, Hanson envisions that an agrarian revolution was well on its way before the military revolution that took place with the creation of the hoplite phalanx. He objects to both "gradualists" and "sudden change" theorists who postulate that new battle tactics, whether at 700 or 650 BC, *followed* the adoption of hoplite equipment.[130] The references to mass fighting of infantry in Homer's *Iliad* may be historical and demonstrate that phalanx tactics of some type existed *before* the complete adoption of the hoplite panoply.[131] "Most likely a less rigid style of massed attack had already been present in the eighth century [apart from formal hoplite equipment]."[132] On the other hand, Hanson sees little merit in arguing for men fighting in the hoplite panoply apart from the phalanx, in *any* formation.

> Could a man in heavy armor battle in small groups or alone outside the phalanx in all sorts of terrain? Consider carefully the particular elements of the hoplite panoply, especially the concave wooden shield. Seventy pounds of arms and armor were difficult to wear and somewhat expensive to fabricate. They were also disadvantageous for fluid fighting and individual combat. The image of a metal-encased pikeman scrambling alone over rocks, darting across a plain in groups of twos and threes, or perched on a charger is unconvincing.

How did this agricultural revolution, which lies at the base of all the changes associated with the rise of the polis, take place? Hanson views the increase in population as the force behind the need to intensify agriculture. By contrast, the Late Bronze Age was characterized by a command economy controlled by an autocratic, centralized, and bureaucratic government that stifled innovation in farming.

> The Mycenaean bureaucracies apparently practiced collectivized agriculture under central control, the age-old anathema to productive agriculture. Such a system could never have led to the free farming of the *polis* era. Much of the land in Mycenaean times had been allotted to local political and religious officials. They supervised vast herds of sheep, crop selection, and agricultural technique, closely monitoring returns, reimbursing seed, and bringing produce back up to the palace stores. True, there was a certain efficiency to such regimentation, but it was a redistributive system of both public and private landholding that ensured little agricultural innovation. Its rigorous complexity could not have allowed much for personal initiative, and thus maximum utilization of both human and natural resources. No city-state, no community of peers could have emerged out of that environment.[133]

Mycenaean society had had a narrow distribution of wealth. The elites of the palace controlled most of the land, food production, and social life. There seems to have been little advance in viticulture and arboriculture, and a small range of domesticated species of fruit trees and olives. The moderate population density resulted in a low intensity of labor and productivity. Either external or internal pressure or some combination of the two destroyed the elite of the agricultural hierarchy in the twelfth century. That led to the collapse of the vulnerable Mycenaean system. The majority of farmers who had depended on palace authority were now left without directors to organize them. The ensuing Dark Age of 1100–800 BC, however, laid the groundwork for the agrarian revolution that followed in the eighth century.

> Paradoxically, for all the ensuing human misery, the disruption and devastation of this "banking system" [which received, stored, exchanged, and lent surplus crops, both locally and overseas] at the end of the twelfth century could in time facilitate real agricultural change. *If* Greek farmland was eventually allowed to fall into as many private hands as possible, and *if* farmers themselves could retain their own crop surpluses, people could quickly learn new potentialities for land use, novel methods of food storage, grafting and propagation of an entire range of domesticated species of vines and olives. Dissemination of agricultural knowledge and expertise was practicable if—and only if—a large number of farmers gained title to their own pieces of ground, if they became freed from outside interference from the top. In the case of Greece, the process took nearly four hundred years.

In the eighth century these conditions began to be met when individual decision-making authority came into the hands of the middling farmers. This was made possible by the decentralization of the Dark Age.

> Once Mycenaean palace authority was done away with, there was a second opportunity for agrarian transformation by the sheer *process of neglect and unconcern*, should other critical factors—mainly population growth—ever come into play. The Dark Age chieftain, in an environment where efficient land use was not necessary, seems to have been indifferent to agriculture. He was more intent on raiding by land and sea, and in acquiring large herds of cattle, sheep, goats, and pigs; if anything, he was more a thug than a bureaucrat.[134]

The low population density and physical environment of Greece lent itself to livestock and nomadic herding in preference to intensive agriculture. Since the food needs of the people were easily met as long as the population remained stable there was little incentive for agricultural change even in the absence of a powerful and rigid hierarchy. "Both Mycenaean and Dark-Age Greeks were relatively ignorant of intensive farming technique for entirely different reasons."[135] It was not until the rise of the Greek *polis* that domesticated species were cultivated on a wide scale and came to predominate over wild varieties of trees, vines, and cereals.

At the end of the Greek Dark Age there was a gradual increase in domesticated species as population pressure forced the end of traditional land use. Hanson's idea of a renaissance in viticulture and arboriculture opposes the common view that there was little change in farming technique or crop species from Mycenaean to Hellenistic times. This is critical for his argument that innovative farmers from the eighth century on liberated agriculture from the control of Mycenaean palace authority and the neglect of Dark Age nobles. "They [the *georgoi*] found specialized varieties for particular locales, thus increasing the potential for viticulture and arboriculture as a whole in

Greece."[136] In order to feed a growing population a greater number of farmers transformed the conditions of agriculture. These farmers "must have changed the fundamental conditions of land tenure. Thus arose the *kleros*, or the idea of a privately held plot attached not to any one person, but rather in perpetuity to a single farm-family or *oikos*." The autonomy of farmers who owned their own plots fostered a new ideology.

> Renters, serfs, indentured servants, or lessees cannot invest in capital crops such as trees or vines in any efficient manner. Nor will they take the considerable risks entailed in viticulture and arboriculture without clear title to the land they farm. Farmers, especially planters of trees and vines, will soon demand to own their own land if they are to invest labor and capital in order to enrich the surrounding community. Once they own land, and plant permanent crops there, a transformation in both values and ideology ensues.[137]

The slow but steady population growth of the late Dark Age ensured the spread of revolutionary family-owned, independent, and intensively worked small farms. "In the case of Greece, like many other nonindustrial societies, population growth may have come first: it often initiates, drives, and maintains agricultural intensification." Growing numbers of people needed to eat, so they had to develop better methods of producing food and organizing themselves in the countryside. "After centuries of strict agronomic control, followed by the other extreme of relative agrarian neglect, agriculture in Greece was finally becoming the property of numerous individual and autonomous families."[138]

Hanson suggests what caused the population growth and how this facilitated the development of the new agrarianism. The process started with a breakdown of "age class" systems or the discouragement of early marriage and procreation by the elite clans of the Dark Age. The age class culture, characteristic of warrior societies, ensured the political power of the few Greek aristocrats over their subjects; this delayed for centuries the dramatic rebound from the chaos that followed the collapse of the Mycenaean centers. The modification and erosion of the old "system" led to social experimentation as "military regimentation gave way to other pursuits like agriculture."[139] Hanson credits the agricultural revolution with preventing any large-scale famine in early Greece that might have otherwise accompanied the population increase.

The innovation in land use in mainland Greece preceded the colonization movement of the eighth and seventh centuries. In fact, foreign colonization was not sufficient in and of itself to address the problem of surplus population at home. Local agricultural change at home was necessary in the form of "a more gradual *internal* colonization of land previously unwanted and underdeveloped."[140] The incorporation of "marginal" land (*eschatia*) by middling farmers in response to demographic pressure marked a serious challenge to the existing social order. "In the old Dark-Age social and economic sense, that [cultivation of marginal land] meant less accessibility to manorial centers, and less fertility for native grazing, less suitability for easy ploughing of cereals, but not unsuitability for crops such as vines and trees." The process initiated private ownership of land for the first time in the West.

> "Marginal" land is ubiquitous in many parts of Greece, an ideal, relatively safe springboard for anyone brave enough to embark on a new sort of agricultural strategy of outright private ownership and intensive working of permanent crops. Once private ownership by adventurous farmers was the rule, each Greek rural household sought its own parcel, to improve and pass on. Previously unused and unowned land was thus developed by men on their own, marking the real beginning in the West of individual property holding on any wide scale.[141]

When the *georgoi* did leave the mainland, the colonists agreed on the new role of agriculture, and "were often not critics, but supporters of agrarianism; not the poor, but members of the lower middle stratum who saw little chance of obtaining a hereditary plot for themselves inside Greece."[142] In addition to private ownership of marginal lands and overseas colonization, Greek farmers applied their new intensive strategies to the estates of wealthier landowners. But the repressive forms of tenancy, where the owner could draw off the surplus of another's work, compromised agricultural success, which depends on private ownership. On the other hand the gradual transition from pastoralism to intensive farming "liberated" the *georgoi* of the eighth century from the traditional social patterns and military castes. The majority of farmers chose to remain in the mainland of Greece rather than to move overseas in mass. Hanson attributes the agrarian renaissance of the eighth century and later to a combination of three factors: "(1) a quiet revolution in agricultural technique and rural social organization in general, (2) an incorporation of new technologies and crop species, [and] (3) an intensification of labor."[143] Key techniques such as grafting applied to the domesticated olive along with other trees and vines "allowed for a lasting alternative to pastoralism," which sustained the population increase into the polis period.

Hanson points out why this kind of farming was such an important element for the rising class of smallholders; the liberation of agriculture helped create a new type of human being. "People who choose this kind of agriculture have confidence that they can and will stay put, that they can and will keep the countryside populated, prosperous, and peaceful. They are not just a different sort of farmer, but a different sort of person as well." Farming bears on the quality of the infantry soldier as well.

> In a military sense . . . there is little doubt that the superiority of Greek citizen infantry, the "planters of trees," in wars both foreign and domestic derived from the resoluteness, conservatism, independence, and physical courage prerequisite to the intensive farming of trees and vines, the need to protect and to honor the visible inherited vineyards and orchards of past generations.[144]

How might agriculture shape the character of the smallholder? Hanson details the differences between an intensive farmer of vines and fruit trees in the polis and a Dark Age pastoralist and grower of grain.

> The picture that emerges from even a small Greek vineyard is clear: constant decisions, endless searching for the precise but always elusive equilibrium between multifarious choices, the need for constant attention and labor, and reverence for ancestral practice. Much different from cereal or livestock

production, these complexities in viticulture and arboriculture help explain the new intensified Greek agriculture of homestead residences, slave labor, incorporation of rough terrain, and mastery and control of food processing.[145]

Where did this emerging class stand in relation to other citizens in the polis? "It is impossible accurately to gauge their numbers, possible only to approximate their relative position between a smaller entrenched elite and a slightly larger group below of landless poor, and some less successful subsistence "peasants."

> There is intense dislike on the part of the landed and wealthy elite for these upstart farmers, the *georgoi* who in early Greek literature are predictably dubbed the *kakoi*, the "bad" (in opposition to the *agathoi*, the "good" traditional aristocrats by birth), and second, recognition appears among more enlightened Greeks that the presence of an agrarian class of small farmers (properly called *hoi mesoi*, "the middle ones") was responsible for both the creation and preservation of the Greek city-state, and that their political agenda was both reasonable and proper. . . . This "class" is clearly not mercantile or commercial in the modern sense, but rather entirely agrarian, sandwiched between the few wealthy and the most numerous poor.[146]

Hanson finds strong support for his thesis in Aristotle's *Politics*.

> Aristotle writes of middling farmers in realistic, rather than utopian terms. He implies that agrarians of the middle had been widespread throughout the early *polis* history of Greece. . . . He . . . confirms that the "middle ones" were, in fact, those who farmed on their own, and who provided the city-state with the social and political stability that led to the "best" type of government . . . but possible only when they are present in sufficient numbers to prevent class strife between the very rich and the abject poor. . . . Aristotle writes that this most stable form of government by small farmers had an ancient pedigree, and was to be associated with the foundation of the *polis*.[147]

Aristotle discussed the effect the early lawgivers had in shaping their governments to protect the interests of the growing number of independent farmers. They seem to have designed their legislation to protect the land and the economic gains of the farmers from aristocratic backlash.

> Philolaus of Corinth (about 730 B.C.?) had supposedly enacted regulations ensuring that the farms at Thebes might remain the same number in perpetuity. The Corinthian Pheidon, "one of the most ancient of the lawgivers," purportedly argued that the population and the number of plots ought always to remain roughly equal. An even more shadowy figure, Phaleas the Chalcedonian, advanced the concept that all citizens of the polis ought to hold equal amounts of property.[148]

In addition to the texts of Aristotle and Plato, Hanson sees evidence for property egalitarianism and small farm size in the Greek colonies from the eighth through the fourth century. "Surely the formal organization of colonists and their creation of equitable plots and a complex social structure presupposes the prior formation of a *polis*, and suggests a preexisting, ongoing agrarian ideology." The standard size for allotments of land in the colonies was rectangles around fifty *plethra* (about 11 acres). "This practice may suggest that farm plots between forty and sixty *plethra* (8.9 and 13.3 acres), the so-called exemplary hoplite farms we discussed earlier, were being duplicated afresh in early colonies. . . . Would be *georgoi* were seeking to reproduce—or given this second chance, to perfect or to improve on—an agrarian ideology they had seen at home."[149]

There is a pattern in Greek literature of agrarian legislation and practice (about 700–550 BC) that ensured widespread equality in landholding by about 550–400 BC. He stresses above all "the actual conditions of landowning, the size of farms as expressed in the literary and epigraphical record, oratory for the most part, and leases and sales recorded on stone." Authors in the fifth and fourth centuries most often speak of farms from ten to twenty acres; there were on occasion larger estates between fifty to seventy acres, but holdings over one hundred acres were very rare until the Hellenistic and Roman period. It appears that an enforced code or social ethic of the Greek polis discouraged the accumulation of property. "How else can we explain why the inherited rich, the more gifted *georgoi*, the more successful in commerce and mining, all failed to accumulate vast tracts, failed to transfer their off-farm capital into landed estates—phenomena that were commonplace after the demise of the free and autonomous Greek *polis*."[150] The new middling class of farmer-citizen-soldiers became numerous enough to prevent agriculture from reverting back to the fragile palace bureaucracies. Their prosperity and ability to provide for the increased population ensured that the agricultural neglect of the Dark Age clans would not return.

> All of Greek history in the *polis* period follows from the successful creation of a new agriculture and the efforts of the many to protect a novel agrarian way of life. The rural system of the *georgoi* created the surplus, capital, and leisure that lay behind the entire Greek cultural renaissance. It was an agrarianism that was highly flexible and decentralized economically, socially egalitarian, and politically keen to avoid the accumulation of power by a nonagricultural elite. No surprise that the later *polis* Greeks envisioned the rise of agrarianism—which had created their city-state—primarily in moral terms.[151]

The development of hoplite warfare took place in this context of novel agrarianism, which promoted a particular type of moral excellence.

> Small and equitable farm size inculcated a number of values in the citizenry and created a shared vision of what a Greek city-state might be. In the early agrarian polis, modest, equal-sized plots ensured that all Greek citizens would have to work with their own hands. All would look at the ensuing (most natural) challenges pragmatically, rarely theoretically. All would acquire capital largely through their own sacrifice and toil. All would rely on their own resolve and bodily strength to reclaim land or ward off invasion. All would be secure in the thought that a whole cadre of like citizens was

> presented with about the same challenges, with about the same opportunities to succeed or fail.[152]

Victor Hanson's *The Other Greeks* provides the fullest and most vivid account of those who might have comprised the middling class of the orthodox tradition of hoplite warfare. He has developed his picture of the late Dark Age and early polis period through examination of the early Greek lawgivers and the extensive site surveys that have been conducted in Greece since the 1980s. Yet it is from the archaeological sources that Hanson's thesis has met with some of its strongest criticism.

Revisionism and the Hoplite Orthodoxy

The first sustained challenge to the orthodoxy came with Anthony Snodgrass's seminal work of the 1960s. He developed the earlier suggestion of Nierhaus[153] to indicate that the introduction of hoplite arms was a "long drawn out, piecemeal process"[154] and that it did not lead to an immediate change in tactics. For Snodgrass the double-grip shield does not imply the phalanx. In a transitional stage, aristocratic soloists took up new items of equipment before the invention of the phalanx. The date of 650 that Snodgrass proposed for the fully developed phalanx refuted the idea that hoplites played a role in the rise to power of the tyrants or in any other revolutionary changes associated with the early Greek polis. These arguments throw light on some of the problematic aspects of Lorimer's thesis.

Lorimer had contended that the literary evidence confirmed her conclusions based on the archaeology. The *Iliad* depicts prehoplite equipment and tactics. Shields have telamons, and the heroes often carry spears in pairs and cast them at long range. Homeric heroes never throw their shields away but fling them around their back for protection in flight. They wear an open-face helmet and a corselet, which Lorimer identified with the leather jerkin depicted on the Warrior Vase and on other late Mycenaean monuments. She imagined that the Greek warrior's arms, armor, and fighting style changed little from the collapse of Bronze Age civilization in the twelfth century till the hoplite revolution in the early seventh century.[155]

On the contrary, Nierhaus had proposed the theory of the piecemeal and gradual adoption of hoplite equipment, which was still far from complete at the end of the seventh century.[156] The process began with the introduction of the round shield in the eighth century, which he identified with the hoplite shield. He reasoned that, since artistic representations of the plate corselet were rare in the first half of the seventh century and limited in the second half, its adoption was slow and tentative. Lorimer dismissed his hypothesis as a priori improbable owing to the inseparable link she posited between hoplite equipment and the phalanx and its tactics. She pointed out that he overlooked the Corinthian helmet, greaves, and spear in his thesis; for example, the helmet is already present with the plate corselet on the Perachora aryballos, which was unknown to Nierhaus. In addition, the greaves appear on the Hymettus amphora, while both vases show the exclusive use of the single spear. The aim of adopting the single heavy thrusting spear and the *porpax* shield in place of the pair of light throwing spears and the single-grip shield was to supersede the long-range fighting of the Geometric period; greaves added protection and completed the panoply intended for hand-to-hand fighting by troops with uniform equipment arranged in an unbreakable line. "These items form a natural and logical combination, and they all appear on one of our earliest monuments, the Perachora aryballos." "If they [the Carians] invented the *porpax* shield," she proposes, "[they] must also have invented the cohesive tactics of which it was to be the instrument."[157]

But in light of the finds of the panoply at Argos in 1953 and of the armor at Dendra in 1960, Snodgrass could argue for the "piecemeal" adoption of hoplite arms with far greater force than Nierhaus. The eighth-century Argos discovery made it impossible to maintain that a metal corselet was specific to hoplite tactics, which were unknown to Geometric art. The Dendra metal corselet and greaves from the Bronze Age gave even more striking proof that protecting the body with bronze armor was not exclusive to the archaic period. In fact, most of the essential items of the "hoplite panoply" were known to Mycenaean Greece, including the metallic helmet and the single thrusting spear.[158] The plate corselet, for example, traces its ancestry back to the type of corselet used seven hundred years earlier at Dendra. But Snodgrass traces the origin of the technique for producing the bronze corselet found at Argos to central Europe before it returned to the Aegean in the eighth century through trade and colonization in the West.[159] Elite Geometric fighters used the bronze body armor with neither a Corinthian helmet nor a double-grip shield. His ideas have inspired all subsequent attempts to revise the hoplite orthodoxy.

> The originality of the 'hoplite panoply' has been disproved by the emergence of Bronze Age precedents for many of its parts, and its homogeneity dispelled by the differences in origin and chronology between them. The fact that Mycenaean soldiers, to whom hoplite warfare was most decidedly unknown, fought with metal helmets, corslets, greaves, and ankle-guards, suggests that their similarly-equipped successors were not so armed with new and specific tactics in mind. The sole point of difference is the porpax-shield, and its tactical significance, hitherto rather taken for granted, needs re-examination. Further, the Argos discovery, in addition to all its other valuable testimony, also gives a hint that 'hoplite' armour was first known as the possession of the few.

The existence of hoplite armor and weapons by no means implies the phalanx. "The essential components of the hoplite's armament (the greave excepted), are thus all known to the Aegean world before 700, and their association together is first portrayed about 25 years later; while another full generation elapses before we have any archaeological evidence for the adoption of 'hoplite' tactics."[160]

Snodgrass not only challenged ideas about the origins of the phalanx; he made several other important arguments against the notion of hoplites playing a revolutionary part in the rise of the polis. First, the initial adoption of new arms starting in the mid-eighth century emboldened the aristocratic warrior to fight at closer range. He would close with his sword after throwing two or three javelins, or substitute his javelins for a single, heavy thrusting spear as his main weapon. Yet these changes in fighting style required neither greater manpower nor the close-packed formation of a phalanx. Second, the qualification of wealth, namely, the ability for the individual soldier to provide his own panoply, is the basis for a hoplite army. In an agricultural society such as archaic Greece, the recruits must have come from the farmers who were substantial landholders. He suggests that the farmers concerned about the devastation of their property and their absence from it had no vested interest in war. In fact, there would have been "no enthusiastic rush to arms on the part of the more substantial property owners, the future 'hoplite class.'[161] Even if the bait of political power had been held out from the first—which is perhaps improbable—this would hardly be enough to launch a voluntary movement which ran so entirely against historical precedent."[162] Third, the aristocracy remained as a traditional warrior class after the introduction of hoplite *equipment*; it was only after the sharp increase in the number of soldiers required by the adoption of hoplite *tactics* that the new class could affect their military supremacy. Fourth, Snodgrass sees in Etruria and Rome examples of societies that can adopt hoplite tactics without immediate and far-reaching social and political consequences. He presents his view in the following.

> The Greek hoplite entered history as an individual warrior, probably in most cases an aristocrat. The adoption of the phalanx meant that he was joined by men, for the most part substantial land-owners, who had come not to seek a way to political power nor by any wish of their own, but because they were compelled to. These men, however stout-hearted as warriors, are not likely to have become, all at once, a revolutionary force in politics, even in Greece. The political rights which they came to possess could have been acquired gradually and peacefully, *ton en tois hoplois ischusanton mallon*, as Aristotle says. They must have had political leaders, but I doubt whether we can number the early tyrants among them. Hoplites, in short, were an instrument before they became a force.[163]

In sum, Snodgrass's treatment of the development of Greek arms suggests that the traditional picture of the early history of Greek warfare is too simplified. The evidence does not support the idea of Lorimer that in about 700 BC some genius, in one of the great military reforms of history, imposed order on the loose, disorganized skirmishing of the Dark Age. In the light of the precedents for bronze armor, Snodgrass views the military developments of the seventh century as a continuation of what went before, not a radical break, and denies any military or political impulse to equip massed heavy infantry. Warriors adopted greaves, for example, in the era of long-range warfare as a barrier against missiles, and that had nothing to do with massed infantry tactics. The double-grip shield existed in the late eighth century, yet the first plausible portrayal of the phalanx does not occur until the Berlin aryballos. This does not indicate that artists were unable to paint the phalanx earlier, but that the classical formation did not exist at the time of the first panoplies, which were worn by the few.[164] In the case of the *porpax* shield and the metal corselet, the two items were alternative pieces of equipment, not necessarily meant to be worn together. Corinthian art of the mid-seventh century bears witness only to the initial stage of the adoption of the true hoplite phalanx; the poleis with a large enough body of wealthy citizens completed the process, which ended when the heavily armed foot soldier discarded the throwing spear as his equipment became more and more standardized. "Finally, at a date unknown but possibly not much before the fifth century, the Greeks coined a word to define the final status that the heavy infantryman had reached—hoplitēs. We, too, should be hesitant in our application of the term to the earlier stages of Greek armament."[165]

Since the 1965 article of Snodgrass, several schools of thought have established themselves, with two emerging as especially critical. First, it has been held that use of the broad hoplite shield marked only a single stage in an evolutionary process that culminated in about 650 BC, the date of the first known artistic representations of the classical phalanx. Second, scholars have argued that the classical hoplite phalanx took shape rather suddenly with the introduction of hoplite armor, between 725 and 700 BC. In his 1977 article Cartledge proposed some nuances to the "sudden change" theory:

> Briefly, the change was relatively sudden and due *imprimis* to the widespread adoption of what became regarded as the hoplite accoutrement *par excellence*, the shield with *porpax* and *antilabe*. This was not, however, a case of brute determinism (as it is presented by Lorimer; *cf.* Detienne 132 n. 68). For, to borrow the careful phraseology of Greenhalgh (71), the new shield was 'not impossibly ill-adapted to the unorganised warfare of the javelin era'. But Greenhalgh, although he does at least make the points that it *was* ill-adapted and that pre-hoplite warfare was *un*organised, does not go far enough. As an invention for use in pre-hoplite warfare the hoplite shield would not merely have been barely (if at all) superior to its single-handled predecessors but also in certain circumstances positively and dangerously inferior. For what the invention of *porpax* and *antilabe* tells us is that concern for protection in the front was outweighing the need for manoeuvrability and for protection in the flank and rear—in other words, that a change in tactics in the direction of organized, hand-to-hand fighting was *already* in progress.[166]

Cartledge stresses the fact that the Greeks *invented* the double-grip shield: "why should it not have been invented with the phalanx in mind rather than the other way around?"[167] He has less trust in the often insecure visual and literary evidence; instead, he looks to the "whole gamut of economic, social and political conditions in this 'Age of Revolution'" (c. 750–650) to explain how the development of the hoplite shield was soon followed by hoplites operating in phalanx formation; this took place "somewhere in the first quarter of the seventh century, the precise date varying naturally from state to state." No one polis was responsible for the entire process, and by 650 all of the more important states had gone hoplite. Cartledge details the dominant trends. Relative overpopulation in Greece resulted in colonization abroad and in a shift from pasturage to arable farming. Land hunger also had military implications:

> Warfare became more frequent as each political community sought to secure for itself the maximum amount of land compatible with its convenient

> utilisation and defence: throughout Greek antiquity the ownership of land was the most important single cause of interstate wars. Secondly, the shift from stock-raising to arable farming determined thereafter the general pattern of warfare on land, for the basic objectives everywhere in this game of 'agricultural poker' (Snodgrass 1967, 62) became the menacing, temporary possession or destruction of the enemy's crops and the protection of one's own.[168]

The idea of the polis has significance as a community of equal citizens and for the consequent decline of monarchy. The upheavals of the "Age of Revolution" led to the rise of a solid peasantry of substantial farmers with the psychological independence to challenge the injustice of the "bribe-swallowing" aristocrats. In this scenario, the aristocrats were the "reluctant hoplites" forced by the new circumstances to invite the "wealthy and well equipped commoners" to join them in the phalanx, whose success depended on fielding the greatest possible numbers on a given occasion.

> Indeed, it had the makings of a brilliant compromise. The relevant commoners were enabled at a stroke to defend not only their own property but also the *polis* of which they were citizens. At the same time the devolution of military responsibility did not obviously imperil the aristocratic structure of society. Rather, it could have reasonably been hoped that phalanx-warfare would defuse the potentially explosive contradiction between aristocratic *arete* and *polis*-equalitarianism. For although membership of the phalanx was open in principle to all who could provide their own *hopla*, and although sheer numbers were an advantage in the hoplite style of fighting, rarely was as much as one half of a state's citizen-body able to turn out as hoplites in practice.[169]

The advent of hoplite warfare not only destroyed the monopoly of political suzerainty of the aristocrats; it excluded militarily "the poor peasantry and 'wearers of skins' in the country, . . . the shopkeepers, petty traders, handicraftsmen and casual labourers in the town. . . . The hoplite 'reform' brought on a change in conceptions of bravery, but hoplite ideology retained the indelible stamp of its aristocratic origins."[170]

In the same 1977 *Journal of Hellenic Studies* volume, John Salmon, a "gradualist," accepts the thesis that the phalanx came into existence after the piecemeal adoption of the hoplite panoply.[171] But he argues that as soon as the aristocrats adopted massed tactics, which he dates to 675 using vase painting, new fighters joined them on the battlefield. Salmon agrees with Snodgrass, moreover, that the representations of warfare in paintings in the period 700–650 may provide "the documentary evidence of a transitional stage in the development of Greek warfare."[172] This is for three main reasons: (1) unlike later hoplite practice many warriors are shown carrying two spears; (2) they sometimes use swords as primary weapons; and (3) they often are equipped with less than the full panoply. Salmon does not thus conclude, however, that massed tactics were unknown in the early form of phalanx warfare. "[The] phalanx has two essential features: its cohesion and its relatively large size; both can be achieved without following the later canonical pattern closely."[173] He notes that even when the phalanx existed, after 650, paintings still show hoplites carrying two spears: presumably a shorter spear to throw before the opposing forces met in hand-to-hand combat, and a longer spear for thrusting at close quarters. Therefore, Salmon suggests a second transitional stage after the invention of the phalanx, in which "the new style of fighting saw the gradual development, through experiment with throwing spears, swords and various items of body armour, of the canonical version."[174] He dates the beginning of this second transitional stage to no later than 655, the time of the Macmillan vase, but probably at least as early as the flutist on the Perachora aryballos of circa 675. In either case, the hoplites might have had a role in the revolutions of Cypselus, Orthagoras, and Theagenes.

Salmon compares the Roman tradition that Servius Tullius organized the centuriate assembly at the same time as he reformed the military. He notes that the political situation in Greece was far different from the one in Rome in view of the background of political unrest, which renders the analogy false.

> Comparatively wealthy men with a grievance were given, for the first time, major military importance; it would hardly be surprising if they used their new strength to set their grievance right—or if ambitious men like Cypselus took advantage of this new pressure group to achieve their own ends. There are no reasons in principle to deny that the invention of hoplite tactics had an effect on political development solely because of the analogy with what may have happened in Etruria and in Rome.[175]

Salmon agrees that economic grounds restricted a place in the phalanx to a relatively small class, resulting in a seventh-century phalanx of hundreds compared to that of thousands in the fifth century. The unpleasant character of hoplite warfare also might have made many wealthy landowning farmers reluctant to serve, as Snodgrass suggests; but Salmon does not see this standing in the way of revolution. "Wealthy men have never been slow to press what they see as their interests, and that has often made them support revolution, from the non-Eupatrid wealthy who supported Solon through the great plebeian families of Rome who fought the struggle of the orders." Citizens in the more advanced Greek poleis were growing discontent with aristocratic methods of government in the mid-seventh century. At the same time aristocrats were losing their monopoly on fighting skills with the development of phalanx tactics. "In such a situation it was the wealthy who were *most* likely to attack the *status quo*; they were doubtless contented enough with their economic position, but they felt a stark contrast between that and their social and political poverty.[176] For the less well off there was no such contrast, and therefore no impulsion to political change."[177]

Salmon finds the adoption of the new style of fighting to be the most powerful explanation for the many political revolutions that took place in mid-seventh century Greece. However, he does not attribute them to the development of a self-conscious hoplite class. The hoplites gave positive support to tyrants in not rescuing the aristocratic regimes under attack; but more wide-ranging claims of hoplites demanding political power commensurate with their new military status seem to him unlikely. The length of time to develop such feelings is perhaps longer than the gap between the adoption of the phalanx and its political consequences allows. The complaints against exclusive rule of aristocrats and their failure to provide *dike* would not depend on hoplite status.

Second, if hoplite demands were for greater political power, these demands were rarely met. At Corinth, Sicyon, and Megara control passed from traditional aristocracies to tyrants, and in Argos there is no evidence the hoplites were conscious instruments of change. "It is not easy to believe that one generation of Corinthian hoplites raised Cypselus to the tyranny in order to gain influence for themselves through him only for a succeeding generation to acquiesce in its effective exclusion from political power."[178] In the case of Sparta, Salmon finds it incredible that a politically inexperienced group such as the hoplites could demand the positive political rights formulated in the *rhetra*. "Hoplites were probably incapable of formulating even a coherent statement of their grievances; but they were sufficiently discontented for an aristocratic faction to attempt to turn their discontent to its own advantage."[179] On the model of Pheidon's success at Argos, Salmon posits that the two Spartan kings attempted to enhance their power by gathering hoplite support in political life. Thus the *rhetra* enshrines royal power in the *gerousia* to help preserve their declining power. In sum, special circumstances in Greece beyond simple participation as a hoplite contributed to political change, whereas those other factors were not significant in places such as Etruria. "We cannot look to the hoplite reform for a simple explanation of the political upheavals of the mid-seventh century, for the essential causes will have been different in each case." The role of the hoplite was far more modest. "The hoplite reform played an important part; it supplied the weapon for change, but not the will for it."[180]

The gradualist position not only calls into question the political role of hoplites in the seventh century; in the last few decades scholars have mounted vigorous challenges to the orthodoxy on the topic of tactics. Hans van Wees, for example, has argued for a much-reduced role for the mass formation of the phalanx as an instrument of change. "I believe that the process of change was not only less rapid than that envisaged by e.g. P. A. Cartledge, but also longer drawn-out than the piecemeal development suggested by Snodgrass. By implication, I do not believe that the introduction of the double-grip shield greatly accelerated the growth of the phalanx-formation."[181] In his 1994 article, he states that Krentz's 1985 piece in *Classical Antiquity* and Cawkwell's paper in *Classical Quarterly* 1989 "appear to me worthy of more positive attention than they have received thus far."[182]

Krentz developed the idea that the change to hoplite tactics was gradual and did not bring about a hoplite revolution in archaic Greece. He argues against the view that in a hoplite battle the two sides met in tight formation with each of its soldiers stationed about three feet apart and (usually) eight rows deep with the objective of literally pushing through and breaking up the opposing line.[183] Instead he contends that "the essence of a hoplite battle remained [throughout its history] the hand-to-hand fighting of individual hoplites in the front rank, one-on-one, two-on-one, three-on-two, etc."[184] Two of the main points of the orthodoxy with which he takes issue are the spacing between the troops in the phalanx and maneuverability of the two-handled hoplite shield.

Regarding the distance between hoplites in formation, Krentz disregards Polybius' statements about the width between Macedonian phalangites as inapplicable to hoplites; he doubts that Thucydides refers to a distance as tight as three feet per man. For instance, he takes *sunklesis* in one passage of Thucydides to mean "a gap large enough to hold 2/7 of the Spartan army." "He might have thought three feet per man impossible, too cramped for hand-to-hand fighting. Such fighting requires room to fake, to dodge, to sidestep, to wrong-foot the opponent by stepping backward as he delivers his blow or thrust."[185] On the other hand the two-handled hoplite shield is in no way incompatible with fighting as a soloist. Its advantages include the *porpax* or central armband, which helped support the weight of a larger shield that could be held at an angle more firmly than a single-handed shield to deflect blows more easily. The double-grip shield also made it possible for the hoplite to hold a spare weapon in his left hand. He discounts the often cited difficulties of using the less maneuverable hoplite shield to protect the more vulnerable right-hand side outside a tight formation.

> Its [the double-grip shield's] disadvantages were that it protected the left side better than the right, and that it did not effectively protect the back. But given that it is difficult for a right-hander to reach the right side of his opponent, and given that a hoplite could protect his right side by turning his body as well as by moving his shield (and would naturally do so in order to deliver a spear thrust), an individual fighter would find the double-handled shield preferable to its predecessors.[186]

In reference to hoplites in land battle, as opposed to marines who fought on triremes armed as hoplites, Krentz addresses some of the main tactical issues his theory raises.

> How close did [a hoplite] need to be to his neighbor to feel reasonably protected? Within a spear's thrust, I should think. Consider the position from the point of view of the enemy hoplite: how far would hoplite A have to be from hoplite B for an enemy to enter the gap and attack A from the side? Far enough so that the enemy would not have to worry about a spear or sword in his back from B while his attention was directed toward A. The comfortable limit, therefore, would be about six feet per man, as the Roman legionaries had (Polybius 18.29.6-8).[187]

Krentz allows for formations tighter than six feet apart per man under various scenarios, "but the typical battle order allowed significantly more than three feet per man." He draws further support for this idea from Tyrtaeus 8.35–38, who pictures javelin and stone throwers seeking cover behind the shields of seventh-century hoplites. In sum, Krentz relates his position to earlier challenges to the orthodoxy. "The effect of my argument that hoplite battle consisted of a multiplicity of individual combats is to increase the emphasis A. M. Snodgrass and John Salmon have placed on gradual transition rather than sudden revolution in the switch from 'Homeric' to 'hoplite' warfare."[188]

For Krentz, the phalanx was not an invention of the seventh century; it is fully present in Homer's *Iliad* and only became more *standardized* later. He pictures a small number of aristocrat hoplites fighting in the eighth-century phalanx alongside a much larger number of more vulnerable men who could not afford the new equipment. "The Homeric *laos* did not instantly disappear or move to the side. When the rank and file could afford it, no doubt they acquired the new panoply too—with the approval of the existing hoplites."[189]

G. L. Cawkwell's paper questions the orthodox model for how hoplites fought as far too rigid: "the only confidence one can have is that things were not as simple as the orthodox would have us believe."[190] The main thrust of his argument is that hoplites and phalanxes were far more flexible in their battle tactics and use of weapons than the orthodoxy allows.[191] For example, the orthodoxy draws heavily on Thucydides' description of the battle of Mantinea to explain the hoplite's need to protect his vulnerable right-hand side by maintaining a tight formation so as to seek protection from the shield of his right-hand neighbor. But Cawkwell is unconvinced. Hoplites may have advanced in close formation, but once they closed with the enemy they would have required more room to fight in the actual battle. Plato speaks in the *Laws* about the need for a full and regular system of military training organized by the polis, including teaching by experts in *hoplomachia*. This implies that fighting skills were important. Dancing, moreover, was part of [Spartan] hoplite training, and in the *Laws* (815a) Plato speaks of the Pyrrhic depicting "the motions executed to avoid blows and shots of all kinds (dodging, retreating, jumping into the air, crouching)."[192] He notes that "when 'the Mantineans and some of the Arcadians' from the Ten Thousand danced, they did so in hoplite equipment, and in general the place of dancing in Greek life was such that we may be confident that most young men of the hoplite class got from dancing whatever was of use in it for soldiering."[193]

The discussion of tactics in Xenophon's *Constitution of the Spartans*, especially the description of the Spartan countermarch and the thinning of the ranks, suggests that hoplite phalanxes were "flexible on the field of battle." Cawkwell finds it "very hard to conceive of a hoplite using his weapons at all effectively in the crowded space orthodoxy assigns him," aside from using the spear in an overhand motion or the sword solely to cut.[194]

> In the use of weapons as in all games that involve the delivery and avoidance of blows, it is footwork that is all important. Hoplites may have been heavily armed, but they would surely duck and dodge in the way that Plato would have had them train (*Laws* 815a). One cannot do that, if one's neighbour gets in the way. Likewise the delivery of blows would require some freedom of movement. Of course, they may have fought in a highly constricted way and very ineffectively and longed for a chance for single combat where their real skills could be exploited, but if the evidence lends any encouragement to the view that hoplites fought, as opposed to advanced or followed up, in open order, one should take the possibility most seriously.[195]

On the other hand, Cawkwell points out, "Variations of formation could be, and indeed were on occasion, made in the course of a battle, but this is far from disproving that normally hoplites fought as Thucydides made them advance, i.e. as close as possible to each other to secure the partial protection of the shield of the man on the right."[196]

Another area that Cawkwell addresses is the iconography. He confines his comments to scenes representing rows of fighters going into combat.

> In most scenes that I am aware of, the shield is held not across the body but is extended forwards and at an angle, as if the hoplite was using his shield to give a 'straight left'. (Indeed if they did not use it in this way, their shields would have been unnecessarily wide.) In those few scenes where the shield is held directly in front, it is held well forward to leave the hoplite free to use his legs, but the Chigi vase is the typical scene, and in it hoplites, with spears held high ready to strike, all have their shields on their left and their right legs forward, the very posture necessary for the effective use of the spear. Was this how the fighting in line was conducted?

Based on the depictions of vases Cawkwell believes that hoplites fought in open order. "If one is to take seriously the archaeological evidence, it is plainly the case that hoplites did not fight as Thucydides made them advance." One concern is for safety: "If the man on one's right is fighting with left leg forward and with shield advanced to ward off his opponent's spear, the closer one got to him the greater the danger of his opponent's spear sliding off one's neighbor's shield and damaging oneself. Another concern would be tactical: "Common prudence would require that there be some space between one and one's neighbor. Such space would give the hoplite room to move and make good use of his weapons. Nor was there need to fear that he would be attacked on his open right side. He had the man behind him to defend him."[197]

An open formation, he suggests, is the best way to imagine a hoplite having the room to employ the type of skills Plato (*Laws* 815a) mentions. "He was still in line, fighting man beside man, still dependent on his neighbor's courage, but had enough room to do more than just make ineffectual jabs."[198]

Before looking at the arguments of van Wees, it is critical to examine in detail the enormous impact that Homeric studies have had on the way scholars understand early Greek warfare.

Homer and the Hoplite Phalanx

Lorimer's view of Homeric warfare is in its essentials similar to that of Grote a century earlier.[199] The fighting takes place at long range and privileges the actions of heroic champions over those of the mass of common soldiers; the picture of warfare in the *Iliad* predates the invention of the hoplite phalanx. Like Grote, she appears to assume a written text composed by Homer in the eighth century. Her ideas on late passages and interpolations are consistent with the types of debates that took place in the nineteenth century.[200] For example, she points out that a reference to the plate corselet occurs only twice in the poem within a short space (13.371–72; 397–98), which indicates it is an interpolation. She treats the apparent reference to the hoplite phalanx in a similar manner. "Corslets are called *neosmektoi* [newly cleaned] in a passage (13.339–44), which can only be an attempt, unique in the poem, to describe hoplite formation, and is therefore an interpolation, presumably of the seventh century." Homer's diction might indicate the weapons and armor of a hoplite as well. "The emphatic *makreis* [long] marks the spears as the heavy thrusting weapon, while *neosmektoi* can only apply to a corslet of metal."[201] The main differences in her reading of the epic seem to depend on the archaeological evidence to which Grote did not have access.

In the 1970s Snodgrass and Latacz developed two of the most influential approaches to the Homeric poems as sources for early Greek warfare. Their theories respond to the problem of Homeric society that Finley stated in *The World of Odysseus*.

> The serious problem for the historian is to determine whether, and to what extent, there is anything in the poems that relates to social and historical reality; how much, in other words, of the world of Odysseus existed only in the poet's head and how much outside, in space and time. The prior question is whence the poet took his picture of that world and its wars and its heroes' private lives.[202]

In the light of the work of Parry and Lord on oral composition and oral traditions, certain key ideas have impacted all subsequent work on this subject. The first recognizes that the bard or singer composes his epic during his performance of it. The second emphasizes the importance of the interaction between the poet and his audience in shaping the content of his narrative. The result is that the poet seeks consistency in providing his audience with a coherent view of society that might appear remote or "heroic," but, to be intelligible, must resemble their shared experience. For ancient warfare, therefore, the description in the *Iliad* must represent a fighting style familiar to the audience in order to be realistic and compelling.

Snodgrass answered an unequivocal no to the question whether Homer presents an historical society in the *Iliad* and *Odyssey*.[203] Yet he finds that Homer combines and conflates features from different eras. The Homeric description of fighting and equipment does not derive from one single period of history, but "is composite and shows internal inconsistency." Cartledge agrees on this point: "The problems of interpreting 'Homer' (i.e. our Homer) as history are legion, but for my limited purposes the most important is whether it is possible to locate a coherent Homeric 'world' or 'society' in space and time. To avoid multiplying references, I need only cite Snodgrass, with whose negative I am in complete agreement, against e.g. M. I. Finley."[204] But in a more recent work, Cartledge discusses the problems that face the historian who wishes to make use of the epics for evidence.

> They were the products of a centuries-long oral tradition unconstrained by properly historical attention to accuracy, authenticity, and consistency—indeed, of a tradition constrained rather to mutate and evolve in accordance with the changing circumstances and expectations of the poets' audiences. If it is indeed the case that no imaginative poet can be expected to be as consistent

> and authentically realistic as the historian might wish or demand, then this is true to the ultimate degree of the poets of the Homeric tradition of oral epic.[205]

However, the revisionists, Latacz first of all, have shown that the common soldier in the *Iliad* plays a critical role in the fighting. Indeed, Latacz and scholars since have argued persuasively that mass action, not individual combat between heroic champions, is decisive in most Homeric battles.[206]

For his part Hans van Wees accepts that phalanx-style fighting is already widely—not just occasionally—detectable in Homer's *Iliad*, which he dates to the early seventh century. But he does not see a clear-cut break between the Homeric and hoplite styles of fighting. For example, Homeric heroes use spears as weapons far more frequently than warriors depicted on Geometric vases. On the other hand Geometric warriors use bows and arrows about three times more often than epic heroes; and swords, the least mentioned weapon in Homer, are the most used weapon in the paintings.[207] He concludes that "the usage of weapons in the *Iliad* corresponds, not to Geometric, but to early seventh-century practice." Van Wees summarizes his findings:

> In the eighth century, warriors are armed with a pair of spears, which they use primarily as missiles: hence the prominence of the sword in Geometric scenes of close combat. In the seventh century, and in the *Iliad*, men are armed with either one or two spears, which they use for both thrusting and throwing, with roughly equal frequency: the *Iliad* features 87 spear casts (52.4%) and 79 spear-thrusts (47.6%). By the classical period, warriors are without exception equipped with a single large spear used exclusively as a thrusting weapon.[208]

The old view saw a dramatic break between the fighting styles of heroic soloists and that of hoplites; the new consensus led by Latacz proposed that the masses play as decisive a role in Homer as they do in the phalanx. Van Wees suggests a compromise. He agrees on the importance of the masses in both styles of fighting but sees no increased participation of the masses in warfare from the eighth to the seventh century; therefore there was no change in the balance of power between aristocrats and commoners. On the other hand he notes development in the evolution of warfare from Geometric, through Homeric, to hoplite fighting, whereas Latacz does not. For example, there is a shift from the sword to the spear as the main weapon of close combat; a gradual disappearance of chariots from the battlefield; light-armed troops become differentiated from heavy-armed warriors and lose status; and, "most importantly, there is a marked development of cooperation, coordination, and central leadership."[209] This process culminates in the increasing uniformity, equality, and solidarity associated with the rise of the phalanx.

But van Wees's conclusions differ from the traditional narrative. Mass combat did not lead to political changes. Not only was the process drawn out over several generations or more; "it is doubtful whether without the crucial ingredient of the introduction of mass combat the remaining changes would have had much effect on relations between aristocracy and commoners." The rise of the phalanx simply reduced further the elite's claim on political power. "By reducing individual mobility and finally excluding chariots and horses from the battlefield, the phalanx made it even harder than it had previously been for anyone to stand out in the melee, and even more obvious that the course of battle was never really determined by noble champions."[210]

Van Wees employs his understanding of "mass fighting, but not in dense or regular order" in the *Iliad* to develop perhaps the most ambitious thesis of the revisionists. Latacz had suggested that Homeric warriors wear the equivalent of hoplite panoplies because they fight in the close formation of a phalanx. For van Wees, however, not only is Homeric armament similar to that of hoplites, but it is also "by no means incompatible with mobile, open-formation."[211] He explains the apparent contradiction between the combat of champions (*promachoi*) and mass fighting in the epic (13.576–655).

> The situation is clear: the fighting takes place among the *promachoi*, while behind them a mass of *hetairoi* are in relative safety. A man picks an adversary and moves as near to him as is necessary to shoot an arrow, cast a spear or stone, or stab with spear or sword. Unless killed in combat, he then falls back upon the mass. The pattern recurs in every battle. Warriors go "through the *promachoi*" and "run" or "jump" at their opponents before they fight. All kinds of weapon, including arrows and stones, are used simultaneously. The spear, either thrown as a javelin or thrust as a lance, is by far the most commonly mentioned. Men may come close to their target to strike, or to retrieve their spear, or, if they have killed, to try to take spoils, but in each case they will quickly retreat to safer surroundings. This style of fighting presupposes that individual combatants are separated by a considerable distance from one another as well as from the enemy.[212]

In sum, either common fighters or heroic champions may fight among the *promachoi*. "This is depicted quite consistently, so it would appear that the poet had a clear vision of what battles in heroic times were supposed to be like."[213]

Van Wees places Homeric warfare in the context of the interaction between the oral poet and his audience. The battle narrative alternates between close-ups of the front-rank fighters and panoramic images of the mass of men in action.

> To the modern reader, unfamiliar with the kind of fighting described by the poet, the panoramic scene of "shields clashing" at the beginning of the first battle may suggest a collision of two close-order phalanxes, while missiles flying all morning at the beginning of the third battle may sound like long-range skirmishing. But to audiences who understood how the heroes fought it would have been obvious that such images simply represented two sides of the same coin. In the fluid, open-order action of the epic, mass fighting takes place close range and long range at the same time.[214]

The open order and fluid combat of the *Iliad* provides a model for van Wees of how Greek hoplites fought in the seventh century. In addition, he finds support for his thesis in the poetry of Tyrtaeus.

Tyrtaeus has long figured into the orthodoxy and has often been cited as proof of the existence of the classical phalanx. Van Wees concedes that "some of the main themes of Tyrtaeus' surviving work may indeed at first glance deceptively suggest phalanx tactics."[215] There is the importance of close combat: "Set foot against foot, press shield against, fling crest against crest, helmet against helmet, and chest against chest, and fight a man, gripping the hilt of a sword or a long spear." A second theme is cohesion: "Fight while staying together, young men" (F 10.15 West); "those who [fight] while staying together die in smaller numbers and save the men behind them" (F 11.11–13); "speak encouraging words to the next man when you stand beside him" (F 12.19). Tyrtaeus also stresses the need to stand one's ground: "legs well apart, both feet planted firmly on the ground, biting your lip, covering thighs and shins below and chest and shoulders with the belly of the broad shield, shaking a mighty spear in your right hand" (F 10.16–32; 11.4–27). However, van Wees points to other elements of the poetry that appear in both pre-selected passages and especially in fragments that survive by chance on papyrus, "which show that our poet did *not* have the classical phalanx in mind."[216] In these the poet must exhort the soldier to make his way to the front line: "those who *dare go into close range and towards the front-line fighters* (*promachoi*), while staying together, die in smaller numbers" (F 11.11–13).

> Tyrtaeus' Spartans, in other words, have the space and freedom to move around the battlefield. They are still able to behave just like the warriors of the *Iliad*, who wander around their battlefields quite freely, individually and in small groups, moving "towards the front-line fighters" or dropping back "beyond the range of missiles," leaving and entering battle as they see fit. Just like Homer's heroes, the Spartans must be fighting in an *open and fluid order*.[217]

Van Wees sees other aspects of the poetry that contradict the idea that the warriors in the martial elegies of Tyrtaeus have a fixed place in a tightly organized formation. For instance, light-armed missile troops play a prominent role. Instead of fighting outside the phalanx as in the classical period, the light- and the heavy-armed "are part of a single, undifferentiated formation." One exhortation by the poet to fight hand-to-hand is especially telling. "And you, light-armed, squatting under a shield here and there, must throw great rocks and hurl smooth javelins while you stand close by the heavy-armed (F 11.35–8)." "The light-armed here are clearly not a separate body of troops, but scattered 'here and there' among the hoplites," van Wees points out, "and 'squatting' for cover behind the latter's shields. The same mode of operation is described in the *Iliad*, where archers are protected by other men's shields, and only briefly break cover to shoot their arrows."[218]

Using both the literary and iconographical evidence, van Wees traces the slow transformation of Greek warfare from the Dark Age to the creation of the hoplite. Dark Age Greek warriors wore little or no armor; they fought with a light shield and a sword in close combat; the weapons they used at long range included either a pair of throwing spears or bow and arrows. Both archers and spearmen fought independent from one another in a wide, open formation. The relative status of different styles of fighting changed with the emergence of the hoplite in the last quarter of the eighth century. The heavy armor and heavy shield enabled the hoplite to engage the enemy at closer range. Therefore, he could use his spear for thrusting as well as throwing. As formations became denser, archers started to play a subordinate role as auxiliary troops; they moved among the ranks and behind the shields of the hoplites. "Not until the last third of the seventh century did the majority of hoplites stop carrying throwing spears and begin to rely on the single thrusting spear and sword only. Even then, as Tyrtaeus shows, formations remained relatively open and fluid: hoplites and light-armed intermingled and soldiers continued to enjoy considerable freedom of movement on the battlefield."[219]

When did the classical phalanx emerge with its closely packed ranks? Van Wees considers the possibility that the phalanx continued to evolve until after the Persian Wars in the fifth century.

> Perhaps we can only say that the type of phalanx described by Thucydides and Xenophon must have developed some time after 600 BC and before the Peloponnesian War. Either way, it is clear that the emergence of the hoplite was only the beginning of a lengthy process, which certainly lasted more than a century and may have lasted more than two centuries, leading to the creation of a close-order, hoplites-only phalanx. The classical hoplite formation, then, was not the long-lived military institution of scholarly tradition, but merely one phase in a history of almost four centuries of slow change towards ever denser and more cohesive heavy infantry formations, culminating in the mid-fourth century with the creation of the Macedonian phalanx.[220]

If the hoplite phalanx did not fully develop until the fifth century, this rules out any hoplite-led political revolution in archaic Greece. But in this volume, van Wees argues that something like the agrarian revolution Victor Hanson details in *The Other Greeks* took place about two centuries later. The thesis that van Wees presents in the present volume builds on some of the arguments in his book *Greek Warfare: Myths and Realities*,[221] which Hanson addresses in his chapter.

Notes

1. Lewis Mumford, *The Transformations of Man*, New York, 1956, 46–47.
2. *Laws* 1.626A.
3. Thucydides 3.82.2.
4. George Grote, *A History of Greece*, New York, 1846, II, 106.
5. Grote, II, 106.
6. Grote, II, 107.
7. Grote, VII, 84.
8. Grote, III, 16.
9. In arguing for a ninth-century Homeric society Grote (II, 160) reasons that "there is nothing either in the *Iliad* or *Odyssey* which savors of *modernism*, applying that term to the age of Peisistratus; nothing which brings to our view the alterations, brought about by two centuries, in the Greek language, the coined money, the habits of writing and reading, the despotisms and republican governments, the close military array, the improved construction of ships, the Amphiktyonic convocations, the mutual frequentation of religious festivals, the Oriental and Egyptian veins of religion, etc., familiar to the later epoch."
10. Grote, II, 155.

11. Grote, II, 107.
12. Grote, II, 107.
13. Grote, II, 107–8.
14. Grote views (I, 340–69) the period immediately following the first Olympiad as momentous in the passage from an age of imagination, emotion, and religious feelings to one of recorded history and science, and concern with the present. The early Greek myths, the *Iliad* and *Odyssey* specifically, furnished a quasi history and a quasi philosophy that "filled up the vacuum of an unrecorded past." The vast majority of Greeks still clung to mythopoeic ways of thinking, "the staple of the uninstructed Greek mind," throughout the historical period. But the meaning of the word myth changed, and it "came to carry with it the idea of an old personal narrative, always uncertified, sometimes untrue or avowedly fictitious [pointedly opposed to *historia*]. And this change was the result of a silent alteration in the mental state of society,—of a transition on the part of superior minds (and more or less on the part of all) to a stricter and more elevated canon of credibility, in consequence of familiarity with recorded history, and its essential tests affirmative as well as negative." The transition to historical time is remarkable: "a sensible progress is made in the Greek mind during the two centuries from BC 700 to BC 500, in the record and arrangement of historical facts: an *historical sense* arises in the superior intellects, and some idea of evidence as a discriminating test between fact and fiction."
15. Grote comments (II, 65) on Aristotle's inability to explain the voluntary obedience his ancestors paid to their early heroic chiefs, "such remarks [of Aristotle] illustrate strongly the revolution which the Greek mind had undergone during the preceding centuries, in regard to the internal grounds of political submission. But the connecting link, between the Heroic and the republican schemes of government, is to be found in two adjuncts of the Homeric royalty . . . the boule, or council of chiefs, and the agora, or general assembly of freemen."
16. Grote, III, 14.
17. Grote, II, 93.
18. Grote, III, 17.
19. Grote, III, 31.
20. Since he dated Pheidon of Argos to between 770 BC and 730 BC, Grote placed this controversial figure outside the age of tyrants proper. On the other hand, Grote presumably would have attributed the despot's remarkable military success to a hoplite army, which he also dates in the eighth century.
21. Grote, III, 28.
22. Grote, III, 31.
23. Grote, III, 21.
24. Grote, III, 23.
25. Grote (II, 276–77) comments further, "These Thessalian cities exhibit the extreme of turbulent oligarchy, occasionally trampled down by some one man of great vigor, but little tempered by that sense of political communion and reverence for established law, which was found among the better cities of Hellas. Both in Athens and Sparta, so different in many respects from each other, this feeling will be found, if not indeed constantly predominant, yet constantly present and operative."
26. Grote, III, 30–31.
27. Grote, II, 456.
28. Grote, II, 455.
29. Grote, II, 453.
30. Grote, II, 389.
31. Grote, II, 400.

32. Grote, III, 128.

33. Grote, III, 128.

34. P.D.A. Garnsey, *Famine and Food Supply in the Graeco-Roman World: Responses to Risk and Crisis*, Cambridge, 1988, nuances this "22 percent cultivable" figure.

35. G. B. Grundy, *Thucydides and the History of His Age*, London, 1911, 248.

36. For example, Grundy commented on the weight of the Corinthian helmet (244), "I have tried on a Greek helmet found at Delphi, and I have also tried on various helmets of genuine armour dating from various periods in the Middle Ages. The iron [*sic*] of the Greek helmet was extraordinarily thick, and its weight was, I should say, nearly double that of the heaviest helmet of the medieval period, even than those used by the Spanish common soldiers of the sixteenth century, which were naturally made of inexpensive metal."

37. Grundy, 267–68.

38. Grundy, 268.

39. Grundy, 271.

40. Grundy, 271.

41. Grundy, 271.

42. Grundy, 270.

43. Grundy, 268.

44. Grundy, 256.

45. Grundy, 257.

46. Grundy, 260.

47. Grundy, 261.

48. Grundy, 262.

49. Grundy, 274.

50. Grundy, 279.

51. Grundy, 281.

52. Martin P. Nilsson, "Die Hoplitentaktik und das Staatswesen," *Klio* 22 (1929), 240–49, p. 240, translations by Gregory Viggiano.

53. Ulrich von Wilamowitz-Moellendorff, *Die Textgeschichte der griechischen Lyriker*, Berlin, 1900; see fragment 11, 23–24.

54. Nilsson, 241–42; Nilsson accepts that Tyrtaeus is problematic on these grounds but remarks, "one cannot help finding also in the words of fragment 11, V.11 παρ 'ἀλλήλοισι μένοντες, which stick fast, a prefiguring of the phalanx." See fragment 12 and fragment 11, 29–34.

55. Grote (II, 106 n. 1) had also commented on the problematic nature of using to Tyrtaeus to date the introduction of the phalanx regarding both the content and language of his poems: "Tyrtaeus, in his military expressions, seems to conceive the Homeric mode of hurling the spear as still prevalent, — δόρυ δ 'εὐτόλμως βάλλοντες. Either he had his mind prepossessed with the Homeric array, or else the close order and conjunct spears of hoplites had not yet been introduced during the second Messenian war."

56. Nilsson, 243; See the note in the introduction on the Spartan dedications.

57. Nilsson, 242.

58. Nilsson, 244.

59. Nilsson, 248.

60. Nilsson, 245.

61. Nilsson (248) discusses the analogous situation in Rome. "The story that in the year 432 the dictator A. Postumius Tubero had his son beheaded, because he leaped out from his assigned post (Diodorus XII, 64; Livius IV, 29), has by no means a legendary character. . . . On the contrary, it is an occurrence of the type that leaves a deep impression on the heart and memory

and therefore survives. It must only be understood in the circumstances of the time. It was not even long before that the hoplite tactic had been introduced, in which the gravest fault was to leave one's place in the line; However, the old way of fighting, according to which the individual needed to prove his worth in single combat, had not yet been forgotten, and the young man had given way to his thirst for glory. The father had maintained and inculcated the hoplite discipline with ruthless severity. Such conflicts between the old and the new way of fighting must have taken place when the former was replaced by the latter, because the hoplite discipline is difficult to learn and the old way is deeply rooted in human nature. Such a tragic outcome as this remained unforgotten. For us, the story is valuable because it teaches us at which time the change took place."

62. Nilsson, 247.

63. H. L. Lorimer, "The Hoplite Phalanx with Special Reference to the Poems of Archilochus and Tyrtaeus," *The Annual of the British School at Athens*, 1947, 76–138.

64. Lorimer, 76.

65. Lorimer, 107; see illustrations for Perachora aryballos.

66. Lorimer, 92; see note in introduction.

67. Lorimer, 81.

68. Lorimer, 82–83.

69. Lorimer, 83.

70. Lorimer, 105.

71. F. E. Adcock, *The Greek and Macedonian Art of War*, Berkeley and Los Angeles, 1957, 2, 3, and 4.

72. Adcock, 2.

73. Adcock (3 n. 5) points out, "the word [phalanx] was first generally applied to the famous Macedonian phalanx, which was a variant of the hoplite formation with special characteristics of its own."

74. Adcock, 14.

75. Adcock, 5.

76. W. Rüstow and H. Köchly, *Geschichte des griechischen Kriegswesens von der ältesten Zeit bis auf Pyrrhos*, 1852, 145; *Cambridge Ancient History* IV, 166.

77. Adcock, 7–8.

78. Andrewes, *The Greek Tyrants*, 1956, 31.

79. Andrewes, 32.

80. Andrewes, 32–33.

81. Andrewes, 33.

82. Andrewes, 34.

83. Andrewes, 36.

84. Andrewes, 36; note that "Similars" or "Peers" is a preferable translation for *Homoioi*.

85. Andrewes, 37–38.

86. Andrewes, 38.

87. Other important examples include Oswyn Murray's *Early Greece* (Harvard, 1978, 2nd edition 1993), John V. A. Fine's *The Ancient Greeks: A Critical History* (Harvard, 1983), and more recently the second edition of Robin Osborne's *Greece in the Making 1200–479 BC* (Routledge, 2009) and the popular textbook by Sarah B. Pomeroy et al., *Ancient Greece: A Political, Social, and Cultural History* (Oxford, 2008), as well as Ian Morris and Barry B. Powell's *The Greeks: History, Culture, and Society* (Pearson, 2nd edition 2010).

88. Victor Davis Hanson, *The Western Way of War: Infantry Battle in Classical Greece*, Berkeley and Los Angeles, 1989, 2nd edition 1998.

89. Hanson (1989, xvii); see below for the arguments to which Hanson is in part responding to here.

90. Hanson (1989, xxviii).

91. V. D. Hanson, *Warfare and Agriculture in Classical Greece*, Pisa, 1983.

92. Hanson (1989, 4).

93. Hanson (1989, 5).

94. Hanson (1989, xxiv–xxv).

95. Hanson (1989, 30–31).

96. Hanson (1989, 4).

97. Hanson (1989, xxiv).

98. Hanson (1989, 9).

99. Hanson (1989, xxv); for more in-depth discussion of the nature of terrain, geography, etc., see V. D. Hanson, "Hoplite Battle as Ancient Greek Warfare: When, Where and Why?" in H. van Wees, *War and Violence in Ancient Greece*, London, 2002, 167–200.

100. Hanson (1989, xxviii).

101. Hanson (1989, 22–23).

102. Hanson (1989, 22–23).

103. Hanson (1989, 24).

104. Hanson (1989, 24); Y. Garlan, *La Guerre antique de Sumer a Rome*, Paris, 1973.

105. John Keegan, *The Face of Battle*, New York, 1976.

106. Hanson (1989, 25).

107. Hanson (1989, xxvii).

108. Hanson (1989, 56); See Krentz in this volume on the weight of hoplite armor.

109. Hanson (1989, 57).

110. Hanson (1989, 65–66).

111. Hanson (1989, 71).

112. Hanson (1989, 156–57); for the sake of comparison, Hanson (159) cites Oman's detailed account of medieval warfare's collision of a German phalanx and a square of Swiss pikemen: "The two bristling lines of pikes crossed, and the leading files were thrust upon each other's weapons by the irresistible pressure from behind. Often the whole front rank of each phalanx went down in the first onset, but their comrades stepped forward over the bodies to continue the fight. When the masses had been for some time 'pushing against each other,' their order became confused and their pikes interlocked" (2.274).

113. Hanson (1989, 157).

114. Hanson (1989, 159) quotes Thucydides: "Large armies break their order just as they meet the enemy" (5.71.1).

115. Hanson (1989, 159).

116. Hanson (1989, 169–70) sees in Xenophon's remark (*Hellenica* 4.3.16) that Koroneia "proved to be such as none of the battles of our time" evidence of the anomaly that the two phalanxes locked together in slaughter without the expected advance.

117. Hanson (1989, 172); Xenophon, *Hellenica* 2.4.34; 6.4.14; 7.1.31; *Agesilaos* 2.12; *Cyropaedia* 7.1.33; Thucydides 4.96.2; 4.35.3; 6.70.2; Herodotus 7.224–25; 9.62.2; Polybius 18.30.4; Arrian, *Tactica* 12.10.20; 14.16; Pausanias 4.7.7–8; 13; Plutarch, *Agesilaos* 18.2.

118. Hanson (1989, 172–73); Thucydides, 4.96.2.

119. Hanson (1989, 174).

120. Hanson (1989, 174–75); Polybius 18.30.4.

121. Hanson (1989, 175).

122. Hanson (1989, 35–36).

123. Hanson (1989, 36–37).

124. For an example of recent criticism and revisionism of Hanson's overall thesis see Harry Sidebottom, *Ancient Warfare: A Very Short Introduction* (Oxford, 2004). Sidebottom (preface) explains: "Some modern scholars have picked up on the classical cultures' ideas of their distinctiveness in war-making and, linking this to classical influences on modern Western culture, have come up with the concept of a 'Western Way of War'; a continuity of practices that they claim runs from ancient Greece to the modern West." Sidebottom continues his critique, "the 'Western Way of War' is not so much an objective reality, a genuine continuity of practices, but more a strong ideology which since its creation by the Greeks has been, and still is, frequently reinvented, and changed with each reinvention. Those who subscribe to the ideology do not necessarily fight in a different way to others, it is just that often they genuinely think they do."

125. Many scholars have stressed the importance of a new commercial class in the eighth century that exploited settled conditions in Greece to generate a level of movable wealth that could rival the landed wealth of the traditional aristocracies. For example, Forrest suggested that safer conditions for travel, more stable markets, better goods, and the momentous effect colonization had had on trade resulted in a shake-up of the existing society that was the starting point of a political revolution. This led to a change in how commoners might view aristocrats and their power based on greater landed wealth and divine ancestry. The expanded economy allowed some to advance beyond their peers or even to surpass their betters. The physical dispersion of the Greeks created the psychological independence that made it possible for the new middle class to first question and then outright oppose their superiors. "It is at least certain that this new economy . . . provided the necessary conditions for the rise of the hoplite army (in a very loose sense); let us say for the first military adventures of a new middle-class" (94).

126. Victor Davis Hanson, *The Other Greeks: The Family Farm and the Agrarian Roots of Western Civilization*, New York, 1995, 220, emphasis Hanson.

127. Hanson (1995, 116).

128. Emphasis Hanson (1995, 39).

129. Hanson (1995, 237).

130. Hanson (1995, 227).

131. This argument was first put forth by J. Latacz, *Kampfparanese, Kampfdarstellung, und Kampfwirklichkeit in der Ilias, bei Kallinos und Tyrtaios*, Munich, 1977.

132. Hanson (1995, 228).

133. Hanson (1995, 29–30).

134. Hanson (1995, 32).

135. Hanson (1995, 33).

136. Hanson (1995, 35).

137. Hanson (1995, 35).

138. Hanson (1995, 37).

139. Hanson (1995, 38).

140. Hanson (1995, 39).

141. Hanson (1995, 39–40).

142. Hanson (1995, 38).

143. Hanson (1995, 41).

144. Hanson (1995, 42–43).

145. Hanson (1995, 173).

146. Hanson (1995, p103, 106–7, 113).

147. Hanson (1995, 113–15); Aristotle, *Politics* 4.1318b7–15; 1295b40–1296a22.

148. Hanson (1995, 119); see Aristotle, *Politics* 2.1274b1–6; 2.1265b13–16; 2.1266a40–1266b6; cf. 2.1274a23–30.

149. Hanson (1995, 192–93).
150. Hanson (1995, 184, 186).
151. Hanson (1995, 44).
152. Hanson (1995, 199).
153. R. Nierhaus, *Eine fruhgriechische Kampfform, Jdl* 53 (1938), 90–113.
154. A. M. Snodgrass, "The Hoplite Reform and History," *JHS* 85 (1965), 110–22, p. 110.
155. Lorimer, 111.
156. Nierhaus, 90ff.
157. Lorimer, 107–8.
158. Snodgrass (1965, 34, 115–16).
159. Snodgrass (1965, 73, 89).
160. Snodgrass (1965, 89–90).
161. Paul Cartledge, "Hoplites and Heroes: Sparta's Contribution to the Technique of Ancient Warfare," *JHS* 97 (1977), 11–27, pp. 20–21; reprinted 1986 in K. Christ, ed., *Sparta*, in a German translation with new addenda) strongly denies this point on the grounds that wealthy nonaristocrats would be keen to enlist to defend their own substantial plots—warfare at this point being largely a matter of defending crops.
162. Snodgrass (1965, 115).
163. Snodgrass (1965, 122).
164. Snodgrass (1965, 198).
165. Snodgrass (1965, 204).
166. Cartledge, 20.
167. Cartledge (1977, 20 n. 71).
168. Cartledge (1977, 21–22).
169. Cartledge (1977, 23).
170. Cartledge (1977, 23–24).
171. John Salmon, "Political Hoplites?" *JHS* 97 (1977), 84–101.
172. Snodgrass (1965, 113).
173. Salmon, 90.
174. Salmon, 90–91.
175. Salmon, 94.
176. Cf. Cartledge (1977, 22).
177. Salmon, 95.
178. Salmon, 99.
179. Salmon, 99.
180. Salmon, 101.
181. Hans van Wees, "The Homeric Way of War: The Iliad and the Hoplite Phalanx (part II)," *Greece & Rome* 41.2 (1994), 155 n. 100.
182. Van Wees (1994, 155 n. 100).
183. Peter Krentz, "The Nature of Hoplite Battle," *Classical Antiquity* 4 (1985), 50–61.
184. Krentz, 61; Krentz sites the painting by the C painter on the bowl of a tripod-pyxis in the Louvre to support his thesis. See illustrations.
185. Krentz, 53.
186. Krentz, 53.
187. Krentz, 54.
188. Krentz, 59–60; Snodgrass conceded Salmon's point in A. Snodgrass, *Archaic Greece*, Berkeley, 1980, 106.
189. Krentz, 61.
190. G. L. Cawkwell, "Orthodoxy and Hoplites," *CQ* 39 (1989), 375–89, 389.

191. Peter Krentz in this volume discusses the nature of the *othismos* and the orthodoxy's use of the rugby analogy, which Cawkwell discusses in detail.

192. Penguin translation by T. J. Saunders.

193. Cawkwell, 379; Xen. *Anab.* 6.1.11.

194. Cawkwell, 381.

195. Cawkwell, 381.

196. Cawkwell, 384.

197. Cawkwell, 384–85.

198. Cawkwell, 386–87.

199. See the introduction in this volume.

200. In the second edition of his classic study, *The World of Odysseus*, originally (1954) written close to a decade after Lorimer's article on hoplites, Finley (1977, xxi) commented on the delayed impact that theories of oral composition had had on Homeric studies: "About oral poetry and its techniques, in contrast [to the negligible changes made to the rest of the first edition], the alterations (in the first two chapters) are significant, though not numerous. I originally wrote at a time when the discoveries of Milman Parry, which revolutionized our understanding of heroic poetry, had just been digested by scholars in the English-speaking world, and were still largely ignored."

201. Lorimer, 113.

202. Finley, 21.

203. Anthony Snodgrass, "An Historical Homeric Society?" *JHS* 94 (1974), 114–25.

204. Cartledge (1977, 18 n. 59).

205. Paul Cartledge, *Spartan Reflections*, Berkeley and Los Angeles, 2001, 157.

206. Anthony Snodgrass, "The 'Hoplite Reform' Revisited," *Dialogues d' Histoire ancienne* 19 (1993), 47–61, accepts this aspect of Latacz's argument.

207. Van Wees (1994, 131–55, 143–44).

208. Van Wees (1994, 145–46).

209. Van Wees (1994, 148).

210. Van Wees (1994, 148).

211. Van Wees (1994, 131).

212. Hans Van Wees, "Kings in Combat: Battles and Heroes in the *Iliad*," *CQ* 38 (1988), 1–24.

213. Van Wees (1988, 14).

214. Hans Van Wees, *Greek Warfare: Myths and Realities*, London, 2004, 157; see *Iliad* 4.446–56 and 11.90–91.

215. Hans Van Wees "The Development of the Hoplite Phalanx: Iconography and Reality in the Seventh Century," 149, in Van Wees, ed., *War and Violence in Ancient Greece*, London, 2000, 125–66; scholars have dated Tyrtaeus as early as 680.

216. Van Wees (2000, 149).

217. Emphasis that of van Wees (2000, 150).

218. Van Wees (2000, 151); *Iliad* 4.112–14; 8.266–72; 15.436–44.

219. Van Wees (2000, 155).

220. Van Wees (2000, 156); for a more detailed discussion see van Wees (2004, 166–83, 195–97), which tries to show that the phalanx did indeed develop c. 550–450 BC.

221. Hans van Wees, *Greek Warfare: Myths and Realities*, London, 2005.

CHAPTER 2

The Arms, Armor, and Iconography of Early Greek Hoplite Warfare

GREGORY F. VIGGIANO AND HANS VAN WEES

The Greek Hoplite (c. 700–500 BC)

Although elements of the bronze panoply associated with the classical hoplite began to appear in the late eighth century, what set the hoplite apart from his predecessors was above all his distinctive heavy wooden shield with a double handle, which is first attested circa 700 BC (see below, fig. 2-4). This date may therefore be regarded as the beginning of the hoplite era. A great deal of the debate about the origins of the classical phalanx centers on what the adoption of this type of shield might imply about the nature of hoplite fighting and battle formations.

The Hoplite Shield

The simple scene of combat shown in figure 2-1 is representative of a very common type in archaic vase painting. It is a scene from heroic legend—explicitly identified by captions as Menelaus facing Hector over the dead body of Euphorbus (described in the *Iliad* 17.1–113)—but the combatants are equipped with the panoply of the contemporary hoplite. It is included here primarily to illustrate the nature of the double grip of the hoplite shield, as shown on the figure on the left: the shield has a central metal armband (the *porpax*), through which the bearer thrust his left forearm up to the elbow, and a hand grip (*antilabe*), at the rim of the shield, that he grasped with his left hand.

It is worth noting that in archaic art the hoplite shield is almost always shown in scenes like this, used by combatants who are "dueling" or otherwise engaging in what looks like combat in a quite open order, rather than in a regular, close formation of the classical type. On a view widely adopted since the study of Lorimer, all such images show a combination of contemporary arms and armor with unrealistic "heroic" combat tactics. Alternatively, it could be argued that early hoplite tactics were not yet like those of the classical phalanx and that both the equipment and the manner of fighting shown on the vases may reflect contemporary reality.

The common view is that the double-grip hoplite shield could be effectively employed only in a dense formation because the bearer used the protection of only half

FIGURE 2-1. Rhodian plate, c. 600 BC. London, British Museum 4914. Redrawn by Nathan Lewis.

the shield, leaving him vulnerable on his right unless he exploited the cover of the "redundant" half of his right-hand neighbor's shield, as shown in figure 2-2a. If so, the presence of the shield implies the existence of a close-order phalanx in which the intervals between men are such that their shields nearly touch, that is, about three feet. On Victor Hanson's view, the shield was adopted to meet the needs of an already existing form of massed combat; more commonly, it has been argued that the invention of the shield immediately, or in the course of some fifty years, brought about the adoption of close-order formations. Others, by contrast, have argued that the double-grip system was invented primarily to enable warriors to carry heavier shields that offered more protection, and that the hoplite shield could be used without serious disadvantage in more open formations. In particular, van Wees has suggested that hoplites stood sideways (left side forward) when in close combat with their opponents, as shown in figure 2-2b, and that in this position they would make full use of the cover of their entire shield, leaving no "redundant" section and thus little opportunity or need for men to rely on the shelter of their neighbor's shield. He argues that this pose is both the more natural stance to adopt in fighting with a spear, and is frequently shown in Greek art; see figures 2-2c and d.[1] If so, the hoplite formation could have been more open, with intervals of, say, six feet between soldiers, which are attested elsewhere and would have allowed room for brandishing spear and sword, as well as for some movement between the lines, without losing the cohesion of ranks; in archaic hoplite combat, the formation may have been still more open.

Other significant features of the large wooden hoplite shield are its more limited maneuverability compared with the single-grip shield and its greater weight compared with a variety of types that were smaller and/or made of lighter materials such as leather or wicker. A hoplite shield could be held out no farther than the length of the upper arm, whereas a single-grip shield could in principle be held out at arm's length, though if it was carried on a strap (*telamon*) the range of its forward movement was in practice limited. The hoplite shield could not be brought over to the right-hand side as far as a single-grip shield, though in practice the lateral range of the latter was restricted by how much space the bearer needed in order to wield the spear or sword in his right hand. A hoplite shield was not carried on a *telamon* and could thus not be slung across the shoulders, as a single-grip shield on a strap could; it thus offered no protection for one's back in retreat or flight, though the bronze corselet, which was introduced at the same time, would have at least partly compensated for this.[2] The greater weight of the hoplite shield made the bearer less mobile, but how much less mobile depends on one's estimation of its actual weight (see Krentz, chapter 7 this volume), and literary and iconographic evidence show that it did not stop hoplites from being able to charge into battle at a run (see fig. 2-2e and the Chigi vase, fig. 2-8).

Many scholars argue that the cumulative effect of the above factors was enough to make the bearer of a hoplite shield a largely static fighter who relied heavily on the protection of a close-order formation. For some, however, the effect of the shield was primarily to provide much greater frontal protection, and neither the reduced mobility nor the reduced protection for the right flank and the back were significant enough to produce (or reflect) a fundamental change in manner of combat. On this latter view, "If this change to the shield did not necessarily entail a change in formation, it does suggest that in the late eighth century BC the trend in warfare was towards more frequent or prolonged hand-to-hand fighting, where improved protection was vital since blows landed with more force and were less easily dodged than in missile exchanges."[3]

Finally, Victor Hanson has argued that the bowl-shaped hoplite shield was particularly well suited to physical "shoving" of the enemy: the bearer could lean his shoulder into the hollow of the shield and thus push with his whole bodily weight against the enemy, or into the back of the comrade in the rank ahead of him.[4] Krentz, however, has argued that most references to "pushing" refer to a forward drive in combat, not to a physical shove,[5] and van Wees has suggested that hoplite shields were tilted back (see figs. 2-2e and 2-2f), so that the upper rim rested on the shoulder and the lower rim pointed outward, and any physical "pushing of shields" could not have involved shoving with one's whole bodily weight into the shield, but rather "shoving the protruding lower part of one's shield against the corresponding part of the enemy's shield—with the aim, no doubt, of driving him back, disturbing his balance, or at least breaking his cover."[6] The rear ranks would not engage in this type of pushing, but played a more passive role, including replacing fallen or tired men from the front ranks.

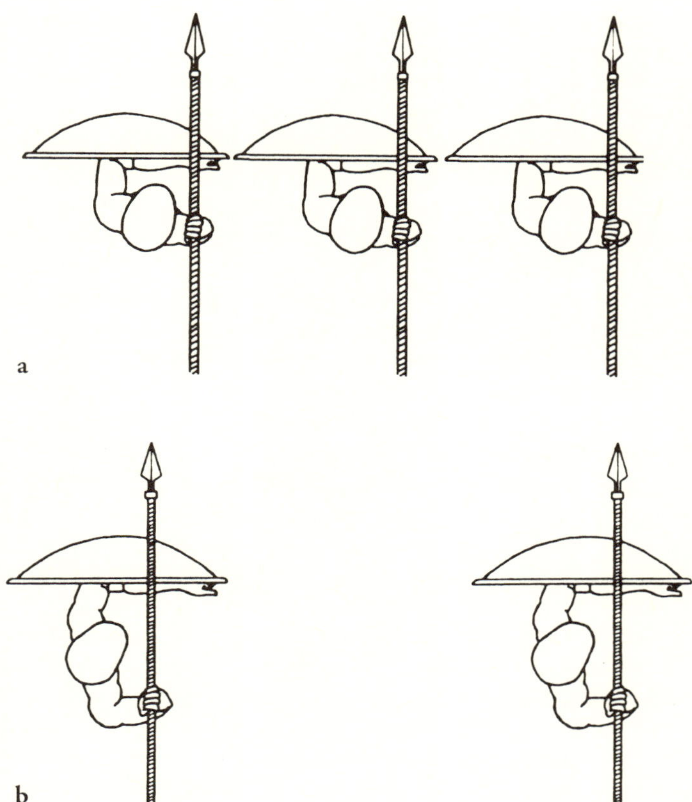

FIGURE 2-2. Line drawings illustrating the use of the hoplite shield. (a) Phalanx formation, assuming three-foot intervals and a frontal stance. (b) Phalanx formation, assuming six-foot intervals and a sideways stance. (c and d) Profile views of hoplite shields as carried in combat, tilted back against the left shoulder, on (c) a Middle Protocorinthian vase, the Berlin aryballos attributed to the Chigi/Macmillan Painter, c. 650 BC, from Kamiros (Berlin inv. 3773), and (d) a Siana cup by the Heidelberg Painter, c. 560 BC, from Boeotia (Athens, NM 435). (e and f) Hoplites running and squatting with left shoulder turned forward, torso almost at a right angle to the shield, on (e) a terra-cotta plaque from Athens, c. 520–510 BC (Acropolis Museum 1037) and (f) an Attic red-figure cup, c. 520–510 BC, from Chiusi (Louvre G25). Drawings courtesy of Hans van Wees.

Hoplite Body Armor

After the hoplite shield, the Corinthian helmet has been regarded as the piece of equipment with the greatest impact on the manner of fighting.[7] Its weight may have contributed to making warriors less mobile, but more importantly its extensive cover restricted the hoplite's range of vision and reduced his ability to hear. It is commonly

argued that these limitations meant that the wearer of a Corinthian helmet could operate in relative safety if he were surrounded by comrades in a close-order formation; as in the case of the shield, the counterargument is that the limitations were not so severe that a hoplite could not still operate in a relatively independent fashion.

The hoplite corselet was composed of two bronze sheets: a breastplate modeled to the shape of the chest, and another plate for the back connected by metal bands and leather lacing over the shoulders and down the sides. Corselets are commonly worn by hoplites in archaic art, but it has been noted that they are very much less common than helmets and shields in actual finds, which may suggest that only about one in ten hoplites wore a bronze cuirass.[8]

The panoply also included greaves, which were hammered out of a sheet of bronze, and customized to fit the fighter and the shape of his calf muscles. The greaves covered the warrior's ankles and shins, and were held in place by the pliability of the metal itself. The clear differences between the greaves that first appear on vase paintings of the seventh century, and the types known from the Mycenaean period, argue against continuity.[9] Although it was once argued that greaves were the last major addition to the hoplite panoply, circa 650 BC, it is now clear that they were introduced at about the same time as the rest of the armor, in the late eighth century.[10] As in the case of the corselet, greaves are much more common in archaic art than among actual finds, and it has been suggested that only about one in three hoplites wore them.[11]

Thigh guards and arm guards are also attested in archaic archaeology and iconography, but were probably quite rare. By contrast, finds and images from the classical period (fig. 2-3) suggest that hoplite body armor at this time was generally very

FIGURE 2-3. Classical hoplite equipment. Attic tombstone, late fifth century BC. Berlin. Staatliche Museen zu Berlin. Photo: Anderson 1970, pl. 12. Redrawn by Nathan Lewis.

limited: a simple *pilos* (conical cap) helmet, protecting only the top of the head, and a tunic were all the cover most classical hoplites seem to have enjoyed, apart from their shields. Whatever restrictions body armor may have imposed on the most heavily armed hoplites, they evidently were no longer in force by the late fifth century.

The Early Hoplite Phalanx in Greek Art

Representations of battle in archaic vase painting have played a major role in the debate about the origins of the phalanx. A series of images on Protocorinthian vases in particular has often been adduced as evidence for the development of the classical phalanx in or before the seventh century. Some doubts about this interpretation have been raised, however; it has been suggested that these vases represent scenes which have parallels in Homer's *Iliad*. If so, the images do not provide evidence for the existence of the phalanx but may instead reflect a more open and fluid battle order. The captions below set out the main points of contention.

The scene reproduced in figure 2-4 is the earliest to show the inside of a shield and therefore the earliest to show an unmistakable hoplite shield, with central armband and peripheral handle. However, a few Geometric vases from circa 700 BC show round shields with figured blazons, which almost certainly also represent hoplite shields.[12] Unlike his classical successors, the hoplite on the Lechaion aryballos is equipped with two spears, the second of which is held in the left hand gripping the shield handle; most other hoplites on later Protoattic and Protocorinthian vases also carry two spears in the same way, and it seems very likely that at least one of the spears would be thrown rather than thrust at the enemy. The other figures in the scene are differently equipped. To the left of the hoplite, a kneeling archer may be thought of as fighting the enemy from behind the shelter of the other man's shield, as described in the *Iliad*. The fighters on the right all carry Boeotian shields, with their distinctive scalloped edges; one man has the shield slung across his back, which shows that it must be suspended by a *telamon*.

The first iconographic appearance of a hoplite is thus as a single figure backed by an archer and opposed by nonhoplites. The hoplite shield here may be interpreted as a contemporary element in an otherwise unrealistic "heroic" scene (based on epic poetry and/or the conventions of Geometric art), in which case the image provides no further evidence for the nature of seventh-century battle. Alternatively, one or more of the other elements may also be derived from contemporary warfare, in which case

FIGURE 2-4. Protocorinthian aryballos from Lechaion, c. 690 BC. Source: Snodgrass 1964a (plate 15b). Reprinted by permission of Edinburgh University Press, www.euppublishing.com.

FIGURE 2-5. Protocorinthian aryballos from Perachora, c. 675 BC. Plate 57 from *Perachora*, vol. 2, *Pottery, Ivories, Scarabs, and Other Objects* edited by T. J. Dunbabin (Oxford, 1962). Reproduced with the permission of the British School at Athens.

the image may imply that in the early seventh century the hoplite shield was not yet used to the exclusion of other types, that hoplites still used throwing spears, and that archers mingled with hoplites on the battlefield.

The surface of the vase in figure 2-5 has suffered extensive damage, so that many details are lost or uncertain. In the center, two figures on each side are locked in combat. On the right, one man appears to be attacking another while a third figure comes to the backward-leaning fighter's aid; the advancing attacker may be imagined as belonging to the same side as the two men on the left of the central group. On the far left, a kneeling archer has released an arrow that is about to penetrate the shin of the leading fighter on the right of the central group. Behind the archer, a flute player, unarmed and wearing a chiton, has turned his feet to the left and is about to leave the battle for safety.

The armor of the figures shows a mix of hoplite and nonhoplite elements.[13] Judging from the crest and the neck protection, the five helmets that are visible seem to be Corinthian, though only the lead fighter on the left has what looks like a cheek piece. There are no greaves but, apart from the archer, the warriors are armed with single thrusting spears, which they use in an overhand style aimed at the opponent's throat. The lead fighter on the left carries a hoplite shield; though the *porpax* and *antilabe* are not visible, the position of the arm leaves no question. Lorimer inferred corselets on several of the men as well. As for the nonhoplite elements, she argued that the figure between the archer and the lead fighter on the left is nude and that the warriors on either side of the figure with the hoplite shield carry Dipylon or Boeotian shields. However, whereas in Geometric art the Dipylon shield is always held vertically, here the fighters carry them slantwise like a hoplite shield.

Lorimer concluded from the mixture of hoplite and nonhoplite equipment and the presence of "heroic nudity" that, "though I have no doubt that one object of the Perachora aryballos was to depict the encounter of two hoplite forces, I have also felt certain from the first that the scene was at the same time meant to be heroic."[14] On the suggestion of Dunbabin, she identified the scene as the slaying of Achilles by Paris. Whether or not the scene represents a specific legend, and whether or not nudity is an indicator that the image is "heroic," the Boeotian shield and the presence of an archer are not necessarily fictional or archaizing, so alternatively one could take the scene as evidence that hoplite and Boeotian shields continued to be in simultaneous use, and that archers still mingled with hoplites.

Apart from the use of hoplite equipment, further possible evidence for this image representing a closed phalanx in action, rather than a purely "heroic" scene, is the presence of a piper, who is assumed to have set a marching rhythm to help keep the formation intact (as in classical Sparta, according to Thucydides 5.70). However, the piper may instead have been present "for religious reasons" (as Thucydides implied was customary elsewhere in Greece), that is, to accompany the singing of a paean by the soldiers as they advanced into battle, without implying a regular formation.

An aryballos in the Berlin museum (fig. 2-6), which dates to about 650, depicts the encounter of four men on the far left opposing an advancing group of five, and then three men on the left of center face three on the right of center. On the far right, at the back of the vase, two hoplites attack two men that have fallen to their knees, and a third is in retreat. The wounded man to the left is about to receive the death blow in the back of his neck. It is not clear whether the three groups represent different stages of battle, or simultaneous actions on the right, center, and left of the battlefield, as one sometimes finds in the *Iliad* (esp. 13.308–29).

The fading paint has caused most of the spears to disappear, but there is no indication that any soldier had a second spear. All ten warriors on each side hold shields with blazons, including flying birds, bulls' heads, a lion's head, and a hare; all wear Corinthian helmets with crests, and greaves, and the left-hand man of each group, the only men whose torsos are visible, wear corselets. Lorimer inferred corselets where the border of a chiton is visible. The equipment is thus typical of the hoplite, although, as in the whole Protocorinthian battle series, there is not a single representation of a sword or dagger, which every man presumably carried.[15]

This is the first image that shows lines of hoplites with significantly overlapping figures, and this has generally been interpreted as an indication that the artist is trying to represent a high-density formation, specifically closely spaced organized ranks, as in the classical phalanx. It has been suggested, however, that what appear to be straight ranks may rather be stylized images of dense but irregular crowds, and it has been pointed out that the spacing of the different groups of figures on this aryballos varies. Van Wees argues that the closeness of the men on the far left and their short

FIGURE 2-6. Battle frieze from the Berlin aryballos. Middle Protocorinthian, c. 650 BC. Berlin 3773; drawing after E. Pfuhl, *Malerei und Zeichnung der Griechen* (Munich, 1923), no. 58. Redrawn by Nathan Lewis.

stride indicate that "they are standing still, packed tightly together," while the wider strides of their opponents suggest that the enemy is "moving towards them in rather more open formation." In the central groups, the even more generous spacing and long strides of the men suggest "a much looser order as the troops briskly advance into battle."[16] He suggests that even the densest of these formations, on the far left, may not represent a regular phalanx, but rather an irregular stationary crowd massed together in defense, as occasionally described in the *Iliad* ("leaning their shields against their shoulders, raising their spears," 11.592–5; also 13.126–35, 152).[17]

The Macmillan aryballos (fig. 2-7), ca. 650, was painted by the same artist as the Berlin aryballos and the Chigi olpe. Nine figures moving from right to left are apparently in the process of defeating nine opponents. From the right, the first five victorious hoplites are dispatching four opponents who have fallen to their knees in flight. The sixth hoplite on the winning side is meeting with resistance from a retreating enemy. The seventh hoplite has exceptionally been defeated by an opponent on the side that is otherwise losing. The final group on the far left shows another two victorious hoplites driving back two retreating opponents who are evidently trying to cover a wounded comrade collapsed behind them. All wear Corinthian helmets and greaves; almost all, including the defeated, carry two spears.

This is the first scene in Greek art to represent a collective rout and pursuit; in classical hoplite battle, a rout almost always meant defeat without any chance of rallying and resuming the fight, so the attempt to portray this crucial moment may reflect the emergence of the phalanx.[18] On the other hand, rout and pursuit are inevitably part of most kinds of infantry combat, and are frequently described in the *Iliad* in a manner similar to the image on this vase, that is, as a series of hand-to-hand combats in which the casualties are all on one side, even if a few put up some resistance (e.g., 5.37–84; 16.306–56).[19] Supplication of the victor by a defeated soldier is also a new feature; it is prominent in epic (e.g., *Il.* 21.72ff.) and might be a "heroic" feature, as Lorimer suggested, but could equally reflect contemporary practice. Again the use of two spears, in the Homeric manner, could be either a heroizing element that "crops

FIGURE 2-7. Battle frieze from the Macmillan aryballos. Middle Protocorinthian, c. 650 BC. British Museum, London 1889.4-18.1; drawing after *JHS* 11 (1890), pl. II 5.

FIGURE 2-8. Chigi vase. Middle Protocorinthian olpe from Veii, c. 640 BC. Museo di Villa Giulia 22679. Redrawn by Nathan Lewis.

up to mar the perfect picture of hoplite equipment"[20] or else an indication that mid-seventh-century hoplites were indeed still equipped in this way, and sometimes used spears for throwing.[21]

Most complex of all surviving battle scenes in seventh-century art, the Chigi vase (fig. 2-8) shows four groups of hoplites, two on each side, about to engage in combat. On the far left, two men are arming themselves. Each of the hoplites carries two spears, one in the right hand and another, apparently larger, in the shield hand. Snodgrass has refuted Lorimer's attempt to explain these second spears as representing an extra rank of hoplites not shown: "contrary to what she says, in the original illustration of the scene in *Antike Denkmaler*, the shafts of at least two of the spears are visible, passing across the shields of the main group of the left, and grasped in their left hands together with the *antilabe*."[22] The men arming on the far left each have two spears planted in the ground beside them, and here it is clear not only that the spears are of unequal sizes but also that they have throwing loops attached to their shafts.

This is the first scene, and one of the very few scenes ever, to show hoplites in more than one rank, and as a result scholars since at least Nilsson have regarded the Chigi vase as the first undeniable depiction of the classical phalanx; Snodgrass describes the image as follows: "the men fight in close-packed ranks; they advance and join battle in step, to the music of a piper; they balance their first spear for an overhand thrust; they are all equipped with Corinthian helmet, plate-corselet, greaves and hoplite shield."[23]

But the image raises some questions. First, if, as Snodgrass pointed out, the two front ranks of hoplites are raising the smaller of their pairs of spears with loops, the implication seems to be that they are preparing to throw. The two sides, despite standing so close together, would thus be engaging in missile rather than hand-to-hand combat.

Van Wees concludes that "whether we have here a picture of close combat with the wrong weapons, or of missile warfare at the wrong distance, we do not have a picture that matches the classical phalanx."[24]

Second, van Wees observes the extra pair of legs in the front line on the left. He doubts that this can be a careless mistake by the meticulous Chigi Painter. He also notes the redundant spear in the other army (i.e., the third, shorter, upright spear that protrudes behind them), which "must belong to some other, unseen hoplite. In other words, these rows of overlapping figures are not realistic images of single ranks, but schematic representations of larger groups of hoplites—whether in regular formations or bunched together, we cannot tell."[25] Third, he points out that the second rank of hoplites is in each case larger than the first, and is not marching in step with the men ahead of them, but "unmistakably *running*." The running hoplites on the left, moreover, are still carrying their spears upright rather than leveled, which may suggest that they are imagined as farther from the front than the second rank on the right, which has begun to level its spears. His overall interpretation of the scene is as follows:

> In the centre, two groups of hoplites are about to join battle and throw javelins at one another. The army on the right is about to be reinforced by a larger group of hoplites who have come running up and are just raising their spears to join the fray. In danger of being overwhelmed, the troops on the left call for help in turn, but their reinforcements, the largest group of all, still have some way to run, and indeed some are only just getting armed. The role of the piper in this scenario is not to set a marching rhythm, but to sound a call to arms, as trumpeters do elsewhere: this explains why he is evidently blowing at the top of his lungs, and why we see no piper on the other side, which has the temporary advantage.[26]

On this interpretation, the Chigi vase does not, after all, represent a classical hoplite phalanx, but a stylized version of the scenes of escalating combat by sizable but irregular crowds of warriors that one finds described in the *Iliad* (e.g., in the sequence at 13.330–495; men arming while their comrades are already fighting has a parallel at 13.83–128).[27]

Van Wees thus contends that these three remarkable vase paintings "prove nothing about the existence of a fully developed phalanx." Unlike earlier Greek art, they show armies moving into battle and armies in flight and pursuit, as well as "an unprecedented degree of overlapping between figures to create an impression of density."[28] However, van Wees sees closer analogies to Homeric battle narratives than to the classical phalanx in the work of the Chigi Painter.

Further explicit evidence that hoplites in the seventh century were sometimes armed with throwing spears comes from the alabastron from Corinth (fig. 2-9). The still-life arrangement of a hoplite's equipment shows both a long (i.e., thrusting) spear and a shorter javelin with a throwing loop. The fact that this appears in a still life rather than a battle scene makes it unlikely to be a "heroic" feature. "It seems an inescapable conclusion," Snodgrass argues, "that the early hoplite often, though not invariably, went into battle carrying two or more spears; and it is very probable that one at least

FIGURE 2-9. Alabastron from Corinth, c. 625 BC. Formerly Berlin 3148; after Snodgrass 1964, pl. 33. Source: Snodgrass 1964a (plate 33). Reprinted by permission of Edinburgh University Press, www.euppublishing.com.

of these was habitually thrown."[29] He also argues that the use of throwing spears in the Geometric age "took such a strong hold on current practices that the advent of the heavy infantry panoply, and even of the rudimentary hoplite phalanx, did not at first expunge it."[30] It is not clear how the use of throwing spears by hoplites was compatible with a dense phalanx formation—which in classical times engaged only in hand-to-hand combat—and it could be argued that the use of this weapon implies a more open and fluid formation even as late as 625 BC.

A battle scene from a badly broken Corinthian krater (fig. 2-10) presents a group of at least five hoplites crouching—some stooping slightly, others almost down on one knee—behind a scene of combat. They hold their spears horizontally in an underarm grip, or rest them on the ground, pointing diagonally forward and upward. These rear

FIGURE 2-10. Middle Corinthian krater, c. 600–575 BC. The Metropolitan Museum of Art, Gift of John Marshall, 1912; New York 12.229.9. Redrawn by Nathan Lewis.

ranks are not represented in the way one would expect to see in the classical phalanx. They seem closer to the relatively passive "crowd of companions," waiting some way behind the "frontline fighters," which is often mentioned in the *Iliad*. The scene may be taken either as "heroic" or, as Van Wees has suggested, a reflection of the looseness of the battle order even in the early sixth century.[31]

There are no images of the phalanx, archaic or classical, that illustrate the traditional views regarding the part played in the battle by the rear ranks in either adding weight to the phalanx or pushing on the front ranks.

As an alternative to the classical phalanx as a model for the style of fighting adopted by hoplites in the archaic age, van Wees has suggested an open and fluid kind of combat often attested in "primitive" warfare. He illustrates this with the particular example of battles as they were still fought in the 1960s by warriors in the Highlands of Papua New Guinea.

A series of remarkable photos[32] illustrates their fighting techniques.

> Before combat, Highlands warriors gather round their leaders in dense crowds [fig. 2-11a] and after a harangue set off at a run towards the battlefield, scattering as they do [2-11b] and slowing as they draw closer to the enemy [2-11c], until they come within firing range of the opposing lines. At this point the warriors are widely dispersed [2-11d] and in constant movement, not only across the front line 'to avoid presenting too easy a target,' but to and from the front: 'men move up from the rear, stay to fight for a while, and then drop back for a rest.' Warriors fight as archers or spearmen as a matter of personal preference. Spears, as in Homer, are used both for thrusting and throwing. At any one time, only about a third of each army takes an active part in the battle, while two-thirds stand or sit well back and observe the action. In the course of a day's fighting, a man spends much time at the back, but he will also go several times to take his turn at doing battle.
>
> In the course of this open order skirmishing, 'the front continually fluctuates, moving backwards and forwards as one side or the other mounts a charge'. 'As the early afternoon wears on, the pace of battle develops into a steady series of brief clashes and relatively long interruptions. . . . An average day's fighting will consist of ten to twenty clashes between the opposing forces', lasting between ten and fifteen minutes each.[33]

Van Wees argues that, in essence, this model fits the depictions of combat in Geometric and archaic art, and the descriptions of battle in the *Iliad* (as well as the allusions to battle in the seventh-century martial poems of Callinus and Tyrtaeus); he concludes that this is also how archaic hoplites actually fought.

Whether this "primitive" model is viable depends largely on one's interpretation of hoplite equipment. The Papua New Guinea Highlanders do not carry shields or swords, or wear body armor, so that they are certainly more mobile and more dependent on missile fighting than were archaic hoplites. If one believes that the weight of their armor made hoplites largely immobile, that they fought only with thrusting

a

b

c

d

FIGURE 2-11. Battle in the Highlands of Papua New Guinea. Source: R. Gardner and K. G. Heider, *Gardens of War: Life and Death in the New Guinea Stone Age*. (Harmondsworth, 1974).

spears, and that the double-grip shield was designed for use in dense formations, then they clearly cannot have fought in the Papua New Guinea manner. If however one believes that hoplites were relatively mobile despite their armor, that the double-grip shield and the rest of the bronze panoply could be effectively used also outside dense formations, and finally that hoplites used throwing as well as thrusting spears in the seventh century and mingled in combat with archers and infantry carrying lighter Boeotian shields, as the vase paintings suggest, then it is conceivable that they practiced a rather slower and denser form of Papua New Guinea combat.

Notes

1. Hans Van Wees "The Development of the Hoplite Phalanx: Iconography and Reality in the Seventh Century," 128, in Van Wees, ed., *War and Violence in Ancient Greece* (London, 2000), 125–66; drawing (c) after a terra-cotta plaque, c. 520–510 BC, from Athens (Acropolis Museum 1037; photo in J. Charbonneaux et al., *Archaic Greek Art* [London 1971], 313, fig. 359); (d) after an Attic red-figure cup, c. 520–510 BC, from Chiusi (Louvre G25; photo in P. Ducrey, *Warfare in Ancient Greece*, New York, 1986), 120, pl. 84.

2. Van Wees (2000, 127).

3. Van Wees (2000, 130–31).

4. Victor Davis Hanson, "Hoplite Technology in Phalanx Battle," in Hanson, ed., *Hoplites: The Classical Battle Experience* (London, 1991), 63–84.

5. Peter Krentz, "The Nature of Hoplite Battle," *ClAnt* 4 (1985), 50–61; Krentz, "Continuing the *Othismos* on *Othismos*," *AHB* 8 (1994), 45–49.

6. Van Wees (2000, 131).

7. A. M. Snodgrass, *Arms and Armour of the Greeks* (Ithaca, NY: Cornell University Press, 1967), 51, explains the significance of the helmet's craftsmanship: "To beat a complete headpiece out of one sheet of bronze has always been a feat requiring exceptional skill on the part of the smith; in the seventeenth century AD, for instance, armourers seem to have lost this art, and resorted to constructing helmets in two or more pieces with a join over the crown; while even in 1939 a modern Greek artificer, making a replica of a similar form, found it difficult to beat out the back of the helmet unless a deep recess was left over the forehead. So far as we can tell, the Greek bronzesmiths at the end of the eighth century had no foreign model or precedent for their achievement."

8. E. Jarva, *Archaiologia on Archaic Greek Body Armour* (Rovaniemi, 1995), 111–13, 124–80, with n. 10 below.

9. Snodgrass (1967, 52–53).

10. A. Snodgrass, *Early Greek Armour and Weapons* (Edinburgh, 1964), 86–88; E. Kunze, *Beinschienen. Olympische Forschungen* XXI (Berlin, 1991), 4–5 n. 10.

11. Hans Van Wees, *Greek Warfare: Myths and Realities* (London, 2004), 50 n. 10.

12. See, e.g., the Benaki amphora: H. Lorimer, "The Hoplite Phalanx," *BSA* 42 (1947), 76–138, pl. 19.

13. Lorimer (1947, 94).

14. Lorimer (1947, 95).

15. Lorimer (1947, 85).

16. Van Wees (2000, 140).

17. Van Wees (2000, 140–42).

18. Lorimer (1947, 104–5).
19. Van Wees (2000, 142).
20. Lorimer (1947, 104).
21. Van Wees 2000, 142.
22. Snodgrass (1964, 138).
23. Snodgrass (1967, 58).
24. Van Wees (2000, 136) quotes W. Helbig, "Über die Einführungszeit der geschlossenen Phalanz," *Sitzungsberichte der Königlichen Bayerischen Akademie der Wissenschaften. Philosophisch-philogische und historische Klasse*, (Munich, 1911), 3–41.
25. Van Wees (2000, 138).
26. Van Wees (2000, 139).
27. Van Wees (2000, 139).
28. Van Wees (2000, 142).
29. Snodgrass (1964, 138).
30. Snodgrass (1964, 139).
31. Van Wees (2000, 132).
32. Originally published in R. Gardner and K. G. Heider, *Gardens of War: Life and Death in the New Guinea Stone Age* (Harmondsworth, 1974).
33. Van Wees (2004, 154).

CHAPTER 3

Hoplitai/Politai: Refighting Ancient Battles

PAUL CARTLEDGE

I was myself at one time an actively engaged participant in the intellectual gymnastics that are, inevitably, the default mode for the study of early Greek hoplite warfare.[1] But, in or around 2001, I effectively retired from the lists.[2] So my involvement here is largely that of a former combatant, and interested spectator, somewhat bloodied by the latest thrusts and cuts of scholarly rapiers and bludgeons but yet largely unbowed.

Once, perhaps, "2001" might have conjured up images of Stanley Kubrick and futurology, but today it is all too gloomy retrospective visions of the destructive mayhem in New York City on 9/11, and its ongoing military consequences in Iraq, Afghanistan, and elsewhere, that weigh like a nightmare on our brains. I highlight our present circumstances, not just because war seems, like Jesus' poor, always to be with us, but because all history is in Benedetto Croce's sense present history: we historians of ancient Greek warfare cannot, however much we might like to, avoid bringing a present (though not, we trust, a viciously presentist) consciousness to bear on our strategic studies of the ancient Greek past.

I suppose the first thing that has struck me most forcefully as I have tried to review the scholarship on early Greek warfare of the past thirty years or so is the extent of the shift away from the more narrowly technical toward sociopolitical issues and approaches. The message that what we should aim to do ultimately is not "war studies" or "military history" in the abstract, but polemology, a totalizing history of war-and-society, seems to have been firmly driven home. Hence, presumably, all those collective volumes, excellent ones too, with that sort of a title.[3] From this welcome welter I should like to single out for special commendation, as the twin pioneers in the 1960s, Yvon Garlan of Rennes and my Cambridge colleague and fellow congressist Anthony Snodgrass.[4] Gratifyingly, for example, religion has begun to be given its due place in the story.[5] The other thing that strikes me palpably now is just how much work has been published recently on ancient Greek warfare—the Croce syndrome at work again, presumably.[6]

What follows is intended as a continuation of our editors' introductory lucubrations, a scene-setting attempt to frame the discussions or polemics that ensue. I shall state what I take to be the most compelling or pressing issues, and sometimes too give an idea of what my own views of them are, and how they have or have not changed over the past thirty years.[7] But this remains above all a position paper, a thinkpiece.[8] To begin with, therefore, let me try to deconstruct the "rise" or evolution of the hoplite phenomenon (a question-begging catchall label). As I (still) see it, we have to deal with a number of concomitant and I should say causally related variables or factors: first, and above all others, and indeed most generally, an "accelerated dynamic" as it has been nicely called[9] toward the formation of poleis or citizen-states with distinct identities, distinct territorial boundaries (including those of the especially dynamic "conquest states" such as Sparta), and distinct political, legal, and administrative institutions, as well as some idea of collective—including, not least, military—action; and, second, such further enabling or conditioning phenomena as demographic growth, the emergence of written law, struggles for power between old and new elites, intensified interstate relationships, and, last but not least, changing forms of warfare, especially greater or lesser degrees of hopliticization.

The process of polis formation was of course by no means universal, and I have some sympathy with those who wish to emphasize in parallel or opposition the rise of non-polis political entities,[10] or those who, more radically, wish the debate to transcend conventional polis-ridden categorizations altogether.[11] Nor of course was "hopliticization" any more universal.[12] But I hope I am not mistaken in thinking that—as is the case of the Archaic phenomenon of tyranny—what really matters is not so much universality, but significance: that is, what we today think matters historically, as we look back with the privilege of 20/20 hindsight. It is thus because of what I (again, still) see as the inseparable, inextricable connection between warfare and politics, and specifically the rise of poleis in the century between 750 and 650 (though of course not just then), that I have given my contribution its punning, near-anagrammatic title.

In sketching out some aspects of the many contentious issues, I have adopted the well-known Spartan organizational preference for groupings of five:

1. The source problem(s): contemporary as opposed to noncontemporary sources, documentary as opposed to imaginative (or imaginary), literary as against archaeological or documentary.
2. The developmental problem: What tipped massed fighting over into mass, phalanx fighting? Why, and how, did this tactical development occur, and how widespread how soon did it become?
3. Did (any) states need to "go hoplite" for purely utilitarian, functional, military reasons? Or rather was it ideology that drove, or at least severely inflected, the change?
4. But, if so, what was "hoplite" ideology? Were there rules of agonalism? Was it, for example, an ideology that included—or was specially focused upon—an ultimately political notion of equality?
5. Finally, to return to issue 1, above, the source problem(s): Did Aristotle get it at all right—not just in postulating an intimate causal connection between form of warfare and form of polity but in identifying the precise nature of that

connection? Or was he either wildly anachronistic or concerned only with peddling theoretical dogma, or both?

1. Sources

It is quite right to remind us sharply, as Peter Krentz has done (2007b), that we know nothing much for sure about Greek warfare in practice (we know or are told rather more about the theory or ideology) before the fifth century. That is true, after all, of almost all aspects of Archaic, or pre-Classical, Greek history. But it does mean that a great deal is made to hang upon those few scraps of especially contemporary evidence that are deemed to be unambiguous, accurate, and relevant; and, in particular, upon those that are claimed to be probative, whether they are literary or archaeological.[13] I shall give two illustrations, one contemporary, one noncontemporary, both Spartan, of the problems of the literary evidence, and a third illustration that combines literary evidence with archaeological (both representational and artifactual). My overall point is to show that we can and should do more than just throw up our hands and retreat to the imagined safety of a "we don't know anything, or anything much significant, before the fifth century" position.

i. Tyrtaios

Let us assume, for the sake of this argument, that Tyrtaios was indeed Tyrtaios, that is, a genuine Spartan poet of the seventh century BC rather than, say, an Athenian of the fourth, or even a non-Spartan literary fabrication. How, or how best, can his surviving verses be used to throw light on, or even explain, real Spartan military evolutions and developments of his own or an earlier generation (ex hypothesi, we are dealing with roughly the first half of the seventh century)? Two interpretative constraints have to be scrupulously observed—constraints, that is, operating on any interpretation we may wish to advance. First, there are the literary qualities or dimensions of his poems. He belonged to, if not the first, at any rate one of the first generations of post-Homeric, non-Homeric poet-creators, which means that he was, on the one hand, desperately original, but also, on the other hand, that he was just as desperately cabined, cribbed, and corralled by the overwhelming cultural-linguistic legacy of Homeric-style oral epic. Second, his poems, anapaests as well as elegiacs, continued to be sung by Spartans for centuries after his own, putative seventh century; that is, they were preserved and rehearsed through and into military and political circumstances unimaginably different from those of their original creation without that difference being felt as an insuperable obstacle to their positive reception. His verses apparently detailing real tactics cannot and must not therefore be read as if they are merely a poetic form of an early seventh-century Spartan general's campaign manual.[14]

ii.

Early Greek "lawgivers" were apparently by no means all equally concerned or preoccupied with military matters, though they must all have taken at least some interest and devoted some care and attention to the issue of the security, if not the power, of their respective polities. The most famous—or fully documented—of these pioneers were Solon of Athens and Lykurgos of Sparta. The latter, if it's not too disrespectful to say so, was little more than an urban myth; that he is not so much as mentioned by Tyrtaios is at least suggestive. Yet I judge it to be neither accidental nor coincidental that "Lykurgos," as represented by our earliest even vaguely reliable historical source Herodotus (1.65), was thought to have had military concerns centrally at the heart of "his" reforms.

Well in advance of the current trend of minimalist downdating of key Archaic phenomena, Moses Finley (1968, 1981) summed up his revisionist view of Archaic Sparta's development in the phrase "the sixth-century revolution." By that he meant that by 500 Sparta was, taken overall, the unique political, cultural, social, and economic entity that entered the brightish light of history in the Graeco-Persian wars. But how long before 500 it had assumed that overall profile, and how long before 500 its individual components—the military and so forth—had come into being, the state of the evidence he believed precluded us from stating. This is fair enough—up to a point. Yet, as Finley himself pointed out later in his *Politics in the Ancient World* (Finley 1983), one useful way of characterizing and categorizing the Spartan state entity is to label it a "conquest-state." In other words, it was not the case merely that the state of Archaic Sparta made conquests, but that it had acquired its very being and identity as a state precisely through such acts of (permanent) conquest and acquisition, both external and (at least as important) internal. Putting Finley and Herodotus together therefore, as it were, one might very well be tempted to claim, on prior theoretical grounds, that for Sparta to have become as it did and to have done what it did by 500 not only must it necessarily have undergone some major structural military transformation but it must have done so relatively early on (whether or not one also wants to claim that the transformation occurred very or relatively swiftly). Just exactly how one describes and construes that major military transformation is of course a separate question. But the theoretical considerations, for me, tend to argue strongly against such notions as four centuries of slow evolution, or a denial of any dramatic politico-military change anywhere in Greece before 500.[15]

iii.

My third and final illustration of a source problem concerns what I am still firmly minded to claim as the decisive, and possibly literally, hoplitic innovation: the hoplite shield.[16] No one, I think, denies that the very large, round, double-handled hoplite-type shield was an innovation, or that the invention can be pinned down quite closely to the years around 700. What I think not all discussants are always willing to acknowledge is just how peculiar—in both senses—this invention was. Two-handled shields can indeed be used effectively in less as well as more massed, phalanx-like formations, but this particular version (regardless of local or individual variations) was designed, purpose-built, to be held only on the left arm, in an unalterably fixed position that severely restricted free movement, so that it had to be used in close association with other shields so held and fixed.

Plato, predictably unorthodox, objected to this enforced dextrosity, to this systematic disadvantaging of the natural southpaw (who might have been able safely to wield a double-handed shield on his right arm in any more open-order style). But that objection came many centuries after an innovation, the impact of which must have been felt most fiercely in the original phase or stage of introduction, or rather imposition. The basic design of the hoplite shield remained unaltered for over three centuries, and later articulate Greeks, anecdotally and otherwise, recognized its absolutely cardinal, central, and definitional function in a variety of ways: by criminalizing "shield throwers" (the very existence of the single word *rhipsaspides* is telling) or by urging ideologically that, whereas one wears other items of defensive equipment for one's own self-protection, one bears the shield for the sake of the battle line or formation as a whole. If it was an ancient etymological mistake to derive the word *hoplitês* from *hoplon* meaning "shield," the mistake is itself a revealing one.

2. The Developmental Problem

I have given a hint already as to how I see the tipping point from mass to full-blown phalanx fighting happening operationally. Very briefly, the invention and very widespread adoption for many centuries thereafter of such a peculiar form of double-handled shield implies that it supplied efficiently a functional need: the need, that is to say, for much greater defensive protection and a correspondingly decreased emphasis on offensive maneuverability—just such a need as would have been created by the sort of increasingly mass style of fighting inferred from Homer by Joachim Latacz, an insight further developed by Hans van Wees, Kurt Raaflaub, and others.[17] We are of course all now hypersensitive to the difficulty of reading Homer as in any sense "history," but to identify this trend within the epic as it were against the grain (of the dramatic, ideological, and narratological highlighting of heroic individualism) as Latacz did seems to me a very impressive feat indeed of historical deduction.[18] But the inferences to be drawn from that discovery remain as contested as ever.

3. The Follow-My-Leader Problem

A hoplite style of fighting was unarguably quite widely adopted in Greek lands during the seventh and sixth centuries.[19] But did all or most or any poleis need to "go hoplite" for similar utilitarian, functional, military reasons to those that favored or required the adoption of the hoplite shield? Or was it rather ideology that drove, or at least gravely inflected, the issue?[20] I used myself once to be overimpressed by Herodotus's wonderful send-up (as I now see it to be) of the absurdity of hoplite warfare in terrain such as that which characterized most of mainland Greece (Hdt. 7.9). That this send-up was placed in the mouth of Mardonius should have been a sufficient clue. He was after all a "barbarian" who had not, actually, managed to defeat the Greek (especially Spartan) hoplites at Plataea, despite ridiculing their mode of fighting. So, yet another case of Herodotean dramatic irony. On the other hand, the fact does remain that the adoption of a hoplite style of warfare was not the most obvious purely military solution to a strategic-tactical problem. It does therefore remain a strong possibility that a very large dose of ideology might have been involved, if not solely or mainly in the original decision by a state to "go hoplite" then at least in the states' refusal for so long to diversify within—or out of—the hoplite mode.

4. (A) Hoplite Ideology?

The classically trained historical sociologist W. G. Runciman seems to me to have put his finger on the nub of this issue when he wrote: "it is difficult to see how the persistence of hoplite warfare can be accounted for without reference to the distinctive set of norms, values and beliefs which encouraged and legitimated it" (Runciman 1998: 733). But if so, what exactly was this hoplite ideology? What were the norms, values, and beliefs involved, and were they essentially or only contingently so connected? Were there quasi laws of warfare, or at least informal rules of agonalism, honored not only or mainly in the breach? Was there, for instance, a properly hoplite ideology that included—or was especially focused upon—an ultimately political notion of equality?

Possibly one of the most unguarded formulations of just such a point of view, not unconnected to the author's nationality perhaps, is the following, by the Japanese scholar Hiroshe Ando (1994: 23): "the system of the hoplite army created new human beings who carried on their shoulders a new polis which was nearing completion." That formulation is not incompatible with the overall thesis of one of the most challenging of recent general interpretations of Archaic Greek politics, Victor Hanson's *The Other Greeks*: hoplite warfare, Hanson argues, "cannot be understood apart from the economic, cultural and political agenda of a new group of middling agrarians, whose unique notions of private property, landed timocratic government, free economic practice, and distrust of rich and poor established the foundations of the Greek polis."[21] One might even wish to rescue something of Herodotus's Mardonios and invoke it in favor of a notion of hoplite agonalism, even perhaps egalitarianism, so long as that is not understood in strictly mathematical terms. At any rate, Peter Hunt (2007: 138) is surely right that "hoplites were the citizen army par excellence."[22]

Yet if these thoughts are on the right lines, they have failed to persuade, for example, Peter Krentz, according to whom "the case for new [agonal] protocols evaporates" and hoplites "did not *qua* hoplites drive political changes in Archaic Greece."[23]

5. Aristotle

So, let us turn finally to the political issue, also of course a source issue, and reconsider whether Aristotle was entirely off the mark in his postulated organic connection between form of warfare and form of polity in early Greece.

> The first political community [*politeia*] that arose in Greece after the kingships was based on the men who did the brunt of the fighting. These were originally the cavalrymen, because the strength and superiority in war lay with the cavalry. (Heavy-armed infantry are useless without formation, but the ancients had no experience of ranks and such matters, which is why their strength lay in the cavalry.) But as cities grew and the heavy-armed grew in strength, more began to share in ruling the state. That is why what we now call Polities were formerly called democracies. The ancient communities were of course oligarchically and monarchically ruled. (*Politics* 1297b16–26, trans. R. E. Robinson, slightly modified)

Revolution, I would suggest, is at the heart of our discussions here, though it is a problematic term, the application of which to ancient Greece has been denied by no less a historian than Moses Finley.[24] But Finley chose to apply what I consider to be an unduly restrictive, even anachronistic definition. So, although I agree with him on the absence from ancient Greece of an economic or socioeconomic infrastructure that would have allowed a permanent progressive transformation of the social conditions and relations of production (one thinks immediately of the persistence of slavery and other forms of unfree labor), I see no contradiction between that absence and the possibility of both the fact and the concept of political revolution: what the Greeks, Aristotle not least, called *metastasis* or *metabolê*. That notion, explicit in the Aristotelian *Ath. Pol.*, is, I suggest, implicit here, where Aristotle employs a military-based schema to account for successive political developments not merely within one polis but on the grandest scale of Archaic Greek political development in general and as a whole.

The problem with this schema, empirically speaking, is that its generality is—ironically for the advocate of golden mediocrity—excessive. Structurally, as often in the rather disjointed *Politics*, it does not follow organically from what immediately precedes. Moreover, not all of its meaning is transparently clear. Nevertheless, that does not seem to me to invalidate its utility precisely as a thought experiment, or model. That is, it constitutes a set of simplifying assumptions about what sorts of conditions and variables must necessarily be present to account for, not just the differences between the various sorts of Greek "constitution," but also the causal connections, the developmental interrelations, between them. Above all, the general context of Aristotle's thinking here is not only abundantly clear—the military dimension of a polity can serve, or be made to serve, to inflect or determine its fundamental nature—but also, to me, persuasive. But, no doubt, that will not necessarily persuade all readers altogether.[25]

Conclusion

I should like to end on a more general than a narrowly hoplitic note, quoting from a Theban praise poet writing, for once, not in a triumphalist vein: "War is sweet to the inexperienced but anyone who has experienced it fears its approach in his gut" (Pindar fr. 110).[26] But let us not only fear war's approach, but rather, with Donald Kagan, actively seek, and seek to promote, "the preservation of peace."[27] One useful way to do that, perhaps, is to reexamine the mainsprings of Western warfare in Archaic and Classical Greece: let the *ôthismos* commence.[28]

Notes

It was a huge honor for me to be invited by Don Kagan and Greg Viggiano to give at Yale on April 4, 2008, the opening talk of their Hoplites conference, held under the auspices of Yale's International Security Studies program and Department of Classics. This chapter reproduces substantially that quite informal presentation, with the addition of some rather light annotation.

1. I began my participation, as an undergraduate student of Geoffrey de Ste. Croix at New College, Oxford, just about the time Victor Ehrenberg was writing his *From Solon to Socrates* book (1st ed. 1968). Referring back to the struggles over early Spartan history of his academic youth, Ehrenberg wrote there of his involvement in a form of "intellectual gymnastics" (1968: 380 n. 2).

2. Cartledge 1977, 1986, 1996, 2001 (where fuller documentation, ancient and modern, may be sought).

3. Rich and Shipley 1996; Raaflaub and Rosenstein 1999; Meissner, Schmidt, and Sommer 2005 (rev. E. L. Wheeler, *BMCR* 2006.07.55); Pritchard, ed., forthcoming.

4. Garlan's *La Guerre dans l'Antiquité* (originally Paris 1972, 3rd ed. 1999) was translated as *War in the Ancient World* (London 1975) for a series edited by Moses Finley. Garlan 1989 marked a further development of his polemological thought, in a specifically economic direction: see my review in *Gnomon* 62 (1990): 464–66. The book of Snodgrass's Oxford doctoral thesis, published in 1964, quickly gave rise to Snodgrass 1965 (reprised, together with essential contextual material, in Snodgrass 2006).

5. Especially of course in the work of Kendrick Pritchett (1991), but also for instance in Hanson ed. 1991 (two essays out of the nine). Cf. Krentz 2007a: 158.

6. Rawlings 2007; Sabin et al. 2007; De Souza 2008.

7. It is perhaps somewhat risky to find oneself lined up in the ranks with my old friend Victor Hanson, but I have to say that the very title of his present contribution did cheer me. Revisionism has its place, here as elsewhere; indeed, insofar as "progress" may be made in any field of historiography, revisionism must have a place. The question, always, is what sort of a place? Conversely, orthodoxy is probably to be rejected *eo ipso* only if it is orthodoxy of a caste-imposed and -enforced kind. Cawkwell's review of "orthodoxy and hoplites" honestly "ends on an agnostic note" (1989: 389).

8. Compare Hanson 1999; Hanson and Strauss 1999.

9. The phrase of Sitta von Reden, in a forthcoming work on money and coinage in the ancient world.

10. As Morgan 2003; but see my review in *CR* n.s. 55 (2005): 198–200.

11. As Vlassopoulos 2007.

12. Wheeler 2007a: 187 has done well to remind us of that.

13. Hall 2007: 155–75 is an especially strong account from the methodological point of view, all the more so for being embedded in a general history of Archaic Greece. Van Wees 2000 conscientiously distinguishes between the *realia*, the actual pieces of equipment extant, and

the more or less idealized representations. For the latter see now Muth 2000 Part III, "Das Spektrum der Hoplitenkämpfe: Vielfält an Siegern und Vielflt an Opfern," esp. "Die nicht-narrativen Hoplitenkämpfe: Pendeln zwischen Sieg und Tod?" 142–238.

14. For very different recent readings of Tyrtaios, see Hall 2007: 166–67; and Singor 2009: 591–92.

15. Krentz 2007a, 2007b, and this volume; van Wees 2000: 156, and this volume; Singor 2009.

16. Dr. V. Stamatopoulou kindly shared with me the findings of her Athens doctoral thesis on the "Argive" shield: Stamatopoulou 2008.

17. Latacz 1977; developed by van Wees 1994, 2000, and 2004: 183; and see very recently Raaflaub 2008.

18. Snodgrass 2006: 346 pays due tribute to Latacz's pioneering interpretation.

19. Pritchett 1986 convinced H. W. Pleket, *Mnemosyne* 45 (1991): 266, that there was indeed "massive hoplite warfare in early Archaic Greece," though Hornblower (1996: 396, *ad* Thuc. 4.96.2) may well be right that "only an unusually arrogant scholar could claim to know what really went on in a hoplite battle." (I owe that reference to Dan Tompkins.) Hunt 2007: 108–9, 111–13 airs the propositions that the hoplite panoply innovation spread within a generation but that classical hoplite fighting developed slowly and hoplite dominance was less long and less complete than the traditional view would hold. Krentz 2007b, following and citing Raaflaub 1997, argues that there was no space for a hoplite revolution, or even a serious hoplite reform. Osborne 2009 has only a couple of (good) pages on hoplite warfare.

20. A possible analogy for the general type of question under consideration might be drawn with the introduction of silver coinage in the sixth century BC. For all the differences in detail, this likewise is a case of a compound of the severely pragmatic-utilitarian with the heavily ideological.

21. Hanson 1999: 403, referring to Hanson 1995. See also Hanson, this volume; and, especially, Viggiano, this volume.

22. Cf. Santosuosso 1997. On equality and citizenship in early Greece, see now Cartledge 2009. Note that, according to Burckhardt 1996, even in the fourth century BC citizen-armies were the norm as well as the ideal.

23. Krentz 2007b: 76, 80; and Krentz, this volume.

24. On the theoretical issue of "revolution" in antiquity, see, with caution, Finley 1986. The Goldhill and Osborne 2007 "revolutions" collection does not, unfortunately, consider warfare.

25. For my most recent engagement with Aristotle's political thought, see Cartledge 2009.

26. I have used the translation of Krentz 2007b: 79.

27. Kagan 1995.

28. Matthew 2011 unfortunately appeared too late for my consideration here.

Bibliography

Ando, H. 1994. "The ethos of hoplites and democracy in ancient Greece." *KODAI* 5:17–25.

Burckhardt, L. A. 1996. *Bürger und Soldaten: Aspekte der politischen und militärischen Rolle athenischen Bürger im Kriegswesen des 4. Jahrhunderts v. Chr.* (*Historia* Einzelschr. 101). Stuttgart.

Cartledge, P. 1977, 1986. "Hoplites and heroes: Sparta's contribution to the technique of ancient warfare." *JHS* 97:11–27. [German trans., with add., in K. Christ, ed., *Sparta* (WdF 622, Darmstadt 1986), 387–425, 470.]

Cartledge, P. 1996. "La nascita degli opliti e l'organizzazione militare," in S. Settis, ed., *I Greci* II.1: 681–714.

Cartledge, P. 2001. "The birth of the hoplite: Sparta's contribution to early Greek military organization," in his *Spartan Reflections*, 153–66. London and Los Angeles.

Cartledge, P. 2009. *Ancient Greek Political Thought in Practice*. Cambridge.

Cawkwell, G. 1989. "Orthodoxy and hoplites." *CQ* 39:375–89.

De Souza, P., ed. 2008. *The Ancient World at War: A Global History*. London and New York.

De Souza, P., and J. France, eds. 2007. *War and Peace in Ancient and Medieval History*. Cambridge.

Ehrenberg, V. 1968, 1973. *From Solon to Socrates: Greek History and Civilization during the Sixth and Fifth Centuries B.C.* London. [2nd ed. (1973) reprinted by Routledge in 2010 with a new foreword by Paul Millett.]

Finley, M. I. 1968, 1981. "Sparta and Spartan society," in B. Shaw and R. Saller, eds., *Economy and Society in Ancient Greece*, 21–40. London.

Finley, M. I. 1983. *Politics in the Ancient World*. Cambridge.

Finley, M. I. 1986. "Revolution in antiquity," in R. Porter and M. Teich, eds., *Revolution in History*, 41–60. Cambridge.

Garlan, Y. 1989. *Guerre et économie en Grèce ancienne*. Paris.

Goldhill, S., and R. Osborne, eds. 2007. *Rethinking Revolutions through Ancient Greece*. Cambridge. [Nothing on war.]

Goldsworthy, A. 1997, "The *Othismos*: Myths and heresies—the nature of hoplite battle." *War & History* 4:1–26.

Hall, J. M. 2007. *A History of the Archaic Greek World ca. 1200–479 BCE*. Oxford.

Hanson, V. D. 1989, 2000. *The Western Way of War: Infantry Battle in Classical Greece*. London and Los Angeles.

Hanson, V. D., ed. 1991. *Hoplites: The Classical Greek Battle Experience*. London and New York.

Hanson, V. D. 1995. *The Other Greeks: The Agrarian Roots of Western Civilization*. New York.

Hanson, V. D. 1999. "The status of ancient military history: Traditional work, recent research, and on-going controversies." *Journal of Military History* 63:379–414.

Hanson, V. D., and B. S. Strauss. 1999. "Epilogue," in Raaflaub and Rosenstein 1999:439–53.

Hornblower, S. 1996. *A Commentary on Thucydides*, vol. 2. Oxford.

Hunt, P. 2007. "Military forces," in Sabin et al. 2007:108–46.

Kagan, D. 1995. *On the Origins of War and the Preservation of Peace*. New York.

Krentz, P. 2007a. "War," in Sabin et al. 2007:147–85.

Krentz, P. 2007b. "Warfare and hoplites," in H. A. Shapiro, ed., *The Cambridge Companion to Archaic Greece*, 61–84. Cambridge.

Latacz, J. 1977. *Kampfparänese, Kampfdarstellung und Kampfwirklichkeit in der Ilias, bei Kallinos und Tyrtaios* (Zetemata 66). Munich.

Matthew, C. 2011. *A Storm of Spears: Understanding the Greek Hoplite in Action*. Barnsley.

Meissner, B., O. Schmitt, and M. Sommer, eds. 2005. *Krieg—Gesellschaft—Institutionen*. Berlin.

Morgan, C. A. 2003. *Early Greek States beyond the Polis*. London.

Muth, S. 2008. *Gewalt im Bild. Das Phänomen der medialen Gewalt im Athens des 6. und 5. Jahrhunderts v. Chr.* Berlin and New York.

Osborne, R. 2009. *Greece in the Making, 1200–479 BC*, 2nd ed. London.

Pritchard, D. M., ed. 2011. *War, Democracy and Culture in Classical Athens*. Cambridge.

Pritchett, W. K. 1979. *The Greek State at War*, vol. 3. *Religion*. Los Angeles.

Pritchett, W. K. 1986. "The topography of Tyrtaios and the Messenian Wars," in his *Studies in Ancient Greek Topography*, 5:1–86. Los Angeles.

Raaflaub, K. A. 1997. "Soldiers, citizens and the evolution of the early Greek *polis*," in L. G. Mitchell and P. J. Rhodes, eds., *The Development of the* Polis *in Archaic Greece*, 49–57. London and New York.

Raaflaub, K. 2008. "Homeric warriors and battles: Trying to resolve old problems." *Classical World* 101.4: 469–83.

Raaflaub, K., and N. Rosenstein, eds. 1999. *War and Society in the Ancient and Medieval Worlds*. Cambridge, MA.

Rawlings, L. 2007. *The Ancient Greeks at War*. Manchester.

Rich, J., and G. Shipley, eds. 1996. *War and Society in the Greek World*. London and New York.

Runciman, W. G. 1998. "Greek hoplites, warrior culture, and indirect bias." *JRAI* 4.4: 731–51.

Sabin, P., H. van Wees, and M. Whitby, eds. 2007. *The Cambridge History of Greek and Roman Warfare*, vol. 1, *Greece, the Hellenistic World and the Rise of Rome*. Cambridge.

Santosuosso, A. 1997. *Soldiers, Citizens and the Symbols of War: From Classical Greece to Republican Rome, 500–167 BC*. Oxford.

Singor, H. 2009. "War and international relations," in K. A. Raaflaub and H. van Wees, eds., *A Companion to Archaic Greece*, 585–603. Oxford.

Snodgrass, A. M. 1965, 2006. "The hoplite reform and history." *JHS* 85:110–22. [Repr. with new introductory discussion in Snodgrass 2006:309–30.]

Snodgrass, A. M. 2006. *Archaeology and the Emergence of Greece: Collected Papers on Early Greece and Related Topics (1965–2002)*. Edinburgh.

Stamatopoulou, V. 2008. "HOPLON. I argoliki aspidha kai i tekhnologia tis." PhD diss., University of Athens.

Van Wees, H. 1994. "The Homeric way of war: The *Iliad* and the hoplite phalanx (II)." *G&R* 41.2: 131–55.

Van Wees, H. 2000. "The development of the hoplite phalanx: Iconography and reality in the seventh century," in van Wees, ed., *War and Violence in Ancient Greece*, 125–66. Swansea.

Van Wees, H. 2004. *Greek Warfare: Myths and Realities*. London.

Vlassopoulos, K. 2007. *Unthinking the Greek Polis: Ancient Greek history beyond Eurocentrism*. Cambridge.

Wheeler, E. L. 2007a. "Battle. Land battle," in Sabin et al., eds., 2007:186–224.

Wheeler, E. L., ed. 2007b. *The Armies of Classical Greece*. Farnham, UK.

CHAPTER 4

Setting the Frame Chronologically

ANTHONY SNODGRASS

If there is nowadays a consensus that discussion of the Greek hoplite must start from Homer and the descriptions of fighting in the *Iliad*, then this is a fairly recent development. For most historians and Homerists of little more than a generation ago, Homer stood outside the issue and the *Iliad*'s battles would be mentioned only to be excluded from the discussion. There is an obvious analogy here with a bigger topic, one so closely linked with the hoplite as to be often thought inseparable from it: the rise of the polis. The same shift has occurred here: where there was once widespread agreement with Finley's view of the *Iliad* and *Odyssey*, that "neither poem has any trace of a *polis* in its classical political sense" (Finley 1956: 39), it is common practice today to scrutinize both texts, the *Odyssey* especially, for features that betray the poet's familiarity with elements of early polis society. Recent scholarship has detected a number of such elements there and indeed has held that, for the *Iliad*, the hoplite style of fighting is itself one of them.

In the specific case of hoplite warfare, this collective change of heart is, I think, relatively easily accounted for. It began with the appearance of Joachim Latacz's *Kampfparänese, Kampfdarstellung und Kampfwirklichkeit in der Ilias, bei Kallinos und Tyrtaios* in 1977. I would not go so far as to say that, without Latacz, the old orthodoxy would have continued to prevail, and the Homeric evidence to be set aside; but I would maintain that the momentum and concertedness of this change in opinion derived from the publication of his book and, more especially, to its favorable reception on the part of historians. The prime contention of that book, that mass armies and mass combat play a far more important role in the battles of the *Iliad* than anyone had hitherto been prepared to admit, has won almost unanimous acceptance and, on its own, constitutes a major advance in the debate.

For Latacz, however, it served as the foundation for a series of more far-reaching inferences, which carry his argument far beyond the philological domain and progressively further into the historical one. At this point, radical dissent intervenes. It begins with a mainly philological issue: how far is Latacz justified in arguing that the picture of fighting in the *Iliad*, his *Kampfdarstellung*, is a homogeneous, consistent, unified, and coherent one? One critic who, at an early stage, gave a firmly negative answer was Latacz's reviewer in *Gnomon*, Rüdiger Leimbach (Leimbach 1980). In his view, Latacz had quite failed to establish the coherence of detail of the Homeric battle scenes: his analyses tended to illustrate just the opposite qualities, of incoherence and internal incompatibility. For instance, the allegedly regular sequence of an engagement at long range, giving way to a phase of exploits by individual heroes, then to a mass engagement at close quarters, was simply not there in the text. A passage singled out by Latacz to exemplify the first phase of long-range engagement and specifically discussed at the Yale hoplite conference, *Iliad* viii, 60–67, gives an ideal illustration of this. This and other points were later to be taken up by historians and archaeologists, the present writer (Snodgrass 1993) and Hans van Wees (1994) included.

But we remained in a minority. Just as, on the philological side, most of the reviewers had reacted favorably, so most commentators on the historical implications took their lead from the late Kendrick Pritchett (Pritchett 1985), who followed the lead given by Latacz far beyond the point that we have reached so far. A useful roll call of these largely favorable responses has been given by van Wees (1988: 1–2, n. 3; supplemented in 1994: 14, n. 2): as we shall see, they include a number of historians and archaeologists. For Latacz and for many of his converts, not only was there a coherent *Kampfdarstellung* of massed battles, but it was historically a realistic one, rather than some kind of poetic construction; not only was it real, but it was based on a type of phalanx formation familiar from historical times; not only was it a kind of phalanx warfare, but it was the *same* kind of phalanx warfare that we know from later descriptions of the hoplite. This is the *Kampfwirklichkeit* of Latacz's title: it goes without saying that, at almost every point, its validity depends on the integrity of the *Kampfdarstellung* that we were just now criticizing.

It will be apparent by now that, after the first, indisputable demonstration of the importance of mass armies in the *Iliad*, I question every subsequent stage in this sequence of arguments. The "consistency" of the poet's battle descriptions seems to me largely imaginary. Even if it were genuine, it does not necessarily follow that the descriptions should be credited with the historical authenticity that Latacz confers on them: they might have been designed simply to fit the plot of the *Iliad* (as, in the main, they do, playing down but not entirely suppressing the effectiveness of the large forces arrayed on each side so as to highlight the deeds of individual warriors). But from this point on, the issues become increasingly historical ones: can the descriptions of mass engagements in the *Iliad* be closely compared, let alone identified, with the evidence that we have for the early historical phases of hoplite phalanx battle?

To assert that they can, Latacz had to venture unusually far outside the purely philological sphere. The fact that he nevertheless convinced historians and archaeologists of high repute on this whole issue, up to and including the final step of identifying the hoplite phalanx in the *Iliad*, must be reckoned a powerful argument for the strength of his case. No doubt I remain in a minority in continuing to find in this mass conversion a source of amazement. I cannot understand how my historical and archaeological colleagues were lulled into overlooking what seem to be glaring contrasts between the two methods of fighting. These contrasts range from the higher conceptual level, in the multiple linkage of the hoplite phalanx with the condition of citizenship, to the lower levels of organization (the presence *or* absence of pipers) or of mundane accoutrements (the total dichotomy between shields of hide and shields of wood). I can only echo a phrase that we earlier heard from Paul Cartledge, "a world of difference."

It is true that I have jumped directly to the last step in Latacz's argument, the identification in Homer of the hoplite phalanx and the consequent denial of any post-Homeric "hoplite reform," passing over many complex intermediate arguments. It might be asserted that his case could anyway stand without the support of these intervening steps: that is, even if the battle descriptions of the *Iliad* were confused and incoherent, and consequently lacking in all historical verisimilitude, the mere occurrence, even once or twice, of a descriptive passage recognizable as an account of the hoplite phalanx would be enough—enough to show (short of having recourse to the old tactic of denouncing such lines as later interpolations) that the hoplite phalanx was something present in the poet of the *Iliad*'s experience. In some opinions, we do have one or two passages of just this kind, notably in book xiii (130–33, 339–43). We shall return to this issue of single passages later; but in any case, I do not think that it was this line of argument that won over so many distinguished scholars. Rather, it was a feeling of intellectual dissatisfaction (shared by myself) with the established view against which Latacz was rebelling: the view, enshrined in Lorimer's classic article (1947: 111), that Homeric and hoplite fighting were two utterly different, sharply contrasting phenomena, the latter having fairly abruptly replaced the former in post-Homeric times; and that any Homeric passage suggesting otherwise was to be excised as a later interpolation. Like the denial of any trace of the polis in the Homeric poems, this doctrine had come to seem too absolute, too "pat."

But next, I wish to move for a moment into a fully archaeological field: that of dedications of actual armor in sanctuaries. Here we have a class of evidence that is robust in itself, and central to the issue of chronology with which we are concerned: indeed, for the early chronology of the hoplite and the phalanx, it constitutes the firmest evidence that we have. From a date in the mid-seventh century BCE, it suddenly became common practice to dedicate, to Zeus at Olympia and to other deities elsewhere, specimens of the bronze armor of the hoplite. None of these items of equipment was altogether new, but never had they appeared in anything resembling these quantities. The highly protective bronze Corinthian helmet becomes a very much more frequent dedication, along with the less common bronze breastplate; more important than either, and more abrupt in the scale of increase in dedications, are the bronze facings and bronze armbands from the round, wooden hoplite shield. The figures in Snodgrass 1980: 105 today stand to be greatly enhanced by new finds and publications, particularly in the additional category of the bronze greave: Kunze 1991. Kunze's periodization is slightly different, with the phases beginning and ending somewhat later: the marked surge in the dedication of greaves thus becomes clearly visible only from around the 630s BCE, rather than at the mid-seventh century, rising from about thirty-four examples in the "Early Archaic" phase to about eighty in the "High Archaic" (a phase of similar duration, extending perhaps from about 630 to about 560 BCE), dedicated at Olympia or Delphi. But some of the "Early Archaic" specimens—perhaps as many as fourteen—are specifically dated to the third quarter of the seventh century (Kunze 1991: 14, 20–21) so that the "surge" at the midcentury may have been comparable with those apparent in the other categories of armor.

Each item on this list—hoplite shield, breastplate, Corinthian helmet, cuirass, and greaves—had been seen on the battlefield for a generation or two before circa 650 BCE, and indeed, most of them feature in the battles of the *Iliad*. But when taken together, they comprise the first, and heaviest, standard panoply of the Greek hoplite, and there is good reason to see in this upsurge in dedication a significant step in the development of the hoplite. To explain it as a mere change in votive fashion would be to overlook the exact coincidence in time with a small group of Corinthian vase paintings, which give us our best iconographic evidence of this same, standardized heavy panoply, together with the first and clearest depictions of the phalanx.

It is important to realize that this "mature" phase of heavily armed hoplites, fighting in a phalanx, had an end as well as a beginning. Something over a century later, in the final generation of the sixth century BCE, there is a similar conjunction of archaeological (a falloff in dedications) and iconographic evidence, but this time demonstrating that armor was becoming lighter. Perhaps in the cause of increased mobility, the bronze cuirass began to be discarded in favor of lighter materials and the Corinthian helmet to be made of thinner metal, or replaced by less protective forms (though the greave evidently lived on). This lightened form of the panoply was to prevail permanently: the hoplite familiar from the Classical written sources was thus a different animal from his ancestor of the period between circa 650 and 525 BCE.

But this if anything increases the significance of that earlier phase: it is perhaps the most prolonged, stable, securely attested, and well-dated episode in Greek warfare. It is also the period of the widespread overseas exploits of the Greek hoplite (John Hale, this volume), in what might be called his "export model"; and, as a direct consequence, the period during which certain non-Greek peoples, most famously the Etruscans, first paid the Greek hoplite the compliment of adopting his equipment and imitating his formations. It is not the beginning of the hoplite's story, but it provides a fundamental benchmark against which we should judge both earlier and later Greek warfare—including the warfare of the *Iliad*.

Each of the approaches to these problems that has been mentioned—the philological, the historical, and, less often, the iconographical—has its characteristic strengths and weaknesses, which in turn may have a chronological application; the weaknesses are often apparent at the point of junction with, or transition to, a different field of study. To take first an example of the philological approach: every discussion of the battle tactics of the *Iliad*, by comparison with those of the historical hoplite, must take account of the fact that the word *phalanx* occurs repeatedly in the poem, though almost always in the plural: I recall my own unease, many years ago, in seeking either to explain away this fact, or alternatively to use it as an argument against the then established orthodoxy. For the philologist, it is natural to attach greater weight to a terminological factor of this kind and, if pressed too far, this tendency becomes a weakness. The fact is that a given Greek word could, and often did, change its meaning through time: Peter Krentz (this volume) considered the interesting case of the verb *ôtheo*, which (like *phalanx*) makes frequent appearances in the battle scenes of the *Iliad*, but is also a basic feature in descriptions of Classical hoplite fighting. Even within a single period, Greek terminology is notorious for its failure to use the same word to denote a given thing in anything like a one-to-one relation: rather, it seems to revel in richness and variety of vocabulary. The Greek nomenclature of pot shapes, or of weapons, would provide clear examples. All of this means that too close a reliance on the terminology of literary descriptions can become a weakness of the philological approach: the mere presence of a word like *phalanx* (or *phalanges*) may mean little on its own. I am not suggesting that Latacz himself is vulnerable on this account, but I do suspect that this factor has played a part in persuading others.

But the historical approach has its weaknesses too. In this context, there is one tendency that I have found as prominent as it is unfortunate: the detachment from, or disregard for, the most recent shifts of opinion in philological scholarship. Historians and archaeologists are, I think, by now generally aware of the movement (already of some thirty years' standing) on the part of philologists and others toward lowering the date of the completion of the *Iliad* and *Odyssey*, in essentially the form in which we have them, from the later eighth century BCE to the earlier seventh: indeed, some of them have themselves contributed to it. Its effect on the whole issue of the relation between hoplite fighting and the battles of the *Iliad* is potentially quite a profound one.

What I have missed altogether, however, is any reference to a more recent, and even more far-reaching, movement of opinion. I refer to the "evolutionary model" for the Homeric texts, which in its fully fledged form, first pioneered in the 1990s by Gregory Nagy, has today made such a rapid advance as to have reached "almost the status of orthodoxy" among the younger generation of American philologists, according to one of their number who does not himself accept it (Reece 2005: 52). The doctrine is conveniently summarized in a succinct, two-page outline that Nagy appended at the end of his paper in the volume *New Light on a Dark Age* (Nagy 1997: 206–7). According to this model, there were "five ages of Homer," each showing progressively less flexibility and greater rigidity:

1. the most fluid period, with no written texts, extending from the second millennium to the later part of the eighth century BC
2. a more formative or "Panhellenic" period, still with no written texts, from the later eighth to the mid-sixth century BC
3. a definitive period, originating in the Athens of the Peisistratids, with potential transcripts being taken down at any of several points from the mid-sixth to the later fourth century BC
4. a standardizing period, perhaps with texts that were not mere transcripts, from the later fourth to the mid-second century BC
5. a most rigid period, with texts as "scripture," from the mid-second century BC onward.

All this, but especially the description of the first two "ages," poses a direct and obvious threat to any theory of consistent and coherent Homeric battle tactics, belonging to a single period. The most important feature for us is perhaps the continued absence of written texts down to the mid-sixth century and the fact that even the second stage is still merely "more formative," not definitive. Yet in one respect, by bringing the first "age" to a close in the later eighth century rather than the seventh, this model restores some of its significance to a long-established, but now increasingly disputed, landmark: an important quality, namely, Panhellenic status, differentiates the second "age" from the first. At the same time, the model would undermine the recent fashion for detecting the latest diagnostic features in the Homeric *Realien* and using them to lower the date of the main composition of the epics from the eighth century to some point within the seventh, and so setting up a comprehensive *terminus post quem* for their consolidation into essentially the form that we know. Instead, the whole concept of "consolidation" becomes premature for this stage, and any such features may simply be assigned to a further stage in the development of the epics.

We may wish to reject the entire evolutionary model, but I do not think we can silently ignore its existence. On the positive side, the model opens the door to a variety of potential solutions to the problems that we have been discussing. An example might be the occurrence in the *Iliad* of single passages with distinctively hoplite overtones, which we were discussing earlier. Under the "evolutionary model," it is no longer necessary to stigmatize such lines as "interpolations," if the whole received text was still potentially exposed to the influence of the age of the hoplite: on the contrary, it may now be their extreme rarity that occasions surprise.

The ramifications of the evolutionary model of course extend very much more widely. New explanations may emerge, whether for long-standing textual debating points such as the description of the shield of Achilles in *Iliad* xviii, with its surprisingly advanced development, both in the society portrayed and implicitly in the techniques of artistic execution; or for notorious iconographic problems such as that posed by the "Euphorbos plate," showing the fight to secure the body and arms of Euphorbos, with Menelaos apparently prevailing against Hektor in a way that not merely differs from, but flatly contradicts the narrative of *Iliad* xvii, 1–113. In these as in other cases, the main effect of the model may appear to be that of increasing the range of the uncertainties—not necessarily a bad thing.

The iconographical approach, in general, is perhaps the one whose weaknesses are most apparent to us. I content myself with quoting a couple of phrases from the paper published earlier by Adam Schwartz (Schwartz 2002: 54): "any attempt towards interpretation is bedeviled by the sheer amount of ambiguity inherent in such early iconography. There is no external criterion of control to iconography." One might contest the last comment by saying that actual finds of objects, corresponding to those shown in the images, constitute a partial external control. But in general these comments are truer of the iconographical approach than of either the philological or the historical one.

None of these three approaches can in fact progress very far on its own, without recourse to the other two. Above all, this must not degenerate into a game of stone/scissors/paper, in which the "stone" of the textual evidence competes with the "scissors" of history and the "paper" of iconography. Our difficulty is that few of us can muster the skills necessary to judge authoritatively in more than one of these categories, let alone all three. We have instead to assess the reliability of the conclusions reached by colleagues in other disciplines; and the essence of my argument so far has been that we have sometimes fallen short in such assessments.

Yet my conclusion, in the light of the contributions to this volume intended to represent the full range of divergent views, and of the conference at Yale from which the volume sprang, is an optimistic one. I recall something said by Donald Kagan in the first session at Yale. He referred to the "search for self-differentiation" that once preoccupied the epic poets, but which today instead affects research—in that scholars tend to accentuate, rather than play down, the differences between their own views and those of colleagues. I agree: I think that the degree of consensus present in the current study of hoplites is greater than has often been acknowledged by the participants in that study. I would include myself, and this present article, in that judgment: it is more important that I share in the fundamental consensus, founded on Latacz's work, that mass armies are the decisive force in the warfare of the *Iliad*, than that I reject every one of the later inferences that he bases on that insight.

Some of the apparent disagreements have turned out to be derived from simple misunderstanding. Thus, Hans van Wees did *not* deny the presence of mass combat in the *Iliad*, but that of *massed* combat, a different thing (van Wees 1994: 15, n.7); and Kurt Raaflaub (this volume) does *not* support Latacz's identification of the close formations described in the *Iliad* with the hoplite phalanx. It is helpful to have these matters clarified, but what I argue is that there is a deeper level of convergence between ostensibly competing views.

I do not wish to overpress this point. But one man's "hoplite revolution" may not differ all that much from what is merely a significant advance in the course of another man's "evolution of the hoplite." Nowadays, in fact, nearly everyone seems to accept some kind of gradualist account of the onset of the Greek hoplite, though we differ in the degree of gradualism that we favor, and in the chronological settings to which we extend it. Thus the nascent phalanx of the *Iliad*, even on Latacz's own account, has some further developments to undergo before reaching the form recognizable from historical accounts; while, for Hans van Wees, these further developments had still not run their full course by the end of the seventh century BCE. A combination of these two views would extend the evolution of the hoplite over a century or more.

Against this trend toward gradualism, however, one substantial obstacle has remained: the adoption of the two-handled arrangement for the hoplite shield, that single, once-for-all advance, apparently widely and rapidly accepted. It is absolutely certain that this invention was in place by the early decades of the seventh century, and very likely that it had already happened in the late eighth. But was it desirable, or even practicable, to combine this new piece of equipment with any battle formation other than the fully fledged, close-order phalanx, whose members were uniformly armed with it?

Here a genuine conflict of views persists. Paul Cartledge (now joined by Greg Viggiano at this conference) has been prominent among those who champion the inseparability of shield and formation; Victor Hanson has brought home to everyone the features of weight and concavity that distinguish the hoplite shield from just any two-handled form; while Hans van Wees has been tireless in the search for other contexts of use for the two-handled shield. For now, I would only plead for flexibility in our interpretations. Is it not possible, even likely, that the developed form of the hoplite shield—heavy, wooden, concave, partly bronze-faced—did not appear immediately upon the invention of the double handles? Could it have been precisely this final form that introduced and characterized the slightly later phase of the "standardized heavy panoply" that I identified earlier? Certainly the decorated bronze arm armband, the most diagnostic surviving feature of the developed hoplite shield, begins to appear among the dedications only from this time. In that case, the earlier round, two-handled shields, though undoubtedly real and of similar dimensions, could have been made of different, lighter materials, and so perhaps been usable in a wider range of battle formations.

I note, too, how often those involved in recent discussion of hoplites have seen themselves as seeking compromises between different views, and I am happy to join their number. My paper has concentrated heavily on the beginning and the early phases of the age of the hoplite, to the detriment of the far better documented Classical period, let alone anything later. So let me end with a pointer in the direction of something that is very seldom discussed, no doubt because it is heavily deficient in written documentation and almost entirely lacking in iconography: the final disappearance of the hoplite.

Some may be tempted to say that the age of the hoplite had come to a close on the battlefield of Chaironeia in 338 BCE, when the hoplite phalanx met with immediate defeat and ultimate replacement at the hands of the Macedonian army. Yet the evidence shows that many elements of the hoplite system and, especially, of the enrollment of citizens for it, still remained in place in the Greek cities for generations after this; nor did the tactics and armor change everywhere overnight. This was not necessarily a token of localized backwardness or conservatism. Rather, as has been argued in an illuminating paper by John Ma (Ma 2000), the system was a central characteristic of the small intercity wars of the Hellenistic age. However much our literary sources may have neglected them in their preoccupation with the major clashes of the successor kingdoms, such wars, documented primarily in the epigraphic record, continued to occur and, for them, established systems were still found most appropriate.

A possible example of such a survival, apparently much regarded at the time although there are interesting differences between the various later accounts of it, is the story of Philopoemen's reforms of the equipment and tactics of the army of the Achaean League. As told by Pausanias (viii.50.1), Philopoemen actually introduced the traditional phalanx tactics and equipment of the Classical hoplite to the Achaean army, till then entirely equipped as lightly armed: Pausanias makes this explicit by his use of the phrase "Argolic shields," the time-honored designation for the large round wooden shield of the hoplite; his "longer spears" will then also presumably be those of the hoplite. But this is not quite how our other two sources, Plutarch (*Philopoemen* 9.2–3) and later Polyainos (*Strategemata* 6.4, 3) tell it. For them, the new equipment was that of the Macedonian phalangite: Plutarch implies this by having Philopoemen directly seek to emulate the superior arms of the Macedonians, while Polyainos explicitly uses the word *sarisa* for the longer spear that he now introduces. This latter version is the more likely to convince: the episode must belong in or close to the year 208 BCE, a time not long after the Spartans had abandoned the hoplite spear and shield in favor of their Macedonian counterparts (Plutarch, *Cleomenes* xi.2). But even so, the "last hoplites" of John Ma's account (Ma 2000: 353–57) were still a reality in some Greek cities of this era. This gradual, protracted decline of the hoplite may even have some lessons to teach us about the other end of the story, when, I have argued, gradual change had also been the order of the day.

The disparities in the speed and direction of military development, whether in Archaic or Hellenistic times, as between different regions of Greece, serve to remind us how far the hoplite system fell short of being a Panhellenic phenomenon. The long lapse of time that is attested toward the end, with hoplite equipment still being in use many years after its critical limitations had been exposed on the field of Chaironeia, does at least warn us against the general dangers of any periodization that is too rigid and clear-cut. The hoplite system of fighting was a successful, but not a self-evidently irresistible, mode of warfare: the idea of an immediate and near-universal rush to embrace it still seems to me just as improbable as the notion of a "sudden death" for the system has turned out to be. Even in the Classical period, and surely in the early years too, it had to undergo the occasional serious setback, long before things deteriorated into any kind of steady eclipse. Whether politically or tactically, its greatest strength seems to have lain in defense, which might in certain circumstances limit its value. Admiration for it seems to have been widespread, but we may doubt whether it was at any stage unquestioning. Yet even when faced, toward the end, with evidently superior external methods of warfare, we see that it could still be found fully serviceable by some Greeks in more limited, internal contexts. All these factors, cumulatively, encourage me still to join in supporting a gradualist account of the advent of the hoplite.

Bibliography

Finley, M. I. 1956. *The World of Odysseus*. London: Chatto and Windus.

Kunze, E. 1991. *Beinschienen* (*Olympische Forschungen* 21). Berlin: Walter de Gruyter.

Latacz, J. 1977. *Kampfparänese, Kampfdarstellung und Kampfwirklichkeit in der Ilias, bei Kallinos und Tyrtaios* (*Zetemata* 66). München: C. H. Beck.

Leimbach, R. 1980. Review of Latacz 1977. *Gnomon* 52:418–25.

Lorimer, H. L. 1947. "The hoplite phalanx with special reference to the poems of Archilochus and Tyrtaeus." *BSA* 42:76–138.

Ma, J. 2000. "Fighting *poleis* of the hellenistic world," in H. van Wees (ed.), *War and Violence in Ancient Greece*, 337–76. London: Duckworth.

Nagy, G. 1997. "The shield of Achilles: Ends of the *Iliad* and beginnings of the polis," in S. Langdon (ed.), *New Light on a Dark Age: Exploring the Culture of Geometric Greece*, 194–207. Columbia/London: University of Missouri Press.

Pritchett, W. K. 1985. *The Greek State at War*, vol. 4. Berkeley and Los Angeles: University of California Press.

Reece, S. 2005. "Homer's *Iliad* and *Odyssey*: From oral performance to written text," in M. C. Amodio (ed.), *New Directions in Oral Theory: Essays on Ancient and Medieval Literatures*, 43–90. Tempe: Arizona State University.

Schwartz, A. 2002. "The early hoplite phalanx: Order or disarray?" *Classica et Mediaevalia* 53:31–64.

Snodgrass, A. 1980. *Archaic Greece: The Age of Experiment*. London: J. M. Dent.

Snodgrass, A. M. 1993. "The hoplite reform revisited." *DHA* 19:47–61.

Van Wees, H. 1988. "Kings in combat: Battles and heroes in the *Iliad*." *CQ* 38:1–24.

Van Wees, H. 1994. "The Homeric way of war: The *Iliad* and the hoplite phalanx." *G & R* 41:131–55.

CHAPTER 5

Early Greek Infantry Fighting in a Mediterranean Context

KURT A. RAAFLAUB

Some of my work has long focused on two projects: to understand "Homeric or epic society," including epic battle descriptions, and to situate the emergence of political thinking in archaic Greece in a broader Mediterranean context.[1] I posit that the Greek polis with its institutions, and political thought or, to put it differently (without intending to pursue this here), the polis and "the political," developed in a long interactive process.[2] Polis institutions included political (assembly, council, offices) as well as religious (cults, festivals, rituals), social (for instance, ritual dining in public contexts), and military ones. I have therefore suggested that the polis as a type of community, the form and composition of its army, and its fighting tactics evolved together and in interaction as well.[3] If I see this particular evolution as a long process, I do not exclude ruptures or accelerated spurts of development, but I expect continuity and integration of innovations into an ongoing process to prove more important than revolution or abrupt new beginnings. Among others, Hans van Wees, too, emphasizes a "slow and steady process" that, he thinks, lasted "throughout the archaic and classical periods which transformed Greek infantry tactics from the kind of fluid long-range skirmishing found in 'primitive' societies into the kind of close-order hand-to-hand combat found in more developed city-states."[4] I shall return to this later. I have discussed elsewhere why and to what extent I think "epic society" reflects a historical society, and take this for granted here.[5] To forestall criticism, even if I deliberately simplify and generalize here, suggesting a uniform "Greek" development, I am very much aware of vast differences among Greek regions, individual poleis, and between poleis and *ethnē*, but this is not the place to emphasize these.[6]

To return to my overall thesis, if polis, institutions, and political thought evolved in an interactive process, political thought must be studied in this broader social and political context. It matters, for example, that already around the mid-seventh century in Cretan Dreros "the polis decided" (literally: *tad' ewade poli*) to enact a law limiting iteration of the chief office, and the Spartans regulated the process of communal decision making and formally attributed the final decision (*kratos* and *nikē*) to the assembly.[7] Such rules and laws reflect a high level of communal awareness and a certain priority attributed to the community (as opposed to individual leaders or groups of elite families).[8] This could not but influence the political thinking that emerged in these communities and among their members. The same, I suggest, is true if members of this community (whatever the criteria determining participation) regularly met for communal feasting, eating, and drinking, or if many of its men (whatever criteria determined inclusion or exclusion) fought in the communal army to defend community and territory. I am therefore interested in early Greek military practices in themselves (because of Homer's description of wars and battles) but also because they were a crucial part of the social context in which early Greek political thinking evolved.

Moreover, the archaic Greeks interacted intensively with the highly developed civilizations in the ancient Near East (from Anatolia to Egypt). They absorbed an enormous range of cultural impulses, from crafts and technology to law and literature.[9] My project tries to assess the impact of all this "orientalizing" on early Greek political thought.[10] Here I wonder about "orientalizing" influences on early Greek military developments, especially, of course, on that of the hoplite phalanx.

After Anthony Snodgrass's seminal work,[11] little attention has been paid to this aspect. As far as I can see, Hans van Wees pretty much ignores it. In the recent *Cambridge History of Greek and Roman Warfare*, Everett Wheeler observes: "A definite command structure and the use of column and line formations characterize state (as opposed to pre-state) warfare, so the phalanx need not be a Greek peculiarity. A lack of detailed information for Bronze and Iron Age Near Eastern infantry deployments precludes proving either that the phalanx developed independently or that it imitated Near Eastern practice."[12] True enough: such detailed information is lacking, but this does not need to be the end of the story.

Although some continuities in equipment are documented through the Dark Age, I do not think that Near Eastern influences on Greece in the Bronze Age matter for our present purposes. At the end of the Bronze Age and again from the tenth century Greek civilization experienced major changes, if not ruptures, and these deeply affected military culture and customs as well. Moreover, by the eighth century pieces of equipment that may have been "imported" from the Near East more than four hundred years earlier would long have been firmly integrated into Greek military tradition.[13] For my present purposes the period in which polis and phalanx developed (eighth to early fifth century) is more immediately important. From this period we have some information about warfare in the Near East, especially about Neo-Assyrian and, later and to a lesser degree, Persian military practices.[14] A comparison seems promising, and I suggest focusing on three aspects. One is the composition and organization of armies, that is, their recruitment (citizens vs. professionals, seasonal vs. standing), the categories of fighters, and the emphasis placed on each category (chariots, cavalry, infantry, and, among the latter, heavily vs. lightly armed and specialists such as spearmen, archers, and slingers). A second aspect concerns arms and armor: here we explore possible connections between early Greek military equipment and Near Eastern models, and examine the way the Greeks adapted such "imports" to serve their own (and possibly new and different) purposes. A third aspect involves formations and fighting tactics. By combining comparison of these three aspects, we may be able to determine more precisely what the Greeks borrowed from the Near East, how they adapted it, and how this contributed to the development of phalanx fighting. This in turn will allow us to define more precisely the Greeks' own contribution, and especially how this contribution relates to communal development.

I limit my comparison primarily to the Neo-Assyrian empire because the evidence (both textual and pictorial) is rich and authentic (rather than, as is the case with the Persians, seen and conveyed largely through Greek eyes and pens) and because we know that Greeks both served as mercenaries in the Near East from at least the early seventh century and were aware of military and other aspects of Assyrian culture.[15] It suffices to mention here Sarah Morris's brilliant explanation of the Trojan horse as reflecting knowledge of Assyrian siege engines that indeed look somewhat like giant battle horses, and Erwin Cook's recent comparison of Alkinoös' palace in the *Odyssey* with specific features of Near Eastern palaces.[16]

First, then, the composition of armies. Although Homer mentions agrarian property only when speaking of the leaders and Hesiod largely ignores war when talking about the life of his farmers, there is no good reason to doubt that Greek polis armies (as opposed to raiding bands of individual warlords) consisted early on of independent farmers (elite and "middling," wherever the line was drawn on the lower end): all members of the community who were capable of doing so and met the criteria set by each community fought in the polis's wars.[17] These same men (and those beyond fighting age) formed the assembly and played there a communally indispensable political role.[18] A couple of generations after Homer, Tyrtaeus' Sparta illustrates all this well, and Sparta was not unique even if these matters for specific reasons were probably more pronounced there than elsewhere. Importantly, already Alcaeus alludes to the formula "the men are the polis."[19]

True, archers and other lightly armed missile specialists initially seem to have played a more significant role and may have continued to do so longer than we used to think:[20] early poetry, images on vases, as well as, for example, Spartan lead figurines of bowmen leave no doubt about this. Yet this role should not be overestimated, and it seems to have decreased over time. For example, the masses of Spartan lead figurines from the sanctuary of Artemis Orthia show two types of archers in the seventh century and only one in the sixth, but a large variety of "hoplite" types, increasing from fifteen to twenty-six in the same period; those from the Menelaion reflect the same distribution; moreover, the "hoplites" are spearmen and always wear helmet and shield, sometimes greaves; the archers do not.[21] The fragments of Archilochus' poetry mention (non-Greek?) archers in the context of a siege and the storming of a city but spears, javelins, and swords everywhere else; as we shall see, heavy protective armor appears already by the late eighth century, the *Iliad* emphasizes the dominant role of heavily armed fighters in large numbers, and by the second half of the seventh century illustrations on vases, dedications in sanctuaries, reflections in poetry (esp. Tyrtaeus), and new polis institutions leave no doubt that, despite the presence of missile specialists (lightly armed archers, slingers, javelin or stone throwers), in military importance, social prestige, and communal status the hoplite predominated.[22] As far back as we can see, therefore, the Greek polis army consisted of soldiers who were "citizens," farmers, and primarily heavily armed spearmen.

Assyrian evidence reveals a different picture. True, the Assyrians, often receiving land assignations in border areas, were obliged to serve in the army. In the early phase of the Neo-Assyrian state (the "Old Empire"), Assyrian armies consisted largely of citizen levies. But the kings of the "New Empire," beginning with Tiglath-pileser III in the mid-eighth century, used large-scale citizen levies mostly in emergencies but otherwise relied on standing armies under their own command or assigned to provincial governors.[23] These were largely recruited among provincial populations and regularly replenished by large contingents of soldiers from among defeated enemies and thus from newly subjected peoples. For example, after his conquest of Carchemish, Sargon says: "I created a contingent of 50 chariots, 200 men on horseback and 3,000 foot soldiers and added it to my royal corps." At another occasion, he integrated into his standing army 10,000 archers from Philistia and 30,500 from Bit-Jakin and Elam (as well as the same number of shield bearers).[24]

These figures are illuminating: bowmen apparently were by far the largest force in the army, several times outnumbering all the others together. According to Sargon II's *Annals*, the king assigned to the governor of a new province an army consisting of 150 chariots, 1,500 horsemen, 20,000 bowmen, and 1,000 spearmen.[25] Such disproportion is all the more remarkable as each bowman, naturally unable to protect himself with a shield, worked in tandem with a shield bearer. The preponderance of archers is confirmed in other texts and in pictorial reliefs where they are highly prominent.[26] The Assyrian army thus relied primarily on the long-distance impact of a hail of arrows and on the assault of cavalry and chariots. Infantry capable of hand-to-hand fighting was limited to relatively small units of spearmen armed with a heavy spear and shield.

The Achaemenid Persian armies that invaded Greece in the early fifth century reflect similar preferences. They too were recruited in the whole empire and thus were ethnically mixed (although, as Pierre Briant has demonstrated brilliantly, the fighting army must be distinguished from the "parade army" displaying the ethnic contingents' native dress and equipment).[27] According to Herodotus, Persians preferred to fight in terrain that was suitable for cavalry. At Marathon, he says, they were shocked to see the Athenians attack without support of archers and cavalry—by implication, Greeks commonly expected Persians to rely heavily on such support. Miltiades ordered his hoplites to attack on the run—obviously to minimize their exposure to Persian arrows, and the Persians were handicapped decisively by lacking (for whatever reasons) the support of their cavalry. In close combat the more lightly armed Persian infantry was no match for Greek hoplites, hence the extraordinary disproportion in losses.[28] Herodotus says so explicitly when describing the battle of Plataea, where Persian cavalry and archers, bombarding the enemy from behind their shield barrier, caused serious problems for the Greeks but resistance faded quickly once the cavalry general had fallen, the cavalry retreated, and the shield barrier was overrun; the latter also sealed the fate of the Persians at Mycale.[29] In his description of the Persian army on the march Herodotus gives for the core contingent of Persians equal numbers of horsemen and spearmen, which may indicate that the Persians placed more emphasis than the Assyrians on the capacity of their armies to sustain close combat, but archers and cavalry apparently still dominated the battlefield. In *Persae*, Aeschylus famously pits the Greek spear against the Persian bow. Yet Herodotus's report about the Persians fighting at Plataea seems to suggest that, unlike their Assyrian predecessors, Persian infantrymen were both archers and spearmen: they pelted the enemy with arrows before the armies closed, then fought in the melee with spears and swords.[30]

Next, equipment. The Greeks themselves were aware of their military borrowings from others. According to Herodotus, they appropriated three inventions from the Carians: "fitting crests on helmets, putting devices on shields, and making shields with handles." Modern scholars have doubts about these "Carian inventions" or modify them.[31] Overall, despite the debt the Greeks owed to the Near East in terms of technology—most importantly, the knowledge of ironworking[32]—imitation of specific armor and weapons is surprisingly limited.

The first Greek iron swords may have come from Cyprus and the Levant, but Greek smiths soon mastered the challenge.[33] The bronze-plate corselet appears first around 725; it is definitely not Near Eastern (where the scale corselet dominated) and was most likely modeled after a European type ultimately derived from the Celtic urnfield culture, which may in turn have been influenced by Greek Bronze Age technology.[34] While earlier helmet types have analogs in a wide area of the eastern and western Mediterranean, the "Corinthian" helmet, usually hammered out of one sheet of bronze and covering the entire head except for a small opening for eyes, nose, and mouth, is Greek and originated in the late eighth century.[35] The same is true for the greaves, first visible on vases about 675 but now archaeologically attested some fifty years earlier.[36]

Round shields were used by the sea peoples, in late Bronze Age Greece, and through the Dark Age; their bronze bosses have analogs on Cyprus. Round shields are frequent too in Neo-Assyrian battle depictions. Where we see their interior, it is clear that they were light, made of wicker, and covered with leather. All these shields were held by a single grip in the middle and could presumably be carried by a strap around the neck. Scholars assume a common origin of this shield type in late Bronze Age Anatolia or Assyria.[37] The Greek hoplite shield, larger than earlier round ones, made of wood with bronze applications around the rim or even covering the entire surface, and markedly concave, with its characteristic two handles (*porpax* and *antilabē*), was an entirely new, Greek invention, even if it is possible that, as Snodgrass thinks, the "very large round shield of sheet bronze carried by Assyrian infantrymen, though it had only a single central hand-grip, . . . influenced the evolution of the Greek type." But this, he emphasizes, "detracts little from the Greek achievement." This shield, too, was in use by the end of the eighth century.[38]

In the aspects, then, that are most characteristic of the Greek hoplite, his defensive body armor made of sheet bronze and his shield with double handle, borrowings from the Near East are not decisive, perhaps even marginal; many of the crucial technological advances were made in Greece. Most remarkably, all this equipment shows up in the late eighth century. Although initially not many fighters may have worn all of it, by the second half of the seventh century vase paintings show the entire assemblage and document that a uniformly equipped line of hoplites had become the ideal.[39] Although Snodgrass concludes "that the archaeological facts give little ground for believing that any unity of purpose lay behind the development of the various items of the panoply," it seems worth thinking along the lines suggested by Victor Hanson:[40] all pieces of this equipment, whatever their origin and original purpose, and whenever they appeared in Greece, were ultimately adapted or combined for one single purpose: fighting straight forward in relatively dense formation. Hence, for example, the Corinthian helmet radically prioritized safety over hearing and peripheral vision. If the spear broke, the sharp iron butt provided a useful weapon before the hoplite had to use his even shorter sword. Corselet and shield were heavy: again, protection was more important than maneuverability. True, the perfection of this fighting system took time, and missiles initially played a significant role. Still, the *idea or principle* of close-order frontal fighting must have been developed early on, apparently earlier than 700. It is tempting to think, as Hanson does, that fighting mode and equipment developed hand in hand, in an interactive process—for which there was no Near Eastern model either—but this is not provable, and I will not press it here.

Third, fighting tactics. Snodgrass thinks that "massed heavy infantry had long been in use among the Oriental kingdoms," but finds it remarkable that the Ionian Greeks, with their close contacts to the Near East, were not among the Greek pioneers of these tactics. Kendrick Pritchett refers to the famous "Stele of the Vultures," interpreted by Yigael Yadin as a "heavily armed phalanx of soldiers in a column of six files."[41] Unfortunately, a third-millennium relief is not helpful to us. Neo-Assyrian texts, although effusive about royal campaigns and victories, and often describing the difficulties the king had to overcome, suffice only to make clear that the Assyrian army, in Arther Ferrill's words, "was an integrated force of heavy and light infantry, consisting of spearmen, archers, slingers, storm troops, and engineers," relying on chariot corps and cavalry as its major strike force.[42] But these texts do not give detailed descriptions of battle formations and tactics. The pictorial record is rich, though, like the Greek vase paintings, stylized, using its own conventions and "language," and thus not necessarily realistic enough for our needs.[43]

At any rate, these images delight much more in dramatic sieges than in field battles.[44] With good reason. As Israel Eph'al writes, "After the Assyrian Empire had consolidated its power and its military supremacy had been duly demonstrated, there was a considerable decline in its involvement in pitched battles. Assyria was so much more powerful than most of its opponents that only rarely did they dare to confront her in the open field. Accordingly, the massive offensive activities of the Assyrian army, both within and, to some extent, beyond the empire, were aimed at ensuring victory by conquest of cities." This helps explain the importance of archers in the composition of Assyrian armies: in siege warfare, where walls separate the armies and the attackers fight largely from a distance, archers necessarily assumed a crucial role. Where we do see infantry in battle, archers therefore dominate; the spearmen with shields, helmets, and swords are shown in intensive, chaotic fights in the open field, intermixed with horsemen and archers, and, more often, in their advance, in single files, against a besieged city.[45] The latter is due to the constraints of relief sculpture with largely two-dimensional representation that, moreover, juxtaposes in one image sequential scenes and is thus limited in space. Still, so far I have seen evidence for mass battle but nothing that would suggest dense formation, even in the stylized way the Chigi vase and other Greek vase paintings represent this.

In Greece we know the result of the evolution: the hoplite phalanx, arranged in somewhat dense formation, with a wide front, several rows deep. After clashing, the two armies engaged in fierce hand-to-hand fighting, those in the hind rows replacing those who fell in front, perhaps at some point engaging in a veritable shoving match, until one line broke, turned, and fled.[46] The details (how closely packed and how "purely hoplite" this phalanx was, how much fighting occurred before the "shoving match," and how exactly we should imagine the latter) can be endlessly debated, but they matter less for my present purpose than that, as far back as we can see, the Greeks fought intercommunal wars primarily by meeting each other in frontal assault and fighting it out in person-to-person combat: missile-to-missile, spear-to-spear (by throw and thrust), hand-to-hand. Although the hoplite could fight individually, his strength lay in the formation.[47] We grasp this formation in the second half of the seventh century.

In our intense debates over every detail we tend to forget what seems to me crucial: both Tyrtaeus's poetic exhortations and Homer's descriptions of armies marching into battle, clashing, and fighting convey in numerous ways an impression not only of mass fighting but also of relatively dense formations. I have argued for this in detail elsewhere and will say here only that all the Homeric evidence adds up to an impression that made at least Polybius, an experienced general, think of a phalanx. We may try to prove him wrong, but that is the way he read it, and, I think, this corresponds to the poet's intention.[48]

I have also suggested that Homeric battles, lasting all day, are stitched together from large-scale but infinitely varied type scenes by alternating between "normal battles" and "chaotic flight and *aristeia* scenes," in which the poet gives his fantasy free rein, heroes reach spectacular levels of achievement, "special effects" are frequent, and gods as well as chariots play an important role. By contrast, I argue, the "normal battles," lasting from march into battle in dense formation and intense fighting in a long line of duels to flight of one side, essentially reflect a reality familiar to poet and audience. If we look for anything coming close to historical reality, we have to focus on these "normal battles."[49] Even here, as I have insisted all along, Homer does not describe anything resembling the fully developed hoplite phalanx. But what he depicts is much closer to at least a "proto-phalanx" than the much looser and disorganized model, the "kind of fluid long-range skirmishing found in 'primitive' societies," that Hans van Wees sees in Homer.[50]

At any rate, my reconstruction of epic fighting fits well with the date established by archaeology for the emergence of various pieces of hoplite equipment. By the time Homer's epics were composed, therefore, that is, by the early seventh century at the latest, the Greek development toward the hoplite phalanx was well under way.[51]

Let me summarize and draw some conclusions. The Assyrian kings' armies consisted of levies from among citizen farmers, mostly for seasonal campaigns, and, from the mid-eighth century, increasingly of standing armies composed largely of provincials and replenished by units formed from among subject populations. These armies combined various types of arms; in numbers and importance, archers (protected by shield bearers), chariots, and cavalry dominated, while shock troops of spearmen (some more heavily, some more lightly armed) seemed to be less important. The Persians continued to rely heavily on archers and cavalry, while assigning a more significant role to shock troops: their archers were also spearmen. In both empires the latter attacked and fought en masse, though often intermixed with archers and horsemen and apparently not in tight formation. Although Assyrian spearmen are mostly represented as wearing light round wicker shields, it is possible, as Snodgrass suggests, that in some cases the shields were larger, heavier, and covered with metal. If so, this is the only Near Eastern piece of military equipment that may have influenced the development of the Greek hoplite panoply.

On the Greek side independent citizen-farmers fight in the communal army. Despite Homer's focus on the great leaders, it is clear that all fighters matter and contribute, and they all share in the booty that is distributed by "the army," that is, by collective communal authority.[52] Although archers, slingers, and javelin throwers play a nonnegligible role, the battle is dominated already in Homer both numerically and physically by the heavily armed spearmen. As it will be for centuries to come, this battle is decided in frontal clashes of mass (and somewhat massed) armies and in person-to-person combat. With the possible exception of some aspects of the shield, none of the defensive armor of the future hoplite is derived from Near Eastern models. Crucial inventions and adaptations (the Corinthian helmet, the shield's *porpax*, *antilabē*, and typical concave shape, the greaves, and the iron spear butt, among others) that were used to develop and perfect frontal fighting in the phalanx's massed formation—these are all Greek. All parts of the hoplite equipment seem to have been in use before 700. Homer's battle descriptions reflect some awareness of the value of dense formations and close support among fighters.[53] Hence, as said before, by Homer's time the development that would result in the phalanx seems to have been well under way, both in terms of equipment and in terms of fighting tactics. This is why I have been arguing that, as big, profound, and perhaps "revolutionary" as this transformation was overall, it was mostly the result of a long process of gradual change in which I do not see one specific moment for a "hoplite revolution" of the kind that was postulated in the past.[54]

Overall, then, the military development that eventually produced the phalanx was essentially a Greek one.[55] As said at the beginning, by 700, and perhaps earlier, Greek mercenaries and their elite officers were fighting in the Near East; Homer reflects awareness of Assyrian military motifs. Information about Assyrian armies and ways of fighting was thus available in Greece. Yet the Greeks of the early seventh century did not have any use for the Assyrians' highly developed siege technology and tactics, and they did not do what military specialists have been telling them forever they should have done: they did not develop, in imitation of the Assyrians, an "integrated force of skirmishers, light infantry, heavy infantry, and light and heavy cavalry," although, as Ferrill insists, such forces are "more effective and less demanding on society," especially, as already Herodotus's Mardonius points out, in a country that seems mostly unsuitable for hoplite armies.[56] Chariots were not useful for fighting in Greece,[57] but horses were available, at least in modest numbers, outside Thessaly and Macedonia, and bows, arrows, and slings were much cheaper than the panoply. Yet the Greeks did not imitate the eastern empires' systematic use of large corps of archers. Archery remained the specialty of geographically marginal areas (Crete and Thrace), and the tendency, clearly attested in the fifth century, to look down on the archer is perceptible already in the *Iliad*.[58] Instead, the Greeks developed an army focused predominantly on heavily armed spearmen.

In the military aspects of Greek social culture, it seems, therefore, that Near Eastern influence can be ruled out almost entirely. Why this is the case is of great interest and crucial importance. Many scholars have tried to explain this Greek peculiarity, focusing on the phalanx as part of the Greek "way of life, a code of manliness and morality" and on the essential correspondence, characteristic of Greek social values, between tilling the land and fighting.[59] Reluctantly, I refrain from entering this debate here: it would exceed the scope of this chapter. Instead, I mainly want to draw attention to what this tells us about the nature of early Greek polis communities. I suggest that by the time information about Assyrian armies and modes of fighting began to arrive in Greece, conveyed by credible informants (that is, Greeks, and preferably elite Greeks who had personal experience of these matters),[60] Greek poleis were already well under way in developing their characteristic social and political institutions and achieving an increasing degree of cohesion, based not only on their elites but on a much broader class of independent farmers. These were the men who mattered in the early polis and who therefore manned the assembly and the polis army. In Homer they fight not for prosaic goals such as defending or conquering land—as they did in contemporaneous real life (after all, this is the age of the Messenian Wars and other well-attested wars between neighboring poleis about the control of contested territory)—but they already fight in straight man-to-man combat. They are the ancestors of those whom we see a little later fighting on their land for their land and in those increasingly competitive and ritualized forms that have sometimes been exaggerated but should not be entirely discarded.[61]

This brings me back to my initial thesis about the interactive development of polis, institutions, and political thought. I draw two conclusions—which in turn serve as hypotheses for my continuing research. One is that the crucial role in the early polis of these "citizen" farmer-soldiers was responsible for the communal ethos that pervades the earliest extant epic and elegiac poetry. Clashing with growing elite aspirations and tendencies toward exclusiveness, this communal ethos underlies the earliest attestations of Greek political thinking.[62] The other conclusion is that the Greek poleis around 700 were no longer entirely open communities, ready to absorb any outside influences.[63] They did this in many ways, but as far as communal structures were concerned, they were already set in their ways and, I think, more developed than is usually believed. Hence, based on a number of partial explorations such as that conducted here,[64] I begin to think that in the sphere of "the political"—and perhaps only in this sphere—Greek borrowings from the Near East were much more limited than one might expect. Naturally, a much broader investigation will be required to confirm or refute this.

Notes

1. The paper I offered at the conference at Yale University was based largely on one that has now been published (Raaflaub 2008a). Although several parts of that paper await further development, I prefer to offer for public discussion a related paper that was presented at meetings of the European Network for the Study of Ancient Greek History at Oxford University in late March and the Midwestern Consortium of Ancient Historians at the University of Michigan in late April 2009. I thank all participants for valuable criticism and suggestions; in addition, I am grateful to Ryan Balot and Adam Schwartz and to two anonymous referees for helpful comments. This is work in progress. I am aware that more needs to be done to confirm and solidify my results, but what I need most at this point is feedback from knowledgeable colleagues.

2. Raaflaub forthcoming. On "the political," see Meier 1990: pt. 1.

3. Raaflaub 1997b; see also 1999. On the emergence of the Greek polis, see, e.g., Hall 2007: ch. 4; Osborne 1996: ch. 4, and chs. by Snodgrass and Raaflaub in Hansen 1993.

4. Van Wees 2004: 152. For recent summaries of scholarly debates about the emergence of the hoplite phalanx, see Osborne 1996: 170–85; van Wees 2004: ch. 12; Hall 2007: ch. 7; Singor 2009.

5. Raaflaub 1998; see also Ulf 1990; van Wees 1992; Donlan 1999. Osborne 1996: ch. 5; Osborne 2004; and Shear 2000, among others, offer differing views.

6. See also Paul Cartledge's important chapter in the present volume.

7. Dreros: ML 2. Sparta's "Great Rhetra": Tyrt. 4 West; Plut. *Lyc.* 6; on the general issue of communal awareness and "people's power" in early Greece, see Raaflaub and Wallace 2007.

8. See, from different approaches, I. Morris 2000: pt. 3; Raaflaub and Wallace 2007.

9. See, recently, Burkert 1992, 2004; S. Morris 1992; West 1997. A more complete bibliography is in Raaflaub 1993: xvii–xix.

10. See esp. Raaflaub 2008b, 2009, in preparation a; see also 2004a, 2004b.

11. Snodgrass 1964b, 1965, 1999 (1967); the update (1999: 134–38) does not record major changes.

12. Wheeler 2007: 193.

13. On Greek Bronze Age military equipment, see Snodgrass 1999: 14–34, 132–34. Dark Age: ibid., ch. 2; 1964: ch. 20. On changes and ruptures: e.g., Snodgrass 1971; Raaflaub 2003: 312–23; Dickinson 2006.

14. For recent work on Assyrian warfare, see Malbran-Labat 1982; Stillman and Tallis 1984; Bahrani 2008; see also Ussishkin 1982; Bleibtreu 1990; Eph'al 1995. Hamblin 2006 covers the period to 1600 BCE. (I thank J. Novotny for some of these references.) On Persian warfare, see Briant 1999: 107: there "exists at this point no comprehensive monograph on the Achaemenid armed forces, their composition, the methods of their recruitment, their financing, their command structure, or their fighting tactics." Owing to the scarceness of Persian evidence, which forces us to rely far too heavily on Greek sources with their specific agendas and biases, this has not changed (Briant, written communication); see generally Briant 2002.

15. Evidence: Kuhrt 1995: II, 500–505. Greek mercenaries: Bettalli 1995: 43–52; Raaflaub 2004: 206–10 with biblio. See also Luraghi 2006.

16. See Morris 1995 on Near Eastern sources for the Trojan horse; Cook 2004 for Alkinoös's palace.

17. Homer and agrarian property: Hennig 1980; Donlan 1999: 303–20; cf. id. 1997: esp. 654–61. Hesiod and war: Wade-Gery 1949: 91–92. Farmers and fighters: No direct contemporaneous evidence exists to support this view (nor, for that matter, any other). When we first see such evidence (in Sparta at the time of the Great Rhetra and the emergence of the *homoioi*

system, and Athens at the time of Solon's timocracy: Raaflaub 2006), the hoplites are farmers; I don't see why their predecessors should have been different. See also Raaflaub 1999: 134–38. Van Wees 2004: chs. 3–4 emphasizes elite hoplites. Polis army: this requires dropping the model of a "hoplite revolution" based on Arist. *Pol.* 1297b16–18 and outdated views of tyrants relying on hoplites and early Greek warfare being predominantly an affair of elite warriors; see n. 54 below.

18. Assembly: Ruzé 1997; Raaflaub 1997a; Hölkeskamp 1997.

19. "The men are the polis": Thuc. 7.77.7; cf. Hdt. 8.61; Alc. fr. 112.10; 426 Campbell. On Sparta, see, e.g., Murray 1993: ch. 10; Osborne 1996: 177–85; Thommen 1996; Luther at al. 2006; Hall 2007: 178–209.

20. See esp. van Wees 2000; 2004: ch. 12.

21. Spartan lead figurines (I thank L. Foxhall, J. Hall, and Stephen Hodkinson for references): for Artemis Orthia, see Wace 1929: 262, 269, pls. 183, 191, 197 (archers: 2 varieties throughout the seventh century BCE, only one in the sixth; hoplites: 15 varieties 700–635, 18 or 21 635–600, 26 in the sixth century); Menelaion: Wace 1908–9: 130, 137 with pls. 10 and 7; Cavanagh and Laxton 1984. See also Boss 2000: 55–72 (warriors), 78 (naked archers; are they hunters?), and in the future Cavanagh's chapter on the lead votives in the forthcoming publication of the BSA Menelaion excavations.

22. Archilochus (West 1971; Gerber 1999) fr. 98 (siege with attack by Thracian [?] archers); frs. 2, 3, 91, 96, 113, 139, et al. (spears, javelins, swords). Predominance of hoplites: Snodgrass 1980: 99–106; Raaflaub 2007: 134 with biblio. Battlefield evidence might be helpful, but I doubt whether reliable statistics are available; D. Blackman (oral communication) has seen large piles of arrowheads at Himera, but these could be more Carthaginian than Greek.

23. Manitius 1910; though outdated, this article is still cited with approval; cf. Saggs 1963; Reade 1972.

24. Recruitment and replenishing of standing armies: Manitius 1910: 220–24; see also Dalley 1985; Oded 1979. Specific examples: Yadin 1963: II, 293; Manitius 1910: 128, 131.

25. New provincial army: Manitius 1910: 129. Preponderance of bowmen: confirmed by the evidence of the Sargonid letters found in Niniveh: Malbran-Labat 1982: 79–80 (often also recruited for specific campaigns from the local population).

26. Bowman working in tandem with shield bearer: Manitius, 1910: 130–32; Malbran-Labat 1982: 81–82 (though pointing out that shield bearers appear in other contexts too); see illustrations, e.g., in Yadin 1963: II, 418, 424. Spearmen armed with heavy spear and shield: Manitius 1910: 125–27; Yadin, 1963: II, 420.

27. Fighting army vs. "parade army" (described by Hdt. 7.61–99): Briant 1999: 116–20.

28. Preference for "horse country": Hdt. 6.102 (Marathon); 9.13.3 (Boeotia). References to battle of Marathon: 6.112.1–2. Losses: 6,400 vs. 192 (6.117.1).

29. Superiority of heavily armed hoplites over much more lightly armed enemy: Hdt. 9.62–63. Significance of shield barrier: 9.61–63; cf. 102.2–3 (Mycale). Archers at Thermopylae: 7.218, 225–26 (when the Persians shoot their arrows, the sun disappears). Plataea and Mycale: archers shooting hails of arrows protected by barricade of wicker shields: 9.61, 99, 102; cavalry attacks at Plataea: 9.20–25, 40, 49–50, 52, 57; cavalry blocking passes of Kithairon to prevent reinforcements and supplies from reaching the Greeks: 9.39. On Persian use of cavalry, see now Tuplin 2009.

30. Persian army on the march: 12,000 horsemen and spearmen (Hdt. 7.40–41). Greek spear vs. Persian bow: Aesch. *Pers.* 813; cf. 280, 725, 1001–3. Archers and spearmen identical: Raaflaub in preparation b.

31. Borrowings from Carians: Hdt. 1.171.4; cf. Asheri et al. 2007: 192–93; Snodgrass 1964a.

32. Ironworking: Snodgrass 1967: 36; 1971: ch. 5; Wertime and Muhly 1980.

33. Swords: Snodgrass 1964b: ch. 4; 1967: 37.

34. Corselet: Courbin 1957; Snodgrass 1964b: ch. 3; 1967: 41–42; see also Catling 1977; Jarva 1995.

35. Corinthian helmet: Snodgrass 1964b: 11, 13, 20–28; 1967: 51; J. Borchhardt 1977: esp. 72.

36. Greaves: Snodgrass 1964b: 66–68; 1967: 52; Kunze 1991.

37. Round shield and bosses: Snodgrass 1964b: ch. 2; 1967: 43–44; H. Borchhardt 1977: 28–36; on Assyrian depictions: H. Borchhardt 1977: 36–37; Hrouda 1965: 90–91; Yadin 1963: II, 294–95, with ill.; common origin: H. Borchhardt 1977: 39 with biblio.

38. Hoplite shield: Snodgrass 1964b: 61–68 [quotes 66, 68]; 1967: 53–55. On the crucial significance of this shield for hoplite fighting: Cartledge 1977; 2001; this vol.; Osborne 1996: 175–76.

39. Hoplite ideal: Snodgrass 1967: 58; see illustrations in Salmon 1977. Uniformity prevails even if, for example on the Chigi vase, the fighters still carry both javelin and spear.

40. Snodgrass 1964b: 90. Adaptation to straight-forward fighting: Hanson 1991.

41. Snodgrass 1967: 59; Pritchett 1985: 8, with reference to the third millennium "Stele of the Vultures" (Yadin 1963: I, 134–35).

42. Ferrill 1997: 70, 99.

43. See Eph'al 1995: 51 on the questionable realism of the reliefs. Spearmen in battle: Yadin 1963: II, e.g., 431–32, 442–43. Stylized mass formation on Greek vases: Salmon 1977; van Wees 2004: 178 fig. 21; pls. 18–21. A systematic investigation of battle depictions on Greek vases with the purpose of "deciphering" the artists' conventions and "language" is an urgent desideratum.

44. E.g., Ussishkin 1982; Bleibtreu 1990. Eph'al 1995 (quote: 50).

45. See, for example, for a battle in the open field, Yadin 1963: II, 442–43; for sieges: ibid., 418–25, 428–37, 448–49, and passim; Ussishkin 1982; Bleibtreu 1990.

46. On phalanx fighting, see, e.g., Thuc. 5.66–74; 6.66–71; Anderson 1970; Pritchett 1985: 1–93; Hanson 2000. Further biblio. in Raaflaub 1999: 149 n. 12. More recently, see van Wees 2004: ch. 13; Hall 2007: 163–70 raises important questions, as does Osborne 1996: 170–85. This is not the place to deal with these. For counterarguments, see, e.g., Schwartz 2002 and 2009.

47. Schwartz 2002: 31 reemphasizes what seems essential: "hoplites were unfit for single combat, and the weaponry was invented for use in the already existing phalanx. Assessments of iconography and literature yield the same results: the hoplite was always intended for phalanx fighting." See also Schwartz's contribution to this volume.

48. Homeric fighting: Raaflaub 2008a. Pol. 13.3.4; cf. Walbank 1967: 416.

49. "Normal battle" vs. "chaotic flight and *aristeia* scenes": Raaflaub 2008a: 479–83.

50. Van Wees 1997: 690: "The heroic army is composed of many small and loosely organized bands of warriors, held together by personal ties of subordination and companionship. Battles are fought in open order; at any particular moment the majority of men remain at a distance from the enemy, while a substantial minority of individual 'front-line warriors' venture closer to fight with missiles or hand-to-hand. There is much mobility back and forth as every man in the army is expected to join combat at least occasionally, and even the bravest heroes retire from battle every so often." See also 2000; 2004: ch. 11, with figs. 14–17. Contra: Schwartz 2002. Further biblio. on Homer's battle description is listed in Raaflaub 2008a: 470 n. 8.

51. I have defended this date in Raaflaub 1998: 187–88.

52. Raaflaub 2008a: 476–78 (booty: 478).

53. Ibid., 477–78.

54. For discussion of the "hoplite revolution," see, among others, Snodgrass 1965, 1993; Cartledge 1977, 2001; Raaflaub 1997b; 1999: 132–41; Hall 2007: 157–59.

55. So too Snodgrass 1965: 110: "The combination of all these elements [of the panoply] together was an original Greek notion; as was their later association with a novel form of massed infantry tactics, the phalanx."

56. Criticism of the inadequacy of Greek hoplite fighting: Ferrill 1997: 144; cf. Hdt. 7.9b. A rare testimony for an archaic battle about a fortified city is Arch. fr. 98 West, where the attackers are non-Greek (n. 22 above).

57. Crouwel 1992; see also Greenhalgh 1973.

58. For contempt of archers, see, e.g., Soph. *Ajax* (Teucer) and Eur. *Heracles*. Typically, in the *Iliad* Paris and Pandaros are bowmen, and Odysseus left his prized bow at home! Conversely, despite the primacy of the spearman in the *Iliad*, Troy cannot be taken without the assistance of Philoctetes, an archer, and the use of deception; see Mackie 2008: 70 and ch. 3.

59. Ferrill 1997: 145. Values: Aymard 1967. See also, generally, Cartledge 2001; Hanson 1995.

60. Raaflaub 2004a; on mercenaries and elite Greek mercenary commanders: 206–10. Hdt. 2.152, 154 comments on the flow of information to Greece from mercenaries settled in Egypt.

61. Ritualized warfare: Connor 1988. On the model of the early polis underlying my reconstruction, see Raaflaub 1991, 1993, 1997b, 1999; also, for example, Starr 1977, 1986, 1992; Stein-Hölkeskamp 1989: chs. 2–3; Donlan 1999.

62. Early Greek political thought: Raaflaub 2000; Hammer 2002. That armies (such as those of Assyria and Persia studied in this paper) drafted to a large extent from subjected populations and serving an autocratic, divinely sanctioned king and his officers, who were wielding absolute power over them, did not and could not develop a comparable communal ethos is obvious. The structures of leadership, command, and obedience would offer another fruitful aspect of comparison.

63. Open and closed communities: Ulf forthcoming.

64. See n. 10 above.

Bibliography

Anderson, J. K. 1970. *Military Theory and Practice in the Age of Xenophon*. Berkeley.

Asheri, D., A. Lloyd, and A. Corcella. 2007. *A Commentary on Herodotus Books I–IV*, ed. O. Murray and A. Moreno. Oxford.

Aymard, A. 1967. "Hiérarchie du travail et autarcie individuelle dans la Grèce archaïque." In Aymard, *Etudes d'histoire ancienne*, 316–33. Paris.

Bahrani, Z. 2008. *Rituals of War: The Body and Violence in Mesopotamia*. New York.

Bettalli, M. 1995. *I mercenari nel mondo greco*, vol. 1: *Dalle origini alla fine del V secolo a.C.* Pisa.

Bleibtreu, E. 1990. "Five Ways to Conquer a City." *Biblical Archaeology Review* 16.3.

Borchhardt, H. 1977. "Frühe griechische Schildformen." In Buchholz and Wiesner 1977:1–56.

Borchhardt, J. 1977. "Helme." In Buchholz and Wiesner 1977:57–74.

Boss, M. 2000. *Lakonische Votivgaben aus Blei*. Würzburg.

Briant, P. 1999. "The Achaemenid Empire." In K. Raaflaub and N. Rosenstein (eds.), *War and Society in the Ancient and Medieval Worlds*, 105–28. Washington, D.C.

———. 2002. *From Cyrus to Alexander: A History of the Persian Empire*. Winona Lake.

Buchholz, H.-G., and J. Wiesner (eds.). 1977. *Kriegswesen*, I. *Archaeologia Homerica*, pt. E. Göttingen.

Burkert, W. 1992. *The Orientalizing Revolution: Near Eastern Influence on Greek Culture in the Early Archaic Age*. Cambridge, MA.

———. 2004. *Babylon, Memphis, Persepolis: Eastern Contexts of Greek Culture*. Cambridge, MA.

Cartledge, P. 1977. "Hoplites and Heroes: Sparta's Contribution to the Technique of Ancient Warfare." *Journal of Hellenic Studies* 97:11–27.

———. 2001. "The Birth of the Hoplite: Sparta's Contribution to Early Greek Military Organization." In Cartledge, *Spartan Reflections*, 153–66, 225–28. London.

Catling, H. W. 1977. "Panzer." In Buchholz and Wiesner 1977:74–118.

Cavanagh, W. G., and R. R. Laxton. 1984. "Lead Figurines from the Menelaion and Seriation." *BSA* 79:23–36.

Connor, W. R. 1988. "Early Greek Land Warfare as Symbolic Expression." *Past & Present* 119:3–29.

Cook, E. 2004. "Near Eastern Sources for the Palace of Alkinoos." *AJA* 108:43–77.

Courbin, P. 1957. "Une tombe géométrique d'Argos." *Bulletin de Correspondance Hellénique* 81:322–86.

Crouwel, J. H. 1992. *Chariots and Other Wheeled Vehicles in Iron Age Greece*. Amsterdam.

Dalley, S. 1985. "Foreign Chariotry and Cavalry in the Armies of Tiglath-pileser III and Sargon II." *Iraq* 48:31–48.

Dickinson, O. 2006. *The Aegean from Bronze Age to Iron Age: Continuity and Change between the Twelfth and Eighth Centuries BC*. London.

Donlan, W. 1997. "The Homeric Economy." In Morris and Powell (eds.), *The Aristocratic Ideal and Selected Papers*, 649–67. Wauconda, IL.

Eph'al, I. 1995. "Ways and Means to Conquer a City." In S. Parpola and R. M. Whiting (eds.), *Assyria 1995*, 49–54. Helsinki.

Ferrill, A. 1997. *The Origins of War from the Stone Age to Alexander the Great*. Boulder, CO.

Gerber, D. E. (ed., trans.). 1999. *Greek Iambic Poetry*. Cambridge, MA.

Greenhalgh, P.A.L. 1973. *Early Greek Warfare: Horsemen and Chariots in the Homeric and Archaic Ages*. Cambridge.

Hall, J. 2007. *A History of the Archaic Greek World, ca. 1200–479 bce*. Malden, MA, and Oxford.

Hamblin, W. J. 2006. *Warfare in the Ancient Near East to 1600 BC: Holy Warriors at the Dawn of History*. London.

Hammer, D. 2002. *The* Iliad *as Politics: The Performance of Political Thought*. Norman.

Hansen, M. H. (ed.). 1993. *The Ancient Greek City-State*. Copenhagen.

Hanson, V. D. 1991. "Hoplite Technology in Phalanx Battle." In Hanson (ed.), *Hoplites: The Classical Greek Battle Experience*, 63–84. London.

———. 1995. *The Other Greeks: The Family Farm and the Agrarian Roots of Western Civilization*. New York.

———. 2000. *The Western Way of War: Infantry Battle in Classical Greece*. 2nd ed. Berkeley.

Hennig, D. 1980. "Grundbesitz bei Homer und Hesiod." *Chiron* 10:35–52.

Hölkeskamp, K.-J. 1997. "*Agorai* bei Homer." In W. Eder and K.-J. Hölkeskamp (eds.), *Volk und Verfassung im vorhellenistischen Griechenland*, 1–19. Stuttgart.

Hrouda, B. 1965. *Die Kulturgeschichte des assyrischen Flachbildes*. Bonn.

Jarva, E. 1995. *Archaiologica on Archaic Greek Body-Armor*. Rovaniemi.

Kuhrt, A. 1995. *The Ancient Near East c. 3000–330 bc*. 2 vols. London.

Kunze, E. 1991. *Beinschienen*. Oympische Forschungen 9. Berlin.

Luraghi, N. 2006. "Traders, Pirates, Warriors: The Proto-History of Greek Mercenary Soldiers in the Eastern Mediterranean." *Phoenix* 60:21–47.

Luther, A., M. Meier, and L. Thommen (eds.). 2006. *Das frühe Sparta*. Stuttgart.

Mackie, C. J. 2008. *Rivers of Fire: Mythic Themes in Homer's* Iliad. Washington, D.C.

Madhloom, T. A. 1970. *The Chronology of Neo-Assyrian Art*. London.

Malbran-Labat, F. 1982. *L'Armée et l'organisation militaire de l'Assyrie*. Paris.

Manitius, W. 1910. "Das stehende Heer der Assyrerkönige und seine Organisation." *Zeitschrift für Assyriologie und verwandte Gebiete* 24:97–149, 185–224.

Meier, C. 1990. *The Greek Discovery of Politics*. Trans. D. McLintock. Cambridge, MA.

Morris, I. 2000. *Archaeology as Cultural History*. Malden, MA, and Oxford.

Morris, S. P. 1995. "The Sacrifice of Astyanax: Near Eastern Contributions to the Siege of Troy." In J. B. Carter and S. P. Morris (eds.), *The Ages of Homer: A Tribute to Emily Townsend Vermeule*, 221–45. Austin.

Murray, O. 1993. *Early Greece*. 2nd ed. Cambridge, MA.

Oded, B. 1979. *Mass Deportations and Deportees in the Neo-Assyrian Empire*. Wiesbaden.

Osborne, R. 1996. *Greece in the Making, 1200–479 BC*. London.

———. 2004. "Homer's Society." In R. Fowler (ed.), *The Cambridge Companion to Homer*, 206–19. Cambridge.

Pritchett, W. K. 1985. *The Greek State at War*, vol. 4. Berkeley.

Raaflaub, K. A. (ed.). 1991. "Homer und die Geschichte des 8. Jh. v. Chr." In J. Latacz (ed.), *Zweihundert Jahre Homer-Forschung*, 205–56. Stuttgart.

———. 1993. *Anfänge politischen Denkens in der Antike: die nahöstlichen Kulturen und die Griechen*. Munich.

———. 1997a. "Politics and Interstate Relations among Early Greek Poleis: Homer and Beyond." *Antichthon* 31:1–27.

———. 1997b. "Soldiers, Citizens and the Evolution of the Early Greek *Polis*." In L. G. Mitchell and P. J. Rhodes (eds.), *The Development of the* Polis *in Archaic Greece*, 49–59. London.

———. 1998. "A Historian's Headache: How to Read 'Homeric Society'?" In N.R.E. Fisher and H. van Wees (eds.), *Archaic Greece: New Evidence and New Approaches*, 169–93. London and Swansea.

———. 1999. "Archaic and Classical Greece." In Raaflaub and N. Rosenstein (eds.), *War and Society in the Ancient and Medieval Worlds*, 129–61. Washington, D.C.

———. 2000. "Poets, Lawgivers, and the Beginnings of Political Reflection in Archaic Greece." In C. Rowe and M. Schofield (eds.), *The Cambridge History of Greek and Roman Political Thought*, 23–59. Cambridge.

———. 2003. "Die Bedeutung der Dark Ages: Mykene, Troia und die Griechen." In C. Ulf (ed.), *Der neue Streit um Troia. Eine Bilanz*, 309–29. Munich.

———. 2004a. "Archaic Greek Aristocrats as Carriers of Cultural Interaction." In R. Rollinger and C. Ulf (eds.), *Commerce and Monetary Systems in the Ancient World: Means of Transmission and Cultural Interaction*, 197–217. Stuttgart.

———. 2004b. "Zwischen Ost und West: Phönizische Einflüsse auf die griechische Polisbildung?" In R. Rollinger and C. Ulf (eds.), *Griechische Archaik: interne Entwicklungen—externe Impulse*, 271–89. Berlin.

———. 2006. "Athenian and Spartan *eunomia*, or: What to Do with Solon's Timocracy?" In Josine Blok and André Lardinois (eds.), *Solon: New Historical and Philological Perspectives*, 390–428. Leiden.

———. 2007. "The Breakthrough of *Demokratia* in Mid-Fifth-Century Athens." In Raaflaub et al. 2007:105–54.

———. 2008a. "Homeric Warriors and Battles: Trying to Resolve Old Problems." *CW* 101:469–83.

———. 2008b. "Zeus und Prometheus. Zur griechischen Interpretation vorderasiatischer Mythen." In M. Bernett, W. Nippel, and A. Winterling (eds.), *Christian Meier zur Diskussion*, 33–60. Stuttgart.

———. 2009. "Early Greek Political Thought in Its Mediterranean Context." In R. Balot (ed.), *A Companion to Greek and Roman Political Thought*, 37–56. Malden, MA, and Oxford.

———. Forthcoming. "Perfecting the 'Political Creature' (*zōion politikon*): Equality, *demokratia*, and 'the Political' in the Evolution of Greek Democracy." In Johann Arnason, Kurt A. Raaflaub, and Peter Wagner (eds.), *The Greek Polis and the Invention of Democracy: A Politico-Cultural Transformation and Its Interpretations.*

———. In preparation a. "Frühgriechische Gerechtigkeitsvorstellungen im interkulturellen Zusammenhang des Mittelmeerraumes: methodologische Überlegungen." In R. Rollinger and K. Schnegg (eds.), *The Complex World of Cultural Contacts in Antiquity*. Leuven.

———. In preparation b. "Persian Army and Warfare in the Mirror of Herodotus's Interpretation." In R. Rollinger and B. Truschnegg (eds.), *Herodot und das Perserreich*. Darmstadt.

Raaflaub, K. A., J. Ober, and R. W. Wallace (eds.). 1997. *Origins of Democracy in Ancient Greece*. With chs. by P. Cartledge and C. Farrar. Berkeley.

Raaflaub, K. A., and R. W. Wallace. 2007. "'People's Power' and Egalitarian Trends in Archaic Greece." In Raaflaub et al. 2007:22–48.

Reade, J. E. 1972. "The Neo-Assyrian Court and Army: Evidence from Sculptures." *Iraq* 34:87–112.

Ruzé, F. 1997. *Délibération et pouvoir dans la cité grecque de Nestor à Socrate*. Paris.

Sabin, P., H. van Wees, and M. Whitby (eds.). 2007. *The Cambridge History of Greek and Roman Warfare*. 2 vols. Cambridge.

Saggs, H.W.F. 1963. "Assyrian Warfare in the Sargonid Period." *Iraq* 25:145–54.

Salmon, J. 1977. "Political Hoplites?" *JHS* 97:84–101.

Schwartz, A. 2002. "The Early Hoplite Phalanx: Order or Disarray?" *C&M* 53:31–64.

———. 2009. *Reinstating the Hoplite. Arms, Armour and Phalanx Fighting in Archaic and Classical Greece*. Stuttgart.

Shear, I. M. 2000. *Tales of Heroes: The Origins of the Homeric Texts*. Crestwood, NY.

Singor, H. 2009. "War and International Relations [in Archaic Greece]." In K. Raaflaub and H. van Wees (eds.), *A Companion to Archaic Greece*, 585–603. Malden, MA, and Oxford.

Snodgrass, A. M. 1964a. "Carian Armourers: The Growth of a Tradition." *JHS* 84:107–18.

———. 1964b. *Early Greek Armour and Weapons from the End of the Bronze Age to 600 B.C.* Edinburgh.

———. 1965. "The Hoplite Reform and History." *JHS* 85:110–22.

———. 1971. *The Dark Age of Greece*. Edinburgh.

———. 1980. *Archaic Greece: The Age of Experiment*. Berkeley.

———. 1993. "The 'Hoplite Reform' Revisited." *Dialogues d'histoire ancienne* 19:47–61.

———. 1999 (1967). *Arms and Armour of the Greeks*. London and Ithaca, NY, 1967. Repr. with a new afterword, Baltimore 1999.

Starr, C. G. 1977. *The Economic and Social Growth of Early Greece, 800–500 b.c.* New York.

———. 1986. *Individual and Community: The Rise of the Polis, 800–500 b.c.* New York.

———. 1992. *The Aristocratic Temper of Greek Civilization*. New York.

Stein-Hölkeskamp, E. 1989. *Adelskultur und Polisgesellschaft*. Stuttgart.

Stillman, N., and N. Tallis. 1984. *Armies of the Ancient Near East, 3,000–539 bc*. Devizes.

Thommen, L. 1996. *Lakedaimonion Politeia: Die Entstehung der spartanischen Verfassung*. Stuttgart.

Ulf, C. 1990. *Die homerische Gesellschaft*. Munich.

———. Forthcoming. "Die komplexe Welt der Kulturkontakte. 'Kontaktzone' und 'Rezeptivität' als Mittel für ihre Beschreibung und Analyse." *Ancient West & East* 9.

Ussishkin, D. 1982. *The Conquest of Lachish by Sennacherib*. Tel Aviv.

Wace, A.J.B. 1908–9. "Laconia: Excavations at Sparta, 1909. The Menelaion: The Lead Figurines." *BSA* 15:127–41.

———. 1929. "Lead Figurines." In R. M. Dawkins (ed.), *The Sanctuary of Artemis Orthia at Sparta*, 249–84. London.

Wade-Gery, H. T. 1949. "Hesiod." *Phoenix* 3:81–93. Repr. in Wade-Gery, *Essays in Greek History*, 1–16. Oxford 1958.

Walbank, F. 1967. *A Historical Commentary on Polybius*, vol. 2. Oxford.

Wertime, T. A., and J. D. Muhly (eds.). 1980. *The Coming of the Age of Iron*. New Haven.

Wees, H. van. 1992. *Status Warriors: War, Violence, and Society in Homer and History*. Amsterdam.

———. 1997. "Homeric Warfare." In I. Morris and B. Powell (eds.), *A New Companion to Homer*, 668–93. Leiden.

———. 2000. "The Development of the Hoplite Phalanx: Iconography and Reality in the Seventh Century." In van Wees (ed.), *War and Violence in Ancient Greece*, 125–66. London and Swansea.

———. 2004. *Greek Warfare: Myths and Realities*. London.

West, M. L. (ed.). 1971. *Iambi et Elegi Graeci Ante Alexandrum Cantati*, vol. 1. Oxford.

———. 1997. *The East Face of Helicon: West Asiatic Elements in Greek Poetry and Myth*. Oxford.

Wheeler, E. L. 2007. "Land Battles." In Sabin et al. 2007:1, 186–223.

Yadin, Y. 1963. *The Art of Warfare in Biblical Lands*. 2 vols. London.

CHAPTER 6

The Hoplite Revolution and the Rise of the Polis

GREGORY F. VIGGIANO

In his seminal 1937 article, "When Did the Polis Rise?" Victor Ehrenberg notes that it is impossible to give exact dates for the "rise" and that the polis was no doubt the product of a long evolution.[1] He acknowledges that "rise" can only mean true origin, which scholars as a rule place long before the sixth or fifth century. However, "some strange pronouncements in a contrary sense," the assertions of Berve in particular, provoked Ehrenberg to reassert the orthodox position. Earlier Ehrenberg had protested[2] against Berve setting the formation of the Greek state as late as the turn of the seventh to the sixth centuries.[3] But he was astonished when Berve later argued for a fifth-century date: in the generation of Pindar and Simonides the "growing spirit of the Polis is scarcely yet apparent"; "not under Cimon but under Pericles, the dynastic form of rule is dissolved totally into the self-accomplishment of the Polis."[4] Ehrenberg points out the fallacy in thinking that realization of the polis does not occur until its climax in the fifth century. Such a model as Berve's limits the polis to about the period of Periclean Athens since it declines soon thereafter (e.g., Thuc. 3.82ff.).[5] In recent years, similar attacks on the orthodox view[6] threaten once again to reduce the polis to a "phantom which would owe its existence perhaps to the speculation of philosophers and rhetors of the fourth century."[7]

Ehrenberg suggested that Berve confused the Polis with the "democratic polis" of the fifth century. In fact, as early as 800 BC, the Greeks knew the polis in a purer and simpler form even before the first legislators and the tyrants. The thrust of Ehrenberg's argument is that the polis existed well before it had reached what many consider its apex if not its predestined form. The first stage involved the emergence of the polis-city. Following the formation of the walled polis-town and its unification with the hinterland, the rule of the town replaced the domination of the pure aristocracy. The concept of *dikē*, which had over time become a traditional and admitted principle of the state, restrained the aristocracy and made it responsible to the will of the community of citizens. This description of the process of the internal formation of the state would not arouse much controversy today. It is the second stage Ehrenberg identifies in the rise of the Greek state that scholars have vigorously challenged in recent years. That is when, in the seventh century, a more egalitarian form of the state resulted from the "family-polis" giving way to the "hoplite-polis."[8] The idea that a rising and middling group of farmer-citizen-soldiers burst the bonds of exclusive political privilege and paved the way for broader oligarchies and later for democracies traces its roots back to Aristotle. One of the most common forms of attacking this position has been to deny the existence of a substantial middling stratum of farmers, to make early Greek political history an affair of elites.[9] This view has drawn much inspiration from attempts to downdate the classical phalanx. Ehrenberg sought to prevent the assumption of a "totally new and arbitrary use of the term 'Polis'";[10] in this light I want to reassert the traditional hoplite narrative in the face of the current challenges and put the phalanx in its proper context in the history of the polis.

In his *Politics*, Aristotle, provides a model for how the constitutions of the Greek polis evolved.[11] Following the early kingships, the earliest form of constitution among the Greeks was made up of those who fought. The first constitutions consisted of the cavalry, the horse-owning aristocrats, who dominated the battlefield. However, once the heavy infantry learned the art of proper formation (*syntaxis*), the hoplites were able to break the aristocrats' monopoly of political power. The early Greeks, Aristotle says, called the hoplite constitution democracy. In a later passage,[12] he remarks that the rowers made the democracy of Athens stronger, having been the cause of the victory off Salamis during the Persian Wars and thus the cause of the city's hegemony due to its sea power. Scholars have criticized this scheme.[13] For instance, except for a few areas, such as Thessaly and Macedonia, cavalry never played a preeminent role in Greek warfare. Yet Aristotle still presents a compelling thesis for how the political institutions of the polis did develop. The orthodox view of historians, moreover, has maintained for a long time that the rise of the polis owed much to the emergence of a middle class of farmer-citizen-soldiers, wealthy enough to provide their own hoplite panoply to fight in defense of their state. The hoplites have often been linked to the early Greek tyrants as well. A brief review of the traditional model for how the early polis developed can help throw light on recent attempts to overthrow it.

The polis emerged in the eighth century after the long Dark Age, which followed the chaos that attended the collapse of Mycenaean society. The centuries of low population density and of depressed economic conditions gave way to demographic and geographic expansion and to renewed long-distance trade. The details are obscure, but Thucydides gives a plausible account of the rise of the polis after the period of the migrations ended and the conditions in Greece settled down. He says that the early constitutions were hereditary monarchies with limitations placed on the powers of the kings.[14] There was no great land war fought during this period. Warfare involved simple border conflicts between neighboring poleis over contested land. The Lelantine War fought between Chalcis and Eretria in which "all the rest of Hellas took sides in alliance with the one side or the other" was the first significant land battle to take place among the Greeks.[15] By this time, around 700, most scholars believe that hereditary monarchies of some sort had yielded to aristocracies of birth in most poleis. The traditional view is that the nature of Greek warfare changed dramatically shortly thereafter.

Above all other factors, the introduction of the hoplite shield in the late eighth century had a revolutionary[16] effect. Use of the shield makes sense only in the context of a phalanx in which a warrior in the massed formation seeks coverage for his vulnerable right-hand side behind the shield of the neighbor on his right (Thuc. 5.71). The hoplite shield underscores the technical differences between Dark Age and classical warfare. Dark Age warriors seem to have worn their shields suspended from their necks by a leather strap and to have thrown their spears as javelins. The hoplite shield, on the other hand, is held in place by a double armband while the warrior uses his spear like a pike. Hoplites fought in close formation and thrust their spears instead of throwing them. Thus the open-order battles in which champions were preeminent must have given way to more cohesive formations of heavy infantry with the introduction of the double-grip shield. This transition in tactics led to radical social and political changes in the Greek world. As the defense of the state came to depend more and more on ever-greater numbers of nonaristocrats who fought in the phalanx, side by side with the aristocrats, the hoplites succeeded in their demands for political power. In many states, a charismatic leader exploited the masses' discontent with their aristocratic peers to champion the cause of the hoplites and establish himself as tyrant.

The model outlined above has been challenged from a number of viewpoints. Perhaps the most influential approach has been to argue that the phalanx did not come about through sudden change with the introduction of the hoplite shield.[17] Snodgrass further maintained that the double-grip shield does not necessarily imply phalanx tactics, and that the two innovations did not occur at the same time. In his view, the phalanx did not achieve its full development until about 650. Since the phalanx as described in the classical sources did not first take shape until after the date for the earliest tyrants, there was no self-conscious hoplite class to back the tyrants and to push for political reform. In addition, the prohibitive expense of the panoply meant that few individuals outside the narrow class of aristocrats could afford to arm themselves as hoplites. These aristocrats continued to fight as soloists, and it was only over a period of half a century or more that they gradually recruited nonaristocrats to join their ranks in the phalanx. Therefore, the "gradualist" position contends that there was a military reform in the seventh century but no accompanying political revolution.

Scholars have based the next major change in their understanding of the phalanx on the new readings of the battle scenes in Homer. They claim that in the *Iliad* mass armies, and not heroic champions, are the decisive element in battle.[18] The mass forces are not only decisive but also engage in hand-to-hand combat and close-order formations that are nearly the same as those of the classical phalanx. Latacz argued that, since the Homeric phalanx likely resembles what must have taken place in historical battles of the same period, there is no need to posit a hoplite "revolution" or even a "reform" for the seventh century. The reform must have come earlier or not at all. From this some have concluded that in Homer "the pitched battle was the decisive element."[19] Pritchett has remarked, "The general impression created by the poems is one of hoplites fighting in formation." Indeed, Raaflaub has combined the idea of piecemeal adoption of the hoplite panoply with the arguments for mass fighting in Homer. He proposes a long evolution of fighting in early Greece that involves *perfection* and *formalization* of tactics rather than the introduction of phalanx warfare. He asserts, "The evidence of Homeric and early Greek warfare leaves no space for a 'hoplite revolution.'"[20] Raaflaub suggests that mass fighting gradually "evolved along with the formation of the polis."[21] Since mass fighting had been developing since the start of the polis, the phalanx did not incorporate a new class of citizens who for the first time fought on equal terms with the aristocrats. For Raaflaub, the integration of the polis, which took place under the leadership of the aristocrats, resulted from the "collective will of the entire citizen body" and served the needs of the entire community.[22]

Some historians have gone much further in rejecting the idea of a seventh-century military reform. Van Wees, for example, accepts the thesis that hoplite warfare is widely represented in the *Iliad* and has advanced a new theory about how warriors used the double-grip shield, the *aspis*. He argues that hoplites fought in a stance resembling that of fencers, with their left shoulder facing the enemy, rather than the position of a wrestler, with their chest to the foe. In this case, the *aspis* covers both flanks of the warrior, so there is no need for him to seek the shelter of a neighbor's shield for the protection of a vulnerable right-hand side.[23] Therefore, he contends that hoplites did not need to maintain a tightly ordered line but could fight in a much looser and less cohesive formation or could even have fought independent of the phalanx. The consequences of the new readings of Homer and van Wees's thesis go beyond just a revision of tactics. For example, in a recent textbook discussing the Greek polis Osborne remarks that warfare in massed ranks replaced warfare of individual champions in the eighth century and that this was both prior to the invention of the double-grip shield and well before the appearance of the first tyrants in the Greek tradition. Osborne also accepts van Wees's ideas on how hoplite warriors used their shield. He concludes that "as a key to the development of tyranny, the invention of the hoplite shield needs to be laid aside: it probably happened too early, and it probably made very little difference to the nature of warfare."[24] These trends have begun to affect how some scholars write authoritative descriptions of archaic hoplite battle, as follows.

> The standard hoplite battle formation, the phalanx, developed gradually over the centuries. In classical times the phalanx was a densely packed arrangement, typically eight ranks deep, optimized for mass shock combat. While Herodotus sometimes anachronistically portrays hoplites fighting in classical fashion, the Archaic phalanx was in reality looser and less structured. Armies did form up in close-ordered lines, but contingents were able to advance or withdraw on their own initiative (5.75, 5.113, and 9.62). Battles could proceed in seesaw fashion, with troops repeatedly charging and falling back (7.225, 9.21, and 9.74). Archers and other light troops occasionally fought mixed in with hoplites (9.22, 9.29–30).[25]

On the contrary, I shall argue that the testimony of Homer does not mean that the innovations in hoplite arms brought about no revolutionary change in warfare, and that van Wees's ingenious interpretations of the iconographical evidence are no cause to throw out the orthodoxy regarding tactics. I shall then maintain that the date of the phalanx does in fact coincide with the introduction of the double-grip shield. This earlier date, moreover, is crucial for understanding the revolution that occurred in the poleis in the political and social institutions of at least several of the major Greek states.

These changes transformed Greek values and culture in general and helped create the egalitarian ethos and rule of law that shaped the polis. None of the recent advances in archaeology or the new readings of the literary sources for the period has refuted the traditional grand hoplite narrative.

I begin with a critique of van Wees's view on how hoplites fought,[26] especially their use of the *aspis*. In a recent article, Schwartz analyzes van Wees's theory.[27] He rejects the view that hoplite warriors were fit for single combat. The hoplite was always meant to fight in a phalanx. Schwartz also disputes the idea that the hoplite phalanx did not evolve until the time of the Persian Wars. To begin with, the hoplite panoply, including the bronze breastplate, the bronze "Corinthian-style" helmet, the iron-tipped ashen spear, the iron sword, the bronze greaves, and, of course, the large shield (the *aspis* or *hoplon*), remained essentially unchanged throughout the archaic and classical periods. The shield itself maintained the same circular shape, the concavity of its inner surface, its wooden core, the bronze band on its rim, and the double-grip system. Examination of the equipment shows that it could only have been made for one style of fighting. The size and weight of the shield made it unwieldy.[28] The double-grip system of the central arm band—the *porpax*—and the gripping handle—the *antilabe*—enabled the hoplite to support the approximately 7.5 kg weight of the shield at two points instead of the one afforded by the single-grip shield. In addition, this meant that the bearer could wield the shield with the left arm only, as opposed to the warrior who could shift a single-grip shield from one hand to the other to relieve its weight. On the other hand, the concavity of the shield allowed the hoplite to rest the lip of the shield on his shoulder. Carrying the shield in this inclining position, with the lower rim jutting out in front of the warrior, has the added advantage of enlarging the zone of protection and serves to make spear thrusts glance off the shield. Schwartz points out[29] that this is in fact the only *possible* way to handle the *aspis*.

However, without the carrying strap (the *telamon*) of previous shields, and owing to the sheer size of the shield, the bearer could not sling the *aspis* around his back, which limited his protection when the hoplite turned to flight. This fact, along with its weight and awkward concavity, made the *aspis* particularly unwieldy, and made the warrior himself far less mobile than previous fighters. Yet van Wees insists that "the shield . . . at most tended to slow down movement on the battlefield: it did not in itself impose a static form of combat," and that the loss of maneuverability that the *aspis* entailed "should not be exaggerated," since no type of shield can be brought very far to the right "without badly impeding the use of weapons."[30] However, as Schwartz maintains, it is nearly impossible to deflect a blow or thrust with a shield in one hand and strike with a weapon in the other hand *simultaneously*. The required technique is to deflect an incoming blow first, say to the defender's right side, and then, only *after* that, to go on the offensive. By this time, the warrior will have transferred his shield to its usual position to the front and slightly to the left, so he can strike with greater force. What van Wees's description misses is that in fast-paced fighting the lighter, single-grip shield is of greater value because the bearer can deflect incoming blows better by more swiftly transferring the shield's center to the point of attack and back again, "in short, by using his shield *actively* in the fighting, truly *wielding* it." In addition, since a fighter can hold the single-grip shield at full arm's length, which decreases the opponent's angles of attack, the shield surface need not be quite so large. The single-grip shield also allows great freedom of movement. For example, even when the bearer reaches across to his own right side, a mere turn of the wrist enables him to rotate the shield to maximize the angle of deflection.

The *aspis*, on the other hand, failed in all these respects. The double-grip system severely limited the warrior's overall range of motion. Unlike the single-grip shield, which could be held out at full arm's length, the *aspis* could only be held out as far from the body as the elbow, or about half the distance. It would have been especially difficult for the hoplite wearing a heavy bronze cuirass to reach across his torso to deflect a thrust aimed at his right side. It would have been even more difficult for him to use his *aspis* to deflect a thrust directed at his legs. For unlike a warrior armed with the single-grip shield who could simply alter his footing and lower his shield arm, the hoplite would have had to stoop down for his shield to deflect the sword or spear of his attacker. In any instance, the weight and size of the *aspis* made it awkward to wield, especially over any prolonged period. The Corinthian helmet can be seen in much the same light as well. Besides the considerable weight of the helmet and the discomfort of wearing it, the highly protective helmet impaired the hoplite's field of vision and made it nearly impossible for him to hear.

When one considers the great skill and workmanship that went into designing and making such engineering masterpieces as both the Corinthian helmet and the *aspis*,[31] it is hard to believe that they were not created for a particular type of fighting. That style would hardly have been fighting a series of duels between individuals with their mobility impaired by awkward armor, which limited their range of motion, restricted their vision, and deprived them of their hearing. The most reasonable way to understand the use of the shield is described by Thucydides' often-quoted passage: "through fear each man draws his unarmed side as close as possible to the shield of the man stationed on his right, thinking that there is the greatest safety in the tightest formation possible (*synkleisis*)."[32] As Greenhalgh remarks, "the significance of Thucydides' observation is that some lateral, not frontal, protection was obtained from the next man's shield, and that it was vital not to allow a gap to develop which might break the line, since a broken phalanx was as good as lost."[33]

Peter Krentz has criticized the traditional understanding of archaic battle for its "excessively literal interpretation of the sources both for the formation and manner of fighting."[34] He makes light of the double-handled shield, which is "like any shield carried on one arm,"[35] and suggests that a hoplite "could have covered himself nicely by turning sideways to the enemy," which "would also have enabled a more powerful spear thrust."[36] In fact, this technique would have worked just as well with a smaller shield, which would have been easier to wield without the double grip and wide diameter, and would have presented a smaller target to the enemy. Of course, the logical reason for soldiers preferring the larger *aspis* is what Thucydides describes in 5.71.1, which is precisely why we *should* "assume that Thucydides did not exaggerate and should be taken literally."[37] Krentz gives his own account of how phalanxes collided, inspired by the Myrmidons' charge in the *Iliad*:[38]

> However neat the phalanx was when it began to move, by the time it reached the enemy it tended to dissolve into small clusters and individuals, the braver men striking out on their own, the less confident men bunching together. Archaic hoplites were amateurs, mostly farmers, who lacked the training necessary to advance in an evenly spaced formation.[39]

Not by coincidence, this reconstruction contrasts sharply with Victor Davis Hanson's vivid portrayal of the terrible shock collision of hoplites in *Western Way of War*.[40] However, it is hard to believe that even the Spartans, the closest archaic and classical Greece came to professional soldiers, lacked the discipline and courage to maintain their ranks during an infantry charge.[41] Yet they did not annihilate every Greek force they faced. For example, the Athenians more than held their own against the Spartans at Tanagra in 457.[42] What would have happened if one side did maintain ranks and a relatively tight formation while the other side became frightened and scattered before impact? I think the side that maintained relatively uniform ranks, which is what Tyrtaeus exhorts the Spartans to do, would break right through the opposing line, assuming that they would even need to make contact to win.

Krentz criticizes the orthodox argument for the ritualistic/agonistic nature of archaic hoplite warfare because it is based on late sources, but he presents an alternative model based on a second-century AD account about the Messenian Wars.[43] This is despite the fact that at least the First Messenian War took place before the Spartans first adopted hoplite tactics. A common feature of "revisionist" challenges is to propose a hypothesis that seems to contradict individual points of the orthodoxy.[44] These hypotheses are then treated as facts that disprove the theory without offering an alternative to help explain the larger picture. Krentz, for instance, concludes, based on his idea that phalanxes did not maintain a tight formation nor crash into one another, that, "Archaic Greece did not experience a military revolution, much less one that led to political revolutions as well." There was an evolution in equipment, but this was "in order to help a man do better what he was already doing."[45] But how did a double-grip one-meter-in-diameter shield and a Corinthian helmet help an amateur farmer charge an opposing phalanx only to retreat into small clusters or individual combat before making contact with the enemy?

There will no doubt continue to be lively discussion about tactics, but it will be difficult to explain why such a shield and grip system was designed for any other style of fighting than that which Thucydides described three centuries after the invention of the *aspis*. Why would it take so long to figure out how to use the shield to its best advantage when mass fighting was already taking place in the eighth century? Why propose an extended period of evolution in technique when close-order fighting was already being practiced, as nearly all scholars agree? Why would the Greeks invent the *aspis* only to change to a style of fighting as duelists[46] in hoplite armor for the next two centuries? It is inconceivable that the Greeks would invent specialized armor only to use it in a manner that contradicts its design.[47] It is even more incredible that they would need over two hundred years before realizing during the Persian Wars[48] how to fight with identical equipment, when those arms clearly perfect the type of mass fighting to which Homer may bear witness.[49] The burden of proof rests with those who want to argue that hoplites in the seventh century fought in a looser, less cohesive phalanx. Evolution in fighting style and technique no doubt took place, such as the use of throwing spears and the use of swords as a primary weapon. Tyrtaeus exhorts the lightly armed men, moreover, to "throw great rocks and hurl smooth javelins while [they] stand close by the heavy-armed men."[50] However, these elements do not in and of themselves change the essential character of hoplite warfare. What was most likely an early experimental stage before warriors adopted the uniformity of weapons and of methods does not change the obvious references of Tyrtaeus to the classical phalanx: "let him stand with his shield . . . with foot placed alongside foot and shield pressed against shield, let everyone draw near, crest to crest, helmet to helmet, and chest to chest, and fight against a man, seizing the hilt of his sword or his long spear."[51]

Why would a hoplite encounter in the middle of the seventh century be fundamentally different from one in the fifth century? The archaeology for the period suggests a different story. Snodgrass has pointed out "there is a substantial class of evidence, that of the actual surviving pieces of armour dedicated at Olympia and other sanctuaries, which is more robust than either new textual interpretations of Homer, or new readings of battle scenes in art. It tells a firmly consistent story, that the middle years of the seventh century saw a sharp rise in frequency of use of the 'classic' items of hoplite armour on Greek battlefields: something in Greek warfare changed significantly in these years."[52] He argues for a period of transition during which Greek armorers worked their way through experiment toward the "classic" forms of hoplite equipment.

This firmly fixes the *terminus ante quem* for the hoplite revolution at 650. However, changes in and refinements of equipment need not indicate an alteration in the basic nature of what became the classical phalanx. This includes the relatively large size and cohesion of its ranks,[53] and the decisive role played by the massed ranks of heavy infantry. The Homeric texts, moreover, may show that some form of mass fighting involving nonaristocratic warriors took place prior to the phalanx. This could have provided a precedent for participation by nonelite soldiers, some of whom must have been able to afford the new arms once the massed close-order tactics did come into use. Therefore, though the Homeric testimony[54] cannot be used to disprove a hoplite revolution by arguing for a pre-polis hoplite phalanx, Homer may show that mass fighting had a long history before the full adoption of hoplite armor,[55] and that aristocratic soloists did not monopolize the battlefield. It appears unclear in light of the current reading of Homer's poetry whether an early stage of *exclusive* aristocratic combat by individual warriors or soloists[56] ever existed. This removes an important objection to the idea that the phalanx had revolutionary consequences, namely, that hoplite warfare "ran so entirely counter to historical precedent."[57] At the same time, there was no hoplite phalanx without the *aspis*.

The reasons for going hoplite were mostly pragmatic but were also consistent with archaic Greek ethics and culture. Recent study suggests that "mass armies, and not heroic champions, are the decisive element in Homeric battle, and the importance of their role is absolutely integral to the battle-descriptions."[58] Though this is not conclusive proof that Homeric warfare is historical, it is at least plausible that such a depiction of warfare had some resemblance to real battles of the eighth century. The key innovation that transformed battle was the introduction of the double-grip system. Even if hoplite phalanxes were organized based on the clans in early Greece, as soon as the new form of fighting was adopted, the lead position in battle was taken away from the aristocrats. The original size of the hoplite class, which was probably small, would not have determined whether the new form of fighting would have had a revolutionary effect. However one defines the aristocracy, its power was lessened once aristocrats took their place in the phalanx next to commoners soon after the invention of the double-grip shield. Scholars have placed too much emphasis on the insufficient time for a separate hoplite class to become a self-conscious political force to create a revolution. The transition, once the *aspis* came into use, would not require a long period of perfection and formalization of phalanx warfare, which continued to evolve throughout the classical period while maintaining its essential character.

The dependence on nonaristocrats in battle by itself would have diminished the political stature of aristocrats. Even a small number of nonaristocrat hoplites was now essential and in a position to contest the exclusiveness of aristocratic privilege or to support an aristocrat looking to challenge his peers. Enough time for nonaristocrats to become unified was provided by the long period of mass fighting before its formalization with the new equipment in the fully developed phalanx. In any case, for a "revolution" to take place it would not have required a "class consciousness" on the part of the many independent, well-to-do farmers with the means to sustain and to arm themselves with their own hoplite panoply. The need and desire to protect their farmland would have provided sufficient motivation to fight and demand a voice in polis decisions. The tension from this middle stratum may be seen in the figure of Homer's Thersites, a man of no account in battle or in council, who is a caricature of the new threat to the established political order. There is also the instance of Odysseus rebuking the *demos* as worthless in war and in council.[59]

Raaflaub rejects the idea of a "hoplite revolution." He acknowledges that military changes not only took place but also were an integral part of the rise of the polis.[60] However, he sees political institutions, military practice, and cultural values evolving throughout the archaic period. The development of the phalanx plays a key role in the emergence of the polis, but it is just one important element in the "integration of the polis" in the seventh and sixth centuries without causing any radical breaks from the past. Raaflaub sees a gradual progression in the individual's relationship to his community.[61]

It is true that in his exhortation to his comrades to fight all together by the ships Hector mentions dying for one's *patrē*: for the soldier "it is not unseemly to die defending his fatherland (*patrē*); but his wife is safe and his children after him."[62] On the other hand, Hector also tells his wife Andromache, when she advises him to station his army where the city is most vulnerable to attack, that he must consider his own honor ahead of saving her freedom and that of his family.[63] Achilles exemplifies the heroic ethic perfectly by allowing his fellow Achaeans to be slaughtered by the ships in order to defend his own *timē*.[64] In addition, the Achaeans themselves recognize his right in this. In the embassy to Achilles in book 9 his friends agree that Achilles was right to withdraw from battle until his individual honor was restored. Phoenix tells him: "if the son of Atreus were not to offer you gifts . . . I would not be the one to ask you to cast aside your wrath and assist the Argives, though their need is great."[65] Even Agamemnon does not fault Achilles' lack of devotion to the community, but instead concedes his own madness in dishonoring the great warrior.[66] This contrasts sharply with the hoplite ethos advanced by Tyrtaeus:[67]

> "This is *aretē*; this is the best human prize and the fairest for a young man to win." The man who fights without pause among the *promachoi* "is a common good (*xynon esthlon*) for the polis and all the people (*demos*)." . . . "If he falls among the *promachoi* and loses his dear life, he brings honor to his town (*asty*) and his people (*laoi*) and his father."
>
> Young and old alike lament him / and his entire polis mourns with painful regret. / His tomb and his children are notable among men, / and his children's children, and his *genos* hereafter . . . / but if he escapes the doom of death . . . having prevailed [in battle], . . . / all men give place to him alike, the youth and the elders. . . . / Growing old he is distinguished among his citizens. Never does his name or his excellent glory (*kleos*) perish, but even though he is beneath the earth he is immortal.

The warrior in Tyrtaeus may receive individual honors and praise for his valor in battle, but that is only because he has placed the common good of the polis above all else. The heroic values of Achilles and Hector, which place individual honor and achievement of glory over the life and safety of both family and community, are unimaginable in this context. However, the words of Pericles in the Funeral Speech over two hundred years later are in much the same spirit.

> You must behold daily the might of the polis and become lovers of her, and when her greatness has inspired you, consider that bold men, who knew their duty, and at times of stress were moved by a sense of honor, acquired this, and, whenever they faltered in an enterprise, thought that at least they should not deprive the polis of their excellence (*aretē*), but gave freely to her their fairest service; for they gave their lives (*somata*) for the common good and won for themselves the praise which is ageless[68] and the most notable of tombs—not that in which they lie buried, but that in which their glory remains in everlasting remembrance on every occasion that gives rise to word or deed. For the entire world is the tomb of famous men. . . . The polis will maintain their children at the public expense until manhood, thus offering a useful prize for the dead and their survivors for such contests; for where the greatest prizes are offered for excellence (*aretē*), there also the best men are citizens.[69]

I agree that there is some development in the concept of the polis. But the words of Tyrtaeus are much closer in spirit to those of Pericles than to the speech of Hector. Yet Homer comes maybe a generation or two before Tyrtaeus, and might even be contemporary, depending on how one dates the *Iliad*. For Pericles, much like Tyrtaeus, the *aretē* of the individual is directed entirely to and derives meaning only from the polis. Indeed, citizens who do not participate in the affairs of the polis (*ta politika*) are useless (*akhreion*).[70] The difference from the values of Homer[71] originated with hoplite warfare, and the ethos of egalitarianism and the devotion to the polis it fostered.

The idea that there was a dramatic increase in the population of eighth-century Greece has had great influence on how scholars conceive the rise of the polis—the notion being that the population pressure on limited land led to the use of more intensive farming techniques, such as the cultivation of marginal lands and farmstead residence.[72] As such farming expands, the pastoralism of dominant aristocrats gives way to the agrarian lifestyle and ethos of the middling farmer. The middling *georgoi*, who make up the bulk of the soldiers that fight in the phalanx, become a potent force, which transforms the culture of the early polis. The new egalitarian spirit leads to broader oligarchies and democracies as the middle class demands political power on par with its military importance.

Lin Foxhall has challenged this thesis based on archaeological survey.[73] She argues that the evidence does not support the idea of overpopulation or of landscapes approaching their carrying capacity in the archaic period. There is little evidence of expansion into the countryside in the eighth and seventh centuries. In the southern Argolid, for example, "there is no evidence for dramatic changes in cultivation practices and most sites seem to be situated near the areas of the best agricultural land."[74] Small isolated rural "farmstead" sites do not show up in significant numbers until the Classical and Late Roman periods. The period of extensification into marginal lands "seems to start no earlier than the late sixth century, and is more generally a fifth- and fourth-century phenomenon across Greece."[75] According to Foxhall, the elite still dominated the polis until at least the late sixth century.[76] Therefore, the middling farmers and, by extension, the hoplites had little to do with the overthrow of aristocratic regimes. Her analysis removes any significant link between hoplites and the Greek tyrants.

Other scholars have criticized Hanson's model. For instance, Forsdyke suggests, "Hanson's focus on isolated farm residence is motivated by his desire to define a class of small independent farmers whose ethos of hard work and whose skepticism of the values associated with the luxurious and urban city was the backbone of ancient Greek culture."[77] In addition, she questions Hanson's association of the lifestyle and values of the small independent farmer with the rise and culture of the polis. On the other hand, her discussion points to some of the limitations of the current survey evidence in denying the existence of a middling farmer class. Forsdyke states that "current historical interpretations of archaic agriculture place too much emphasis on permanent residence on the land as an indicator of intensive land use."[78] The essential element in increasing agricultural productivity is the availability of labor, not farm residence. Therefore, farmers could apply intensive techniques to the most fertile lands closest to settlements first.[79] When cultivating previously uncultivated lands farmers might employ traditional, less intensive methods.[80] This would "neither require residence near the land, nor techniques such as manuring which might leave traces in the archaeological record."[81] Forsdyke warns of the complex relation between land use and the material record. This comes into play when attempting to "make claims for one region based on the evidence of one or more other regions."[82] The survey evidence bears directly on the hoplite question, but at present it is far from being conclusive enough[83] to make general claims for the whole of Greece in the eighth and seventh centuries.[84] In any case, there is no need to conclude that all the growth in population and agriculture in the eighth century was wholly manipulated by elites with no recognizable "middle class" playing a part.[85] For one thing, this would imply a level of centralized state control and bureaucracy similar to that of the Mycenaean palaces, which we know could not have existed at the time.[86]

Despite the challenges to the thesis about explosive growth in the population of eighth-century Greece,[87] strong conclusions are still possible for the rise of the polis. The recent demographic study by Scheidel[88] estimates steady population growth of about 0.25 percent per annum throughout Greece from the tenth through the fourth centuries. The growth from the late eighth through the fifth centuries was particularly strong at up to 1 percent per annum, and was possibly higher at certain times in certain regions. "It remains true, however, that even after every reasonable adjustment has been made . . . present evidence still suggests that there were more people, living in a larger number of settlements, of a larger average size, and spread over a wider geographical area, in the later eighth century than at any time in the preceding four centuries."[89] The accumulated growth of the previous two centuries in addition to the unusually high growth rate of the eighth century could well have helped bring about the significant changes that marked the emergence of both hoplite warfare and the polis. The increase in population certainly led to farmers employing some type of intensive agriculture, which may or may not have left traces in the archaeological record. Relative land hunger (e.g., farmers not wanting to cultivate marginal lands, or to farm lands more than a certain distance from their poleis, or perhaps dissatisfied with the amount and/or quality of the land available to them) could have inspired colonization, without the need for the entire landscape to be filled to its capacity. More importantly for the hoplite question, relative land hunger would have increased competition for and conflict over the most fertile borderlands. The changes in population and the effects this had on agriculture no doubt varied from region to region and polis to polis, and affected different areas in different ways at different times. The point is that in certain major poleis, such as Argos, Corinth, and Sparta, there were simply more farmers who were well-to-do nonaristocrats and more able to afford arms now than in any prior generation. It is irrelevant that most small poleis could not possibly field a full hoplite army. The situation was no different in the fifth century as well.

If an agrarian and military revolution transformed Greek society in the seventh century, what did it look like? The picture conforms closely to the orthodox view, which has enjoyed widespread acceptance in the past. One has to admit that it is impossible to form anything close to a complete narrative owing to the nature of the surviving evidence, which is both sparse, often of a late date,[90] and controversial. Still, it is possible to sketch a plausible and instructive account of what might have taken place without omitting or contradicting any of the extant archaeological or literary material.

A change in the model of settlement occurred in the eighth century, which demonstrates a regular layout and clear planning by a central authority that was concerned with the whole community.[91] The colonizing movement reinforced this trend. The first major change in the formation of the polis, following the various synoecisms, would have been the division of the paramount *basileus*' power among elected magistrates serving in offices with limited tenure and powers. The struggle between the newly established aristocracies and the emerging middle class of citizen-soldier-farmers who at first took part only in the assemblies came to define the history of the polis in the archaic period. The transition from the mass armies of the eighth century to the massed ranks of the phalanx of the seventh century created revolutionary social and political changes.

The idea for the *hoplon* developed after infantry had been fighting in mass formation since at least the first half of the eighth century. During the second half of the eighth century, the time of the so-called Greek "Renaissance," the great colonization movement toward the west began. Chalkis and Corinth, which founded Naxos and Syracuse in about 734, sent out the first foundations proper. The period of colonization coincided with the growth in population and the competition for resources, arable soil in particular. With polis formation and relative land hunger, border conflicts broke out between neighboring city-states. It was at this time that Chalkis and Eretria fought over the fertile Lelantine Plain. During these border wars of increasing intensity warriors must have come to see the advantages of fighting in a scrum for protection. Before the end of the eighth century, someone imagined the possibilities of having a larger shield for greater coverage when fighting in mass formation. The creation of a double-grip shield was not inevitable. However, the invention was surprising and made sense. The next stage involved the decision of the more innovative leaders to organize the new fighting style into a phalanx to make it more formal and more effective. The process likely started by organizing one's family and neighbors and eventually included all those who could fight and provide their own panoply. Certain pieces of armor became desirable, such as the breastplate in case an enemy should drive his spear through the shield. Through experience, warriors came to see what worked best in practice, and the tendency toward uniformity increased. The hoplite revolution took place at different times in different places of the Greek world.

Chalkis had played the leading role in Greek warfare in the eighth century until Argos, which probably invented the hoplite shield, developed the phalanx, I would argue. The earliest figure to succeed in hoplite warfare on a large scale may well have been Pheidon of Argos, the first Greek tyrant for whom there is any evidence. I agree with Salmon's dating of Pheidon's reign to about 675.[92] Being the first to make use of a hoplite phalanx would help explain the tradition of Pheidon's remarkable success in conquering new territory. He would have exploited the novel phalanx to diminish the power of the aristocrats and to defeat his neighbors, Corinth and Sparta in particular. At the height of his powers, Pheidon probably defeated the Spartans at Hysiae in 669.

Shortly thereafter, Cypselus used his position as polemarch to overthrow the Bacchiads in about 655 and to establish himself as tyrant of Corinth. Cypselus rose to power when the Bacchiad aristocrats, who were no longer able to maintain their great success of the eighth century, faced popular discontent with their rule.[93] It is a natural inference that Cypselus either made use of the hoplites or at least had their tacit support. The revolution in the government brought about by Cypselus would have drawn on both the new class of men who had prospered from Corinth's expansion of commerce, which had made men outside the Bacchiad class wealthy, and, of course, the hoplites. The tyrant would have included in his council and minor magistrates the hoplites on whom Cypselus could rely in Corinth's resistance to Pheidon of Argos. Pheidon is said to have been killed in a civil disturbance in Corinth[94] that occurred in the middle of the century, the same time as Cypselus' revolution. Despite the violence and oppression of the Cypselids, and the fact that oligarchy returned after the fall of the tyranny, Corinth was never subject again to the domination of the Bacchiads or any other single clan.

The external example of tyranny on the Isthmus of Corinth and popular demand for a redistribution of the state land helped bring about the hoplite revolution at Sparta. The date for the political solution formulated in the Great Rhetra must follow the defeat suffered at the hands of Argos at Hysiae in 669[95] and the subsequent helot revolt that resulted in the Second Messenian War. A combination of factors contributed to this development, especially the unequal distribution of land that followed the Spartan victory in the First Messenian War. To avoid the civil strife that had destroyed the aristocracies in other states, such as Corinth, the Spartan ruling class decided to base the state on a citizen body of *homoioi*, "equals" or "similars." The military reform detailed in the *rhetra* transformed the old-style army organized by the three Dorian tribes of kinship[96] into one based on the five territorial units, the *obai*. This new Spartan government was the first hoplite constitution in Greece. It was established when it became clear to the *demos* that the aristocrats could no longer preserve the state following the heavy defeat at Hysiae and the long drawn-out war with the helots. The rights of citizens were linked both to possession of an allotment of state-owned land, a *kleros*, worked by helots, and to membership in the all-hoplite citizen army and the elite class of *homoioi*.[97]

After the hoplite phalanx had already been adopted by many major Greek states such as Argos, Corinth, and Sparta, the revolution in Athens came about relatively late, at the end of the seventh century. Despite the synoecism of Attica in the eighth century, Athens did not become a unified polis until the time of Peisistratus (e.g., warfare between Athens and Eleusis, as separate political entities, into the seventh century). In contrast to Sparta, Athens could also depend on "internal colonization" of relatively spacious Attica to deal with the land-hunger problem plaguing many Greek states. In 632 the Olympic victor Cylon apparently failed to gather enough support from the hoplites in his attempt to become tyrant of Athens. However, the laws of Draco in 621 were insufficient to resolve the feuding among the aristocrats.

When Solon was made sole archon to deal with the debt crisis in 594, he addressed the infighting among the aristocrats that had been going on since at least the time of Cylon. The census groups he created not only broke the political monopoly of the aristocrats, the Eupatrids, on the high magistracies but also essentially divided political power according to military function. The *hippeis* (i.e., the cavalrymen) and the *zeugitai* (the "yoke men," i.e., the hoplites) secured the greatest benefit.[98]

Solon probably established the Council of Four Hundred to serve as a counterweight to the traditional aristocratic council. The Council (*boulē*) provided an opportunity for the *zeugitai* to serve in the government. Except for the right to attend the assembly and to sit in the Heliaia, the *thetes* played little role in the new constitution. However, Solon needed to incorporate the *zeugitai* in the Athenian state if he wished to stave off the tyranny, which had overtaken many Greek states in the seventh century. Since the assembly met relatively few times a year, the power of the council would not have been great, but significant enough to hope to satisfy the drive toward broader participation. The powers of council and assembly were enhanced when Solon established regular meetings of the assembly.[99]

The idea of a hoplite revolution goes a long way in explaining both the changes in the political and social institutions of the archaic polis and the rise of the early Greek tyrants. In general, a scheme for how the hoplite "revolution" took place at different times in different places shows the strength of Aristotle's model. Arguments that do away with the revolutionary character of hoplite warfare fail fully to account for the rise of the polis and its subsequent history. The Mycenaean palace system was similar to the monarchies of the ancient Near East. Many scholars, moreover, propose continuity between the Late Bronze Age and the Dark Age of Greece. However, the polis was unlike any political system prior to it in history. For example, there were no Near Eastern models for Greek assemblies,[100] which developed out of the assemblies of fighting men found in Homer. The assemblies rose in importance and power with the emergence of the hoplites. At the same time, a self-conscious aristocratic class came into existence and defined itself in opposition to the middling farmers and merchants. How did the Greek polis develop?[101] A grand narrative involving the hoplite phalanx helps explain the rise of this unique phenomenon, and nothing put forward in opposition has refuted the theory. At best, individual points have been contested, but no combination of the "revisionist" arguments adds up to a coherent theory that even begins to replace the orthodox model. There is simply no reason to retreat to the position that we cannot know.

Notes

I want to thank Paul Cartledge and Donald Kagan for offering many helpful comments and suggestions for this paper. The translations of the Greek are my own.

1. Ehrenberg 1937.

2. Ehrenberg 1969: 60.

3. Berve 1951, 1:176.

4. Berve, "Fürstliche Herren der Zeit der Perserkriege," *Die Antike* 12 (1936): 1ff., and his book *Miltiades*, 1937.

5. Ehrenberg 1937: 158–59.

6. E.g., see van Wees in this volume. Gawantka (1985: 26, 28, n. 43) attacks the use by modern scholars of the ancient Greek word "polis" as an abstraction, a Weberian "ideal type." Morris, on the other hand, argues for an eighth-century polis, but denies any connection with hoplites: "there is absolutely no reason to associate a 'hoplite class' with either the rise of the polis or the rise of the tyrants" (1987: 200).

7. Ehrenberg 1937: 148, n 2.

8. Ehrenberg 1937: 156.

9. For Morris (1996: 40), "*To meson* was not a class but an ideological construct." He suggests (2009: 76–79) that "the elitist vision . . . formed in opposition to middling ideologies in the same period, and the variability of the late-eighth-century archaeological record reflects the use of material culture to express competing visions of the good society" and "there are hints in the texts that the conflicts of the eighth century were sometimes settled by violence, but the main arena of debate was probably cultural."

10. Ehrenberg 1937: 157.

11. *Politics* 1297b 16–28.

12. *Politics* 1304a 22–24.

13. Raaflaub 1999: 129.

14. Thuc. 1.13.

15. Thuc. 1.15.

16. By the term "revolution" I am referring to the fundamental change that I argue took place in the social and political structure of the polis with the introduction of the hoplite phalanx. This change had more dramatic consequences for the development of the early polis than the military "reform" for which Snodgrass has argued (see below).

17. Snodgrass 1965. See "The Hoplite Debate" chapter in this volume.

18. Latacz 1977.

19. Pritchett 1985: 33.

20. Raaflaub 1999: 140.

21. Raaflaub 1993: 80.

22. Raaflaub 1992: 80–81.

23. See van Wees's chapter in this volume.

24. Osborne 2004: 64–65. However, in the second edition of *Greece in the Making, 1200–479* (2009: 164–65), Osborne states, "From around 675 BC vases provide good evidence for the use of the hoplite shield. . . . such a shield was far less manoeuvrable . . . as they [soldiers] advanced at a run the shield offered protection only to the left-hand side of the body. . . . the invention of the hoplite shield makes no sense except in the context of hand-to-hand fighting. The hoplite shield offers clear military advantages only in combination with heavy body-armour or in a very close-packed line, where each soldier (except the man at the right-hand end!) could protect his right side behind the shield of his right-hand neighbor during the advance. Paintings on pots show pipers in association with marching soldiers as early as they show use of the hoplite shield: once one was in very close-packed ranks with interlocking shields keeping in step became important. Inventing and adopting a shield can only have seemed a good idea when fighting in massed ranks was already familiar. Having a heavier and more securely held shield, which forced warriors to pack tightly together for maximum protection and covered the gaps between warriors, then became militarily desirable."

25. J.W.I. Lee, "Hoplite Warfare in Herodotus," appendix N in *The Landmark Herodotus: The Histories*, ed. Robert B. Strassler, 799 (first Anchor Books edition, June 2009). I do not find convincing that these citations in Herodotus necessarily support this description of hoplite battle.

26. Van Wees 2000.

27. Schwartz 2002.

28. Even if Krentz's revised estimates for the weight of the shield and hoplite panoply are correct (see his chapter in this volume), the point remains unchanged: hoplites were fighting in armor that was much heavier and bulkier than anything they wore prior to the innovations in arms. Snodgrass points out that the arms were heavier when first introduced during the eighth

and seventh centuries than in the fifth century, when the revisionists acknowledge that the close-order formation of the phalanx was in place. Krentz himself argues that hoplite armor became lighter over time until it may have been as light as 10 kg less at the time he claims the close-order fighting first came into use during the Persian Wars. Schwartz points out that the hoplites themselves were considerably lighter than originally estimated as well, which would offset some of the possible downward adjustments in weight of armor.

29. Schwartz 2002: 35, and in this volume.

30. Van Wees 2000: 127.

31. Snodgrass 1964: 35, 68.

32. Thuc. 5.71.

33. Greenhalgh 1973: 72.

34. Krentz 2007: 72 uses V. D. Hanson's *Western Way of War* (2000) as an example.

35. Krentz 2007: 72. In this volume, Kurt Raaflaub argues that, though Near Eastern equipment may have served as a starting point, the Greek shield and hoplite arms in general are unique and unlike anything the ancient world had produced.

36. Krentz 2007: 72 cites van Wees 2004b: 168–69 to support his assertions.

37. Krentz 2007: 72–73 suggests that "as close as possible" might mean much more than three feet for Thucydides, but this is unlikely. Three feet is a fair estimate of the distance soldiers would need to stand apart for the passage to make sense. Why propose a much greater distance that explains nothing and only makes one of the most direct extant references to close-order fighting unnecessarily confusing and obscure? At the Yale conference, Krentz said that three feet or something close to it was a possibility for the distance between hoplites.

38. *Iliad* 16.259–67.

39. Krentz 2007: 74.

40. Hanson 2000: 152–59. See Hanson's chapter in this volume on the impossibility that opposing hoplite phalanxes never collided.

41. In this volume, Krentz cites John Keegan (1976) to make his point that out of faintheartedness hoplites would not crash into one another, but this is unconvincing. Scholars have long used the rugby scrum, which Krentz also criticizes in this volume, as an analogy for certain aspects of hoplite battle. In this case, American football is helpful. Football coaches at all levels, even when coaching eight- to twelve-year-old boys, insist that players crash into one another and often judge the success of line play and tackling in part by the sound of the popping together of helmets and shoulderpads when players collide. Special-team play, during which players run the length of the field at top speed and crash into one another, is considered one of the most exciting and important parts of the game. Teams perform drills in practice to develop the skills and toughness necessary for hitting opposing players head-on. Professional football careers in the National Football League are notoriously short (about 3.5 years) due mainly to the violent contact players, especially the huge linemen, who battle in the "trenches" and crash into each other in tight formation, experience. *Sports Illustrated*, a popular American sports magazine, describes a linebacker tackling a running back at full speed (*SI*, September 5, 2011): "There is an unmistakable *crack*—helmets, face masks and upper body pads all colliding, a noise that can't be heard on Sundays in living rooms or from the distant and soft club seats. But it is the soundtrack of the game." A player explains what he was taught as a boy in Pop Warner (youth football): "Make sure you hit as hard as you can. Inflict as much pain as possible. Take 'em out. That's what got me recruited to Miami from high school—the violence that I tackled with. I guess there were rules but I didn't really think about them till I got to the pros." Why would battle-hardened hoplites similarly equipped and fighting for their lands, families and poleis shy away, as a rule, from violent contact that would help break open the enemy's line? It is more

believable that armies would station their most disciplined and fearless warriors in the front two or three rows, and then place the older but relatively brave men in the back two or three lines to keep the relatively fainthearted hoplites in the middle from fleeing and thus to prevent what Keegan describes from happening. In the *Iliad* 4.299–300, for instance, Nestor drives the cowards (*kakoi*) into the middle to make them fight against their will.

42. Thuc. 1.108.1. An objection that Tanagra is a fifth-century battle will not work. If the Spartans had had such a decisive edge over all other Greeks with a close formation between 650 and 500, that would have compelled other poleis to follow suit.

43. Pausanias, *Periegesis*, book 4. The argument being that archaic wars were neither brief nor decisive nor economical.

44. Along these lines, revisionists will often argue that if there is only one or a handful of references in the sources to an idea (e.g., the collision of phalanxes, *synkleisis* in Thucydides, etc.), the point is either false or can be ignored as unproven.

45. Krentz 2007: 79.

46. At the conference, Krentz objected to saying that the revisionist position characterizes hoplites as duelists, but once one abandons the idea of the close formation and warriors seeking cover provided by their neighbors' shields, the phalanx becomes a series of duels fought in an extended line.

47. See Schwartz in this volume for tactics implied by the hoplite panoply.

48. In this volume, Krentz argues that hoplite armor became progressively lighter until it was ultimately used for close-order fighting in the fifth century, following Marathon.

49. See Hanson's analogy to people playing touch football with full gear in this volume.

50. Tyrtaeus fr. 11.35–38.

51. Tyrtaeus fr. 11.29–34.

52. Snodgrass 2006: 345.

53. Salmon 1977: 90.

54. On the one hand, I am aware of the precarious nature of using the poetic and often ambiguous testimony of Homer as historical evidence. On the other hand, certain references in the *Iliad* to mass fighting seem clear enough (e.g., *Iliad* 13.130–33) to point to precedents for the later hoplite phalanx.

55. In this volume, Snodgrass discusses the trend of philologists to lower the date for the completion of the *Iliad* and *Odyssey* from the eighth to at least the seventh century. However, even if one assumes that Homer describes Greek warfare close to the way it was actually fought before the development of the phalanx, and accepts the evolutionary model of Nagy that posits a somewhat fluid transmission of an unwritten *Iliad* down to as late as the mid-sixth century, that does not necessarily imply a later phalanx. The traditional nature of Homeric poetry and the desire of the poet to represent a distant and heroic, though intelligible, past, would compel him to describe the fighting style of a generation before the hoplite era.

56. This does not mean that aristocrats did not play a much more prominent role in prephalanx mass warfare. Raaflaub is correct that Homer downplays the decisive role of the *laoi* for poetic effect, but in order for Homeric battle to be serious and meaningful, the *aristeia* and individual battles of the great champions must too have met the expectations of the audience for a measure of realism. That argument works both ways. If Homer was pretending and heroic demonstrations of *arete* were entirely fanciful, scenes that display them would seem ludicrous. Indeed, Herodotus describes the battle of champions between the Argives and Spartans over Thyrea in the middle of the sixth century (Hdt. 1.82).

57. Snodgrass 1965: 115.

58. Snodgrass 2006: 346.

59. *Iliad* 2.200–202.
60. See Raaflaub 1993, 1997, and 1999.
61. Raaflaub 1993: 41–42.
62. *Iliad* 15.494–98.
63. *Iliad* 6.407–65.
64. I agree that Homer deliberately downplays the role of the *laoi* in order to concentrate on heroic combat and that there was probably never an era dominated entirely by soloist fighters; however, a fundamental change occurs with the introduction of hoplite armor and tactics.
65. *Iliad* 9.515–18.
66. *Iliad* 9.115ff. and 19.83ff.
67. Fragment 12.15–42.
68. Note the contrast Pericles makes with the ageless praise for which the Homeric hero strives to win individual immortality, not the immortality of the community.
69. Thuc. 2.43.1–2; 2.46.1.
70. Thuc. 2.40.2.
71. Thuc. 2.41.4: "We shall not need the praise of a Homer."
72. Hanson 1995: 47–89.
73. Foxhall 1997: 122–29.
74. Foxhall 1997: 123.
75. Foxhall 1997: 127.
76. Foxhall 1997: 131.
77. Forsdyke 2006: 342.
78. Forsdyke 2006: 343 cites Garnsey 1988: 94, "the argument for the prevalence of intensive farming does not depend on farmers residing on their properties rather than in nearby nucleated settlements." In a list of five methods of intensification Cherry et al. 1991: 331 include only one involving farm residence.
79. Isager and Skydsgaard 1992: 112–13.
80. Forsdyke 2006: 344–45 following Gallant 1982: 122–24.
81. Forsdyke 2006: 345.
82. Forsdyke 2006: 346 observes, "it is striking that on Keos 'farms' and expansion into marginal lands arise already in the archaic period while in the Argolid such phenomena appear only in the classical period."
83. Osborne 2004: 170 points out the limitations of the survey data: "survey itself offers no way in to absolute population levels. Survey data yield figures for inhabitants only when we apply a series of assumptions derived from non-survey, and frequently from non-archaeological, evidence. Survey itself cannot even show that the assumption that 'family farms' were on average the residences of five people is justified. The density figures for larger settlements are at best derived from local excavation evidence (via further hypotheses which are not themselves testable on the basis of archaeological material); more normally, they come from cross-cultural data whose comparability is not explored."
84. It is significant that there is some evidence for marginal lands being farmed in the eighth and seventh centuries, even though the surveys produce a much higher volume of rural sites for the fifth and fourth centuries.
85. This argument has become popular in recent years. But Starr 1977: 123 relates that no more than 400 men were assigned the liturgy of maintaining a trireme in the Peloponnesian War, which must have been less than one percent of the adult male citizen population; 300 citizens had that responsibility in the mid-fourth century. Starr observes, "in earlier centuries and in smaller states the numbers of aristocrats must have been fewer." It is unlikely that the

aristocracy in Greece at any point from 700 to 300 BC numbered much above 1 or 2 percent, far less than even the lowest estimates for the percentage of those wealthy in land in archaic Greece.

86. Foxhall 1995: 243–44.

87. E.g., Morris 1987: 57–109 attributed the dramatic increase in burials found for the years 780–720, which Snodgrass 1980 interpreted as a massive growth (4%) in the population, in part to short-term changes in Athenian burial customs.

88. Scheidel 2003: 120–40.

89. Snodgrass's observation of 1993: 32 still applies.

90. Revisionists are especially critical of using any late source to explain what took place in the archaic period. They often reject any source that is not contemporary and question the dating of early sources such as Tyrtaeus. My method is to be critical of all evidence but not to reject writers like Ephorus solely because they are late, if their testimony does not contradict an earlier source and presents a plausible account.

91. Snodgrass 1993: 30–31.

92. Salmon 1977: 92–93.

93. For discussion of Corinth and tyranny in general see Andrewes 1956: 43–53.

94. Nicholas 90 fr. 35.

95. Pausanias 2.24.7.

96. Tyrtaeus fr. 1. 12.

97. Cartledge 2002: 115–17.

98. Cartledge 2001: 16.

99. On Solon's constitution see Ste. Croix 2005.

100. Davies 1997: 34.

101. Raaflaub 2009: 37–56 argues for the uniqueness of early Greek political thought, despite certain "foreign influences" from the Near East and Egypt.

Bibliography

Alcock, S. E. 2004. *Side-by-side survey: Comparative regional studies in the Mediterranean World*, ed. Susan E. Alcock and John F. Cherry. Oxford: Oxbow.

Andrewes, A. 1956. *The Greek Tyrants*. New York: Harper & Row.

Berve, H. 1951. *Griechische Geschichte*. Freiburg: Herder.

Cartledge, P. A. 2001. *Spartan Reflections*. Berkeley and Los Angeles: University of California Press.

Cartledge, P. A. 2002. *Sparta and Laconia: A regional history, 1300–362 BC*. London and New York: Routledge.

Ehrenberg, V. 1937. "When did the polis rise." *JHS* 57:147–59.

Ehrenberg, V. 1969. *The Greek state*. London: Methuen.

Davies, J. K. 1997. "The 'origins of the Greek polis': Where should we be looking?" In *The development of the polis in archaic Greece*, ed. Lynette G. Mitchell and P. J. Rhodes. London and New York: Routledge, 24–38.

Forsdyke, S. 2006. "Land, labor and economy in Solonian Athens: Breaking the impasse between archaeology and history." In *Solon of Athens: New historical and philological approaches*, ed. Josine H. Blok and André P.M.H. Lardinois. Leiden and Boston: Brill, 334–50.

Foxhall, L. 1995. "Bronze to iron: Agricultural systems and political structures in late Bronze Age and early Iron Age Greece." *The Annual of the British School at Athens* 90:239–50.

Foxhall, L. 1997. "A view from the top: Evaluating the Solonian property classes." In *The development of the polis in archaic Greece*, ed. Lynette G. Mitchell and P. J. Rhodes. London and New York: Routledge, 113–35.

Gawantka, Wilfried. 1985. *Die Sogenannte Polis: Entstehung, Geschichte und Kritik der modernen althistorischen Grundbegriffe der griechische Staat, die griechische Staatsidee, die Polis*. Stuttgart: Steiner.

Greenhalgh, P.A.L. 1973. *Early Greek warfare*. Cambridge: Cambridge University Press.

Keegan, J. 1976. *The face of battle*. New York: Viking Press.

Krentz, P, 2007. "Warfare and hoplites." In *The Cambridge companion to archaic Greece*, ed. H. A. Shapiro. Cambridge: Cambridge University Press, 61–84.

Latacz, J. 1977. *Kampfparanase, Kampfdarstellung und Kampfwirklichkeit in der Ilias, bei Kallinos und Tyrtaios*. Munich, *Zetemata* 66.

Morris, I. 1987. *Burial and ancient society: The rise of the Greek city-state*. Cambridge: Cambridge University Press.

Morris, I. 1996. "The strong principle of equality and the archaic origins of Greek democracy." In *Democratia: A conversation on democracies, ancient and modern*, ed. Josiah Ober and Charles Hedrick. Princeton: Princeton University Press, 19–48.

Okin, L. A. 1988. Review of Gawantka 1985. *American Historical Review*, April, vol. 93, no. 2.

Osborne, R. 2004. *Greek history*. London and New York: Routledge.

Osborne, R., 2009. *Greece in the making, 1200–479 B.C.* London and New York: Routledge.

Pritchett, W. K. 1971–91. *The Greek state at war*, vols. 1–5. Berkeley and Los Angeles: University of California Press.

Raaflaub, K. A. 1993. "Homer to Solon: The rise of the polis; the written sources." In *The ancient Greek city-state: Symposium on the occasion of the 250th anniversary of the Royal Danish Academy of Sciences and Letters, July 1–4, 1992*, ed. Mogens Herman Hansen. Copenhagen: The Royal Danish Academy of Sciences and Letters, 41–106.

Raaflaub, K. A. 1999. "Archaic and classical Greece." In *War and society in the ancient and medieval worlds*, ed. Kurt Raaflaub and Nathan Rosenstein. Cambridge, Mass., and London: Harvard University Press, 129–61.

Salmon, John. 1977. "Political hoplites?" *JHS* 97:84–101.

Scheidel, W. 2003. "A model of demographic expansion: Models and comparisons." *JHS* 123:120–40.

Schwartz, A. 2002. "The early hoplite phalanx: Order or disarray." *C & M* 53:31–64.

Snodgrass, A .M. 1964. *Early Greek armour and weapons*. Edinburgh: Edinburgh University Press.

Snodgrass, A. M. 1965. "The hoplite reform and history." *JHS* 85:110–22.

Snodgrass, A. M. 1993. "The rise of the polis: The archaeological evidence." In *The ancient Greek city-state: Symposium on the occasion of the 250th anniversary of the Royal Danish Academy of Sciences and Letters, July 1–4, 1992*, ed. Mogens Herman Hansen. Copenhagen: The Royal Danish Academy of Sciences and Letters, 30–40.

Snodgrass, A. M. 2006. "The 'hoplite reform' revisited." In *Archaeology and the emergence of Greece*. Ithaca: Cornell University Press, 344–59.

Starr, C. G. 1977. *Economic and social growth of early Greece, 800–500 B.C.* New York: Oxford University Press.

Ste. Croix, G.E.M. de. 2005. "Five notes on Solon's constitution." In *Athenian democratic origins: And other essays*, ed. David Harvey and Robert Parker. Oxford: Oxford University Press, 73–108.

Van Wees, H. 2000. "The development of the hoplite phalanx: Iconography and reality in the 7th century." In *War and violence in ancient Greece*, ed. Hans van Wees. London: Classical Press of Wales, 125–66.

CHAPTER 7

Hoplite Hell: How Hoplites Fought

PETER KRENTZ

If W. Kendrick Pritchett built the stage set for our understanding of Greek warfare and Anthony Snodgrass provided the costumes, Victor Davis Hanson made the actors come alive. Hanson's gritty *Western Way of War*, in particular, has had an enormous impact on popular understanding of how Greeks fought, from Steven Pressfield's *Gates of Fire* (1998)—in which Pressfield created an *othismós* drill that he called, memorably, "tree-fucking"—to Zack Snyder's movie *300* (2007), in which the Spartans fight with the underhanded grip favored by Hanson. So any discussion of how hoplites fought (or what one of my friends, after reading *The Western Way of War*, called "hoplite hell") must now start with Hanson's interpretation.

Hanson writes forcefully and shows an excellent eye for vivid details. Using an impressive variety of scattered pieces of evidence, he builds a thick description of a hoplite battle. In his words, cobbled together from different parts of the book:[1]

> for at least the two centuries between 700 and 500 B.C., and perhaps for much of the early fifth century B.C. as well, hoplite infantry battle determined the very nature of Greek warfare, and became the means to settle disputes—instantaneously, economically, and ethically. . . . Unfortunately, nearly all of the conflicts of the seventh and sixth centuries remain unrecorded. At this time hoplite battle remained a "pure," static, unchanging match between men in the heaviest of armor, void of support from auxiliary cavalry, missile throwers, or archers. . . . [M]ost wars involved only an hour or more of pitched battle. . . . The actual battle environment for men who served in the phalanx was nearly identical wherever and whenever they fought. . . . [U]nusual uniformity in both arms and tactics . . . guaranteed that the killing and wounding were largely familiar to many generations—whether they had fought one summer day in the mid-fifth century in a valley in Boiotia, or on a high plain in the central Peloponnese one hundred years earlier. For men aged twenty through sixty—the uninitiated and veteran alike—the charge, the collision of spears, the pushing, trampling, wounding, panic, confusion, even the pile of

the battlefield dead, were all similar events to be experienced one awful, fatal time, or perennially until a man could fight no more.

Perhaps the only sentence here that I would not quarrel with makes the point that we have very limited literary evidence for Archaic warfare. As for the rest, hoplite battles did not decide wars instantaneously. Archaic wars sometimes dragged on and on. Think of the Messenian Wars, the Lelantine War, Sparta's struggle with Tegea, or Athens' conflicts with Megara and Aigina. Nor were these wars particularly ethical. The idea that Archaic Greeks fought fairly, following distinctive Greek laws of war, is a mirage based on later Greek claims about the good old days.[2] But my job is to discuss the nature of hoplite fighting. Let me first summarize, fairly briefly, my views on two aspects of Archaic warfare that will inform what follows. I will begin with the weight of hoplite equipment and the nature of the Archaic phalanx, or rather, the Archaic phalanges or ranks. Then I will focus on three debated aspects of a battle: the charge, the collision, and the pushing.

"The Burden of Hoplite Arms and Armor"

In *The Western Way of War*, Hanson devotes a chapter to "the burden of hoplite arms and armor," in which he reports that modern estimates range from 50 to 70 lbs.[3] The higher figure is the most common estimate. Hanson mentions 70 lbs at least four times in *The Other Greeks*.

This estimate goes back to W. Rüstow and H. Köchly's *Geschichte des griechischen Kriegswesens von der ältesten Zeit bis auf Pyrrhos* (1852).[4] Rüstow and Köchly estimated weights for each piece of equipment, calculating that a fully equipped hoplite carried 72 lbs or—since they were using German lbs (one German lb = 0.5 kg)—36 kg. Hans Delbrück picked up and popularized the Rüstow-Köchly total.[5] In Delbrück's day, European soldiers carried 28–31 kg, so perhaps it is not surprising that he believed Greeks managed 36. Many scholars since have followed his lead.[6]

I have discussed the equipment item by item in two other publications and do not want to repeat myself needlessly here.[7] Drawing on studies of surviving pieces of Greek equipment, especially from the German excavations at Olympia, and on the reconstructions made by reenactment groups in Britain and Australia, I conclude that Hanson's picture of lumbering hoplites must be moderated. A realistic estimate is that a hoplite equipped with a helmet, cuirass, shin guards, shield, spear, and sword carried a total weight of 18–22 kg in the seventh century. By the time of the Persian Wars, helmets and shin guards had gotten thinner, and leather-and-linen corselets had largely replaced bronze-plate cuirasses, which were never ubiquitous. The total weight dropped to 14–21 kg. If a man did without shin guards and relied on his shield for chest protection, he could have carried only 9 kg.[8]

Let me say a bit more about the shield, which a hoplite called an *aspis*, since it has played a significant role in the debate about the origins of the Greek phalanx. This *aspis*, with its central bronze armband (*porpax*) and leather handgrip at the right edge, was made of wood. It could be faced with a thin sheet of bronze, but movies such as *300* give a misleading impression when the actors use metal shields. Wood did the work. And the three shields that have survived with enough wood to be identified were poplar, willow, and poplar or willow—precisely the woods recommended by the Roman naturalist Pliny for shields (*Natural History* 16.209). These rather soft woods tend to dent rather than split. Because their density is so much lower than the density of oak or even pine, a shield made of willow or poplar will weigh roughly half as much as one made of oak and two-thirds to three-quarters as much as one made of pine.

Reconstructors have shown just how light a *porpax aspis* could be. P. H. Blyth's reconstruction of the best-preserved example, a fifth-century poplar specimen now in the Museo Gregoriano Etrusco, weighs 6.2 kg. This shield, which is on the low end of the range in diameter (0.82 m), had a bronze facing on the exterior that weighed 3 kg. The same shield, unfaced, would weigh only 3.2 kg. Craig Sitch of Manning Imperial in Australia makes several versions: one of poplar, 0.84 m in diameter, weighs 4.3 kg, and another of radiata pine, 0.85 m in diameter, weighs 6.5–7 kg (samples vary). The Hoplite Association in London produces shields made of lime (similar in density to pine) and pine, 0.93 m in diameter, that weigh 6.4 kg. In poplar or willow, these shields would weigh about a third less. Sitch's heaviest version, 0.91 m in diameter, faced with brass and lined with leather, weighs 9 kg. Most shields, however, were *not* faced with bronze.[9] In short, while hoplite shields could weigh 7–9 kg, many weighed only half as much.

Did all hoplites carry this *porpax* shield? No. Greek writers applied the term "hoplite" to Egyptians carrying shields that reached to their feet and to Macedonians who used a much smaller shield.[10] Did all Greek hoplites carry this *porpax* shield? Perhaps yes, but there is good iconographic evidence for a significantly different variation, the oblong "Boeotian" shield found in Archaic vase painting and on coins, in addition to the famous figurine from Dodona, now in Berlin. A Boeotian shield appears to have two cut-out arcs, one on each longer side, with the handgrip on a shorter side. Scholars have usually dismissed the Boeotian shield as an unrealistic heroic marker, adapted from Mycenaean figure-of-eight shields and out of place in a hoplite phalanx. But we have to guard against letting assumptions about how hoplites fought prejudge what equipment they used. A number of scholars have followed John Boardman in arguing that the art reflects reality.[11] Handling a Boeotian shield would have differed from handling a round *aspis*, because no one would want to hold a Boeotian shield with the arm bent at a 90-degree angle, positioning the cutouts to expose the throat and groin. But a warrior could rotate the shield quickly by moving his left hand counterclockwise 180 degrees, lessening the likelihood of dislocating his arm. One anonymous reenactor has posted a YouTube video showing how the Boeotian shield could work.[12] He reminds me of one of the stories told about Sophanes, son of Eutychides from Dekeleia, who distinguished himself at the battle of Plataea. It was said that he "had an anchor as an emblem on his shield, which never ceased moving and was always in swift motion" (Herodotus 9.74.2).

No Boeotian shields have been found, but if they were made of organic materials, perhaps by stretching hides over a wooden frame, they would have disintegrated long before now. The drinking song of Hybrias the Cretan, usually dated to the late Archaic period, demonstrates that a leather shield could be a source of pride (Athenaios *Deipnosophistai* 695f–696a). To judge by vase paintings, the Boeotian shield remained an attractive option for a minority of fighters throughout the Archaic period. It would have looked impressive as the warrior twirled it about, and it would have been more comfortable to walk or run with it slung on one's back, positioned with the cutouts at elbow height so one's elbows would not constantly bump the shield. Its continued use has important implications for the nature of the Archaic phalanx.

The Nature of the Phalanx

From a strictly literary point of view, the hoplite phalanx did not exist until the fourth century, when Xenophon refers to "the phalanx of hoplites" (*Anabasis* 6.5.27).[13] The word "phalanx" apparently derives from a root meaning "log." Neither Herodotus nor Thucydides uses it in a military context, and with a single exception, the Archaic poets use it only in the plural, phalanges, with one exception in the *Iliad*.[14] The word "hoplite," which derives from *hopla* (military equipment), first occurs in the fifth century as an adjective in poetry; it becomes common as a noun in the second half of the century, first in Herodotus, then in Thucydides, Aristophanes, Euripides, and inscriptions.[15] When discussing Archaic warfare, we might do well to avoid the expression "hoplite phalanx" and refer simply to phalanges or ranks, without prejudicing the issue of who fought in them.

Who did fight in the Archaic phalanges? By the time of the Peloponnesian War, lightly armed troops fought separately from the hoplites, as emerges clearly from Thucydides' description of the battle of Syracuse (6.69.2): "The stone-throwers, slingers, and archers of either army began skirmishing, and routed or were routed by one another, as might be expected between light troops." Following this inconclusive skirmishing, the seers sacrificed and the trumpeters blew, and only then did the hoplites move forward. So the phalanx of hoplites existed before any surviving source names it. When was the exclusive hoplite phalanx invented? How historians have answered this question makes for an interesting story.

Before George Grote, historians maintained that the Dorians introduced "the method of fighting with lines of heavy armed men, drawn up in close and regular order," since Homer describes a different mode of combat and an anecdote in Polyainos credits the Herakleidai Prokles and Temenos with using pipers to help their men advance in rhythm in an unbreakable formation against the Lakedaimonians.[16] Grote objected that the correctness of this view "cannot be determined . . . we have no historical knowledge of any military practice in Peloponnesus anterior to the hoplites with close ranks and protended spears."[17] Late nineteenth-century scholars then limited themselves to claiming that the Lakedaimonians had a trained mass formation by the time of the Messenian Wars in the eighth and seventh centuries. In his narrative of these wars, the traveler Pausanias says that it was traditional for the Lakedaimonians not to pursue too quickly, because they preferred to maintain their formation rather than to kill anyone running away (4.8.11). Several ancient sources, starting with Thucydides, say that pipers helped the Lakedaimonians maintain formation.[18] "In this context," opined Hans Delbrück, "the piper is nothing other than the tactical formation."[19]

In the nineteenth century, no one mentioned any of the soldiers' equipment as suitable only for a close-order formation. No one was talking about how heavy and unwieldy the *porpax* shield was—no doubt because, according to the conventional wisdom of Rüstow and Köchly, it weighed only half as much as the earlier great oval shield (6–7.5 kg compared with 14–15 kg).[20]

Credit for connecting the *porpax* shield and the phalanx formation goes to Wolfgang Helbig. In 1909 he suggested in a page or two that the phalanx developed gradually.[21] Only after the development of the close-order formation had made considerable progress did Greeks adopt the *porpax* shield, which Helbig pronounced suitable only for fighting in close ranks. Two years later, he developed this view in a long article, "Über die Einführungszeit der geschlossenen Phalanx," in which he looked not to late sources such as Pausanias and Polyainos, but to Archaic poets.[22] He argued that Euboians distinguished between hoplites and lightly armed men, excluding everyone but hoplites from the ranks during the Lelantine War, which he dated to the middle of the seventh century. Since the Lakedaimonian poet Tyrtaios, whom he put in the second half of the seventh century, did not describe an exclusive phalanx, Helbig concluded that the Euboians, not the Spartans, created it. In his view, there was a longish period of development lasting until the sixth century. He cited the Chigi olpe, which was then dated to the early sixth or even fifth century, as the earliest definite depiction of a hoplite phalanx. Though he found this depiction inadequate in some ways, he did think that the piper on the Chigi vase proves a close-order formation advancing in step. This Protocorinthian jug fit his theory that the hoplite phalanx originated on the island of Euboia, because he believed that Protocorinthian pottery was in fact produced in Chalkis.[23]

The details of Helbig's theory no longer seem tenable.[24] Yet many distinguished scholars have accepted Helbig's innovative claim that the *porpax* shield would only work in a close-order formation, so that once Greeks had that shield, they had the hoplite phalanx.[25] These scholars stress that the shield's weight and distinctive handling system meant that it provided better protection for the left side than the right, and they cite Thucydides' comment that in all armies each man, out of fear, gets his unprotected side as close as possible to the shield of the man stationed next to him (5.71.1). They disagree about whether the phalanx or the shield came first, and they credit different Greek poleis with being first in the field: H. L. Lorimer and Paul Cartledge favor Corinth and Athens, Antony Andrewes Argos, Marcel Detienne Sparta. But they all date the invention of the exclusive phalanx to the first quarter of the seventh century.

Other writers, starting with Johannes Kromayer, have argued that the *porpax* shield could have been used in a mixed fight.[26] While it is true that this shield protects the left side better than the right (as any shield carried in the left hand does), a hoplite could get squarely behind the shield by turning sideways with his left foot forward. Greeks found the *porpax* shield suitable for climbing ladders and fighting on ships.[27]

I do not see any way of resolving this dispute through further reading of ancient texts, vase paintings, and monuments. The problem is a practical one, a matter of what

Delbrück would have called "die Realität der Dinge." Since modern soldiers do not fight with *porpax* shields, we have to look at police (who are not using replicas of Greek *porpax* shields) and reenactors (who are not really trying to kill each other).

Police first. Adam Schwartz has cleverly compared hoplites to Danish riot control police using double-handled, Plexiglas shields weighing less than 3 kg each. The police found them "suitable only for defensive fighting: policemen would typically form a line, advance to the combat zone and keep their position. They would . . . stand so close that the edges of their shields actually touched."[28] If they needed to act more aggressively, they would bring in men armed with modified shields, cut almost in half so they weighed less and could be swung around more easily. Unlike the complete shields, "the adapted version could therefore be used offensively, combined with little or no body armour to ensure crucial mobility. These policemen, cowering behind the wall of shields held by the front line in full combat gear, would then be able to dart forward and close with rioters who had ventured too close to the defensive police line."[29]

So the solid wall of riot police was not always solid, but flexible and permeable enough to permit these mobile troops to dart forward and then back for cover. The formation sounds to me like inclusive phalanges, rather than an exclusive hoplite phalanx.

Reenactors next. Anyone who doubts that a *porpax* shield can be manipulated against attacks from various sides and angles should watch Allen Pittman's YouTube video "Allen teaching Hoplite shield and spear." Pittman is admittedly a martial arts expert who spent a year training with a *porpax* shield, but he is also using one that weighs 9 kg without the metal attachments.[30]

To my mind, therefore, looking at police and reenactors supports the view that warriors could have used *porpax* shields in a mixed formation. I can agree with Schwartz that the *porpax* shield was better suited to fighting in phalanges than to fighting an individual duel in an open field, but the protection needed by a warrior armed with this shield could be provided by a lightly armed fighter as well as by other men with *porpax* shields. Depending on the nature of the threat, a lightly armed fighter might provide *better* coverage than someone more weighed down could. Leaders might have organized all their men into phalanges for getting to the killing zone. The old argument that a piper proves hoplites and only hoplites marching in step is invalid. Everyone could benefit from walking in rhythm together.[31]

How far apart were the men in Archaic phalanges? After collecting the evidence for the width of file, Pritchett concluded that hoplites deployed in files spaced about three feet apart.[32] Most writers have accepted Pritchett's conclusions, but two have argued recently for a tighter formation, at least on some occasions. Their ideas deserve attention.

Allen Pittman suggests that hoplites overlapped their shields slightly, each man using his left hand to grab not only the leather loop at the edge of his shield but also his neighbor's shield cord.[33] This cord is visible in many vase paintings, making a complete loop around the interior of the shield. Pittman suggests that its function was to give the next man something to grasp in order to form a shield wall, and he has posted another YouTube video in which he and a friend demonstrate how this wall would work.[34] The two men do move together well, raising and lowering and shifting their shields together. But the idea seems impractical for an entire line of men. What would happen when one man faced a threat to the right and his left-hand neighbor one to his left? They would pull in opposite directions and would have to break the wall. They could separate quickly, as they demonstrate on the video, but such disparate threats would come so quickly that the shield wall would break apart almost immediately. I think we'd do better to find another function for the cord.

Christopher Matthew has revived Delbrück's view that each man sometimes occupied only a foot and a half. He relies on the Hellenistic tactician Asklepiodotos (4.3), who mentions an offensive formation called *pyknosis* in which each man had two cubits (about 90 cm) and a defensive formation called *synaspismos* in which he had only one (about 45 cm). Matthew argues that "the characteristics of the hoplite's shield (*aspis*) demonstrate that the interval of the close-order phalanx had to be the 45 cm outlined by Asclepiodotus. One of the terms used to describe the close-order formation is 'with interlocked shields' (*synaspismois*). For the shields of the hoplite phalanx to effectively interlock, each man can occupy a space no bigger than half of the diameter of the shield he is carrying."[35] Matthews imagines that Greek phalanxes sometimes lined up in *pyknosis* formation and sometimes in *synaspismos* formation, so that hoplite fighting was "much more varied and dynamic in its nature" than scholars have conceived. A battle between phalanxes in the same formation would have differed a lot from a fight between phalanxes in different formations.

While I like Matthew's stress on difference and variety, his interpretation relies heavily on the translation of *synaspismos* as "interlocked shields," though it literally means only "shields together." The word itself does not require interlocked shields. Polybios uses it to describe a formation allotting each man three feet.[36] In fact Polybios uses *pyknosis* and *synaspismos* as synonyms to describe this three-foot formation, so whether there was a tighter formation is doubtful. And even if Asklepiodotos is correct and the Macedonians did sometimes fight with interlocked shields, his description might not apply to the earlier Greek hoplites, who had larger shields and shorter spears. But the biggest difficulty is imagining a battle between one side with shields interlocked and the other with men spaced twice as far apart. However impenetrable the shield wall, it would have been massively outflanked on both wings unless it had overwhelming superiority in numbers. Yet as best we can tell, when facing odds greater than 3:2, Greeks did not go out to fight another Greek army.

On the other hand, van Wees and I have both argued that Greek warriors might have had more space. Polybios says that against the Macedonian phalanx each Roman occupied three feet and had another three feet between himself and the next man in any direction.[37] This spacing seems about the maximum for comfort, and it might satisfy Thucydides' "as close as possible," given that a man would want some space to feint and duck and manipulate his spear and sword.

The Charge

How did the battle begin? Once the men were in position, the general sacrificed the *sphagia*, the simple battlefield sacrifice that meant, in Michael Jameson's words, "I kill.

Let me kill," and led the men in a paean.[38] The biographer Plutarch, who uses the phrase "marching paean" in his *Lykourgos*, seems to have thought the Spartans sang a paean to the accompaniment of pipes all along their advance. But Thucydides' famous passage about the Spartans advancing in step to the sound of pipes (5.70) does not mention the paean and stresses that the purpose of the music has nothing to do with religion. A passage from Xenophon makes clear that doing the paean differed from marching in time to pipes (*Anabasis* 6.1.11). Paeans before battle are best understood as a subset of paeans in general, which Ian Rutherford has elucidated as song-dances performed by men to honor the god and to demonstrate a sense of community among men.[39] Soldiers performed the paean before they began their final advance into battle, as aorist participles often suggest.[40] The commander had to choose the right moment to begin the paean. Too soon, and the men might lose their edge before they reached the enemy; too late, and faint-hearts might have dropped out before the unifying and invigorating chant began. A good commander, such as Cyrus the Younger in Xenophon's *Anabasis*, would walk to within about 600 m from the enemy, perform the paean, and then advance to within 200 m before ordering the final charge (1.8.17).

The prebattle paean served multiple functions. If the men had previously walked some distance, it helped them regain their order, as they found their places and fell into step with the movements of the dance. It helped them to warm up for the fight. It gave them a sense of solidarity, as they joined in doing something familiar, something they had learned to do as young men. And as they chanted and stamped their feet together, they appealed to the god to see them safely through the battle. Performing the paean gave "courage to friends as it rids them of the fear of the enemy" (Aeschylus, *Seven against Thebes* 270). As the paean ended, they found themselves walking confidently forward, ready to fight. In his semifictitious *Education of Cyrus* (3.3.58–59), Xenophon has Cyrus the Great do it just right: After sacrificing successfully, he leads his well-trained forces ahead at a quick pace. Before they come into missile range, he starts the paean. When it finishes his men are walking boldly forward, filled with "enthusiasm, ambition, strength, courage, exhortation, self-control, and obedience." When they step on the first arrows shot by the enemy, they yell and charge.

As hoplites charged, yelling a war-cry such as *eleleu!* or *alala!* they tended to lose their formation (Thucydides 5.70). The Spartans were the exception, for they advanced all the way to the sound of pipes, but Hanson suspects (I think rightly) that Thucydides gives "an idealized picture of even the Spartan army, which often did not follow such a textbook procedure."[41] Once they started moving, hoplites "lost the rigid conformity of finely tailored columns."[42] Obstacles such as ditches, clefts, clumps of trees, ridges and water courses, Polybios says (18.31.5–6), are all sufficient to break up a formation. Men scattered and bunched. By the time they reached the enemy, the line would not have been straight or the files even.

Scholars and reenactors debate how hoplites held their spears when they charged. They began their advance with spears held at the slope on their right shoulders, spearheads and thumbs upward. To judge by Xenophon's *Anabasis* (6.5.25), they lowered them on command to an underhand thrusting position, thumbs forward. Did they change to an overhand grip (thumbs backward, spearheads forward) before they reached the enemy? Vases show both underhand and overhand grips. Hanson and Matthew maintain that hoplites delivered their initial blows underhand; reenactors in Melbourne agree.[43] They would interpret men using the overhand grip as throwing javelins. But J. K. Anderson argues that warriors raised their thrusting spears to an overhand position before they reached the enemy; reenactors in London agree with him.[44] Anderson believes that the hoplites in the second line on the right on the Chigi vase are shown in the act of raising their spears by flipping them up into the air just enough to grab them again with their thumbs reversed. He comments (and I can confirm) that a little practice with a broom handle will show that changing grips is not all that hard. You have to watch closely to catch Alan Pittman doing it in one of his YouTube demonstration videos, so quickly and smoothly does his hand change position as he raises his arm.[45] J. F. Lazenby argues that changing grips would have been more difficult after the fighting started, and this would be particularly true if Matthew is correct that the weights of the spearhead and butt spike mean the spear's center of gravity would be well toward the butt spike, not in the middle, so that perhaps 2 m of his spear would extend in front of the warrior.[46] Lazenby points out that underhand thrusts shown on vases are invariably in duels, while the (admittedly few) vases showing hoplite lines about to engage show raised spears. He therefore inclines to think that hoplites changed to an overhand grip before they charged, while some changed back again after their line broke and they had enough room to change.

The Collision

In his now classic book, *The Face of Battle* (1976), John Keegan claimed that "large masses of soldiers do not smash into each other, either because one gives way at the critical moment, or because the attackers during the advance to combat lose their fainthearts and arrive at the point of contact very much inferior in numbers to the mass they are attacking."[47] Keegan's denial of shock fits the ancient historians, who regularly speak of armies coming "to hands" or "to spear." It also fits the slow, methodical Spartan advance, which would not have aided shock.

Though he was inspired by Keegan, Hanson argues that Greek hoplites crashed into each other. He says:

> a fair reading of the ancient accounts of hoplite battles suggests that in the case of the Greeks—and perhaps among the Greeks alone—the first charge of men usually smashed right into the enemy line: the key was to achieve an initial shock through collision which literally knocked the enemy back and allowed troops to pour in through the subsequent tears in the line. . . . Indeed, the narratives of the battles of Mantineia, Delion, Nemea, and Leuktra, not to mention the accounts of earlier (often nameless) conflicts in the Lyric poets, make no sense unless we understand that both sides literally collided together, creating the awful thud of forceful impact at the combined rate of ten miles per hour.[48]

Hanson actually quotes from only one ancient account, the second part of the battle of Koroneia (not the initial fight), where Agesilaos "made a furious frontal attack on the

Thebans," according to Xenophon, "and clashing their shields together they pushed, they fought, they killed, they died" (*Hellenika* 4.3.19 = *Agesilaos* 2.12).

Perhaps sensing that this single passage is inconclusive—Xenophon describes the battle as "like no other fought in my time" (*Hellenika* 4.3.16), so it's unwise to use it as if it were typical—Hanson offers four reasons "why we must assume that ancient Greek battle within its first few seconds was a terrible collision of soldiers on the run."[49] None is compelling.

1. The depth of the phalanx. "The function of those to the rear," he says, "was literally to push their comrades forward." This statement assumes what needs to be proved.
2. The size and shape of hoplite shield created a feeling of "absolute protection." I doubt it. Shields were neither impenetrable nor unbreakable.
3. "The enemy line was not necessarily an absolutely impenetrable wall of shields." I agree. But why would this increase the likelihood of shock?
4. At this stage men were irrational; "adrenaline and the laws of motion made continued movement forward more likely than a sudden stop." The stop would not have to be sudden. If Keegan is right that in other times and places infantry lines did not crash into each other, we require good evidence for believing that Greeks were different.

Perhaps Everett Wheeler goes too far when he dismisses the idea of shock on the grounds that many men would have died from the impact.[50] I do not doubt that eager hoplites sometimes collided. But I do not think Hanson has made his case for a general collision. As Adrian Goldsworthy points out, "references in our sources to the great noise when battle was joined cannot be used to prove that the two phalanxes literally crashed together."[51] Wolfgang Petersen's 2004 film *Troy* gives a realistic impression of the charge. The Greeks break their formation somewhat as they run toward the stationary Trojans, deployed in a tight formation outside their city wall. But the film is less realistic in having all the leading Greeks slam into the Trojan shields. Computer-generated imagery has created an unrealistic uniformity.

The Pushing (*ōthismós*)

In Hanson's scenario, a brief period of very crowded fighting followed the initial collision, before the battle turned into a shoving match, a sort of inverted tug-of-war. In taking this view, Hanson followed many distinguished scholars.[52] Cartledge, for example, writes that "warfare between massed phalanxes (phalanges) was not a graceful or imaginative affair, but required above all disciplined cohesion and unyielding physical and moral strength . . . fighting consisted chiefly of a concerted shoving (ôthismos) akin to the tight scrummaging of modern rugby football." This rugby analogy has proved to be a powerful one.

For all its prominence in modern discussions of Archaic battle—how many other Greek words made it into Donald Kagan's opening remarks at the 2008 Yale conference?—the word *ōthismós* occurs rarely in the battle narratives of the classical historians: twice in Herodotus (7.225.1, the struggle over Leonidas' body at

Thermopylae, and 9.62.2, the end of the battle of Plataia), once in Thucydides (4.96, the battle of Delion), and never in Xenophon. The word for the great shoving contest supposed to be the essence of Greek battle, in other words, occurs once in a description of Greek fighting Greek. There it does not stand alone, but is modified by "of shields" or perhaps, by analogy with Herodotus 5.30.4, we should understand "of men with shields." From these few passages, it is hard to be sure that Thucydides' *ōthismós* of shields is any more literal than Herodotus' *ōthismós* of words (8.78, 9.26).

Years ago, scholars did not take *ōthismós* to mean something like a rugby scrum on steroids. Look at how translators used to render Herodotus. George Rawlinson in 1858–60 was typical: "a fierce struggle" and "a hand-to-hand struggle."[53] Commentators and lexicographers were no different. In the first American edition of *A Greek-English Lexicon* (1848), Henry George Liddell and Robert Scott gave "a very *hot, close fight*" and "to come to *close quarters*." In 1908, R. W. Macan wrote that "Hdt. seems to use ὠθισμός for fighting at the closest quarters (without special reference to its etymological sense)."[54] As late as 1938, J. E. Powell's *Lexicon to Herodotus* translated *ôthismós* as "hand-to-hand combat."[55]

Nor were nineteenth-century military historians thinking of Greek battles as shoving contests. Delbrück, for instance, wrote that

> In such a phalanx two ranks at most can participate in the actual combat, with the second rank stepping into the holes of the first at the moment of contact. The following ranks serve as immediate replacements for the dead and wounded, but they exercise principally a physical and moral pressure. The deeper phalanx will defeat the more shallow one, even if on both sides exactly the same number of combatants actually manage to use their weapons.[56]

By "physical pressure," Delbrück does not mean shoving, as he makes clear on the next page. There he says that Greeks did not put unarmored men in the rear ranks because

> the realization that they could not really expect to receive any true support from these rear ranks would have seriously weakened the drive, the forward thrust of the foremost ranks, in which, of course, the value of the rearmost ranks normally lies.[57]

If battles were shoving matches, more men in the rear would have helped, whether armed or unarmed. Delbrück must mean that by their reassuring physical presence the rear ranks supported the front ranks and encouraged their advance.

The earliest use of the rugby analogy that I have found occurs in G. B. Grundy's *Thucydides and the History of his Age*, originally published in 1911:

> Under ordinary circumstances the hoplite force advanced into battle in a compact mass. . . . When it came into contact with the enemy, it relied in the first instance on shock tactics, that is to say, on the weight put into the first onset and developed in the subsequent thrust. The principle was very much the same as that followed by the forwards in a scrummage at the Rugby game of football.[58]

Since the forwards are only eight of fifteen players on a rugby team, perhaps Grundy might have had in mind a "scrum" of the first two or three lines, not of eight lines or more. His further explanation of his idea is curious, to say the least. He says:

> People who are unacquainted with military history do not understand the importance of mere avoirdupois weight in close fighting. A regiment of big men meeting a regiment of smaller men in a circumscribed space, such as, for example, a village street, will almost certainly drive the latter back. . . . In the fifth century the appreciation of it [the factor of weight] would seem to have been at least imperfect. It was not till Leuktra that the Greeks really learnt this particular lesson in the military art.[59]

This passage strikes me as really odd. Greek battles did not take place on village streets, and the Greeks were very well acquainted with their own military history. If weight was literally so important in Archaic and Classical battles, how can it be that the Greeks didn't appreciate it until the fourth century?

In any case, Johannes Kromayer and Georg Veith used the word *Massendruck* in their 1928 handbook, though they did not amplify what they meant by it.[60] They may have meant that the entire front rank or two pushed, or they may have meant that all ranks pushed together. W. J. Woodhouse had the latter in mind in his 1933 book *King Agis III of Sparta and His Campaign in Arkadia in 418 B.C.* This is the first clear statement I have found of what became the dominant view:

> a conflict of hoplites was, in the main, a matter of brawn, of shock of the mass developed instantaneously as a steady thrust with the whole weight of the file behind it—a literal shoving of the enemy off the ground on which he stood.[61]

The context for this passage is Woodhouse's peculiar discussion of Thucydides 5.71, where Thucydides says that each man kept close to his right-hand neighbor's shield out of fear. Woodhouse labeled this "notion . . . to put it bluntly, nothing but a fatuous delusion and stark nonsense," and claimed to understand the real explanation: Hoplites advanced with their shields held straight across their chests, forcing them to slant to the right as they walked.

Not surprisingly, the great commentator on Thucydides, A. W. Gomme, objected:

> a Greek battle was not so simply "a matter of brawn, a steady thrust with the whole weight of the file behind it—a literal shoving of the enemy off the ground on which he stood" (did the back rows *push* the men in front?), as Professor Woodhouse supposes. It was not a scrummage. The men all used their weapons, and had their right arms free.[62]

The parenthetical remark drips with sarcasm—Gomme italicized the word *push*. Did the back rows *push* the men in front? Obviously not, he means. No publicity is bad publicity, however, and Gomme had mentioned the rugby scrum again.

The analogy caught on in spite of both Gomme and a short 1942 article by A. D. Fraser called "The Myth of the Phalanx Scrimmage," which takes as its point of departure the assumption that the rugby model dominates the field, at least in England.

Pritchett dismissed Fraser's note as a "strange article . . . [that] claims that there are only 'three literary references' to pushing."[63] By the time Pritchett wrote this put-down, in 1985, the full-scale rugby scrum, all ranks uniting in one giant shove, had become the standard view of how Greeks fought.

I first challenged this model in an article published in the same year in *Classical Antiquity*—in fact, I suspect that an earlier version of that paper, submitted to another journal and rejected by a cranky anonymous reader using a manual typewriter, prompted Pritchett's chapter. Though I have been rebuked by literalists such as Robert Luginbill and Adam Schwartz, I take heart in the number of other writers since 1985 who have declared themselves skeptical about the rugby model.[64]

It is true that, unlike the noun *ōthismós*, the verb *ōtheō* (push) and its compounds occur frequently in the classical historians, in lines such as "on the right the Athenians pushed the Syracusans." The rugby model takes these verbs literally. (Luginbill's "natural reading" really means "literal reading.") Now there is no doubt that the classical historians sometimes use *ōtheō* figuratively. For example, Herodotus refers to Miltiades pushing the Apsinthians away by walling off the neck of the Chersonesos (6.37.1) and speaks of the Greeks pushing the Persians back in reference to Xerxes' invasion as a whole (8.3.2). So *ōtheō* might be meant literally or figuratively in battle narratives. How can we decide which?

The historians worked in a literary tradition going back to Homer, from whom they inherited *ōtheō*. The natural way to understand *ōtheō* in the historians is to assume they use it as Homer does. If he describes mass shoving, so do they. But if he does not, the natural interpretation is that they do not either.

Pritchett opted for the former. "The *ōthismós* is as common in Homer as it is in later hoplite warfare," he writes, "although the noun is not used."[65] In his description of Homeric fighting, he says that "they pushed, leaning their shields against their shoulders . . . while they thrust with swords and spears."[66] This combination of pushing, leaning shields, and thrusting swords and spears never occurs in the poem. Pritchett cites two passages for the leaning of shields on shoulders. Neither mentions pushing. He cites six passages for the thrusting with swords and spears. Only one mentions pushing. It comes in book 13, in what Pritchett describes as "the most informative passage."[67] The Greeks are massed together closely in what sounds like a hoplite phalanx as Hektor attacks (13.145–48):

> But when he met the dense phalanges he came close and stopped. The opposing sons of the Achaians, pricking him with swords and leaf-headed spears, pushed him away from them; he shivered as he retreated.

Here the Greeks are fighting inside their camp wall, their backs to their ships, when a small group of nine champions, each one named by the poet, rallies together. There's no mention of shields clashing, and the stabbing and the pushing happen at the same time. The Greeks used their weapons, not their shields, to drive Hektor back, slowly—he was "pushed" back rather than routed. A figurative "push" makes equally good sense in the other passages Pritchett cites as evidence of an *ōthismós* in the *Iliad*.[68] The *ōthismós* is as common in Homer as in hoplite warfare, but not in quite the sense Pritchett intended.

I want to return briefly to the battle of Koroneia, a favorite of the literalists. It's an interesting case where Xenophon uses the verb *ōtheō* while alluding to a passage in Homer that does not use it. In the *Hellenika* (4.3.19), Xenophon writes:

> Clashing their shields together, they pushed, they fought, they killed, they died.

Xenophon uses the same verb, *symballein* ("clashing their shields"), that Homer does in *Iliad* 4.446–51 = 8.60–65:

> Now as these advancing came to one place and encountered,
> they clashed their [leather] shields together and their spears, and the strength
> of armored men in bronze, and the shields massive in the middle
> clashed against each other, and the sound grew huge of the fighting.
> There the wails of despair and the cries of triumph rose up together
> of men killing and men killed, and the ground ran with blood.

The allusion is clearer in the expanded version of the scene Xenophon gives in his *Agesilaos* (2.12–14). Here we have, as in Homer, the peculiar noise of battle, men killing and men dying, and blood on the ground:

> Clashing their shields together, they pushed, they fought, they killed, they died. There was no screaming, nor was there silence, but the noise that anger and battle together will produce. . . . When the fighting ended, one could see, where they met one another, the ground stained with blood.

And what happens next in *Iliad* 8? Fighting at a distance (*Iliad* 8.66–67):

> So long as it was early morning and the sacred daylight increasing,
> so long the thrown weapons of both took hold, and people fell.

If Xenophon has this *Iliad* scene in mind, "push" cannot be a mass shove in either the *Agesilaos* or *Hellenika* passages.

A few years ago Simon Hornblower commented that "only an unusually arrogant scholar could claim to know exactly what kind of thing went on in a hoplite battle."[69] I am thankful that he included the words "unusually" and "exactly." I feel close to certain that hoplites never carried 30+ kg of equipment. I feel confident that Archaic phalanges included archers, javelin and stone throwers, and slingers as well as men with helmets, breastplates, shin guards, and shields. The men who came to be called hoplites were not equipped identically. A man might use a Corinthian helmet or a felt pilos, a bronze cuirass or a linen corselet, a round or Boeotian shield—or some but not all of these items, depending on personal preference or simply whether he could afford them all. Whether they lined up with three feet per man or had a few feet more, most armies lost their formation as they advanced and charged. The neat blue and red rectangles we draw on battle plans should not seduce us into thinking of untrained Greeks as capable of marching precision. As for a collision and a shoving match, I'm skeptical that a general collision or general shove occurred, but willing to believe that some men ran into each other and that some literally shoved an enemy when they thought it would give an advantage in the hand-to-hand fighting. But above all, I agree with

John Keegan that "all infantry actions, even those fought in the closest of close order, are not, in the last resort, combats of mass against mass, but the sum of many combats of individuals—one against one, one against two, three against five."[70]

The Origins of the Hoplite Phalanx

At the 2008 Yale conference, Anthony Snodgrass repeated a suggestion he had made in print in 2006: Future considerations of the hoplite's development ought to start from the physical evidence, especially the dedications at Olympia.[71] Greeks dedicated helmets, cuirasses, and greaves by the late eighth century. The *porpax* shield first appears in vase painting in the early seventh century, or even the late eighth if a round shield with a figured shield device proves a shield intended to be held right side up (that is, a double-grip shield). Then the dedications of armor increase sharply about the middle of the century. Snodgrass therefore maintains that individual hoplites existed before the hoplite phalanx. In his view, aristocrats adopted the more expensive equipment first. They fought in a mixed force that included more lightly equipped troops until the middle of the seventh century, when the number of hoplites was large enough to exclude all other fighters from the ranks, restricting them to supporting roles.

I think we can squeeze a bit more out of the material evidence. Peter Bol's study of the bronze shield fragments found at Olympia suggests that bronze rims, bronze emblems, and bronze facings came into use no earlier than the last third of the seventh century. For sixty to seventy years, therefore, *porpax* shields were made of perishable materials, wood or wood and leather. How can we explain this time lag in the use of bronze for shields compared to its use for other pieces of defensive equipment?

Perhaps the earliest warrior on a Greek vase who certainly carries a double-handled round shield in action provides a clue.[72] He does *not* wear a bronze-plate cuirass. Perhaps the first men to carry the new shield were not wealthy aristocrats, but poorer men who wanted the superior protection a large, round shield provided a man who could not afford expensive body armor. I think of Thrasyboulos' men in 403, making wooden and wickerwork shields in Peiraieus (Xen. *Hell.* 2.4.25). They had defeated the Thirty's forces once, but as they anticipated the fighting to come, they needed to equip javelin and stone throwers with enough protection to let them join the hand-to-hand fighting. A big shield would be enough, for a brave or desperate man. John Hale may well be right: The first Greeks to use big, round shields might have been mercenaries employed in the east.[73] When they brought their shields home, they used them in the early phalanges, fighting beside or behind aristocrats armed with the best defensive armor available and using lighter shields. If the Boeotian shield on vases is often used by a hero, perhaps that is because it was used by aristocratic *promachoi*, aristocrats who fought in the front line.

As the richer warriors began to adopt the *porpax* shield, they decorated it more impressively with bronze fittings, which then begin to turn up at Olympia. Because a bronze cuirass was less critical for warriors armed with the *porpax* shield, it became less common, so that by the end of the sixth century a hoplite normally wore a leather and linen corselet, if that.

If hoplites could fight successfully in a mixed force, why did the Greeks eventually exclude archers and other lightly armed fighters from the hoplite ranks? I believe the impetus came from the Persians.[74] Herodotus says that the Median king Cyaxares was the first to divide his forces into spearmen, archers, and cavalry, in the late seventh century (1.103). He's likely to be wrong: The Assyrians probably used an integrated tactical system, employing specialist contingents of different kinds, already in the eighth century.[75] The Greeks had no such specialized contingents until much later. Archaic Greek cavalry was really mounted infantry, men who rode to get into position but dismounted and fought on foot. Archers and other lightly armed men fought in the same ranks. Such armies could not match the Persians. The way forward was shown by Miltiades, who armed all the Athenians at Marathon as hoplites and closed with the Persians before their mounted archers could get into position. Thereafter other Greeks emulated the exclusive phalanx and experimented with specialized contingents of archers and cavalry and even, at Athens, Persian-style mounted archers.

Let me close with a comment on the "grand hoplite narrative." I would return to a view close to that articulated by George Grote, who thought that "the gradual rise of the small proprietors and town-artisans" in the seventh and sixth centuries led to heavily armed infantry replacing cavalry and that the Persian threat led to an equally important increase in the number of rowers in new, larger Greek fleets. "All these movements in the Grecian communities," he wrote, "tended to break up the close and exclusive oligarchies with which our first historical knowledge commences; and to conduct them, either to oligarchies rather more open, embracing all men of a certain amount of property—or else to democracies."[76] Provided that we substitute mounted infantry, men who rode to battle in all their fine gear but fought on foot, for Grote's (originally Aristotle's) cavalry, this passage sounds right to me. It isn't that the hoplite phalanx was politically unimportant. In the big picture, it was very important. But its history is complex. Grote rightly linked both an increasing number of men who could afford hoplite equipment and an increasing number of men who rowed in the fleets to the lengthy evolution toward political equality in ancient Greece.[77]

Notes

I am grateful to Gregory Viggiano and Donald Kagan for inviting me to participate in the 2008 conference at Yale University on the origins of the Greek phalanx. In revising my paper for publication, I have not tried to eradicate traces of its origin as an oral communication delivered to a diverse audience in a setting designed to provoke debate.

1. Hanson 2000: xxvi, 37, 153, 221–22.
2. See Krentz 2000, 2002; and Dayton 2006.
3. Hanson 2000: 56.
4. Rüstow and Köchly 1852: 44.
5. First in *Die Perserkriege und die Burgunderkriege* (1887) and later in his multivolume *Geschichte der Kriegskunst im Rahmen der politischen Geschichte* (3rd ed. 1920, translated as *History*

of the Art of War, vol. 1 *Antiquity*, 1975), where he conceded that Rüstow and Köchly lacked evidence (1975: 86).

6. Some authorities writing in English mention the specific figure of 72 lbs, probably misled or confused by the two kinds of lbs, the German and the avoirdupois. I confess to making this mistake myself until Kurt Raaflaub kindly corrected me during a conference break.

7. Krentz 2010a: 45–50, and 2010b: 190–197.

8. Based on his own experience exercising with replicas and his examination of spears in Greek art, Allen Pittman has argued that Greek spears were thinner than the one inch (25 mm) both scholars and reenactors have generally accepted; he suggests that 18 mm is a realistic estimate (2007: 66–69). As far as I know, no one has tested thinner, lighter spears to see whether they would in fact work better.

9. Snodgrass 1964: 63–64.

10. Xenophon *Anabasis* 1.8.9; Arrian *Anabasis* 1.6.2.

11. Boardman 1983: 27–33; Franz 2002: 183–84; van Wees 2004: 50–52; Rawlings 2007: 57.

12. The YouTube video "Boeotian Shield Usage" (http://www.youtube.com/watch?v=IeKuy36OG_g&feature=player_embedded#at=10) demonstrates the maneuverability of the shield.

13. In this section I draw heavily on my paper "Marathon and the Development of the Exclusive Hoplite Phalanx," forthcoming in Carey and Edwards 2011.

14. The exception appears in Homer, *Iliad* 6.6; Homer uses the plural about twenty times. The plural also occurs in Tyrtaios F 12 lines 21–22, where the good warrior "turns to flight the enemy's rugged phalanges," and Mimnermos F 13 line 3, where the warrior breaks "the massed phalanges of the Lydian horsemen."

15. Lazenby and Whitehead 1996: 32.

16. Müller 1839: 85. Rüstow and Köchly 1852: 10 cite Polyainos 1.10.

17. Grote 1869–70: 2. 462–63.

18. Thucydides 5.70; Plutarch *Moralia* 210F; Athenaios *Deipnosophistai* 14.627D; Polyainos *Stratagems 1.10*, *Excerpts* 18.1; Pausanias 3.17.5; Xenophon *Anabasis* 6.1.11.

19. Delbrück 1975: 58, a translation of the third German edition of 1920.

20. Rüstow and Köchly 1852: 16–17. They included this great oval shield in their 36 kg total estimate discussed above.

21. Helbig 1909: 66–67.

22. Helbig 1911.

23. Helbig 1879: 85–86.

24. The Chigi olpe, for instance, was painted in Corinth about 640, from which Martin Nilson concluded that "the Chigi vase gives the lower boundary; hoplite tactics were fully enacted in the second half of the seventh century" (1929: 240).

25. Gomme 1945–56: 1.10; Lorimer 1947: 128; Andrewes 1956: 31–42; Detienne 1968: 140; Cartledge 1977 and 2001: 153–66; Hanson 1999: 222–42; Schwartz 2009.

26. Kromayer in Kromayer and Veith 1928: 21; Nierhaus 1938: 90–113; Snodgrass 1965 and 1993; Greenhalgh 1973: 69–75; van Wees 2000 and 2004: 166–83; Krentz 2002; Wheeler 2007; Rawlings 2007: 54–59.

27. For hoplites outside the phalanx, see Rawlings 2000.

28. Schwartz 2009: 54.

29. Schwartz 2009: 54.

30. For the video, go to http://www.youtube.com/watch?v=OjjU6tSUp34&feature=player_embedded. Pittman 2007: 70 says that adding the metal parts pushed the weight as high as 14 kg, so it isn't surprising that he's training with an unfaced wooden shield in the video. The Hoplite Association in London judges 14 lbs to be about the maximum manageable weight

(http://www.4hoplites.com/Aspis.htm). I would like to see reenactors practicing with lighter poplar and willow shields weighing a realistic 4–5 kg.

31. Note, too, that the Lakedaimonians' use of pipers was exceptional, was worthy of remark: Thucydides 5.70, Athenaios *Deipnosophistai* 14.624D; Pausanias 3.17.5; Polyainos *Stratagems* 1.10. Most armies did not use pipers to keep their advance slow and their formation intact.

32. Pritchett 1971–91: 1.134–54.

33. Pittman 2007: 70–72. More tentatively, he says that a man might have thrust his arm through his left-hand neighbor's rope, then put his hand through his *porpax*, and finally grabbed both his loop and his right-hand neighbor's rope, linking him both left and right. This idea strikes me as entirely unworkable.

34. For the video "Hoplite Shield," go to http://www.youtube.com/watch?v=ZbPSvJt3ERo &feature=player_embedded#at=13.

35. Matthew 2009: 406.

36. Polybios 18.29–30 with Pritchett 1971–91: 1.145, 151–54.

37. Polybios 18.30.5–11. See Krentz 1985, 1994 (where "6 m" and "3 m" are misprints for "6 feet: and "3 feet"); van Wees 2000, 2004.

38. Jameson 1991.

39. Curiously, Rutherford 1995: 114 seems to think the dance was not included in military paeans. My thanks to my colleague Keyne Cheshire for suggesting that stomping feet and other movements would fit a prebattle context nicely. For a helpful review of recent work on paeans, see Furley and Bremer 2001: 1.84–91.

40. Thucydides 4.43, 4.96.1; Xenophon, *Anabasis* 4.3.29–31, 4.8.16, 5.2.13, *Hellenika* 2.4.17.

41. Hanson 2000: 141.

42. Hanson 2000: 121, 140.

43. Hanson 2000: 162–64; Matthew 2009: 400–406.

44. Anderson 1991: 31.

45. "Hoplite shield," at http://www.youtube.com/watch?v=ZbPSvJt3ERo&feature=player_embedded#at=13.

46. Lazenby 1991: 92–93.

47. Keegan 1976: 71.

48. Hanson 2000: 156–57.

49. Hanson 2000: 157–58.

50. Wheeler 2007: 209.

51. Goldsworthy 1997: 17.

52. Hanson 2000: 68–69, 152–59, 171–84, 1999: 262; Anderson 1970: 175–76, 1984; Cartledge 1977: 15–16. Pritchett 1985: 65–73. Important recent advocates of this view include Lazenby 1991: 87–109; Luginbill 1994; Raaflaub 1999: 132–33; Eccheverría Rey 2011: 64–65.

53. See also George Campbell Macauley in 1904 ("a great struggle" and "jostling"), Henry Cary in 1908 ("violent struggle" and "a close conflict"), and Alfred Denis Godley in the 1921 Loeb edition ("a great struggle" and "blows at close quarters").

54. Macan 1908: 730, commenting on 9.62.

55. Powell 1938: 386.

56. Delbrück 1975: 53, a translation of the 1920 third edition. The first edition was published in 1900.

57. Delbrück 1975: 54.

58. Grundy 1948: 1.268. I have not seen the 1911 first edition, but Grundy says in his preface that he made "only one change in respect to matter and a few minor changes in respect to form" (viii). I would not be surprised to find the rugby analogy somewhere earlier. William Mitford

may have anticipated Grundy's view, without mentioning rugby. On Plataia, Mitford says that "the Tegeans, according to Herodotus, made the first impression; the Lacedaemonians then pushed forward, and confusion soon became general among the Persian infantry" (1823: 2.111). And on Delion: "The field was well disputed between the rest; in action so close, they joined opposing shields; and where weapons could not avail against the compact arrangement of defensive armor, they endevored [*sic*] to break each other's line by force of pushing" (1823: 3.27). Mitford clearly has literal pushing in mind, but it is unclear whether he imagines the Greeks in the rear ranks pushing their own men ahead of them.

59. Grundy 1948: 1.268–69.

60. Kromayer and Veith 1928: 85.

61. Woodhouse 1933: 78–79. He cites only Thucydides 4.96 and 6.70 in support of his view.

62. Gomme 1937: 135.

63. Pritchett 1971–91: 4.66 n. 200. Perhaps this dismissal is not quite fair. Fraser does say that the rugby model was founded on only three passages. But the ones he discusses are among those most frequently cited, and what he says can be applied to the rest. Fraser discusses the battle of Syracuse (Thucydides 6.70.2 [the reference is garbled in his text]), the "give me one more step" story from the battle of Leuktra (Polyainos 2.3.2), and the battle of Delion (Thucydides 4.96).

64. To varying degrees, scholars skeptical of the mass shove and favoring individual action, sometimes including a push with the shield, include Cawkwell 1978, 1989; Krentz 1985, 1994; Goldsworthy 1997; van Wees 2004: 188–91, Rawlings 2007: 93–97, and Matthew 2009.

65. Pritchett 1971–91: 4.29.

66. Pritchett 1971–91: 4.29.

67. Pritchett 1971–91: 4.15.

68. Pritchett 1971–91: 4.29.

69. Hornblower 1991–2008: 2.306.

70. Keegan 1976: 100.

71. Snodgrass 2006: 345.

72. A Protocorinthian aryballos, c. 690–680, found at Lechaion (Corinth Museum CP 2096). See Eliot and Eliot 1968: plate 102, 2.

73. See Hale (this volume). Fagan hints at this hypothesis when he comments that "the development of [the mixed early phalanx], perhaps not coincidentally, was more or less contemporaneous with the height of Assyrian military sophistication" (2010: 99 n. 51).

74. See Krentz 2002: 35–37, 2011. Though he would not attribute such significance to Marathon, van Wees 2004 makes a case based on iconographic evidence that the exclusive phalanx developed only in the sixth or fifth century.

75. Fagan 2010.

76. Grote 1869: 3.30–31.

77. On the role of the fleet in developing its rowers' political consciousness, see Strauss 1996.

Bibliography

Anderson, J. K. 1970. *Military Theory and Practice in the Age of Xenophon*. Berkeley: University of California Press.

———. 1991. "Hoplite Weapons and Offensive Arms." In Hanson 1991:15–37.

Andrewes, Antony. 1956. *The Greek Tyrants*. London: Hutchinson's University Library.

Blyth, P. Henry. 1982. "The Structure of a Hoplite Shield in the Museo Gregoriano Etrusco." *Bolletino dei Musei E'Gallerie Pontifice* 3:5–21.

Boardman, John. 1983. "Symbol and Story in Geometric Art." In *Ancient Greek Art and Iconography*, ed. W. G. Moon, 15–36.

Bol, Peter. 1989. *Argivische Schilde*. Berlin: W. de Gruyter.

Cahn, David. 1989. *Waffen und Zaumzeug*. Basel: Antikenmuseum Basel und Sammlung Ludwig.

Carey, Christopher, and Michael Edwards, eds. 2011. *Marathon 2,500: Proceedings of the Marathon Conference 2010*. Forthcoming from the Institute of Classical Studies, London.

Cartledge, Paul. 1977. "Hoplites and Heroes: Sparta's Contribution to the Technique of Ancient Warfare." *Journal of Hellenic Studies* 97:11–27.

———. 1998. *The Cambridge Illustrated History of Ancient Greece*. Cambridge: Cambridge University Press.

———. 2001. *Spartan Reflections*. Berkeley: University of California Press.

Cawkwell, George L. 1989. "Orthodoxy and Hoplites." *Classical Quarterly* n.s. 39:375–89.

Dayton, John C. 2006. *The Athletes of War: An Evaluation of the Agonistic Elements in Greek Warfare*. Toronto: Edgar Kent.

Delbrück, Hans. 1887. *Die Perserkriege und die Burgunderkriege*. Berlin: Walther & Apolant.

———. 1920. *Geschichte der Kriegskunst im Rahmen der politischen Geschichte*, vol. 1, *Das Alterthum*, 3rd ed. Berlin: G. Stilke.

———. 1975. *History of the Art of War*, vol. 1, *Antiquity*, trans. W. J. Renfroe. Lincoln: Greenwood.

Detienne, Marcel. 1968. "La phalange: problèmes et controversies." In *Problèmes de la guerre en Grèce ancienne*, ed. J.-P. Vernant. Paris: École des hautes études en Sciences sociales, 119–42.

Donlan, Walter, and James Thompson. 1976. "The Charge at Marathon." *Classical Journal* 71:339–42.

Ecchevería Rey, Fernando. 2011. "*Taktikè Technè*—the Neglected Element in Classical 'Hoplite' Battles." *Ancient Society* 41:45–82.

Eliot, C.W.J., and Mary Eliot. 1968. "The Lechaion Cemetery near Corinth." *Hesperia* 37:345–67.

Fagan, Garrett. 2009. "'I Fell upon Him like a Furious Arrow': Toward a Reconstruction of the Assyrian Tactical System." In *New Perspectives on Ancient Warfare*, ed. Garrett G. Fagan and Matthew Trundle. Leiden: Brill, 81–100.

Furley, William D., and Jan Maarten Bremer. 2001. *Greek Hymns: Selected Cult Songs from the Archaic to the Hellenistic period*, 2 vols. Tübingen: Mohr Siebeck.

Gabriel, Richard A., and Donald W. Boose, Jr. 1994. *The Great Battles of Antiquity: A Strategic and Tactical Guide to Great Battles that Shaped the Development of War*. Westport, Conn.: Greenwood.

Goldsworthy, Adrian K. 1997. "The *Othismos*, Myths and Heresies: The Nature of Hoplite Battle." *War in History* 4:1–26.

Gomme, A. W. 1937. *Essays in Greek History and Literature*. Oxford: Blackwell.

———. 1945–56. *A Historical Commentary on Thucydides*, 3 vols. Oxford: Oxford University Press.

Greenhalgh, P.A.L. 1973. *Early Greek Warfare: Horsemen and Chariots in the Homeric and Archaic Ages*. Cambridge: Cambridge University Press.

Grote, George. 1869–70. *A history of Greece; from the earliest period to the close of the generation contemporary with Alexander the Great*, 12 vols. London.

Grundy, G. B. 1948. *Thucydides and the History of His Age*. Oxford: Blackwell.

Hanson, Victor Davis, ed. 1991. *Hoplites: The Classical Greek Battle Experience*. London: Routledge.

———. 1999. *The Other Greeks: The Family Farm and the Agrarian Roots of Western Civilization*, 2nd ed. Berkeley: University of California Press.

———. 2000. *The Western Way of War: Infantry Battle in Classical Greece*, 2nd ed. Berkeley: University of California Press.

———. 2004. *Wars of the Ancient Greeks*. Washington, D.C.: Smithsonian.

Helbig, Wolfgang. 1879. *Die Italiker in der Poebene*. Leipzig.

———. 1909. "Ein homerischer Rundschild mit eine Bügel." *Jahreshefte des Österreichischen Archäologischen Institutes in Wien* 12:1–70.

———. 1911. "Über die Einführungszeit der geschlossenen Phalanx." *Sitzungsberichte der Koniglichen Bayerischen Akademie der Wissenschaften. Philosophisch-philologische und historische Klasse*. Munich, 3–41.

Hornblower, Simon. 1991–2008. *A Commentary on Thucydides*, 3 vols. Oxford: Clarendon Press.

Jameson, Michael H. 1991. "Sacrifice before Battle." In Hanson 1991:197–227.

Keegan, John. 1976. *The Face of Battle*. New York: Viking Press.

Krentz, Peter. 1985. "The Nature of Hoplite Battle." *Classical Antiquity* 4: 50–61, trans. Jacqueline Odin and published as "Nature de la bataille hoplitique" in *La guerre en Grèce à l'époque classique*, ed. Pierre Brulé and Jacques Oulhen, Rennes, 1999, 205–17.

———. 1994. "Continuing the *Othismos* on *Othismos*." *Ancient History Bulletin* 8:45–49.

———. 2000. "Deception in Archaic and Classical Greek Warfare." In *War and Violence in Ancient Greece*, ed. Hans van Wees. London: Duckworth and Classical Press of Wales, 167–200.

———. 2002. "Fighting by the Rules: The Invention of the Hoplite *Agôn*." *Hesperia* 71:23–39, reprinted in E. Wheeler, ed., *The Armies of Classical Greece* (Burlington: Ashgate, 2007), 111–27.

———. 2010a. *The Battle of Marathon*. New Haven: Yale University Press.

———. 2010b. "A Cup by Douris and the Battle of Marathon." In *New Perspectives on Ancient Warfare*, ed. Garrett G. Fagan and Matthew Trundle. Leiden: Brill, 183–204.

———. 2011. "Marathon and the Development of the Exclusive Hoplite Phalanx." Forthcoming in a *BICS* supplement edited by C. Carey.

Kromayer, Johannes, and Georg Veith. 1928. *Heerwesen und Kriegführung der Griechen und Römer*. Munich: C. H. Beck.

Lazenby, John F. 1991. "The Killing Zone." In Hanson 1991:87–109.

Lazenby, John F., and D. Whitehead. 1996. "The Myth of the Hoplite's Hoplon." *Classical Quarterly* n.s. 46:27–33.

Lorimer, H. L. 1947. "The Hoplite Phalanx." *Annual of the British School at Athens* 42:76–138.

Luginbill, Robert D. 1994. "Othismos: The Importance of the Mass-Shove in Hoplite Warfare." *Phoenix* 48:51–61.

Marshall, S.L.A. 1950. *The Soldier's Load and the Mobility of a Nation*. Washington, D.C.: Combat Forces Press.

Matthew, Christopher A. 2009. "When Push Comes to Shove: What Was the *othismos* of Hoplite Combat?" *Historia* 58:395–415.

Mitford, William. 1823. *The History of Greece*. Boston: T. Bedlington and C. Ewer.

Müller, Karl Otfried. 1839. *The history and antiquities of the Doric race*, trans. G. C. Lewis and H. Tufnell, 2nd ed. London.

Nierhaus, R. 1938. "Eine frühgriechische Kampfform." *Jahrbuch des Deutschen Archäologischen Instituts* 53:90–113.

Nilsson, Martin P. 1929. "Die Hoplitentaktik und das Staatswesen." *Klio* 22:240–49.

Pittman, Allen. 2007. "'With Your Shield or On It': Combat Applications of the Greek Hoplite Spear and Shield." In *The Cutting Edge: Studies in Ancient and Medieval Combat*, ed. Barry Molloy. Stroud: Tempus, 64–76.

Pressfield, Steven. 1998. *Gates of Fire: An Epic Novel of the Battle of Thermopylae*. New York: Doubleday.

Pritchett, W. K. 1971–91. *The Greek State at War*, 5 vols. Berkeley: University of California Press.

Raaflaub, Kurt, and Nathan Rosenstein, eds. 1999. *War and Society in the Ancient and Medieval Worlds: Asia, the Mediterranean, Europe, and Mesoamerica*. Washington, D.C.: Center for Hellenic Studies.

Rawlings, Louis. 2000. "Alternative Agonies: Hoplite Martial and Combat Experiences beyond the Phalanx." In *War and Violence in Ancient Greece*, ed. Hans van Wees. London: Duckworth and Classical Press of Wales.

———. 2007. *The Ancient Greeks at War*. Manchester: Manchester University Press.

Rüstow, W., and H. Köchly. 1852. *Geschichte des griechischen Kriegswesens von der ältesten Zeit bis auf Pyrrhos*. Uarau: Verlags-comptoir.

Rutherford, Ian. 1995. "Apollo in Ivy: The Tragic Paean." *Arion* 3:112–35.

Santosuosso, Antonio. 1997. *Soldiers, Citizens, and the Symbols of War: From Classical Greece to Republican Rome, 500–167 B.C.* History and warfare. Boulder, Colo.: Westview Press.

Schwartz, Adam. 2002. "The Early Hoplite Phalanx: Order or Disarray?" *Classica & Mediaevalia* 53:31–64.

Seiterle, G. 1982. "Techniken zur Herstellung der Einzelteile (Exkurs zum Schild Nr. 217)." In *Antike Kunstwerke aus der Sammlung Ludwig, II. Terrakotten und Bronze*, ed. Ernst Berger. Mainz: von Zabern, 250–63.

Snodgrass, Anthony M. 1964. *Early Greek Armour and Weapons*. Edinburgh: Edinburgh University Press.

———. 1965. "The Hoplite Reform and History." *Journal of Hellenic Studies* 84:110–22.

———. 1993. "The 'Hoplite Reform' Revisited." *Dialogues d'histoire ancienne* 19:47–61.

———. 1999. *Arms and Armor of the Greeks*. Baltimore: Johns Hopkins University Press.

———. 2006. *Archaeology and the Emergence of Greece*. New York: Cornell University Press.

Snyder, Zach, et al. 2007. *300*. Burbank, Calif.: Distributed by Warner Home Video.

Strauss, Barry S. 1996. "The Athenian Trireme, School of Democracy." In *Dēmokratia: A Conversation on Democracies, Ancient and Modern*, ed. Josiah Ober and Charles W. Hedrick. Princeton, N.J.: Princeton University Press, 313–25.

Van Wees, Hans. 2000. "The Development of the Hoplite Phalanx: Iconography and Reality in the Seventh Century." In *War and Violence in Classical Greece*, ed. Hans van Wees. London: Duckworth and Classical Press of Wales, 125–66.

Van Wees, Hans. 2004. *Greek Warfare: Myths and Realities*. London.

Wheeler, Everett. 2007. "Battle: (A) land battles." In *The Cambridge History of Greek and Roman Warfare*, 2 vols., ed. Philip A. G. Sabin, Hans van Wees, and Michael Whitby. Cambridge: Cambridge University Press, 1:195–202.

CHAPTER 8

Large Weapons, Small Greeks: The Practical Limitations of Hoplite Weapons and Equipment

ADAM SCHWARTZ

Physical Characteristics of the Hoplite Shield

During the entire period when hoplites held sway over Greek land warfare, they were defined above all in terms of their primary offensive and defensive weapons, namely, the spear and the peculiarly characteristic shield; indeed, it is nearly impossible to conceive of the idea "hoplite" without these. Of these weapons, it was first and foremost the hoplite's shield that was his defining characteristic; and it was this shield that effectively set him apart from any other troop type in the Greek world. Moreover, whereas all other items in the hoplite's equipment were subject to differing degrees of change and development over time, the shield and the spear were the only items to remain essentially unaltered throughout the entire hoplite era. The fact that they did not undergo any larger-scale structural change is significant: evidently their design was eminently suited to their purpose right from the outset, and it continued to be so successful that it needed few or no adjustments later on.

Consequently, attempting an assessment of the shield's measurements, weight, and handling characteristics is of crucial importance for an understanding of what could be done with hoplite armor and weapons. What knowledge can be obtained about hoplite shields is largely derived from two types of sources. First, although shields, unlike other arms and armor, were invariably made chiefly of perishable materials and thus have largely vanished, a few have been at least partly preserved. Among these is the famous Spartan shield captured by the Athenians during the fighting at Pylos in 425; an Etruscan shield of the hoplite type found at Bomarzo in Italy; the Basle shield, found in Sicily; and a bronze shield facing, recovered at Carchemish on the Euphrates.[1] To this should be added numerous bronze shield covers excavated at Olympia.[2] Second, there are many representations of shields in iconography—representations that are frequently quite detailed and revealing, and which therefore allow a great measure of accuracy in determining shield measurements.

Based on this, it may be laid down that the shield was circular, noticeably concave, and on average 90 cm to 1 m across. These characteristics are also particularly evident from the large amount of vase paintings of hoplites holding their shields in different ways, offering good views of the weapon from all angles.[3]

The shield core was invariably made of wood,[4] and while almost all original shield cores have therefore long since disintegrated, there are a few archaeological shield finds with some wood still preserved. This is the case with the Bomarzo shield, inside which were found remains of wood identified as poplar, as well as with the Basle shield, which had a core made of willow.[5] The fact that this type of wood was especially suitable for shields is corroborated by Pliny the Elder, in whose *Naturalis Historia* both poplar and willow, and in fact all hardwoods in the group *aquatica*, are described as the most suitable wood for shields (*scutis faciendis aptissima*), because they are not only tough but also comparatively pliable, and thus very resistant to breaking.[6] Several Greek sources, however, indicate that willow (*itea*, also reckoned among the *aquatica*) was in fact the normal material.[7] Its characteristics lent the wood durability and resistance against penetration while at the same time allowing the wood to contract somewhat in the event of a penetration (*plaga contrahit se protinus cluditque suum vulnus*), and so helped minimize damage from edged weapons sustained during combat. In addition to these characteristics, poplar is also suitable for shield making because of its very light weight compared with, for example, oak or ash.[8]

The shield core was made by fastening wooden laths to the rim, running from side to side. The laths would be joined to each other by a system of grooves and tongues that were glued together in order to achieve a maximum of structural stability.[9] According to Adolf Rieth, some shield cores may even have been made from several very thin layers of laths, with each new layer running at right angles to the preceding one.[10] It is obvious that this manufacturing process would have yielded a gain in resilience: a modern parallel is ordinary plywood, which is extremely durable and nearly impossible to break. While it is possible that the views offered of the inward-facing surfaces of shields on the Chigi olpe—those held by the advancing phalanx on the left-hand side—reveal just such a manufacturing technique, it cannot have been ubiquitous, as the Bomarzo shield had only one layer of wood. In this case, then, it was obviously advantageous to affix the handle grips in a way that ensured that, with the shield held correctly, the grain ran *horizontally* across the shield, offering much better flexibility in case of simultaneous pressure on both sides of the shield (rather than simultaneous pressure on the "top" and "bottom" of the shield, an unlikely scenario). This measure would have increased the shield's combat effectiveness in no small degree.[11]

Often the shield was covered by a very thin bronze sheathing (*chalkōma*), which afforded extra protection against the wood splintering, and helped dissipate the force of blows over a larger area.[12] Even in its current state, the Bomarzo shield offers an excellent example of both the thinness of the bronze facing and the remarkable concavity of hoplite shields: "The bronze cover, which is about 0.5 mm thick, forms a shallow bowl about 10 cm deep and between 81.5 cm and 82 cm in diameter, including a rim which projects about 4.5 cm from the wall of the bowl all round."[13] Nevertheless, many vase images of hoplite shields suggest that shield concavity was frequently even more pronounced. The inner surface of the shield was usually padded with a glued-on layer of leather, which was likely mounted in order to decrease wear and tear on the wooden core, and to prevent the wood snagging or pinching the bearer's arm. By Henry Blyth's estimate, however, the leather layer inside the Bomarzo shield is too thin to have afforded any real protection from penetration, and is therefore chiefly decorative.[14]

The bronze shield facing was apparently optional, but whether the shield had one or not, the shield rim (*itys*) was invariably reinforced with a bronze band to protect the vulnerable edges. The *itys* was thin enough to be wrapped around the shield edge itself, and there is at least one case of an *itys* covering the shield rim halfway.[15] This reinforcement was indispensable on any hoplite shield, and the reason is obvious: if the edge were insufficiently protected, it would be very vulnerable in combat. The joints of the laths would be open to blows, especially lateral sword cuts, which could separate the laths from each other and thus cause the shield to disintegrate.

Emil Kunze and Hans Schleif's listings of the numerous hoplite shields dedicated at the sanctuary in Olympia show diameters between extremes of 80 cm and 100 cm (most between 90 and 100 cm); and the famous Spartan shield captured at Pylos in 425, somewhat bent out of shape, measures 95 × 83 cm. Interestingly, Rieth mentions a shield that is in other respects similar to the one examined, but which measures no less than 125 cm in diameter.[16] The large diameter gave the shield a considerable surface area: between 6,362 and 7,853 cm^2, according as the diameter was 90 or 100 cm.[17]

That hoplite shields were of a considerable size seems also to be borne out by a passage in Arrian's *Anabasis*. Here, the garrison of Miletos, consisting of Milesians and mercenaries, panicked and abandoned their positions when the city was stormed by Alexander's invading Macedonian troops in 334:

> Then some of the Milesians and the mercenaries, attacked on all sides by the Macedonians, threw themselves into the sea. On their own inverted shields, they then paddled across to a small, nameless island near the city. Others boarded small vessels and hurried to get past the Macedonian triremes but were caught by them at the harbour entrance. The majority, however, perished in the city itself.[18]

The word *aspis* in itself of course does not necessarily betoken a *hoplite* shield; but the fact that the shields are inverted (ὑπτίων) for the purpose of flotation seems to corroborate this. If these were hoplite shields, they naturally had a wooden core; but what provided the buoyancy in this case was rather the principle of displacement. It is reasonable to assume that the soldiers in this case, as so often, had discarded most of their weapons and equipment, and so weighed considerably less. However, when Alexander turned his attention to the three hundred survivors after taking Miletos itself, he realized that they were ready to fight to the death (διακινδυνέυειν), a fact that prompted him to spare their lives. This seems to indicate that they may after all have kept their offensive weapons as well. Whether the soldiers kept their weapons or not, we should probably estimate that each shield-boat in this situation had to keep some 60–70 kg afloat on average.[19]

If these events actually took place as described by Arrian, a considerable displacement (and, consequently, shield surface area) was therefore necessary. Let us look at the physics involved. The density of the shield in question is extremely difficult to ascertain, since the amount of metal in addition to the wood is unknown, but it may be assumed that the overall density is less than 1. The density of saltwater is slightly higher than that of freshwater: a 5 percent saltwater solution has a density of 1.034, which is probably not too different from seawater. It is difficult to say with any exactitude without precise knowledge of the concentration of salt, however, so water density will not be factored in. At any rate, the actual buoyancy would not have been less than the result of the calculation. Apart from the shield's own buoyancy, the amount of air contained within the shield produces a buoyancy equal to the amount of water it displaces without the shield edges submerging. Therefore, if the shield contains 10 l of air, it can displace 10 l of water, weighing 10 kg, before becoming submerged and sinking.

Now, the volume of the relevant geometrical figure, a spherical cap, is determined as follows:

$$V = \frac{\pi h}{6}(3r^2 + h^2)$$

, in which *r* is the radius of the base of the cap and *h* is the height (or depth) of the cap. This yields, for shields of the following dimensions, the volumes shown in table 8-1.

Apart from the shield's own buoyancy and the possibly increased density of the seawater in question, the shield will float approximately the same amount in kg as the amount of liters of air contained. It may be seen, moreover, that small changes in height and radius yield rather greater volumes. It is reasonable to surmise that the hoplites in question had jettisoned anything but perhaps their spears and swords; and assuming an average body weight between 62 and 65 kg for an adult male,[20] it is apparent that the dimensions of the Bomarzo shield are insufficient for it to float a man. It is also evident, however, that the carrying capacity greatly increases with slight increments in dimensions; and on this assumption it does not seem unrealistic for the Milesian garrison to have paddled to safety on their shields.[21]

Blyth, in his assessment of the Bomarzo shield, estimates the total weight of all its components at 6.2 kg.[22] Of this, the weight of grips, straps, and fittings is assessed at some 0.7 kg, the rest consisting of the wooden core and the bronze sheathing. The weight of the original wood and bronze can of course be no more than an educated guess, because the materials have decayed considerably over the centuries;

TABLE 8-1

Shield radius	Height	Volume
45 cm	10 cm	32.3 l
45 cm	20 cm	67.9 l
50 cm	20 cm	82.7 l
45 cm	25 cm	87.7 l
50 cm	25 cm	106.3 l

but considering that the average hoplite shield had a diameter of 90 cm, rather than only 82 cm as in this case, the combined weight of bronze and wood would have been closer to 6.75 kg. Rieth, in his examination of the Bomarzo shield, reckons with a very pronounced decay of the wooden components and consequently a rather greater mass in the original shield. If we follow Rieth's assessments, then, we arrive at a shield even heavier than any derived from Blyth's estimates, weighing as much as 7 or 8 kg. And this still only allows for one layer of wood in the construction of the shield core.[23] That this weight is probably closer to the norm is brought out by the fact that the shriveled remains *alone* of the Basle hoplite shield, as examined by David Cahn, weigh as much as 2.95 kg—or nearly half of the estimated full weight of a "new" and intact Bomarzo shield by Blyth's estimates.[24]

Using the Hoplite Shield

It seems a straightforward enough assumption that the shape and sheer size of such shields would have had consequences for the men bearing them in combat, but the worst problem with the hoplite shield would no doubt have been the considerable weight. On closer inspection, the sources also seem to bear this out.

It is interesting, for example, that merely being ordered to stand still while holding the shield (τὴν ἀσπίδα ἔχων) was considered a sufficient disciplinary punishment in the Spartan army,[25] which was not otherwise known for being particularly squeamish when it came to maintaining discipline by means of corporeal punishment.[26] The element of physical ordeal in this type of punishment has been downplayed,[27] apparently because Xenophon, in whose *Hellenika* the punishment is mentioned, adds "[which] is regarded by distinguished Spartans as a great disgrace," almost by way of an afterthought.[28] There can be no doubt that *kēlis* certainly does mean "blemish" or "disgrace";[29] but its mention here does not mean that the disgrace visited upon military miscreants was not intended to be a harsh physical punishment as well. This interpretation is in fact borne out by a comparison with Plutarch's *Aristeides*, where the Spartan king Pausanias' harsh treatment of recalcitrant Spartan allies is discussed: "The commanders of the allies always met with angry harshness at the hands of Pausanias, and the common men he punished with lashings, or by compelling them to stand all day long with an iron anchor on their shoulders."[30]

Now, if the punishment that involved standing while holding a shield was merely symbolic (a symbolic value which, one suspects, may not have been immediately appreciable to outsiders), then this case—similar in all respects except for the object actually held—becomes bafflingly pointless. The point was hardly lost, however, on those unfortunate allies who fell afoul of Pausanias and were forced to stand around holding iron anchors all day—even if they were otherwise unaware that this was a particularly shameful brand of dishonor in the Spartan army. The substitute punishment of flogging emphasizes this to an even greater degree: Plutarch evidently sees the anchor punishment as completely parallel to the floggings, the physical nature of which can hardly be denied. Standing τὴν ἀσπίδα ἔχων may very well have been humiliating or dishonorable for the offender (if he was a Spartan, at least), but it is evident that it was also a grueling physical ordeal. Xenophon's remark that it was a *kēlis* for the Spartans should be seen in this light: the physical harshness of such a punishment was obvious to any contemporary reader; that it was also considered disgraceful in Sparta was what needed an explanatory remark.[31]

An amusing passage in Xenophon's *Anabasis* points to the same conclusion. During Xenophon's learning period as commander of the Greek rearguard on the retreat from Artaxerxes' pursuing Persians, a detachment of hoplites commanded by Xenophon (himself on horseback) "race" Persian troops for possession of a hill commanding the only way forward. One of the hoplites, a certain Soteridas of Sikyon, reacts unfavorably to the *strategos*' ill-timed pep talk: "It's not fair, Xenophon! You are sitting on your horse while I'm wearing myself completely out with carrying this shield."[32] Xenophon, tacitly acknowledging his leadership blunder, jumps down, takes Soteridas' shield from him, and tries to keep up. He is soon completely exhausted, since he's also wearing a heavy cavalry *thōrax*; and the other hoplites therefore bully Soteridas to take back his shield. Whether the anecdote is true or not, it must have been acceptable to contemporary readers, so the vignette demonstrates the hoplite shield's very real problem of sheer weight.

The *Hellenika* and *Anabasis* passages afford a glimpse of how the burden of the hoplite shield was perceived, despite the fact that—or perhaps precisely *because*—the question of weight in either statement is treated in a rather offhand fashion, as is natural with allusions to everyday experiences. Yet other essential characteristics of the shield would also have contributed to making it difficult to use in actual combat. The ungainly shape and the sheer size of the shield made a significant contribution to a quite exceptional awkwardness in handling. As we saw above, the shield's mass was spread fairly evenly over a surface area of approximately 6,400 cm^2 at a minimum, but could easily reach an area of as much as 7,800 cm^2. Now, the greater its surface area, the more inertia and thus difficulty in handling any physical object; and one that is the size of a small bridge table is thoroughly unwieldy, no matter how it is held.

Despite these considerable drawbacks, it has frequently been claimed that the hoplite shield is no less apt for single combat than other shield types;[33] but this claim is too optimistic. The shield seemingly afforded good protection against any kind of edged weapon brought to bear against it, but that protection came at a price. Its size, shape and weight were enough to require some sort of alleviation, and this need in turn dictated the well-known combination of the double grip and holding posture peculiar to this shield type, entailing a series of consequences for close combat. When in use, the hoplite shield—uniquely—was supported on no fewer than *three* points: the elbow (the *porpax*), the wrist (the *antilabē*), and, by means of using the unique "lip" of the shield edge to hang or rest its weight there, the shoulder.[34] The left-side-forward posture not only seems natural to assume in combat; it also greatly relieves the strain on the arm and shoulder by taking advantage of all three support points. Furthermore, when the rim is rested upon the bearer's shoulder, the shield is carried aslant, its lower rim jutting out before the hoplite. This has the additional advantage of enlarging the zone of protection considerably. The inclination of the shield would also have served to make spear and sword thrusts glance off the shield, although, as is in evidence from iconography, the upper edge of a shield supported on the bearer's shoulder was also directly under his chin if he was adopting a sideways-on stance. This meant that a thrust delivered to the top half of his shield might glance off the polished surface and straight into his face or throat, just as anything that jolted the shield forcefully upward at the lower edge, such as a swift kick, must have directed the upper edge in the same direction. Nevertheless, vase images clearly bear out that this was in fact the normal grip and defensive stance with a hoplite shield; and people who have actually worn replicas of hoplite armor have assured me that this way of handling the shield is not only the logical but indeed the *only possible* way.[35]

Furthermore, the hoplite shield had certain design drawbacks compared with other, lighter shield types having a single central grip. The double-grip system dictated that the shield could be held with the left arm *only*, whereas a single-grip shield could easily be shifted from one hand to the other to ease the strain on arm and shoulder. The hoplite shield for this reason generated even greater strain on the left arm, and supporting it on the shoulder was an absolute necessity, not simply a convenience. For the shield to afford sufficient protection, it must also be held as far away from the body as possible, and aslant at an angle of approximately 45°. This increased the angle of deflection and kept penetrating weapons farther away from the bearer's body, but it also increased the strain on the left arm considerably.

However, an even more serious drawback was the fact, to my knowledge hitherto overlooked in scholarship, that in order to use a double-grip shield properly, it can only be held out at half an arm's length, since the forearm must of necessity be bent and held at right angles to the upper arm. The zone of protection therefore begins already at the elbow, and cannot be extended beyond it. The frontal range is thus drastically reduced. A single-grip shield, on the other hand, can be held out at a full arm's length, or about twice as far from the body as the hoplite shield. This is important because it means that a hoplite shield's surface area must necessarily be much larger than a single-grip shield needs to be: the single-grip shield, being held at a full arm's length from the body, can afford to be much smaller while still offering the same degree of protection. It decreases the adversary's angle of attack just as effectively as the much larger hoplite shield does, simply by being held at twice the distance from the body. Furthermore, by merely turning the wrist, the single-grip shield can be rotated to maximize the angle of deflection, even when the bearer reaches across to his own right side. Thus, incoming attacks can be countered earlier and perhaps "nipped in the bud" by merely parrying with the shield. That these exact advantages of a smaller, single-grip shield were well understood in antiquity is demonstrated by Diodoros, who comments approvingly on the Iberians' use of such targes.[36]

A hoplite shield could of course also be moved about to a certain degree, but, owing to its awkward size and shape, not exactly briskly; and if it was moved about actively to parry or block incoming blows and thrusts, this was carried out with the shield very near the body: there was little time and room for secondary measures if a parry came too late or was misdirected.

Weight, shape, and size together thus made a hoplite shield very awkward to "wield"; and it is open to serious doubt whether anyone, no matter how strong or how well trained, was able to sustain its weight, let alone wield it, for any considerable amount of time during combat.

Comparison with a Modern Combat Shield

A major problem facing scholars trying to assess the combat aptitude of ancient weapons is naturally the scarcity of possibilities to try to handle them, let alone under anything resembling actual fighting conditions. Accordingly, the next best thing would be if it were possible to obtain this much-needed information from somebody who has actually tried using similar items.

Police forces around the world have regularly used shields against rioters throwing stones, bottles, or even Molotov cocktails; and Danish riot police have often seen action, particularly against squatters in the 1980s, but on many other occasions as well. The police are among the very few today who have any experience with handling a shield in combat, and the theory and practice of shield fighting employed by them is therefore very relevant in a discussion of what can and cannot be done with a shield. For this reason, I contacted the riot squad section of the Danish police academy in Copenhagen. The following is the distilled result of a long interview I conducted with Chief Inspector Claus Olsen of the Danish police, who supervises the combat training section and has taught riot control for many years, including the use of double-grip shields in phalanx-like formations.

Danish police riot control forces regularly used shields from the 1970s until recently, when they were almost completely abandoned in favor of more mobile and offensive tactics. The shield in question is rectangular with rounded corners and made of Plexiglas, and so its shape is possibly more reminiscent of a Roman legionary *scutum*. It is fitted with a double-grip carrying system that allows for ambidexterity, placed in the middle. The grips are affixed at approximately 45° to the vertical edge, so that the arm is inserted at an oblique angle. The shield measures 95 × 60 cm, or 5,700 cm^2 and as such is roughly comparable with the surface area of a hoplite shield, but the weight is nonetheless kept down to a mere 2.74 kg. Despite the shield's weighing no more than between 34 and 39 percent of a hoplite shield, however, it was considered a weapon suitable only for defensive fighting. Policemen would typically form defensive lines (termed "chains"), and stand so close that the edges of their shields actually touched. They then advanced to the combat zone and kept their position. The defensive character of these formations was underlined by the fact that policemen in combat gear would also be equipped with visored helmets, greaves, bulletproof vests, and thick, padded gloves.

According to Chief Inspector Olsen, the shield was deemed too heavy, large, and awkward to be wielded freely, and to be put to offensive use—so much so, in fact, that a provisional concept was devised for offensive action. The stationary shield line might under certain circumstances be supported by hastily summoned plainclothes policemen, who would be equipped only with modified standard shields. The modified shield is identical to the normal type, but is simply sawn off just above the middle near where the grips are affixed, so that a little less than half the shield remains. Much like a buckler, this lighter shield could be swung around with comparative ease; and unlike the large shield, the adapted version could therefore be used offensively, combined with a lack of body armor to ensure crucial mobility. These policemen, cowering behind the wall of shields held by the front line in full combat gear, would then be able to move around the chain, dart forward, and close with rioters who had ventured too close to the line. It should be noted, however, that this was a stopgap measure intended to enable police to arrest the most aggressive individuals, since police generally had no interest in actually *clashing* with the rioters but rather aimed at containing them and driving them away from crowded spaces, thereby protecting the public and property.

The stationary, defensive police line could thus benefit from the unarmored, lighter troops, who could prevent aggressive missile-throwing rioters from coming close to their position with impunity—something that was otherwise a possibility. In other words: policemen with shields, and in combat gear, were considered unable to fight hand-to-hand, whereas they were extremely well suited to braving barrages of thrown cobblestones and bottles. Individually, however, they could do little more than that, and the practice of leaving the line to pursue rioters was discouraged for two reasons: first, this threatened to disrupt the shield wall and endanger the entire position; second, although well protected, policemen were unfit for single combat because of the large, heavy, and unwieldy shield.

It may of course be objected that Danish police shields are rectangular and as such not comparable to hoplite shields; but this is immaterial, since riot squads of other countries' police forces operate with riot shields of other shapes, among them circular, as I have witnessed myself in Greece.[37] Clearly, then, it is possible to make a satisfactory shield line, providing sufficient shelter for the members, with round shields.

The standard police shield, deemed too heavy and clumsy by well-trained and physically fit riot squad policemen, weighed not much more than a third of a typical hoplite shield. It seems unlikely that hoplites in bronze armor would have been able to do what fit and trained policemen cannot, or at least deem hopeless—namely, fight as duelists in serial *monomachiai*, wielding their three times heavier shields with ease against attacks from all corners.

Physiology

Another factor worth considering is the physical characteristics of the men actually wearing the armor. When theories are put forward about what could and could not be done while wearing hoplite armor, frequently based on assessments of what "adult males" are capable of, the tacit assumption must *eo ipso* be that Greek men of antiquity are immediately comparable to modern Western men.[38] However, whereas the weight and measurements of the surviving specimens of armor, and to a certain degree weapons, are naturally constants (leaving aside for the moment the effects of oxidation, corrosion, weathering, and other decay of the materials, and the corresponding compensation estimates made), there is no guarantee that the individuals who had to wear and use them were physiologically similar to modern men. The questions concerning bearer physiology are thus of crucial importance for understanding the "relative" weight of hoplite weapons and armor; yet the problem of this relation has seldom, if ever, been addressed. It is therefore well worth examining the available data supplied by skeletal remains from the Archaic and Classical periods.

John Lawrence Angel, who in 1945 examined skeletal remains exhumed in Attica, put the average height of the Greek male in antiquity at no more than 162.2 cm, and of the female at 153.3 cm. It should be pointed out, however, that these data accrue from a rather scanty sample material: 61 male and 43 female skeletons from Attica, as against a total of 225 datable males and 132 females in all of Greece proper.[39] Similar results accrue from Angel's 1944 analysis of all ancient Greek skeletal remains known at the time: here, the result is given as 162.19 cm for males, with a range between extremes of 148 and 175 cm. The result for females overall remains the same.[40] Angel, whose interest was primarily "racial" analysis, lists crania from Attica, Boiotia, Corinthia, and Macedonia; but unfortunately he does not indicate the distribution of more complete skeletons, which may have formed the basis for the calculations.[41] Nevertheless it must be assumed that the average measurements actually represent the average, geographically as well as chronologically.[42]

The comparatively scanty material notwithstanding, we would be well advised to keep in mind that, in the words of Lin Foxhall and Hamish Forbes, "this sample may be biased in favour of higher socio-economic groups since it is the graves of the comparatively wealthy that are most likely to receive attention from archaeologists."[43] If this is accepted, it follows that the average Greek male was in fact likely *less* well nourished, and the skeletons examined by Angel may well belong in the absolute upper percentile.[44] Walter Donlan and James Thompson give the average height of Greek males in the Classical period as approximately 170 cm, with body weight between 65 and 67 kg.[45] Unfortunately, however, their article gives no information about how these results were arrived at; so Angel's data must assume priority.

The modern European or American adult male, on the other hand, measures approximately 179 cm on average.[46] Determination of body weight is more complicated, as it depends to a large extent on a wide variety of other factors (age being but one); but the average weight of modern males between the ages of twenty and sixty is 80.97 kg.[47] It is therefore certain that Greek men in antiquity were shorter than Western men today; and it is also highly likely that they were noticeably lighter, considering a diet consisting largely of cereals and pulse and to a certain extent vegetables.[48]

These extrapolations from a rather exiguous sample material have recently been confirmed in no small degree by the interesting findings from the survey of the expansive territory of Metaponto (ancient Metapontion) in southern Italy.[49] In the course of this grand-scale survey, field examinations of the remarkably well-preserved necropolises at Pantanello, Saldone, and Sant'Angelo Vecchio were carried out.[50] Here, Maciej and Renata Henneberg examined the skeletal remains of 272 individuals, 251 of which were excavated at Pantanello alone.[51] The Hennebergs' work on these and other necropolises of Magna Graecia now comprises approximately 1,000 individuals, easily "the largest and most comprehensive study of the mortal remains of a population in the Greek world."[52] In addition, while the human remains excavated from the necropolis spanned a period of several centuries (from the sixth to the third centuries BC), the majority could be dated to well within the hoplite era.[53]

Metapontion was a largely rural settlement, focused primarily on agriculture, and with a population who were very likely predominantly farmers.[54] Accordingly, its inhabitants would have been very similar to the average rural population in the rest of the Greek world with respect to—among other things—nourishment, growth, build, overall health, life expectancy, and general physiology.

Now, it is scarcely unreasonable to assume that, on average, more than 50 percent of the population in the Greek world as a whole were occupied with agriculture, arboriculture, and the production of foodstuffs in some capacity, if possibly sometimes in other activities than farming as such.[55] If that is the case, most Greek hoplite armies, drawn from the male citizenry, would likely have displayed the same ratio of, at a minimum, 50 percent farmers (or, at the least, "agriculturalists"). The implications of this should be clear: the Metapontine necropolis not only furnishes a representative selection of a typical population occupied primarily in agriculture, the backbone of any hoplite citizen army who likely possessed the physical qualities most wanted in hoplites—toughness, stamina, strength, and resilience—but the amount of material in question is comprehensive enough to be statistically significant.[56] The examined data revealed that the average height of adult males was between 162 and 165 cm, that of females between 153 and 156 cm (estimates vary according to the applied method of reconstruction), and with a body weight of approximately 60–65 kg for males and 50–55 kg for females: in other words, the findings of earlier examinations were soundly confirmed in this respect.[57] Given this uncharacteristically ample, significant sample material, as well as its thoroughly agricultural setting, the Metapontion necropolis furnishes an excellent opportunity for assessing the physical characteristics of the average Greek hoplite.[58]

Greek men in antiquity—including Greek hoplites—were thus significantly smaller than modern Western men. For this reason alone, what may perhaps seem comparatively light or small to us as moderns may in fact have been considerably harder and more cumbersome for smaller men to bear. Offensive, and especially defensive, weapons and armor would have been even more uncomfortable, heavy, and unwieldy to men frequently more than 15 cm shorter than the modern Western average. The shield, above all, some 90 cm in diameter, would have been even larger for such men, normally no taller than 165 cm: in most cases, the shield's diameter measured considerably more than half of the total body height. In fact, even the lightest of Greek panoplies would have been a much heavier burden to bear when compared to the physical norm of the average modern Western male. All this serves to underline the fact that hoplite weapons and armor were not, by any stretch of the imagination, easily or comfortably manipulated or worn.

It should also be kept in mind that polis armies were normally composed of citizens of all ages between eighteen and sixty.[59] Owing to this tremendously long obligation to perform military service, there must have been a great many older men in the phalanxes, perhaps even a majority.[60] In the words of Victor Davis Hanson, "after all, thirty of forty-two age classes liable to military service were composed of men over thirty years of age."[61] While this is a priori true, it should also be taken into consideration that these age groups would have been exponentially depleted of members because of the increasing mortality resulting from both natural causes and participation in more campaigns and battles. There is no shortage of sources attesting to older men taking their equal share of the grisly work in the rank and file;[62] and all other things being equal, the burden of arms and armor must have been a great deal harder to shoulder for men pushing sixty.

The sources to a large degree bear this out. Personal servants (*hypaspistai*) frequently carried the hoplites' weapons[63] and supplies;[64] at least this seems to have been the case with higher-ranking and wealthier persons. Even when hoplites did hold their own shields, and when supposedly ready for instant action, they normally would not pick them up until the *last possible moment*: the command θέσθαι (τὰ) ὅπλα means to extract the arm from the twin grips and set the shield (and probably spear) down on the ground, leaning against the knees and ready to be picked up again quickly when the order is given. The phrase is unusually common: it is found forty-three times in Herodotos, Thucydides, and Xenophon alone,[65] and so well known was this "stand at ease" position that the Athenian general Chabrias, according to later historians, on one occasion could display his contempt for the advancing enemy simply by ordering his mercenaries to remain brazenly in this position as the enemy approached (δέχεσθαι τοὺς πολεμίους καταπε φρονη κότως ἅμα καὶ ἐν τῇ τάξει μένοντας).[66] We even find that the Phokians guarding the Anopaia pass at Thermopylae in 480—who, it must be supposed, should have been on maximum alert—only picked up their weapons *after* they saw the Persians approaching, surprising the advancing enemy with that strange sight: "Leaping to their feet, the Phokians were in the act of arming themselves when the enemy were upon them. The Persians were surprised at the sight of troops preparing to fight."[67] In fact, Herodotos' choice of verb, ἐνέδυον ("put on," rather than the expected ἀνέλαβον), implies that the Phokian hoplites did not even put on their *body* armor until the last possible moment—even in a "red alert" situation like this.[68]

In Euripides' tragedy *Herakleidai* (datable to c. 430)[69] the weight of a "full set of armour" (ὅπλων πανττευχίαν) also seems to be a consideration. The old Iolaos, about to join battle, is advised by his servant to put his armor on in a hurry, since battle is near. All the same, the servant adds, "However, if you dread the weight of it,/go unarmed for the present, and when you reach the ranks/put all this on there. Meanwhile I'll carry it." With palpable relief, Iolaos quickly accepts (καλῶς ἔλεξας).[70]

Conclusion

The weight and completeness of armor was, if anything, reduced over the centuries, either by perfecting the metalwork techniques, by replacing bronze cuirasses with corselets made of other materials, or simply by increasingly discarding items that were apparently no longer needed. It is interesting to note that the full set of hoplite weapons and equipment was at its heaviest and most cumbersome in its earlier stages of development; and it is equally interesting that Euripides suggests that even by 430—at a time when most defensive body armor was well on its way to becoming obsolete[71]—a set of armor was still considered a significant burden (albeit, in this case, to an elderly man). Reconstructions based on the surviving remains of shields suggest that they were in fact very heavy, as much as 8 kg not being an unrealistic assessment for a combat shield some 90 cm in diameter. Contemporary literary sources testify to the considerable size and perceived burden of hoplite shields, an aspect that was exacerbated by the shield's ungainly shape and the double-grip system, which, although securing good support for the bearer, also drastically reduced his range with the shield when compared with a lighter, single-grip shield. A comparison with probably the only modern use of shields "in anger" reveals that a double-grip shield of roughly comparable size was deemed too heavy and awkward to be used for any sort of soloist fighting, despite the fact that the police shield in question weighs a little more than a third of a hoplite shield.

The tacit but widespread assumption that Greeks in antiquity were physically immediately comparable to ourselves is refuted by analyses of skeletal remains from the Archaic and Classical periods, revealing that the average height of Greek males was between 162 and 165 cm compared with the 179 cm of modern Western males. Obviously the burden of weapons, and especially shield and armor, would have been even greater for such smaller men. Exacerbating this even further is the fact that quite a few old men must have been present in the average phalanx, since men were required to serve until they were sixty years old.

All this serves to underline the importance of assessing the physical characteristics of the weapons themselves in the debate on how hoplites and phalanxes functioned in combat. Furthermore, it seems to me that the evidence, such as it is, points in the direction of a defensive, closed-order system intimately connected with and based on the weapons themselves. The evidence thus suggests that the debate on hoplite fighting, unlike the hoplite phalanx itself, is not closed at all.

Notes

I wish to thank Curtis Eastin, Gregory Viggiano, and Donald Kagan warmly for inviting me to participate in the Origins of the Greek Phalanx conference at Yale in April 2008. It should also be pointed out that, owing to circumstances entirely beyond my control, I found myself with a matter of mere days in which to prepare a paper for the conference. It, and consequently this article, therefore consisted largely of material drawn from my (then forthcoming) monograph, *Reinstating the Hoplite* (2009). However, I have endeavored, as far as at all possible, to rearrange it and add fresh material and new data for this chapter.

1. Blyth (1982) 9, 13–14; Rieth (1964) 104–5; Cahn (1989) 15–16; Shear (1937) 347; Boardman (1980) 75; Millard (1994) 288–89.

2. Kunze and Schleif (1942) 70–93; Mallwitz and Herrmann (1980) 106.

3. The concavity of the shield is apparent also from a number of literary sources: Hdt. 4.200.2–3 (in which an inverted shield is used as a stethoscope to listen for enemy sapping underground, a procedure also recommended in Aen. Tact. 37.6–7); Thuc. 7.82.3 (where four upturned [ὑπτίας] shields serve as vessels for coins confiscated from Athenian prisoners of war); Xen. *Hell.* 5.4.17–18 (where hoplites weigh their shields down with stones to prevent them from blowing away during a storm on a mountain); Plut. *Mor.* 241f 16 (where the shield [again, presumably, inverted] is thought of as a possible stretcher, in the famous anecdote of a Spartan mother saying to her son "ἢ τὰν ἢ ἐπὶ τᾶς"); cf. Σ Thuc. 2.39.1; Stob. *Flor.* 3.7.30 and Hammond [1979–80]). Several notable landmarks were called "the *Aspis*," most famously perhaps a steep hill or slope near Argos with difficult access (ὀχυρὸς τόπος): "[Kleomenes] led his army by night up to the walls, occupied the region about the Aspis overlooking the theatre, a region which was rugged and hard to come at, and so terrified the inhabitants that not a man of them thought of defence" ([Κλεομένης] νυκτὸς πρὸς τὰ τείχη ἦγε τὸ στράτευμα, καὶ τὸν περὶ τὴν ᾿Ασπίδα τόπον καταλαβὼν ὑπὲρ τοῦ θεάτρου χαλεπὸν ὄντα καὶ δυσπρόσοδον οὕτως τοὺς ἀνθρώπους ἐξέπληξεν ὥστε μηδένα τράπεσθαι πρὸς ἀλκήν [trans. Perrin]): Plut. *Cleom.* 17.4–5, cf. 21.3, *Pyrrh.* 32.1–4.

4. Blyth (1982) 9–12. A wooden core is also strongly suggested by Brasidas' shield, which, when dropped from a ship, drifted ashore (Thuc. 4.12.1; cf. Diod. Sic. 12.62.4).

5. Blyth (1982) 9, 13–14; Rieth (1964) 104–5; Cahn (1989) 15–16. There are adequate photographs in both Blyth's and Rieth's articles; but the best illustration of the Bomarzo shield remains Connolly's drawing (Connolly [1998] 53).

6. Plin. *NH* 16.209: "The trees that have the coldest wood of all are all that grow in water; but the most flexible, and consequently the most suitable for making shields, are those in which an incision draws together at once and closes up its own wound, and which consequently is more obstinate in allowing steel to penetrate; this class contains the vine, agnus castus, willow, lime, birch, elder, and both kinds of poplar" (Frigidissima quaecumque aquatica, lentissima autem et ideo scutis faciendis aptissima quorum plaga contrahit se protinus cluditque suum vulnus et ob id contumacius tramittit ferrum, in quo sunt genere ficus, vitex, salix, tilia, betulla, sabucus, populus utraque [trans. Rackham]); cf. Franz (2002) 128–29.

7. Eur. *Heracl.* 375–76, *Supp.* 694–96; *Cyc.* 5–8, *Tro.* 1192–93; Ar. fr. 65. All these are metonymical uses where *itea* is simply used for *aspis.*

8. See, e.g., http://www.ces.purdue.edu/extmedia/FNR/FNR-109.html (at table 1; accessed 02.09.2011).

9. Blyth (1982) 9–13.

10. Rieth (1964) 108 (citing Robinson who in fact only says "crossing pieces of wood," however: Robinson [1941] 444).

11. The situation, as illustrated by Blyth, can easily be imagined: if the shield bearer charged (or was charged by) two enemies at the same time, the shield might as well be caught between their shield edges as hit either frontally (Blyth [1982] 17 fig. 6).

12. Hdt. 4.200.2–3; Xen. *Lac. Pol.* 11.3; Aen. Tact. 37.6–7; Polyaen. 1.45.2, 7.8.1; Cartledge (1977) 12–13. See, however, Snodgrass (1964a) 63–64. The Bomarzo shield's remains of wood and leather were found inside its *chalkōma*: Blyth (1982) 1, 12; Rieth (1964) 101, 106.

13. Blyth (1982) 5–6.

14. Blyth (1982) 12; Cahn (1989) 16; Robinson (1941) 444. Another suggestion is that the leather increased comfort for the bearer, both when the shield was hung on the shoulder and when he pressed against it and cowered inside it during combat.

15. Rieth (1964) 108. Rieth also mentions the finding of a shield at Olynthos: remains of wood, circumscribed by a bronze *itys.*

16. Kunze and Schleif (1938) 70–74; Shear (1937) 347; Rieth (1964) 101. Cf. Paus. 1.15.4.

17. If $r = 45$ cm, then $A = \pi \times 45^2 = 6{,}362$ cm^2.

18. Arr. *An.* 1.19.4: ἔνθα οἱ Μιλήσιοί τε καὶ οἱ μισθοφόροι πανταχόθεν ἤδη προσκειμένων σφίσι τῶν Μακεδόνων οἱ μὲν αὐτῶν ῥιπτοῦντες σφᾶς ἐν τῇ θαλάσσῃ ἐπὶ τῶν ἀσπίδων ὑπτίων ἐς νησῖδά τινα ἀνώνυμον τῇ πόλει ἐπικειμένην διενήχοντο, οἱ δὲ ἐς κελήτια ἐμβαίνοντες καὶ ἐπειγόμενοι ὑποφθάσαι τὰς τριήρεις τῶν Μακεδόνων ἐγκατε λήφ θησαν ἐν τῷ στόματι τοῦ λιμένος πρὸς τῶν τριήρων·οἱ δὲ πολλοὶ ἐν αὐτῇ τῇ πόλει ἀπώ λοντο.

19. I am very grateful to John R. Hale for pointing out the significance of this passage to me.

20. See the "Physiology" section below.

21. I am indebted to Christian Tortzen, Sebastian Persson, and Claus Glunk for these calculations.

22. Blyth (1982) 16.

23. Rieth (1964) 101. Donlan and Thompson (1976) 341 n. 4 give this measurement as the average weight of the shields in Olympia.

24. Cahn (1989) 15.

25. Xen. *Hell.* 3.1.9.

26. See especially Hornblower (2002).

27. Franz (2002) 269–70, criticizing Hanson (2000) 67; but see also Schwertfeger (1982) 263 n. 34: "Daß der schwere Hoplitenschild eine Last war, geht aus dem spartanischen Recht der klassischen Zeit hervor, wo der König im Rahmen seiner Disziplinargewalt gegen ungehorsame Soldaten die Strafe des 'Stehens mit dem Schild' verhängen konnte" (that the heavy hoplite shield was a burden is also evident from Spartan law of the Classical period, where the king, as part of his disciplinary measures, could punish disobedient soldiers with 'standing with the shield'").

28. Xen. *Hell.* 3.1.9: ὃ δοκεῖ κη λὶς εἶναι τοῖς σπουδαίοις Λακεδαιμονίων.

29. Cf. LSJ 9th ed. s.v. κηλίς.

30. Plut. *Arist.* 23.2: τοῖς τε γὰρ ἄρχουσι τῶν συμμάχων ἀεὶ μετ' ὀργῆς ἐνετύγχανε καὶ τραχέως, τούς τε πολλοὺς ἐκόλαζε πληγαῖς, ἢ σιδηρᾶν ἄγκυραν ἐπιτιθεὶς ἠνάγκαζεν. ἑστάναι δι' ὅλης τῆς ἡμέρας (trans. Perrin, modified).

31. Greek literature is rife with Spartans either exacting or threatening physical punishment: the sources are collected in Hornblower (2002) 57–60.

32. Xen. *An.* 3.4.47–49: οὐκ ἐξ ἴσου, ὦ Ξενοφῶν, ἐσμέν· σὺ μὲν γὰρ ἐφ' ἵππου ὀχῇ, ἐγὼ δὲ χαλεπῶς κάμνω τὴν ἀσπίδα φέρων (trans. Warner, modified). See also Lendle (1995) 187.

33. See, e.g., Greenhalgh (1973) 73; Salmon (1977) 85 n.6; Krentz (1985) 60–61; van Wees ed. (2000) 126; Rawlings (2000) 246–49.

34. See especially Hanson (1991) 68–69, (2000) 68; and cf. Franz (2002) 132; van Wees (2000) 128; (2004) 167–69. Van Wees's sample of illustrations (figs. 3, 4a, 6, and 10) demonstrate the posture clearly.

35. I have corresponded with the UK-based Hoplite Association (http://www.hoplites.co.uk/), a reenactment group whose members have kindly (and patiently) answered my questions. I am also grateful to Nino Luraghi, who, having actually tried on a replica, emphasized to me the impossibility of holding a modern replica of a hoplite shield, except with bent arm and supported on the shoulder.

36. Diod. Sic. 5.34.5: "The bravest among the Iberians are those known as Lusitanians, who carry in war quite small shields which are interwoven with cords of sinew and are able to protect the body unusually well, because they are so tough; and shifting this shield easily as they do in their fighting, now in this direction, now in that, they expertly ward off from the body every blow which comes at them" (τῶν δ' Ἰβήρων ἀλκιμώτατοι μέν εἰσιν οἱ καλούμενοι Λυσιτανοί, φοροῦσι δ' ἐν τοῖς πολέμοις πέλτας μικρὰς παντελῶς, διαπεπλεγμένας νεύροις καὶ δυναμένας σκέπειν τὸ σῶμα περιττό¬τερον διὰ τὴν στερεότητα· ταύτην δ' ἐν ταῖς μάχαις μεταφέροντες εὐλύτως ἄλλοτε ἄλλως ἀπὸ τοῦ σώματος διακρούονται φιλοτέχνως πᾶν τὸ φερόμενον ἐπ' αὐτοὺς βέλος [trans. Oldfather, modified]).

37. See also, e.g., www.fotosearch.com/DGV464/766019/ (accessed 02.09.2011) for a photo of unspecified police riot control forces holding round shields, or http://www.securityprousa.com/pabsleglbosh.html (accessed 02.09.11) for a round Paulson BS-6 Lexan Gladiator Body Shield, manufactured by Paulson Riot Equipment.

38. Such a rationale must be behind, e.g., Blyth's assurance regarding the Bomarzo shield. In Blyth's assessment, "the total is little more than the weight of a World War II rifle, a weapon which can be handled quite briskly by a trained man" (Blyth [1982] 17). For comparisons of this type to work, it is evident that ancient and modern men must be equal in terms of physical characteristics.

39. Angel (1945) 284–85 and n. 25. The male skeletons dating from the Classical period—no more than three—are on average 165.4 cm high: Angel (1945) 324. Foxhall and Forbes (1982) 47 correctly warn against possible statistical insignificance due to the relatively small sample material. Insufficient though it may be, however, there is no better way to estimate bodily proportions of ancients, so the material at hand will simply have to suffice.

40. Angel (1944) 334 table 2a.

41. Angel (1944) 331 table 1.

42. Garnsey (1999) 57–59 cites a number of analyses of ancient Roman skeletal material from, among other sites, Pompeii and Herculaneum. He circumspectly concludes that all that may be said for the average male height here is that it is "for the most part within the range 162–170 cm for men and 152–157 for women."

43. Foxhall and Forbes (1982) 47 n. 21.

44. Teeth stemming from several skeletons excavated under the Stone Lion monument at Chaironeia (in all likelihood the human remains of Thebes' "Sacred Band" elite force of three hundred hoplites, wiped out to a man during the battle there in 338) bear signs of linear enamel hypoplasia, an indicator of systemic stress during childhood; the reasons include severe malnutrition or illness. "The presence of these lines in multiple individuals indicates that even for the future military elite, childhood could at times be stressful in ancient Thebes": Maria Liston (personal communication); and cf. Hanson (1999) 152–76.

45. Donlan and Thompson (1976) 341 n. 4; the 170 cm apparently repeated in Stewart (1990) 1:75. Hanson posits some 1.67 m (Hanson 1991) 67–68 n. 14.

46. http://en.wikipedia.org/wiki/Human_height (accessed 02.09.2011). The figure given is the average of German, Dutch, British, and American males.

47. http://www.halls.md/chart/men-weight-w.htm (accessed 02.09.2011).

48. Foxhall and Forbes (1982) and Garnsey (1999) 17–21 suggest that 70–75 percent of the total consumption consisted in cereals. A postwar survey carried out in Crete demonstrated that no less than 29 percent of the calorie intake was olive oil: Allbaugh, cited in Garnsey (1999) 19 n. 12. Even for heavyweight boxers it was a rare occurrence, apparently deserving of mention, to venture outside the staple diet: Harris (1966) 88–89 relates the few instances; cf. Waterlow (1989) 6–9. See also Henneberg and Henneberg (1998) 512–14; Wilkins and Hill (2006) 114–39, esp. 120–21.

49. Carter (1998), (2006).

50. Carter (1998) 5–22, (2006) 21–22, 40–42.

51. Henneberg and Henneberg (1998) 503–37, at 504.

52. Carter (2006) 41.

53. Morter and Hall (1998) 449–54 with table 8.2 and graph 8.2; Carter (2006) 22.

54. Hdt. 4.15.2 (referring to the χώρη); Carter (2006) 9–15. The Metapontine χώρα was large, covering approximately 20,000 ha (or 200 km^2): Fischer-Hansen, Nielsen, and Ampolo (2004) 279–80.

55. For Attica (otherwise probably the most urbanized of the Greek poleis) see, e.g., Thuc. 2.14; and cf. Arist. *Pol.* 1256a 35–40, where there is a list of possible occupations. Aristotle then

adds "The largest group of people, however, live off the land and off cultivated plants" (τὸ δὲ πλεῖστον γένος τῶν ἀνθρώπων ἀπὸ τῆς γῆς ζῇ καὶ τῶν ἡμέρων καρπῶν). The denotations and connotations of the word γεωργός are many and varied.

56. Strangely, however, the ratio of buried females to males at Pantanello is almost 2:1, which is all the more puzzling as no predominantly male necropolis has been found on Metapontine territory: Henneberg and Henneberg (1998) 509; Carter (2006) 41–42.

57. Surprisingly, these average height values are "the same as [those] for Italian peasants in southern Italy before World War II" (Carter [2006] 42; Henneberg and Henneberg [1998] 519–21 with tables 11.14 and 11.15, and 538–41 [appendix 11A.1]). Of other interesting information culled from the skeletons it may be mentioned that life expectancy was on average forty-one years for males, thirty-nine for females (Henneberg and Henneberg [1998] 509–14), and that there were found twelve cases of malaria and also—rather more surprisingly—signs in some individuals of antigens for *Treponema pallidum*, a form of syphilis (Jeske-Janicka and Janicki [1998] 557–59 [appendix 11A.5]). Moreover, there were high rates of dental hypoplasia, indicating either malnourishment or childhood disease, the latter being the likelier cause: Henneberg and Henneberg [1998] 517–19 and tables 11.10–13; Carter (2006) 42, and cf. above, n. 44.

58. It is interesting, therefore, that when the Athenian relief force under Demosthenes put in at Metapontion in 413 on their way to Syracuse, they picked up a force consisting of no more than three hundred javelin throwers (and two ships): Thuc. 7.33.4–5. However, there may be more than meets the eye to the seemingly grudging assistance afforded Athens by Metapontion: see Hornblower (2008) 608–9.

59. Xen. *Hell.* 6.4.17; [Arist.] *Ath. pol.* 53.4, cf. *IG* II 2nd ed. 1926.

60. In Xen. *Hell.* 6.1.5, Jason of Pherai is made to boast of his well-trained, mercenary army: "[b]ut armies made up of citizens must include some men who are already past and some who have not yet reached their prime. And there are very few people in each city who keep constantly in good physical training. But no one serves in my mercenary army unless he can stand physical hardship as well as I can myself" (ἀλλὰ τὰ μὲν ἐκ τῶν πόλεων στρατεύματα τοὺς μὲν προεληλυθότας ἤδη ταῖς ἡλικίαις ἔχει, τοὺς δ' οὔπω ἀκμά ζοντας·· σωμασκοῦσί γε μὴν μάλα ὀλίγοι τινὲς ἐν ἑκάστῃ πόλει· παρ' ἐμοὶ δὲ οὐδεὶς μισθοφορεῖ, ὅστις μὴ ἱκανός ἐστιν ἐμοὶ ἴσα πονεῖν [trans. Warner]).

61. Hanson (2000) 90.

62. Holoka (1997) 342; Hanson (2000^2) 89–95.

63. Hdt. 7.229.1, 5.111; Xen. *An.* 4.2.20 (Xenophon's personal *hypaspistēs* runs away with his shield, leaving him in a tight spot), *Hell.* 4.5.14, 4.8.39; Polyaen. 2.3.10; cf. Lazenby (1991) 89.

64. Hdt. 7.40.1; Thuc. 2.79.5, 4.101.2, 7.78.2; Xen. *Hell.* 3.4.22, *Cyr.* 5.3.40, 6.3.4.

65. Hdt. 1.62.3, 5.74.2, 9.52; Thuc. 2.2.4bis, 4.44.1, 4.68.3, 4.90.4, 4.91, 4.93.3, 5.74.2, 7.3.1, 7.83.5, 8.25.4, 8.93.1bis; Xen. *An.* 1.5.14, 1.5.17, 1.6.4, 1.10.16, 2.2.8, 2.2.21, 4.2.16, 4.3.17, 4.3.26, 5.2.8, 5.2.19, 5.4.11, 6.1.8, 6.5.3, 7.1.22bis, *Hell.* 2.4.5, 2.4.12, 3.1.23bis, 4.5.8, 5.2.40, 5.3.18, 5.4.8, 6.4.14, 7.3.9, 7.5.22; Diod. Sic. 11.5.4, 12.66.2, 14.105.2, 18.26.4, 18.61.1, 20.42.5, 20.88.8.

66. Diod. Sic. 15.32.5; Polyaen. 2.1.2; Nep. *Chabr.* 1.1–2 (*obnixoque genu scuto*), and see Stylianou (1998) 297–98. The Athenians later erected a statue of Chabrias in just this position in the Agora, the base of which has probably been found: Arist. *Rhet.* 1411b 6–10; Nep. *Chabr.* 1.3; Anderson (1963) 411–13; Buckler (1972), esp. 474.

67. Hdt. 7.218.1–2: ἀνά τε ἔδραμον οἱ Φωκέες καὶ ἐνέδυον τὰ ὅπλα, καὶ αὐτίκα οἱ βάρβαροι παρῆσαν. ὡς δὲ εἶδον ἄνδρας ἐνδυομένους ὅπλα, ἐν θώματι ἐγένοντο (trans. de Sélincourt).

68. Cf. Thuc. 6.69.1; Xen. *Hell.* 4.8.37–39; Plut. *Pel.* 32.3.

69. Wilkins (1993) xxxiii–xxxv.

70. Eur. *Heracl.* 720–26: εἰ δὲ τευχέων φοβῇ βάρος,/νῦν μὲν πορεύου γυμνός, ἐν δὲ τάξεσιν/κόσμῳ πυκάζου τῷδ'· ἐγὼ δ' οἴσω τέως (trans. Vellacott).

71. Anderson (1970) 13–42.

Bibliography

Anderson, J. K. 1963. "The Statue of Chabrias." *American Journal of Archaeology* 67:411–13.

———. 1970. *Military Theory and Practice in the Age of Xenophon*. Berkeley.

Angel, J. L. 1944. "A Racial Analysis of the Ancient Greeks: An Essay on the Use of Morphological Types." *American Journal of Physical Anthropology* 2:329–76.

———. 1945. "Skeletal Material from Attica." *Hesperia* 14:279–363.

Blyth, H. 1982. "The Structure of a Hoplite Shield in the Museo Gregoriano Etrusco." *Bollettino dei monumenti, musei e gallerie pontificie* 3:5–21.

Boardman, J. 1980. *The Greeks Overseas: Their Early Colonies and Trade*, 2nd ed. London.

Buckler, J. 1972. "A Second Look at the Monument of Chabrias." *Hesperia* 41:466–74.

Cahn, D. 1989. *Waffen und Zaumzeug. Ausstellung Antikenmuseum Basel und Sammlung Ludwig*. Basle.

Carter, J. C. 1998. *The Chora of Metaponto: The Necropoleis*, vols. 1–2. Austin, TX.

———. 2006. *Discovering the Greek Countryside at Metaponto*. Ann Arbor, MI.

Connolly, P. 1998. *Greece and Rome at War*, 2nd ed. London.

Donlan, W., and J. Thompson. 1976. "The Charge at Marathon: Herodotus 6.112." *Classical Journal* 71:339–43.

———. 1979. "The Charge at Marathon Again." *Classical World* 72:419–20.

Fischer-Hansen, T., T. H. Nielsen, and C. Ampolo. 2004. "Italia and Kampania," in M. H. Hansen and T. H. Nielsen (eds.), 249–320.

Foxhall, L., and H. A. Forbes. 1982. "Σιτομετρεία: The Role of Grain as a Staple Food in Classical Antiquity." *Chiron* 12:41–90.

Franz, J. P. 2002. *Krieger, Bauern, Bürger. Untersuchungen zu den Hopliten der archaischen und klassischen Zeit*. Frankfurt am Main.

Garnsey, P. 1999. *Food and Society in Classical Antiquity*. Cambridge.

Greenhalgh, P.A.L. 1973. *Early Greek Warfare: Horsemen and Chariots in the Homeric and Archaic Ages*. Cambridge.

Hammond, M. 1979–80. "A Famous *Exemplum* of Spartan Toughness." *Classical Journal* 75:97–109.

Hansen, M. H., and T. H. Nielsen (eds.). 2004. *An Inventory of Archaic and Classical Poleis*. Oxford.

Hanson, V. D. 1991. "Hoplite Technology in Phalanx Battle," in V. D. Hanson (ed.), *Hoplites: The Classical Greek Battle Experience*, 63–84. London.

———. 1999. *The Other Greeks: The Family Farm and the Agrarian Roots of Western Civilization*, 2nd ed. New York.

———. 2000. *The Western Way of War: Infantry Battle in Classical Greece*, 2nd ed. Berkeley.

Harris, H. A. 1966. "Nutrition and Physical Performance: The Diet of Greek Athletes." *Proceedings of the Nutrition Society* 25:87–90.

Henneberg, M., and R. J. Henneberg. 1998. "Biological Characteristics of the Population Based on Analysis of Skeletal Remains," in J. Carter (ed.), 503–37.

Holoka, J. P. 1997. "Marathon and the Myth of the Same-Day March." *Greek, Roman and Byzantine Studies* 38:329–53.

Hornblower, S. 2002. "Sticks, Stones, and Spartans," in H. van Wees (ed.), *War and Violence in Ancient Greece*, 57–82. London.

———. 2008. *A Commentary on Thucydides*, vol. 3, books 5.25–8.109.

Jeske-Janicka, M., and P. K. Janicki. 1998. "Detection of Trepomena Pallidum Antigens," in J. Carter (ed.), 557–59.

Krentz, P. 1985. "The Nature of Hoplite Battle." *Classical Antiquity* 4:50–61.

Kunze, E., and H. Schleif. 1938. *Bericht über die Ausgrabungen in Olympia*, vol. 2. Berlin.

Lazenby, J .F. 1991. "The Killing Zone," in V. D. Hanson (ed.), 87–109.

Lendle, O. 1995. *Kommentar zu Xenophons Anabasis (Bücher 1–7)*. Darmstadt.

Mallwitz, A., and H.-V. Herrmann. 1980. *Die Funde aus Olympia*. Athens.

Millard, A. R. 1994. "King Solomon's Shields," in M. D. Coogan, J. C. Exum, L. E. Stager, and J. A. Greene (eds.), *Scripture and Other Artifacts: Essays on the Bible and Archaeology in Honor of Philip J. King*, 286–95. Louisville, KY.

Morter, J., and J. Hall. 1998. "Dating of Tombs," in J. Carter (ed.), 449–54.

Rieth, A. 1964. "Ein etruskischer Rundschild." *Archäologischer Anzeiger* 1:101–9.

Robinson, D. M. 1941. *Excavations at Olynthus, Part X, Metal and Minor Miscellaneous Find: An Original Contribution to Greek Life*. Baltimore.

Salmon, J. 1977. "Political Hoplites?" *JHS* 97:84–101.

Schwertfeger, T. 1982. "Der Schild des Archilochos." *Chiron* 12:253–80.

Shear, T. L. 1937. "The Campaign of 1936." *Hesperia* 6:333–81.

Stylianou, P. J. 1997. *A Historical Commentary on Diodorus Siculus Book 15*. Oxford.

Van Wees, H. 2000. "The Development of the Hoplite Phalanx: Iconography and Reality in the 7th Century," in H. van Wees (ed.), *War and Violence in Ancient Greece*, 125–66. London.

———. 2004. *Greek Warfare: Myths and Realities*. London.

Warner, R. 1949. *Xenophon: The Persian Expedition*. London.

———. 1979. *Xenophon: A History of My Times*, 2nd ed. London.

Waterlow, J. C. 1989. "Diet of the Classical Period of Greece and Rome." *European Journal of Clinical Nutrition* 43:3–12.

Wilkins, J. (ed.). 1993. *Euripides: Heraclidae*. Oxford.

Wilkins, J. M., and S. Hill, S. 2006. *Food in the Ancient World*. Malden, MA, and Oxford.

CHAPTER 9

Not Patriots, Not Farmers, Not Amateurs: Greek Soldiers of Fortune and the Origins of Hoplite Warfare

JOHN R. HALE

In the eighth and seventh centuries BC, Greek soldiers adopted a new way of making war that has become known as the hoplite tradition. Hoplites were heavily armed infantry who carried large shields or *aspides*—circular, convex, and manipulated with double grips—and who typically confronted their opponents in phalanx formation. The first hoplites appeared on the historical scene in the mid-eighth century BC, and remained an essential part of Greek life throughout the Archaic and Classical periods.

What circumstances gave rise to the invention of hoplite arms and tactics? And who exactly were the first hoplites? To answer those questions, we must identify the precise contexts—chronological, geographical, social, and military—in which Greek hoplites first appeared. Were hoplite innovations triggered by class struggles between farmers and aristocrats?[1] Or by an arms race among emerging Greek city-states—one that was launched when the men of each polis almost simultaneously took up the new equipment and tactics?[2] Or were the innovations adopted as symbols of social status and class identity?[3] All these possibilities have their adherents. This paper presents an alternative context for the origin of hoplite warfare, and tracks early hoplites into a realm where private enterprise, not public service, was the guiding star.

The mainstream of current scholarly opinion is united in regarding the polis or city-state as the breeding ground of the hoplite phalanx. The combatants are envisioned by some scholars as patriotic citizens[4] and sturdy agriculturalists defending their fields, and by others as members of a competitive leisure class, but the social and geographical context is always the polis. In accordance with these prevailing views, a tradition of military amateurism is invoked to account for the seeming simplicity of hoplite tactics.[5] Thus the classic and natural opponent of one city-state's army of hoplites is assumed to be a second army of Greek hoplites, a mirror image of the first.

Hanson links the rise of hoplites to the agrarian sector of Greek society. He outlined his theory in *Warfare and Agriculture in Classical Greece* (1983) and has worked it out in detail thereafter in a succession of books and articles. In Hanson's reconstruction, when a pre-Classical Greek landscape of large aristocratic estates gave way to a polis surrounded by small farms, a brand new military situation emerged.

> It led to the formal creation of hoplite weaponry and finally face-to-face, near-ritual duels between agrarian phalanxes. In sum, yeomen emerged from the anonymity of the old mass to reinvent the Greek phalanx as the private domain of heavily armed, mutually dependent small farmers. This "invention" of hoplite warfare was not some utopian enterprise, the "construct" of some agrarian conspiracy. Instead imagine its birth far more pragmatically, as the result of one group of agrarians, perhaps first on the island of Euboea or in the Peloponnese at Argos in the late eighth century, reinventing and rearming the "phalanx" and thus finding themselves invincible on the battlefield. Other agricultural communities were also forced to go "hoplite" to defend their property.[6]

Hans van Wees, though in agreement with Hanson about the centrality of the polis to this issue, locates hoplites in a very different social milieu. In his book *Greek Warfare: Myths and Realities* (2004), van Wees relegates Hanson's fighting farmers to the category of myth, and presents as the opposing reality a set of leisure-class hoplites, motivated by *pleonexia* ("greed for more") and the quest for high social and political status.

> Despite some sense of respect for the toughness of farmers and shepherds, however, the model hoplite was not the working man whose fitness for war derived from hard labour, but the man of leisure who owed his fitness to dedicated physical and mental training. Those who theorised about the ideal state agreed that soldiers should not cultivate land, or do any productive work, but live off the labour of others and devote themselves to war and politics.[7]

The central role played by the city-state in these two contrasting visions gains some support from historical, literary, and artistic evidence. Greeks were indeed fighting other Greeks at an early stage in the evolution of hoplite warfare—in the Lelantine War, for example, and in the momentous Spartan and Messenian wars. Nevertheless, I believe that the theaters of war that originally gave rise to the hoplite tradition lay far from the gathering places and plowed fields of the polis, and equally far from anything that can be described as a civic mentality or ideology.

Judging from archaeological discoveries of Greek arms and armor, as well as artistic representations, the heavily armed hoplite began to evolve in the eighth century BC. By about 650 BC, the hoplite had emerged as both the archetypal Greek fighting man and a dominant figure in Mediterranean warfare. Even at that early date, there were already two distinct strands within the hoplite tradition. The strand that monopolizes modern historical discourse is indeed polis-centered and patriotic.

> Fair and good [*kalòn . . . agathòn*] the man who falls fighting in the front rank, dying for the fatherland.[8]

The exhortations of the poet Tyrtaeus (mid-seventh century BC) have been traditionally linked by both ancient and modern historians to one or the other of the Spartan-Messenian Wars that eventually led to the complete subjugation of Messenia.

The other major "patriotic" war of this age was the Lelantine War between the Euboean cities of Chalcis and Eretria. In that shadowy conflict, each city was aided by allies from the Greek mainland or the eastern Aegean.[9] One specific inter-polis battle may also be assigned to the mid-seventh century: the battle of Hysiae near Argos. This battle is mentioned by Pausanias, and dated by him, using a surprising synchronism with an Olympic victor and an Athenian archon named Peisistratus, to 669 or 668 BC. At Hysiae soldiers from Argos were said to have scored a victory over Spartans.[10]

There were other battlefields where Greek met Greek in the seventh century. A war that broke out between the islanders of Paros and neighboring Naxos during the lifetime of Archilochus (mid-seventh century) may have involved not only a well-attested sea battle but also fighting on land.[11] Several generations earlier at Paros, a late eighth-century mass burial or *polyandrion* of some 150 Parian soldiers may have commemorated the dead from an earlier Naxian war, or from an expedition even farther afield.[12]

How frequent were classic hoplite battles—those phalanx-to-phalanx shoving matches, held like rituals on open plains between neighboring city-states? Lyric poetry and vase paintings provide our only contemporary evidence, since later Greek historians took only sporadic interest in military affairs before the Persian Wars. Were these combats so common that they became mere background noise, taken for granted by ancient historians and therefore underrepresented in the historical record? Such might be the implication of the eminently quotable description that Herodotus put into the mouth of the Persian commander in chief Mardonius, addressing King Xerxes.

> From what I hear, the Greeks are pugnacious enough, and start fights on the spur of the moment without sense or judgement to justify them. When they declare war on each other, they go off together to the smoothest and levellest bit of ground they can find, and have their battle on it—with the result that even the victors never get off without heavy losses, and as for the losers—well, they're wiped out.[13]

Although the "dramatic date" of this passage in its narrative context is 480 BC, the date of composition may be as late as the 420s, with the author either satirizing or deploring (or both) the situation of his own time. Herodotus presents hoplite battles as commonplace yet ceremonial, and also as being extremely costly in human lives. Hanson, although a proponent of ritualized hoplite battles, argues that in reality the early Greeks who served as hoplites had to devote most of their time to farming: hence wars and battles were few. "Hoplite battles were themselves singular and brief. They were also not frequent before the fifth century."[14] By Hanson's own tally of hoplite warfare in the seventh and sixth centuries, "there were not more than a dozen important campaigns in the historical record involving the major Greek city-states in more than two hundred years."[15]

This observation fits well with Hornblower's claim that in Greek literature and art "the prominence of war is disproportionate to its frequency and significance in practice."[16] Yet such sporadic warfare would seem unlikely to stimulate or sustain any cultural tradition, especially a highly specialized military tradition. If the hoplite tradition was *not* fostered through regular combat between Greek city-states, then we must look elsewhere for the conflicts that offered long-term and consistent training in the arts of war. Just such conflicts existed outside the Greek homeland, in the wider Mediterranean world.

Away from the polis, a more extensive and detailed historical record bears witness to the second strand of early hoplite warfare: campaigns undertaken by Greek soldiers of fortune. These men fought not on the fields of Greece but overseas, as pirates, raiders, mercenaries, bodyguards, land-grabbers, and generals for hire. Archilochus of Paros presents their philosophy, which is utterly antithetical both to the "good death" advocated by Tyrtaeus and to the ritualized combat described by Herodotus.

> Some Thracian is waving the shield I reluctantly left by a bush, a flawless piece.
> So what? I saved myself. Forget the shield. I will get another, no worse.[17]

The Greek soldier of fortune of the Archaic age, like his better-known successors of the fourth century, ventured abroad in search of gain and glory. A drinking song asserts the view of the man who fights for himself, not for his city.

> I have great wealth: a spear, a sword, and the fine leather shield which protects one's skin. For with this I plough, with this I harvest, with this I trample the sweet wine from the vines, with this I am called master of serfs. Those who dare not hold a spear, a sword, or the fine leather shield which protects one's skin, all cower at my knee and prostrate themselves, calling me 'Master' and 'Great King'.[18] (Athenaeus 695f–696a, Page)

The mysterious "Hybrias the Cretan," to whom these verses are attributed, is known only from the quotation of this skolion in Athenaeus' *Deipnosophistae*. Archilochus of Paros, however, was a real seventh-century Greek who, by his own account, served both the God of War and the Muses.[19] Archilochus enjoyed drinking the same Ismaric wine that Homer's Odysseus had prized as booty from a shore raid in Thrace. When Odysseus' company of Ithacan soldiers took Ismaric wine from the Kikones, Odysseus was concerned to ensure an equal division of the loot.[20] Archilochus sees the matter from the entrepreneur's point of view.

> In my spear is my kneaded barley bread, in my spear is Ismaric wine,
> and I drink it leaning on my spear.[21]

For early Greek soldiers like Archilochus, warfare became at times a career. These men were professional soldiers, not amateurs. They sought the good things in life not through a display of arms as status symbols, and still less through agricultural labor, but through wielding their weapons successfully on one battlefield after another.

The evidence for this branch of Greek military activity has been summarized by van Wees in two sections of his book *Greek Warfare: Myths and Realities*. He has given these sections the evocative titles "An Army of Wanderers: Mercenaries, Exiles, Adventurers" and "Epikouroi: Mercenaries and Other Outsiders."[22] Their unimportance in his overall scheme of Greek warfare, however, is indicated by a simple page count: 10 pages are devoted to these fighters out of a main text of 240.

Instead of considering that freebooters like Archilochus may have been a primary influence in the evolution of Greek warfare, van Wees ties their activities back to his central focus: the civic tradition. "The abundance of men, citizens and itinerants, who were prepared—indeed keen—to fight for personal prestige and wealth reinforced the willingness of Greek cities to wage war for the honour and profit of the community."[23] He concludes by contrasting these "outsiders" to the Greek "ideal of the citizen-soldier."[24] Yet as we shall see, these soldiers of fortune did in fact lead the kind of highly specialized and professionalized military life, with continuous months and years devoted to the pursuit of war, that Hanson, van Wees, Hornblower, and many other modern scholars routinely deny to the citizen-soldiers of the classical Greek polis. It is time to consider the possibility that hoplite arms and tactics evolved outside the realm of the polis, and not within it.

The Crucible: Eastern Mediterranean Warfare in the Eighth Century BC

In his article "Traders, Pirates, Warriors: The Proto-History of Greek Mercenary Soldiers in the Eastern Mediterranean,"[25] Nino Luraghi presents evidence to show that Ionian Greek soldiers were fighting as mercenaries for the kings of Assyria as early as 732 BC. In that year the Assyrian king Tiglath-pileser III captured Damascus in Syria, and his soldiers plundered the city. Several bronzes that appear to be loot from the royal treasury of Damascus have turned up in excavations at three sanctuaries of the Ionian Greeks: those of Athena at Miletus in Asia Minor, of Hera at Samos in the Aegean, and of Apollo at Eretria on Euboea. These heirloom bronzes consist of elaborate frontlets and blinkers from the headgear of chariot horses. Inscriptions on the pieces themselves identify their previous owner as King Hazael of Damascus.[26]

Stratigraphic contexts at the Greek sanctuaries assign this cluster of finds to the eighth century, thus supporting a direct link to the Assyrian campaign. Luraghi concludes that these Near Eastern bronzes were dedicated by soldiers from three different parts of Greece who took part in the sack of Damascus, and who made gifts to their gods for bringing them home not only alive but rich with oriental booty.[27] If the men from Eretria and Samos and Miletus who collected royal loot from Damascus were prehoplite soldiers, then their presence in the Assyrian army provides a context for the subsequent invention of hoplite arms and tactics. If, on the other hand, these Greeks already fought as hoplites, then we might regard their heavy armament and disciplined close-order formation as the features that made them desirable mercenaries in the eyes of the Assyrian king Tiglath-pileser.

Snodgrass has observed, "The very large round shield of sheet bronze carried by Assyrian infantrymen, though it had only a single central hand-grip, must have influenced the evolution of the Greek type."[28] If Luraghi is right that Ionians fought in Tiglath-pileser's army in 732 BC, then the campaigns that involved the conquest of Damascus would provide a specific context for Snodgrass's theoretical interactions between Greek and Assyrian soldiers.

There was another aspect of eighth-century conditions in the Near East, however, that provides a background for the appearance of Greek soldiers of fortune at

Damascus. Viking-like, the Ionians were at this time venturing overseas in their long ships not only to serve as mercenaries (as the Vikings did in a later age at Byzantium) but even earlier as piratical raiders. Ionian attacks on coastal cities in the Levant between 738 and 732 BC are repeatedly documented in royal Assyrian correspondence. Let us consider the record of these seaborne attackers.

Several years before the capture of Damascus, a royal Assyrian official named Qurdi-Ashur-lamur learned from a mounted messenger that seafaring men "from the land of Iauna" (i.e.. Ionia) had come ashore on the coast of the Levant and attacked a number of cities.[29] Qurdi-Ashur-lamur marshaled his forces and set off to confront the invaders. When the Ionians saw the Assyrian troops approaching, they retreated to their ships (empty-handed, the official assured Tiglath-pileser, his king) and then vanished into the open sea. The threat of these armed seaborne Greeks was serious enough to warrant building new fortifications and shifting more Assyrian troops to the coastal area.

The Ionians persisted. During the reign of Sargon II in 715 BC, the royal annals recorded that the king—a usurper who had seized the kingship after a career as a general—assembled a fleet of ships on the Syrian coast and personally led a counterattack against the Ionians at sea. According to the texts, Sargon intended to stop both their deadly raids on Tyre and Cilicia and also their disruptions of commerce. He succeeded. The annals repeat many variations of Sargon's subsequent boast: "I caught like fishes the Ionians who live in the midst of the sea of the sunset."[30] This poetical phrase suggests that the troublesome raiders were known to be islanders from the Aegean. They may in fact have been Ionians from as far off as Samos and Euboea. The ethnic term "Iauna" or "Iavan" eventually became the generic name for Hellenes throughout the Near East.

King Sargon's son and successor Sennacherib defeated a Greek army in a land battle in Cilicia, probably in 696 BC. Two years later Sennacherib is said to have repelled an Ionian fleet in an engagement off the Cilician coast. The royal annals for the year 694 BC record that Ionian seafarers had been captured by the king and subsequently pressed into service in the Assyrian army.[31] These Greek warriors then continued their military careers under new management, far from home. Did this transformation of raiders into mercenaries repeat a pattern already established in the reign of Tiglath-pileser, four decades earlier? In any case, such Near Eastern adventures foreshadow the exploits of Greek soldiers of fortune in Egypt, which we will consider shortly.

No surviving Greek historical source preserves any record of these early encounters between Ionians and Assyrians. It may be, however, that the traditional narrative material in the *Iliad* was reshaped by Homer to reflect the contemporary epic of Greek fleets voyaging eastward to assault walled towns beyond the sea. Some scholars have in fact suggested that horse-shaped Assyrian siege towers of the eighth century directly inspired the "Trojan Horse" of Homeric tradition.[32] In any case, the archaeological discoveries and Assyrian records prove the reality of—and also provide solid dates for—these early military contacts. The subsequent history of the Greeks shows their importance. As Luraghi concludes,

> If the arguments presented in this paper are accepted, the history of Greek mercenaries begins considerably earlier than is usually thought. Its roots

> would lie in the activities of pirates-traders from Euboea, the Cycladic islands, and Asia Minor, who seem to have started their business in the Levant in the third quarter of the 8th century. They were the ancestors of the Greek mercenaries who fought for almost every single Near Eastern kingdom from the mid-seventh century to the age of Alexander the Great.[33]

The final century of the Greek mercenary tradition looms large in the historical record, thanks to the career and writings of Xenophon. Mercenary armies of the fourth century BC have been closely examined in books by H. W. Parke[34] and Matthew Trundle.[35] The existence of these later Greeks who fought for personal gain has been regarded as an unfortunate outcome of the Peloponnesian War, a degeneration and debasement of the original patriotic, polis-centered tradition of hoplite warfare. Study of the eighth century evidence, however, shows that Xenophon and his companions were in fact reverting to type. Mercenary service and raiding expeditions were part of the environment in which Greek hoplites evolved. Was this type of warfare directly linked to the appearance of hoplite arms and tactics?

The young fighting man of Euboea or Samos or Miletus whose cry was "Eastward, ho!" would follow the path of the rising sun to the margins of mighty empires. There he experienced a kind of warfare very different from the ritualized hoplite battle attested elsewhere in our sources. His company issued not from the walls of his home city, but from oared ships beached on an alien and hostile coast. The situations he faced while wading ashore or proving his worth to foreign kings shaped his approach to war. His arms and fighting methods were designed to score victories, not against others of his own kind, but against non-Greek chariots, horsemen, and lightly armed troops, or in assaults on walled towns. As for agricultural pursuits, our young soldier of fortune took up arms not to protect a farm that he worked himself but, I would suggest, to escape from the routine drudgery of farmwork altogether.

One important work of ancient art may in fact show Greek soldiers fighting in an eastern war of the eighth or early seventh century BC. The oldest-known representation of hoplite soldiers in a phalanx-like formation appears on a silver bowl that was found in a tomb at Amathus, Cyprus (fig. 9-1).[36] This Amathus bowl was probably created in a Cypro-Phoenician workshop in the late eighth or early seventh century BC, and belongs to a type of vessel that was popular from the Near East to Etruria.[37] On the surface of the bowl, embossed or engraved motifs from Near Eastern and Egyptian art fill the central roundel and two surrounding circular bands. The outermost band, however, which runs around the bowl's rim, is decorated with a battle scene rendered in a more naturalistic style.

Here, troops of various types are engaged in combat at a walled city, some attacking, others defending. The towering fortifications appear to be constructed of ashlar masonry, with crenellated battlements. The attacking army has chariots drawn by pairs of horses, cavalry armed with spears and bows, and archers on foot wearing long Assyrian overcoats and tall conical hats or helmets. Along with these standard elements of Near Eastern warfare there appears a line of four hoplites who are striding or running forward. Nearby, some unarmed men are hacking away with double-bladed axes

FIGURE 9-1. Amathus bowl. Source: "Traders, Pirates, Warriors: The Proto-History of Greek Mercenary Soldiers in the Eastern Mediterranean," Nino Luraghi, *Phoenix* , Vol. 60, No. 1/2 (Spring - Summer, 2006), pp. 21-47. Published by: Classical Association of Canada. After Myres, JHS, 1933. Reprinted by permission of Nino Luraghi and *Phoenix*.

at date palms and fruit trees in the orchards outside the city. (Could this custom have been picked up by Greeks fighting in the Near East, and carried back home to become part of the "hoplite tradition"?)[38]

Chief interest rests with the line of hoplites. They wear crested Ionian or Corinthian helmets, along with fringed tunics and greaves. Over their heads they brandish spears. Circular shields cover their bodies from jawline to hip. The shields display blazons: swirling rays, a sunburst or star, and, on the shield of the leading soldier, a crouching griffin or winged lion. Luraghi has suggested that the artist employed an unusual artistic convention to show that the hoplites are advancing in line, abreast. "Notice the interlocking legs of the warriors, visually conveying the close order of the phalanx, a detail that does not occur, to the best of my knowledge, in other depictions of rows of warriors in Phoenician metalwork or in Assyrian art."[39]

The hoplites are shown approaching a scaling ladder that a nonhoplite has just placed against the city wall ahead of them. On the other side of the city, troops are already climbing a similar ladder. These soldiers hold their pointed shields over their heads to protect themselves from the defensive thrusts of a bareheaded spearman on the tower above (or perhaps also from missiles and rocks). Once the running hoplites begin to climb their ladder, however, they will encounter another hoplite, fighting in defense of the city. He also is equipped with an emblazoned shield and a crested helmet, and will certainly attempt to ward them off with his own spear. Among the other defenders are archers and spearmen without heavy armor.

It appears, therefore, that mercenaries equipped as hoplites are fighting on both sides in this example of Near Eastern art. The only visual distinction between the hoplites inside and outside the walls is a stippled pattern on the defending hoplite's helmet. Thus by the end of the eighth or early in the seventh century, soldiers armed as hoplites and arrayed in close formation were fighting as self-contained units embedded within eastern armies that included archers, chariots, cavalry, and lightly armed spearmen. At this date and in this corner of the world, the originals of the hoplite figures on the Amathus bowl are most likely to have been Greek soldiers.

One other possible point of origin for these particular mercenaries is Caria, in the southwestern corner of Asia Minor. Herodotus (1.171.4) credits the Carians with inventing helmet crests, shield devices, and shield grips or handles, and then passing them on to the Greeks. All these items can be plausibly connected to the hoplite tradition. Snodgrass, however, has denied the reality of the Carians' claims to these military inventions.[40] There is no mention of Carians in the surviving Assyrian records to parallel the references to Ionian Greeks.

A Widening Stage: Early Greek Mercenaries in Egypt and Beyond

In about 664 BC, shiploads of Ionian and Carian "Bronze Men" (i.e., hoplites) landed on the shores of the Nile delta and proceeded to loot and pillage the land. So successful were these raiders against the local forces of horsemen and lightly armed troops that an Egyptian ruler promptly engaged them as mercenaries.

According to Herodotus,[41] this farsighted Egyptian king was Psammetichus I, founder of the Saite or twenty-sixth dynasty, who ultimately owed his throne to these soldiers from overseas. Subsequent rulers of the dynasty continued the tradition of hiring mercenaries, so that within a century of the first landing of the original "Bronze Men" up to thirty thousand Carians and Greeks were said to have been employed in Egyptian armies.[42] An immense fort at Daphnae (modern Tell Defenneh in northeastern Egypt) served as one of their bases.[43] The ruins of the fort have been excavated, revealing not only Greek pottery from the seventh and sixth centuries BC but also quarters that in the estimate of the excavators could have accommodated approximately twenty thousand troops.[44]

About seventy years after the first recorded landing of Greek soldiers in the delta region, a group of their successors inscribed their names on one of the ancient colossi of Ramses II at Abu Simbel, far up the Nile in southern Egypt, where they had traveled in the royal service. These mercenaries came from eastern Greek islands and cities, including Teos, Ialysos, and Colophon.[45] Their inclusion of ethnic identifiers after their names at Abu Simbel suggests that as soldiers of fortune they had not settled down permanently in Egypt and "gone native."

In addition, the tradition of service in Egypt was apparently being passed down within Greek families. The graffiti show that one Greek mercenary had actually been named "Psammetichus" by his father Theocles, who had presumably fought for another pharaoh a generation earlier. The same royal Egyptian name of Psammethicus even found its way into the family of Periander, tyrant of Corinth.

A remarkable archaeological discovery in Syria reinforces the impression that in the seventh century more "Bronze Men" may have been fighting overseas in the eastern Mediterranean region than in Greece itself. In fact, the earliest Greek hoplite gear ever recovered from an actual battle site comes not from a plain in Euboea or the Peloponnese but from the Syrian city of Carchemish on the Euphrates River. The *hopla* or gear in this case probably belonged to Greeks in the Egyptian army.

In about 605 BC the Egyptian king Necho—who, like his forefathers, manned his garrisons, field army, and trireme fleet with tens of thousands of Greeks—led his forces north to Carchemish to challenge the power of Nebuchadnezzar II of Babylonia. Necho lost the battle, and during the fierce fighting two of his Greek mercenaries apparently lost pieces of their bronze hoplite armor (if not indeed their lives). These artifacts were unearthed at Carchemish during the 1911–14 excavations conducted by a British archaeological team that included T. E. Lawrence, later known as "Lawrence of Arabia" and a bit of a soldier of fortune himself.

One of the items was a bronze greave of Archaic type, discovered in the ruins of the city gate along with arrowheads and the bones of horses and humans. The other was a bronze hoplite shield found in "House D" outside the walls of Carchemish. This building had been destroyed by fire. Alongside the shield, the diggers found items inscribed with the cartouches of the pharaoh Necho and his ancestor Psammetichus I, as well as hundreds of arrowheads, some javelin points, and a sword. The device on the Greek shield was the head of the gorgon Medusa, surrounded by writhing snakes and circular zones decorated with horses and other animals.[46] House D may have served as an Egyptian supply station or even the royal headquarters of Necho during the siege.

Here again in this conflict between Babylonians and Egyptians, just as in the fighting depicted on the Amathus bowl, Greek soldiers of fortune seem to have been employed on both sides. Nebuchadnezzar II followed up his victory over Necho at Carchemish in 605 BC by campaigning southward to the old Philistine city of Ashkelon and ultimately to the borders of Egypt itself. By this time (if not long before) the Babylonian king was certainly employing Greek mercenaries. One of these men, a soldier named Antimenidas from Mytilene, defeated a Goliath-like champion in one of the enemy armies. Antimenidas happened to be the brother of the poet Alcaeus (late seventh century BC), who wrote congratulatory verses to mark the mercenary hero's homecoming to his native Lesbos. It is interesting to note that Alcaeus' verses seem to imply that by this time Greeks had actually seen the houses of Babylon itself.

> You have returned from the ends of the earth, Antimenidas, with the gold-bound ivory hilt of that sword with which, as you fought for the Babylonians who dwell in houses of long bricks, you did a great deed, preserving them all from evil by killing a fighter who lacked only a palm of standing five royal cubits high.[47]

Greek hoplites of the seventh and early sixth centuries, then, seem more likely to have been professionals fighting in foreign wars than part-time amateurs fighting for their own cities at home. Is there a connection between these two strands of hoplite warfare—between Greek versus Greek wars on the home front, and mercenary service abroad? It may be that the sporadic wars between city-states and political factions in the seventh and sixth centuries were fueled in part by returning mercenaries, to take up the observation of van Wees quoted above. To use van Wees's terms, the large number of individuals who fought for their own prestige and wealth would "reinforce the willingness of Greek cities" to fight for communal honor and profit.[48]

Antimenidas came back to Lesbos from his glorious stint in the Babylonian army at about the time that war broke out between men of Mytilene and some seafaring Athenians who were attempting to settle at Sigeum near the Hellespont. A Mytilenean civil war followed soon after. The soldier-poet Alcaeus fought in both conflicts, and (echoing Archilochus) frankly admitted that he had lost his shield in an engagement with the Athenians. The victors carried it off as a trophy and (Alcaeus imagines) hung it up in a temple.[49] Here, perhaps, we can see the "soldier of fortune" mentality brought home to roost on Greek soil, in "patriotic" contests between armies of different city-states.

Wars of limited scope between Greeks on the home front may have been spurred by competition to possess the river of gold, slaves, and other riches that was flooding the Greek world as veterans like Antimenidas returned from the eastern wars, flush with pay and booty. At the same time, warfare between factions or city-states could have functioned as an incubator that inculcated toughness, fighting skills, and martial spirit among each new generation of young warriors. The seemingly pointless battles described by Herodotus could thus have contributed to a very practical outcome. Strengthened by athletic training and hardened to the rigors of hand-to-hand combat in local battles, Greek soldiers could have maintained their extremely profitable monopoly on providing heavily armed infantry to wealthy monarchs overseas.

Snodgrass has aptly described the mercantile nature of the tradition. "It was the Greek infantryman himself who was found to be more widely exportable than either ideas or objects on their own; in particular his services were keenly sought in the role of mercenary."[50] The most lucrative opportunities for ambitious Greeks during the period we call Archaic lay outside the Hellenic world, not within it.

Viking warfare holds up a distant mirror to the two strands of Greek hoplite warfare. On the one hand, the Norse sagas recount the dynastic struggles and homegrown conflicts between nascent states in the Vikings' home realm—Denmark, Sweden, and Norway. In these home-front contests, Viking armies even practiced a close counterpart to the ritualized and "agonal" Greek hoplite battle—a "battle of the hazelled field," where two armies met by appointment in a big fenced enclosure. On the other hand, historians have reconstructed—from the sagas of the Vikings and the chronicles of foreigners who were their targets—the relentless overseas raids, sieges, mercenary service, and settlement missions that eventually carried Vikings and their fleets of long ships from Byzantium to Newfoundland.[51]

Which branch of war mattered most to the Vikings? Clearly, in the long run, the overseas campaigns and raids counted for much more than the dynastic wars within the Baltic and the North Sea. Seaborne expeditions, by vastly increasing Viking wealth, territory, and contacts with the outside world, did more to shape Viking warfare, society, and culture than did the conflicts between the rival kingdoms. As it was in Scandinavia from AD 800 to 1000, so it had been, I would suggest, in Archaic Greece.

If one considers the impact made by rovers, raiders, and mercenaries on ancient Greek economy, society, and culture, as well as the number of "man-hours" involved in their professional careers, the overseas campaigns undertaken by soldiers of fortune clearly constituted the "main event" of Greek military history in the seventh century BC. By contrast, battles between Greek city-states appear to have been in this early period a sporadically performed and—always excepting the Spartan conquest of Messenia—rather unproductive sideshow.

Hoplite Origins: Of Halls and *Hetairoi*, Ships and Shields

In his book *The Other Greeks*, Hanson observes that the early city-states of Greece owned few warships. He reasons that since the Greek polis was essentially agrarian, and since farmers by nature distrust ships and the sea, modern scholars can rule out "overseas involvement"[52] as the stimulus for military or cultural innovations. However, ships and seafarers often appear in early Greek art, and the Assyrian documents show that Greek ships were venturing regularly to the eastern Mediterranean in the eighth century BC. The nearly contemporaneous waves of Greek settlement expeditions to coastal sites from Asia Minor to Sicily also presuppose the existence of large fleets.

As far as the eighth century BC is concerned, it is indeed hard to believe that any Greek polis possessed a state-owned fleet. But if city-states could not provide ships for overseas campaigns and colonization, then who did? A new evaluation of archaeological evidence from the earliest overseas settlements suggests that ambitious individuals, not city-states, were the driving force behind eighth-century Greek expansion.[53] In all probability, the owner of every *naus* or longship in the Greek world before the age of the tyrants was an individual aristocrat or an aristocratic clan. No one else would have had the resources needed to acquire the raw materials, compensate the shipbuilders, protect and maintain the finished vessel, and assemble the crew of rowers that was required to propel the ship on its voyages. (A pirate or *leistos* could have performed the same functions, but the occupation of pirate chief may have been no more than a temporary role assumed by opportunistic aristocrats.)

In the eighth century the Greek city-state was only beginning its process of evolution. At that time the upper end of Greek society still centered on a much more ancient focal point: the aristocratic feasting hall. Here, the owner of an ancestral estate displayed his riches and power. Standard equipment included iron firedogs for the open-air roasting of spitted meats—forerunners of modern Greek souvlaki. The firedogs were often forged in the shape of long, low warships with pointed rams, and were so highly prized that they were often buried with their owners.[54] The fires banked under the spits made these halls "smoke-filled rooms" where deals and destinies were decided. As the assembled men accepted the food and wine, they also tacitly recognized the paternal and dominant status of the aristocrat who was the founder of the feast. They became bound to him as *hetairoi* or companions.

The poet Alcaeus from Mytilene, brother of Nebuchadnezzar's champion Antimenidas, composed a vivid description of one such great hall where young Greeks could "get on board" and prove their worth through prowess in fighting.

> The great hall [*mégas dómos*] is ablaze with bronze; ranks of bright helmets cover the ceiling and spill white horsehair crests, ornamentation for masculine heads. Glistening metal greaves, legs' rampart against the arrow's force, hang on the wall on unseen pegs. Fresh linen corselets and hollow shields clutter the floor; here are blades from Chalcis; here, belts in abundance and tunics. From the moment we took on this job [*ergon*], these are things we could not forget.[55]

The *ergon* or "work" that called for the distribution of these arms and weapons must have been an enterprise that, if successful, would increase the wealth and fame of every man involved. As for the personality, background, and worldview of the aristocrat who was tempted away from his inherited lands, we can turn to Homer's *Odyssey* for a vivid portrait. The speaker is a fictional Cretan (one of Odysseus' own false identities), the illegitimate son of an aristocrat named Castor, who shared with his half-brothers in the division of the estate after his father's death.

> To me they gave a very small portion, and allotted a dwelling. But I took to me a wife from a house that had wide possessions, winning her by my valor, . . . Such a man was I in war, but labor in the field was never to my liking, nor care of a household, which rears comely children, but oared ships were ever dear to me, and wars, and polished spears, and arrows. . . . For before the sons of the Achaeans set foot on the land of Troy, I had nine times led warriors and swift-faring ships against foreign folk, and great spoil continually fell to my hands. . . . Thus my house at once became rich, whereupon I became feared and honored among the Cretans. . . . then to Egypt did my spirit bid me voyage with my godlike companions [*hetároisin*], when I had fitted out my ships with care. Nine ships I fitted out, and the host [*laós*] gathered speedily. Then for six days my comrades [*hetaîroi*] feasted, and I gave them many victims.[56]

As Homer reminds us in this passage, the Greek aristocrat needed a following of armed companions or *hetairoi*, not only for the sake of his own prestige and glory, but also for very practical purposes of security, survival, and military success. He and his family attracted these followers by offering them hospitality, sustenance, entertainment (including the singing of bards), weapons, and a share in the profits. The existence of a common source for shields and other arms—namely, the aristocratic leader, who also patronized smiths, bronze workers, and other craftsmen—may help account for the startlingly uniform appearance of early hoplite companies in Greek art. Fortune-seeking young men were eager to find a place in such a retinue, for the great halls were jumping-off places for all sorts of opportunities. The hosts planned overseas expeditions not only for warfare but also for trade and new settlements, ceremonial visits to guest-friends, and religious missions to remote sanctuaries. Homer admired the men who crowded into these noble halls, provided they honored their obligations. Hesiod, the farmer-poet of the *Works and Days*, despised them.

Some seaborne expeditions involved coastal raiding, piracy, and mercenary service abroad—the domain of the soldier of fortune. Because early Greek warships were galleys propelled by rowers—thirty, fifty, or even more being required for each vessel—the owner of the ship had to attract large numbers of men for every expedition. A company consisting of an aristocratic leader and his followers would launch one or more *makra ploia* or "long ships" from a beach near the great hall. In these galleys, which were rowed *auteretai* (by the soldiers themselves), the adventurers set out on their voyages. The men formed a "company" in both senses of the English term—a fellowship of kindred spirits, and an entrepreneurial partnership.

Once aboard, the soldiers hung their circular shields along the ship's railings, making a fearsome and very Viking-like show of strength. Round shields are ideal for use at sea, as they have no sharp corners to chip or cause damage or injury. Unlike long oblong shields (which are in other respects better suited to phalanx formations), round shields can also be lifted clear of the water as the men wade to the beach. Assyrian artists depicted Phoenician warships with rows of circular shields in the eighth century. As noted earlier, Vikings followed the same tradition. On reaching land, Vikings typically formed a *schildborg* or "shield wall" for the initial collision with the defending enemy force. Among Greek soldiers of fortune, the Athenian commander Iphicrates shows exactly how the maneuver was carried out.

> Iphicrates was sailing with 100 thirty-oared ships near Phoenicia, where the beach was covered with standing water. When he saw the Phoenicians marshaling on the shore, he gave orders, when he raised the signal, for the steersmen to drop anchor from the stern and to make the landing in formation, and for each of the soldiers [*stratiôtais hoplisamenous*] to lower himself armed into the sea at his oar and to preserve this formation. As soon as he [i.e., Iphicrates] thought the water shallow enough, he raised the signal for disembarking. The thirty-oared ships landed in formation because of their anchors, and the men, throwing themselves in formation before the ships, advanced. The enemy, amazed at their formation and daring, began to flee. Iphicrates' men in pursuit killed some, captured others, seized a great deal of plunder, which they put on the ships, and encamped on land.[57]

This forming of a phalanx in the sea belongs to the fourth century BC, but similar "D-Day" and Normandy-like conditions must have faced Iphicrates' predecessors three centuries before, and may have generated the same response from those earlier "Bronze Men." Certainly it is a truth, universally acknowledged, that a landing on a beach held by enemy troops constitutes one of the most difficult of all military challenges.

Once formed at the sea's edge with the purpose of forcing a landing, the phalanx could maintain itself on land whenever the enemy continued to challenge the invading Greeks. The poet Mimnernus (c. 630–600 BC) describes such a scene.

> So the men of the *basileus* charged when he gave the word of command, making a fence with their hollow shields.[58]

The *basileus* (king or lord) in this passage may have been either the aristocratic leader of the Greek force, or the foreign monarch who had engaged them as mercenaries. On flat plains the early hoplites came into their own, and could successfully withstand attacks of a "home team" composed of archers, slingers, lightly armed infantry, cavalry, or even chariots. The horses of Asiatic and Egyptian armies would have been no more able to break the hoplites' wall of glittering bronze shields than the horses of Marshal Ney's French cavalry were able to face the squares of British bayonets at Waterloo. Should a horse have come too close, even a lone hoplite stood a chance of fending the animal off with his heavy convex shield, or even inflicting a wound with a slash of the shield's blade-like rim. Once the enemy forces were driven back behind their city walls, the hoplites' shields provided superior protection from stones and missiles as the Greeks attacked the gates and fortifications.

To sum up, the Near Eastern and Egyptian evidence suggests that ambitious Greeks may have initially trained as heavily armed fighting men for success in raiding. Ultimately they discovered (or their erstwhile opponents discovered) that, armed and trained as hoplites, they were supremely desirable as soldiers for hire by monarchs throughout the eastern Mediterranean. The aristocratic Greek leader presumably distributed the loot from raids, and negotiated with foreign kings and chiefs for mercenary pay and shares of booty. Rich with these winnings, an upwardly mobile young Greek might dream of one day presiding in his own great hall, and commanding his own warship filled with *hetairoi*.

Greece was a harder land than most. Starting in the eighth century, its sons began to surpass all other dwellers around the Mediterranean in sheer physical strength and toughness, the ability to wield the heavy hoplite arms and carry them over long distances, and a fierce and battle-ready mentality. The cost of this mastery was the physical training required to manage the shield for long stretches of time. From this necessity sprang the masculine Greek mania for physical fitness, the idiosyncratic Greek pride in displaying and depicting their muscular, naked physiques, and the corresponding scorn for the stereotypical pale, soft, untanned bodies of Asiatics. As men who had developed a marketable skill, these early Greeks resembled not only Vikings but also the Swiss pikemen of the Middle Ages, likewise famous as mercenaries, and likewise native to a harsh and rocky homeland. The Ionian mercenaries serving Near Eastern and Egyptian rulers founded a Greek tradition that endured through the campaigns of Xenophon and the Ten Thousand down to the "world wars" of Alexander the Great and his successors.

After the loot from the shore raids and captured towns was divided, the adventurers of early times reboarded their ships for the return voyage to Greece. The homeward passage was enlivened by celebratory toasts and drinking bouts. Archilochus is our eyewitness to the scene.

> But come, make many a trip with a cup through the thwarts of the swift ship, pull off the covers of the hollow casks, and draw the red wine from the lees; we won't be able to stay sober on this watch.[59]

Archilochus and his fellow soldier-poets expressed a uniquely Greek consciousness of the individual as master of his destiny. The peculiar nature of the newborn Greek polis, so much at variance with the ancient Near Eastern model, reflected the entrepreneurial spirit and worldview of these far-voyaging military professionals as they returned home with their hard-won riches, or created new Greek communities abroad. Their successful exploits became an economic engine that pumped vast wealth and cultural baggage from more advanced cultures into the formerly impoverished Greek heartland. By the sixth century BC these soldiers of fortune had extended the limits of the Greek *oikumene* from the coast of Iberia to the Black Sea, and from the Libyan desert to the northern lagoons of the Adriatic. The armed adventurers of the eighth and seventh centuries BC may have been the true progenitors of Classical Greek civilization. I believe that they were also the first hoplites.

Notes

1. Hanson 1999, p. 223. "Do these innovations in arms tell us how *geôrgoi* took land or influence away from entrenched landowners?"

2. Hanson 1999, p. 224.

3. Van Wees 2007, pp. 273–99.

4. Mitchell 1996, pp. 98–101.

5. Concerning the apparent absence of elaborate tactics in hoplite warfare, see Hanson 1989, pp. 19–26, a chapter titled "Not Strategy, Not Tactics."

6. Hanson 1999, p. 224.

7. Van Wees 2004, p. 55.

8. Tyrtaeus fr. 10, West.

9. Herodotus 1.13 and 5.99; Thucydides 1.15. For a list of the opposing allies, see Murray 1993, p. 76.

10. Pausanias 2.24.7.

11. The fragmentary inscriptions that relate to this war between Paros and Naxos are presented in Gerber 1999, pp. 16–33.

12. Zapheiropoulou 2006, pp. 262–65.

13. Herodotus 7.9b, translated by de Sélincourt.

14. Hanson 1999, p. 299.

15. Hanson 1999, p. 300.

16. Hornblower 2007, p. 22. See also Shipley 1993, p. 1.

17. Archilochus fr. 5, Gerber. Translation by D. Mulroy.

18. Skolion of Hybrias the Cretan, in Athenaeus 695f–696a (Page).

19. Archilochus fr. 1, Gerber.

20. Homer, *Odyssey* 9.39–46 and 9.193–215.

21. Archilochus fr. 2, Gerber. In his own translation for the Loeb edition of *Greek Iambic Poetry* (1999, p. 79), Gerber prefers to translate *en dori* as "on board ship" or "under arms," rather than the more common "on my spear." The reference to campaigning is clear, regardless of which meaning is preferred.

22. Van Wees 2004, pp. 40–43 and 71–76. On Greek mercenaries see also Hunt 2007, pp. 140–44.

23. Van Wees 2004, p. 42.
24. Van Wees 2004, p. 76.
25. Luraghi 2006.
26. Luraghi 2006, pp. 38–39.
27. Luraghi 2006, pp. 40–42.
28. Snodgrass 1964a, p. 66.
29. For translations and detailed discussion of these Assyrian documents, see Luraghi 2006, pp. 31–33, and Niemeier 2001, p. 16.
30. From the "Little Annals," line 9; see Luraghi 2006, p. 31.
31. Luraghi 2006, p. 33.
32. Anderson 1970, pp. 22–25.
33. Luraghi 2006, pp. 41–42.
34. Parke 1933.
35. Trundle 2004.
36. Myres 1933, pp. 25–39.
37. Luraghi 2006, p. 36.
38. For Assyrian destruction of orchards as part of siege warfare, see Cole 1997, pp. 29–40.
39. Luraghi 2006, p. 37, note 86.
40. Snodgrass 1964b.
41. Herodotus 2.152.
42. Herodotus 2.163.
43. Herodotus 2.30.
44. Petrie 1888, pp. 47–96.
45. Tod 1946, pp. 6–7.
46. Woolley 1921, pp. 121–29 and figures 43–46, plates 21, 22, and 32.
47. Alcaeus fr. 133 Edmonds.
48. Van Wees 2004, p. 42.
49. Herodotus 5.95.
50. Snodgrass 1980, p. 110.
51. For an overview of Viking arms and warfare, see Griffith 1995.
52. Hanson 1999, p. 290.
53. Osborne 1998, p. 268.
54. Whitley 2001, p. 96.
55. Alcaeus fr. 19, Edmonds (tr. D. Mulroy).
56. Homer, *Odyssey* 14.210–51, tr. Murray (rev. Dimmock).
57. Polyaenus 3.9.63, tr. Krentz and Wheeler.
58. Mimnernus fr. 13a, Gerber.
59. Archilochus fr. 4, Gerber.

Bibliography

Anderson, J. K. 1970. "The Trojan Horse Again." *Classical Journal* 66:22–25.

Cole, Steven W. 1997. "The Destruction of Orchards in Assyrian Warfare," in *ASSYRIA 1995: Proceedings of the 10th Anniversary Symposium of the Neo-Assyrian Text Corpus Project*, ed. S. Parpola and R. M. Whiting. Helsinki.

Gerber, Douglas. 1999. *Greek Iambic Poetry*. Cambridge, Mass.

Griffith, Paddy. 1995. *The Viking Art of War*. London.

Hanson, Victor Davis. 1983. *Warfare and Agriculture in Classical Greece*. Pisa.

———. 1999. *The Other Greeks: The Family Farm and the Agrarian Roots of Western Civilization*, 2nd ed. Berkeley, Calif.

Hornblower, Simon. 2007. "Warfare in Ancient Literature: The Paradox of War," in *The Cambridge History of Greek and Roman Warfare*, vol. 1: *Greece, the Hellenistic World and the Rise of Rome*, ed. Philip Sabin, Hans van Wees, and Michael Whitby. Cambridge.

Hunt, Peter. 2007. "Military Forces," in *The Cambridge History of Greek and Roman Warfare*, vol. 1: *Greece, the Hellenistic World and the Rise of Rome*, ed. Philip Sabin, Hans van Wees, and Michael Whitby. Cambridge.

Luraghi, Nino. 2006. "Traders, Pirates, Warriors: The Proto-History of Greek Mercenary Soldiers in the Eastern Mediterranean." *Phoenix* 60.1: 21–47.

Mitchell, Stephen. 1996. "Hoplite Warfare in Ancient Greece," in *Battle in Antiquity*, ed. Alan B. Lloyd. Swansea.

Niemeier, Wolf-Dietrich. 2001. "Archaic Greeks in the Orient: Textual and Archaeological Evidence." *Bulletin of the American Schools of Oriental Research* 322:11–32.

Osborne, Robin. 1998. "Early Greek Colonization?" in *Archaic Greece: New Approaches and New Evidence*, ed. Nick Fisher and Hans van Wees. London.

Parke, H. W. 1933. *Greek Mercenary Soldiers: From the Earliest Times to the Battle of Issus*. Oxford.

Petrie, W. Flinders. 1888. *Nebesh and Defenneh*. London.

Snodgrass, Anthony. 1964a. *Early Greek Armour and Weapons*. Edinburgh.

———. 1964b. "Carian Armourers: The Growth of a Tradition." in *Journal of Hellenic Studies* 84:107–18.

———. 1967. *Arms and Armour of the Greeks*. Ithaca, N.Y.

———. 1980. *Archaic Greece: The Age of Experiment*. Berkeley, Calif.

Tod, Marcus N. 1946. *A Selection of Greek Historical Inscriptions*, vol. 1. Oxford.

Trundle, Matthew. 2004. *Greek Mercenaries: From the Late Archaic Period to Alexander*. London and New York.

Van Wees, Hans. 2004. *Greek Warfare: Myths and Realities*. London.

———. 2007. "War and Society," in *The Cambridge History of Greek and Roman Warfare*, vol. 1: *Greece, the Hellenistic World and the Rise of Rome*, ed. Philip Sabin, Hans van Wees, and Michael Whitby. Cambridge.

Whitley, James. 2001. *The Archaeology of Early Greece*. Cambridge.

Woolley, C. L. 1921. *Carchemish*, vol. 2: *The Town Defenses*. London.

CHAPTER 10

Can We See the "Hoplite Revolution" on the Ground? Archaeological Landscapes, Material Culture, and Social Status in Early Greece

LIN FOXHALL

Introduction: A Hoplite Revolution?

The issue of the emergence of hoplite phalanxes in early Greek communities offers a challenging case study for exploring the ways in which archaeological and historical data can be combined, or not, to address questions about social and political developments central to Archaic poleis. A hoplite is not just a material cultural assemblage, although at one level he is defined by scholars by the particular assemblage(s) of weaponry he wore and carried (van Wees 2005: 47–52). Hoplite equipment appears to have varied regionally, over time, and even between individuals, but the core elements were the spear and shield (van Wees 2005: 48; Giuliani 2010). Indeed, "a hoplite" is hardly the issue: it is the hoplite phalanx, the emergence of a group of men fighting together as a team (van Wees 2005: 166–68), that has most interested historians. Fundamentally, the historical debates have focused on the emergence of the hoplite phalanx as a tactic and its relationship to the phalanx as a sociopolitical group, generally believed to be synonymous with property owners (Hanson 1999: 69; 223–24; van Wees 2005: 55–57). The logic of the various arguments presented associates (1) the shared experience of being, almost literally, joined in battle with (2) the shared ideologies that (3) fed into the ideals of a shared political community, whose members (4) held a stake in the security (and sometimes expansion) of a territory they owned and farmed for a living, although not always in this order (Hanson 1999: 235–37).

Hanson (1999: 47–88) dates the social and political environment that generated the social group and political community of hoplites to the late eighth century. He takes Laertes as epitomizing the Zeitgeist of the phenomenon, "a representation of an entire new class of farmers" (Hanson 1999: 49). A key element in Hanson's interpretation is Laertes' permanent residence on his rural farmstead, rather than in a nucleated settlement (Hanson 1999: 51). For Hanson, these "middling" farmers, "independent moderate property owners," served as hoplites to defend their farms and communities (Hanson 1999: 69, 87–88 and passim). Hanson (1999: 40, 50, 79–82) also envisages this period as a time when farmers spread onto "*eschatiai*," "marginal lands," as a result, he postulates, of "population pressure and the scarcity of good bottomland" (Hanson 1999: 82). For the most part Hanson supports his argument for dispersed rural residence (in his terms, "homestead residence") with evidence from contemporary (e.g., Homer's *Odyssey* and Hesiod's *Works and Days*; Hanson 1999: 443–45) and later (e.g., Thucydides, Ps-Aristotle, *Ath. Pol.*; Hanson 1999: 445–46) literary sources. However, he also invokes at a general level the discoveries of extensive and intensive archaeological survey and the excavation of farmhouses of the Classical period to support this argument (Hanson 1999: 51–53; 445–46).

Van Wees places both the development of the phalanx as a hoplite infantry force (van Wees 2005: 56) and the rise of hoplites as a political class in Athens (van Wees 2005: 177) in the sixth century BCE (see also van Wees, this volume). His argument for the development of the phalanx as a fighting tactic is based on a combination of early Greek poetry (especially Tyrtaeus), the archaeological evidence of preserved weapons, and the iconographic evidence, especially of Athenian and Corinthian vases (van Wees, this volume; 2005: 166–79). In contrast, his arguments about the enfranchisement of hoplites as a property-holding group are based primarily upon the, mostly later, historical sources relating to Solon's property classes and the reforms of Kleisthenes. In his view, the early sixth-century "reforms" extended political participation and military service in the phalanx to the *zeugitai*, a group that was still part of the wealthy elite in Athens (van Wees, this volume; 2001; 2005: 55–56, 80–81; 2007: 276; Foxhall 1997). The political reorganization of Kleisthenes devolved military organization to the new political units of tribes and demes, although the generals, who held both political office and military command, were elected (van Wees 2005: 99). For van Wees (2001), the key feature is that hoplites in Athens and other Archaic poleis were (prosperous or elite) farmers and property holders within the community; he does not address the specific question of residence.

The exploration of Mediterranean landscapes through archaeological survey over the past thirty years has transformed our understanding of the ancient Greek polis in its territorial setting. We now have a relatively clear picture of the rural countrysides within which the urban centers of the polis developed and were embedded. The growth of this body of archaeological data has provided us with an additional tool for working through the complex spatial, social, and political relationships between town and country. However, this additional source of data has introduced new, and exacerbated existing, methodological issues. Archaeological and historical data differ in character, and historical "events" do not map easily onto archaeological "events" (Foxhall 2000). Can we use archaeological data to address questions of social and political status in Archaic Greece? If so, what questions can we legitimately ask of these data? Can archaeological evidence be mobilized to address the historical issues of whether the hoplite phalanx was coterminous with "middling" (Hanson 1999: 69) or prosperous (van Wees 2005: 55–56) property holders and whether this phenomenon began in the eighth or sixth century BCE?

Using Archaeological Data: Landscape and Survey

If, as historians, we wish to engage with archaeological evidence, we must first be aware of how it is generated and of what, precisely, it consists. It is no use simply swiping the conclusions from the archaeology book without understanding how and on what basis those interpretations were reached (Alcock and Cherry 2004: 5). When historians do this, it can result in the promulgation of major misunderstandings and misinterpretations (and the same is true in reverse, when archaeologists try to use the conclusions of historians on textual data) (Osborne 2004). It is easy to forget that archaeological data are no more "neutral" or "unbiased" than historical data, and that archaeologists, like historians, have often "found" what they were looking for—that is, their results and interpretations are shaped by the questions they were asking in the first place.

The methodologies of intensive archaeological survey were first developed by American archaeologists working in the "New Archaeology" tradition of the 1960s and 1970s (e.g., Binford et al. 1970:1–2, 7–15; Mueller 1974). These techniques were first applied in the Greek world in the 1970s, first in a limited way by the Minnesota Messenia Expedition (McDonald and Rapp 1972)—still really a more precise form of extensive survey—and more fully by Renfrew and Wagstaff in Melos (1982). A number of major survey projects were carried out in Greece and Italy during the 1980s and 1990s, and intensive survey continues to be a major feature of Greek and Mediterranean archaeological projects at present. With the advent in the 1990s and 2000s of GIS (Geographical Information Systems) and other computer-based techniques for analyzing and reconstructing landscapes (Gillings 2000), the techniques and methodologies of collection, recording, and interpretation are continuing to develop in sophistication (Caraher et al. 2006; Tartaron et al. 2006; Sullivan et al. 2007; Lolos et al. 2007).

The fundamental basis of intensive survey, in a very oversimplified form, is the systematic sampling of a landscape by walking small teams over a selection of areas of known size, measured out in a grid where possible, and generally chosen by some explicit sampling methodology. The team then records and, as appropriate, collects or systematically samples all traces *on the surface of the ground* of human use of that part of the landscape, from all periods usually up to and including the present. Although survey teams are sometimes lucky enough to discover architectural features such as towers or structures, the bulk of the archaeological material found and collected is ceramics and lithics (stone tools and debitage from their manufacture). The density of artifacts in any particular part of the landscape is interpreted as significant for the intensity of human activity in that location, and is sometimes important for determining its specific character. So, for example, a settlement (e.g., a village) generally has a much higher density of artifacts than land that appears to have been used as cultivated fields, which might only have a "background" scatter of artifacts, or in some cases none at all. Nucleated settlement sites generally present a different artifactual "signature" than isolated rural sites, lone agricultural installations, graves, or small rural sanctuaries (which often have a particularly distinctive material cultural signature). The overall aim of intensive survey is to build up a picture of a specific landscape in the past, including human activity as a key component, and to understand how that landscape and the relationship of human societies to it changed and developed.

So, what do the raw data look like, and can historians use them? As noted above, most of the finds are ceramics—small fragments of pottery (sherds). Because these are surface finds, they are often very small indeed, and many are very worn, probably because they have been tumbled about in the plowing zone for many centuries. (However, the question of artifact taphonomy—i.e., how an artifact comes to rest where the archaeologist finds it—is much debated in the survey literature, and may result from a complex combination of human activity and geomorphohological processes, e.g., Jameson et al. 1994: 222–23; James et al. 1994.) Most of the time, for any one specific area within a survey, the sherds collected are few in number and often range over a number of periods. This is true even on the "hot spots" of human activity in the landscape, which most survey projects call "sites" (Jameson et al. 1994: 221–22). Even this term is not unproblematic: distinguishing "sites" in areas of heavy "background" scatter can be very difficult (Pettegrew 2001 with responses from Osborne 2001, Foxhall 2001a, and Bintliff et al. 2002), and some archaeologists have questioned whether the term "site" is even meaningful (Caraher et al 2006; Dunnell 1992) for the interpretation of landscapes. Sites are often occupied in more than one period, and not necessarily continuously—there may be substantial gaps in the habitation record. Archaeologists have long recognized that there can be no straightforward translation of survey data into population or even settlement data for any particular period (Cherry et al. 1991: 327–28).

The key problem for the identification of survey pottery is that material collected on the ground surface usually consists of a mix of periods and has no stratigraphic context as excavated material would. Generally the shapes, decoration, and sequences of fine wares are much better known (from excavated parallels) than for most utilitarian wares. This creates an instant "bias" in data interpretation if we privilege the fine wares (and we thus try not to do so, though that often proves difficult). On many sherds the surface has worn away altogether, and the pottery may then be identifiable only by the fabric (the specific mix of clay and temper of which it is made), if this is sufficiently distinctive (and it may not be). If the surface (especially any surface decoration) survives, it may provide more information. Specific parts of pots, especially rims, bases, and to some extent handles, are also potentially informative and can often be matched with typological sequences of excavated material to determine form and date, and to a limited extent function. Body sherds (the bulk of finds) are usually less informative. However, it is easier to find excavated parallels for some sherds than others since the ceramics of certain periods (e.g., classical antiquity) have been studied in much more detail than for other periods (e.g., early modern household wares).

Nonetheless, survey pottery finds vary considerably in their diagnosticity, and thus in the degree to which we can pin down their date and other attributes. Some distinctive and well-preserved sherds can be pinned down to as narrow a frame as a quarter of a century. Some pottery styles and fabrics are so distinctive that even a very small fragment can be informative, for example, Late Geometric (eighth century BCE) decorated fine wares or Late Roman combed wares or African Red Slip. However, many sherds cannot be dated at all or can be dated only to broad categories such as "prehistoric," "ancient," "medieval," or "early modern." Most problematic of all for the specific question addressed here is that a great many survey sherds in the Greek world, particularly black-slipped fine wares, can be identified as "classical" in a broad generic sense, but could date to any period between the later Archaic and the Hellenistic periods (ca sixth through third/second centuries BCE). Even where a form can be identified, some shapes in black-slipped wares (e.g., drinking cups such as skyphoi or bowls) may have a very long life span (and the most diagnostic elements may be missing), allowing us to narrow the time frame only to several hundred years, e.g., Archaic-Classical or Classical-Hellenistic. Cherry et al. (1991: 328) state that for the Keos survey data nearly 75% of the sherds of the Archaic through Roman periods (over 1,300 in total) can be dated only to within the several hundred years represented by two ceramic periods (e.g., Archaic-Classical). About 35% can be dated to a single period, but only around 10% (i.e., around 130 sherds) can be dated to within a century (fig. 10-1). It has even been argued that the pottery of some periods (e.g., Prehistoric) appears underrepresented in the survey record because of the abundant archaeological deposition of other, later periods (e.g., Classical-Hellenistic) (Bintliff et al. 1999; Bintliff et al. 2007: 13; Jameson et al. 1994: 223), although this idea has been much contested (Davis 2004).

Obviously such floppy chronologies, useful as they are for investigating long-term changes in landscapes and their exploitation, are not helpful or appropriate for addressing chronologically fine-tuned historical questions, and generally should not be used to do so. An interesting example of this is offered by the Boeotia Survey's intensive exploration around the city of Thespiai. Tuplin's detailed analysis of the historical sources has established that sometime between 373/2 and summer 371 BCE the

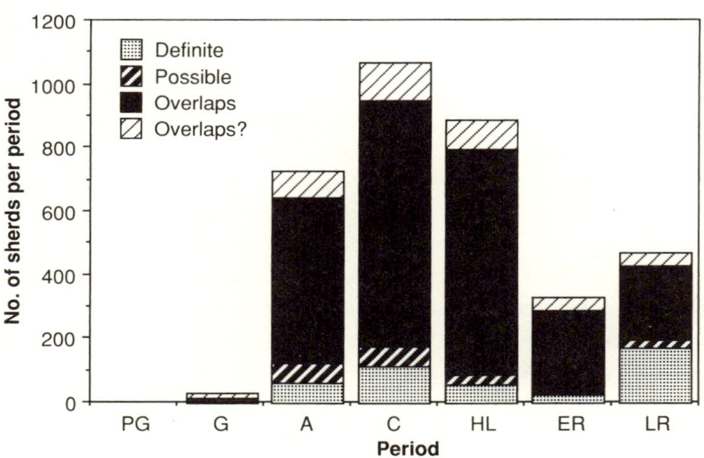

FIGURE 10-1. Keos Survey: numbers of sherds that can be dated to a single century (Cherry et al. 1991: 331, fig. 17.2). Courtesy of John Cherry, Jack Davis, and the Cotsen Institute.

Thebans destroyed Thespiai and removed the population (Tuplin 1986: 337). Whether this was done by expelling them from their land or by mass execution or enslavement is not clear; Tuplin's preferred solution on the basis of the texts is that the urban center was demolished, the population was moved to small settlements in the countryside, and the polis ceased to exist as a political entity (Tuplin 1986: 325, 339). This situation seems to have continued at least down to the Peace of Philokrates in 346, when it is specifically highlighted as an issue (Dem. 5.10; 19.20–21, 112, 325; cf. Aesch. 2.116, 137; Tuplin 1986: 326). However, this dramatic episode in the history of the polis cannot be detected in the archaeological survey record, and the landscape remained intensively cultivated throughout the period, possibly by deposed Thespians living in the countryside, presumably working for the benefit of the Thebans, during this time (Bintliff et al. 2007: 143). In other words, the archaeological data inform us about the intensity and sometimes the type of land use, but usually provide no information about land tenure or patterns of property ownership.

No chronology based on pottery sequences will have the precision of historical dates in well-understood periods (Cherry et al 1991: 328–31). Worse yet, not all survey projects use the same chronological boundaries for identifying pottery and dating sites, which makes comparing data from different survey projects quite difficult except from a very wide-angle perspective. For the most part, survey projects set a threshold (e.g., five sherds) for positively identifying activity/human presence, *sensu lato*, during any particular period, but this is hardly an exact science. And, there are many different ways to quantify pottery data (e.g., number of sherds, weight of sherds, the application of scaled quantitative measures to allow for inequalities in length of periods, deposition and visibility at different times in the past, etc.). This is why it is important that historians move beyond just looking at the dots on the maps; they need to understand, as well, *precisely* on what basis particular sites identified in survey have been dated, and how their function has been interpreted by the archaeologists.

In summary, then, survey tells us an enormous amount about long-term changes in a landscape at a broad level. It is useful for understanding general trends and patterns, and these may both result from large-scale historical processes and have historical implications, but the quality and granulation of the data are such that we cannot push them too far within any specific period. Nonetheless, these broad trends can be usefully deployed to address the question at hand, at least in a limited way.

Survey Data and the Development of the Greek Countryside

This section provides an overview of eight survey projects in Greece, focusing particularly on the data for the Geometric through Hellenistic periods. The data presented are also summarized in table 10-1. As will become clear in the individual subsections, different projects have divided up this time period in slightly different ways, but the data can usefully be compared nonetheless. What emerges is a considerable degree of regional variation in terms of settlement and occupation history within the overall broad trends that appear to apply to almost all areas.

TABLE 10-1

Survey	Protogeometric-Geometric	Geometric	Geometric-Archaic	Archaic
Boeotia	Practically nothing.	Evidence of activity from LG only.		Small amount of archaic rural settlement and activity, mostly 6th c.
Keos	Excavated material from A. Irini. One certain PG sherd, site 20.	A few possible, but no definite G sherds.		Almost all dates to 6th c., nothing certain before 7th c. Numerous 6th c. sherds in countryside.
S. Argolid	Only one site, which also has EG component.	MG: 3 certain and 3 uncertain sites; LG up to 22 sites, but many uncertain.		Later Archaic (700/655–480 BCE) increase in site numbers.
Methana	3 sites (1050–700 BCE).			6 sites in total (600–480 BCE).
Berbati-Limnes	1 PG sherd.	2 excavated graves (1 EG, 1 MG).	12 find spots: 9 with 8th c. BCE material; 9 with 7th–6th c. BCE material	Late 6th–early 5th c. BCE material largely missing.
Laconia		Only activity at 2 sanctuaries at very end of 8th c. BCE.		Early archaic (700–600 BCE) missing; much material from second half of 6th c. BCE.
Pylos	Virtually nothing Submyc-G.		3 certain sites	
Kea	Nothing.	Nothing.		Small numbers of sites.

Archaic-Classical	Classical	Late Classical–Early Hellenistic	Hellenistic
	Period of dramatic increase in rural settlement. For Thespiai, band of cemeteries followed by hamlets/large farms, followed by (a few) small farms.	Peak of rural settlement	Decline after c. 200 BCE.
	A-H most dense phase of sherd deposition, of which a large proportion are probably Classical.		Less material than Classical period, but still quite a lot down to 3rd c.; after that steep drop-off in diagnostic material until Late Roman.
	Even more increase in site numbers in Classical (480–338 BCE), 42 sites.	Peak of rural dispersed occupation, 75 sites (350–250 BCE)	Decline in site numbers in later Hellenistic phase (250–50 BCE).
	22 certain sites (480–323 BCE), Classical component on 48 sites; peak in isolated rural sites appears to be the last third of the 5th c. BCE.		28 certain Hellenistic sites (323–100 BCE); 54 with Hellenistic component.
	13 definite 5th c. BCE find spots.	peak of settlement activity appears late 4th–early 3rd c. BCE	decline in site numbers from 2nd c. BCE.
600–450 BCE , 87 definite sites, 9 new sanctuaries; some activity on 72 further sites.	450–300 BCE, sharp reduction in number of sites to 64.		3rd–1st c. BCE; 48 definite, 27 probable sites.
7th–4th c. BCE increase in settlement, but relatively few dispersed farmsteads.			Peak period of occupation.
	A peak period for site numbers.		Decline in site numbers.

Boeotia

The major, and pioneering, survey project carried out across the rural territories of the cities of Boeotia between 1978 and 1991 is still not fully published, although many important and full publications have appeared. Overall, it is clear that the Geometric occupation was largely restricted to a few key settlements that later became urban sites (Bintliff 1999: 15–18). The sixth century (Late Archaic) appears to be the period when urban sites acquired walls, and a limited amount of activity, possibly dispersed farmsteads in some cases (see below), first appears in the rural territories of these cities (Bintliff 1999: 19). The peak of rural sites (and populations) comes in the fourth century BCE (Bintliff 1999: 23), with a fairly dramatic shrinkage from around 200 BCE (Bintliff 1999: 27). However, it is clear that in the Classical period the distribution of different types and sizes of rural sites (e.g., hamlets/large farm, small isolated farmsteads) varies considerably from one part of Boeotian territory to another (Bintliff et al. 2007: 146–47).

The area south of Thespiai has recently been published in more detail (Bintliff et al. 2007). Between the Late Bronze Age and the Late Geometric period there is almost no evidence of rural settlement, and the earliest documented rural activity is Late Geometric (Bintliff et al. 2007: 173). Geometric-Archaic settlement was largely focused on the center of Thespiai. Ten sites in the southern approaches to the city belonging somewhere in this period are mapped (Bintliff et al. 2007: 132, fig. 9.3) (fig. 10-2). Most of these appear to be hamlets with the occasional sanctuary or cemetery site (Bintliff et al 2007: 131–32, 172–73), but the actual ceramic evidence on which this map is based appears very thin when scrutinized in more depth. From the data helpfully published with the report, it is clear that there is almost no certain Geometric pottery and there are very few certain Archaic sherds per site; of the closely datable material most appears to be sixth century BCE (table 10-2). This contrasts dramatically with the very large numbers of Classical–Hellenistic sherds recovered.

For the Classical period, the authors argue for several "bands" of occupation: a zone of cemeteries on the city's edge, then a band of large estates or hamlets, then farthest out an area occupied by a few small scattered farms (fig. 10-3). This pattern seems to begin in the Late Archaic period (sixth century BCE) (Bintliff et al. 2007: 132). The cemetery zone appears to be an agglomeration of small family grave plots, not big civic cemeteries (Bintliff et al. 2007: 134). In the next band, the sites are all relatively large and thus seem most likely to be either the headquarters of large, wealthy estates or hamlets with several farming families occupying them. All these sites have easy access to (and from) the city. They are also close to good agricultural land, which, judging from the very heavy background scatter, was extremely intensively exploited in Classical times. The third, outermost group consists of only two examples in this sector of the Boeotian landscape, but other areas in Boeotia Survey territory show many more of these small rural "farmstead" sites (Bintliff et al. 2007: 135–36).

Keos

The Keos Survey was carried out in the 1980s in northwest Keos, mostly in what would have been the territory of the Classical city of Koressos, though the eastern sector of

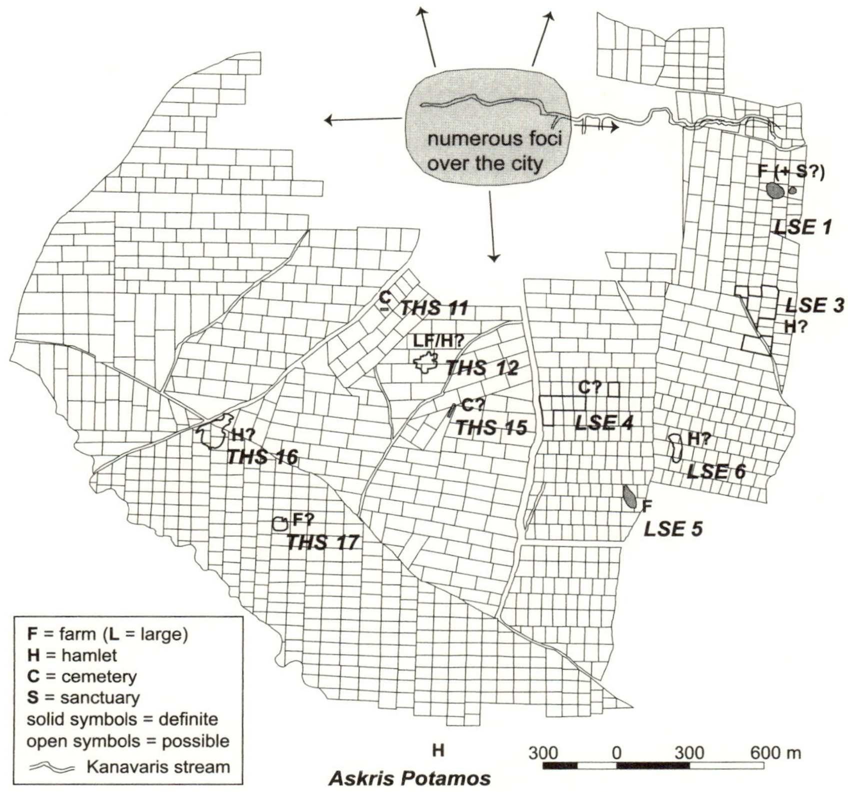

FIGURE 10-2. Thespiai, southern approaches, Geometric-Archaic sites (Bintliff et al. 2007: 132, fig. 9.3). Courtesy of John Bintliff.

the survey area would almost certainly have fallen within the territory of Ioulis. Also included within the survey area was the important prehistoric site of Aghia Irini (Cherry et al. 1991: 5–6). The only significant amount of Protogeometric and Geometric material came from the excavations at Agia Irini where a sanctuary of this period was built over the Bronze Age sanctuary. Few sherds can be dated earlier than the Archaic period (Cherry et al. 1991: 329). Only one single certain Protogeometric (tenth century BCE) sherd was found in the countryside at site 29. All sherds identified as "Geometric" (ninth–eighth century BCE) in the survey, and they are few, are possible but not definite. There is little evidence for any Geometric presence at the polis site of Koressos from either survey or excavation (Cherry et al. 1991: 332) (fig. 10-4).

The Archaic period sees a significant increase in activity both in the countryside and at the polis center of Koressos (fig. 10-5). However, almost all the Archaic pottery discovered is later than the seventh century BCE (Cherry et al. 1991: 330), and the great majority of Archaic sherds that can be identified with certainty date to the sixth century (Cherry et al. 1991: 331, fig. 17.2). It is clear that the overall amount of

TABLE 10-2
Finds from the sites identified as Geometric and Archaic in the southern approaches to Thespiai (derived from data in Bintliff et al. 2007)

Site	Ceramic finds	Comments
THS11	2A in survey	Small cemetery site ca. 200 m from edge of Classical city. 1981 excavation revealed Late Archaic and Late Classical tombs constructed in two separate phases of use (Bintliff et al. 2007: 69–70).
THS12	no certain G or A	"Settlement before the end of the archaic period remains a possibility only" (Bintliff et al. 2007: 73).
THS15	1 possible A, no definite	"Its use may just possibly have begun in Late Archaic times" (Bintliff et al. 2007: 79).
THS16	1 G?-A	"May conceivably have originated before the end of the Archaic period" (Bintliff et al. 2007: 81).
THS17	2 possible A	"'Possibly beginning in the Archaic period" (Bintliff et al. 2007: 83).
LSE1	1 G-A; 1 probable G-A; 1 certain A; 6 probable A; 6 possible A; 1 M/L Corinthian-6th c.; 2 Late A/Early C; 1 6th–5th c.	Interpreted as a sanctuary in this period (Bintliff et al. 2007: 44).
LSE3	1 aryballos mouth c. 600; 2 A; 6 probable A	Hamlet site that was perhaps already large in the Archaic period (Bintliff et al. 2007: 49).
LSE4	8 Late A ca. 500 BC; 2 A; 1 Late A-C; 12 probable A	Interpreted as Classical period burial site (Bintliff et al. 2007: 52).
LSE5	1 A; 1 probable G-A; 7 probable A; 1 probable 6th c.	"Seems likely that main settlement begins during the Archaic period" (Bintliff et al. 2007: 54).
LSE6	2 G-A; 6 A; 2 probable A; 2 possible A	"Occupation of site must begin at this time [G-A and A]" (Bintliff et al. 2007: 55).

deposition of sherd material was greater in the Archaic through Hellenistic period than in the Roman period (Cherry et al. 1991: 329). Indeed, the bulk of sherd deposition appears to belong to the Classical–earlier Hellenistic (down to the third century BCE) phase (Cherry et al. 1991: 330–31). However, the Keos authors explain particularly clearly and straightforwardly just how few sherds can be pinned down in date to a precise time period (see above, Cherry et al. 1991: 328–31). There were fewer certain fifth-century BCE sherds than sixth-century sherds, but the sherd total for the fifth century is much higher if the possible fifth century sherds are included (Cherry et al. 1991: 330–31 and fig. 17.2). There is a significant decrease in the number of diagnostic sherds in the fourth and third centuries BCE (Cherry et al. 1991: 331, fig 17.2), and little diagnostic material postdating the third century was found until Late Roman times (Cherry et al. 1991: 330).

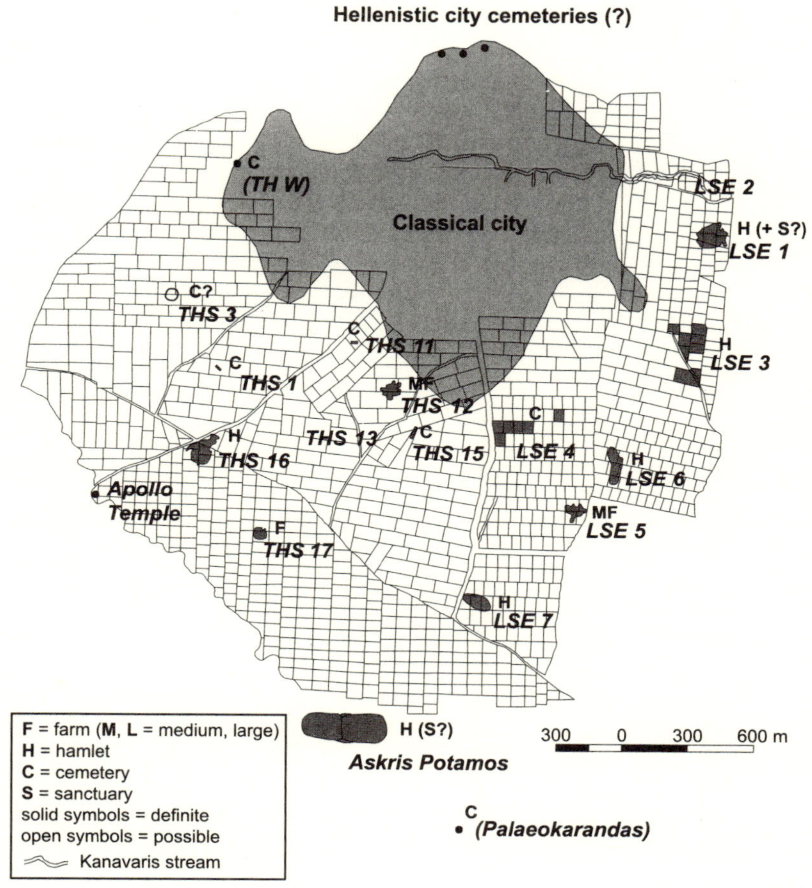

FIGURE 10-3. Thespiai, southern approaches, Classical-Hellenistic sites (Bintliff et al. 2007: 133, fig. 9.4). Courtesy of John Bintliff.

In summary, most of the sites discovered in the countryside appear to have been isolated "farmsteads." They date mostly to the later Archaic (probably mostly sixth century BCE) and Classical periods, and the numbers decline in the Hellenistic period. Such sites do not appear to have been a feature of this part of the Kean countryside before the seventh–sixth century BCE. (Cherry et al. 1991: 336–37).

Southern Argolid

The Southern Argolid Survey was carried out during the 1980s in the southernmost part of the Argolic Peninsula, in the area that would probably have been the rural territory of the Classical cities of Hermion and Halieis, which also included the important prehistoric site of the Franchthi Cave (Jameson et al. 1994: 29–48 and 25, fig. 1.7).

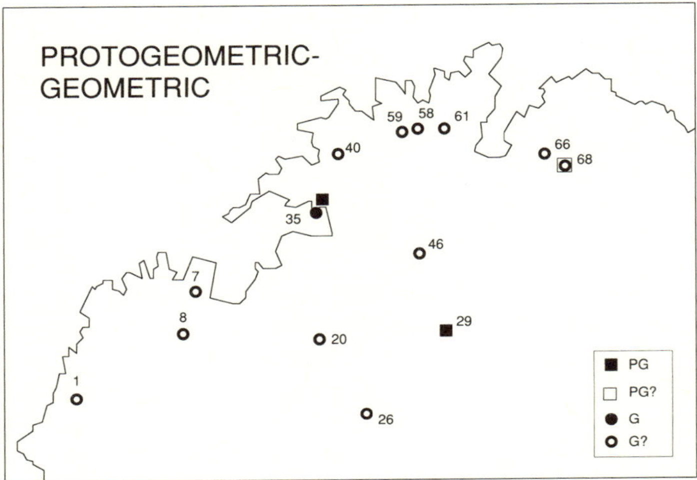

FIGURE 10-4. Keos Survey, Protogeometric-Geometric sites; no. 35 is Aghia Irini (Cherry et al. 1991: 333, fig. 17.5). Courtesy of John Cherry, Jack Davis, and the Cotsen Institute.

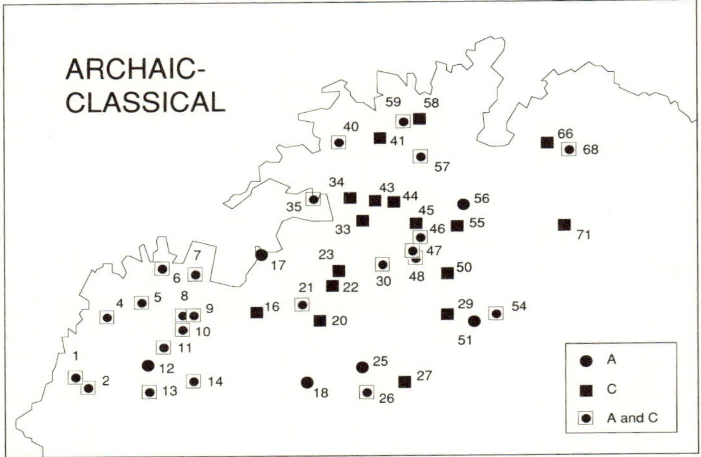

FIGURE 10-5. Keos Survey, Archaic-Classical sites; no. 7 is Koressos, the polis site (Cherry et al. 1991: 334, fig. 17.6). Courtesy of John Cherry, Jack Davis, and the Cotsen Institute.

After a rich Late Helladic record (Jameson et al. 1994: 236, fig. 4.16) very little early Iron Age (1000–700 BCE) material was found. Only one site with a Protogeometric (1000–900 BCE) component was discovered (Jameson et al. 1994: 236, fig. 4.17, 372), and the same site also has an Early Geometric (900–850 BCE) presence, but of uncertain date (Jameson et al. 1994: 237, fig. 4.18). There are three uncertain and three certain Middle Geometric (850–750 BCE) sites (Jameson et al. 1994: 236, fig. 4.19). Up to twenty-two sites have Late Geometric (750–700/675 BCE) pottery, but many are uncertain in terms of date and site size (Jameson et al. 1994: 238, fig. 4.20). The real boom in rural sites appears in the later Archaic (700/675–480 BCE) and Classical periods (480–338 BCE; forty-two sites documented) and even more in the Late Classical/Early Hellenistic period (350–250 BCE; seventy-five sites): the latter period is defined as a discrete phase in the Southern Argolid Survey (Jameson et al. 1994: 238, fig. 4.21; 239, figs. 4.22 and 4.23; 253, table 4.7). Site numbers decline in the later Hellenistic (250–50 BCE) period.

Site locations also change somewhat in different periods. Generally 25%–30% of all sites are located within 500 m of the coast, with the exception of the Geometric and Medieval periods, times when security may have been more of an issue (Jameson et al. 1994: 257 and 245, table. 4.4). During the Geometric period only small sites appear to have existed, and in Late Geometric a couple of medium-size sites (Jameson et al. 1994: 252 and 238, fig. 4.20). The overall settlement pattern for the Protogeometric–Late Geometric/Subgeometric phase is interpreted as nucleated, each area of the landscape having one dominant nucleated site. During the Archaic-Hellenistic period dispersed settlement around urban centers (Jameson et al. 1994: 253–54, table 4.8; 374–83) characterized the countryside. The Late Classical/Early Hellenistic (350–250 BCE) is singled out as the period with the largest number of sites, especially small rural sites (Jameson et al. 1994: 383–85). A preference for fertile valley bottoms for settlement sites appears in Geometric times; but valley slopes and rolling hills in are preferred locations in the Classical through Middle Roman phases (Jameson et al. 1994: 257–58, 373). The settlement and exploitation of thin soils and "marginal" lands began only in the Classical period, not earlier (Jameson et al. 1994: 258).

Methana

The Methana Peninsula is located at the top of the Argolic Peninsula, just to the east and north of Epidauros and Troezen (Mee and Forbes 1997). The Methana Survey was carried out during the 1980s. Protogeometric pottery of the Early Iron Age (1050–700 BCE) appears at the three key settlement sites (fig. 10-6). Two of these are villages: MS69 (Ogha) and its related sanctuary at MS68, and MS60 (Maghoula). The other settlement eventually became the polis center of Methana (MS10). All these settlements are located within easy reach of the sea and good agricultural land (Gill and Foxhall 1997: 57). In this period settlement was clearly nucleated, and land was exploited from villages. During the Archaic period (600–480 BCE) six sites in total were occupied, and the three main sites grew substantially and continued to dominate their respective sectors of the peninsula. Limited exploitation of the Plain of Throni and the interior begin, but only in areas of excellent agricultural land. There is also an increase in the number of rural sanctuaries (Gill and Foxhall 1997: 57–59). The Classical period shows (480–323 BCE) twenty-two certain sites (but a Classical component appears on forty-eight) (fig. 10-7).

The growth of the polis center (MS10) as the main site of the peninsula occurs at this time. There is now also an increase in the number of isolated rural sites, which

a

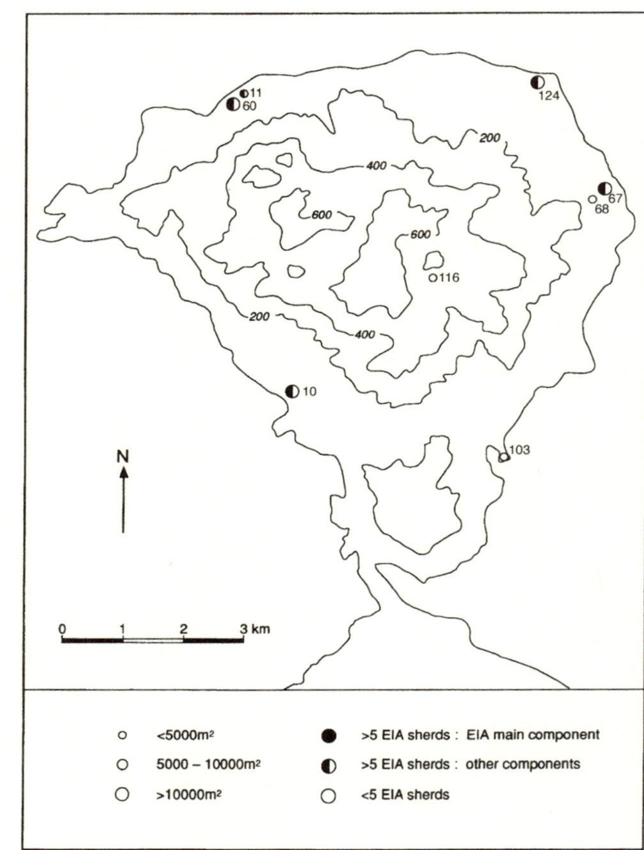

FIGURE 10-6. Methana, Early Iron Age and Archaic sites (Gill and Foxhall 1997: 58, figs. 5.1 and 5.2).

appear to date largely to the last third of fifth century BCE and generally seem to have been very short-lived. For the first time there is substantial exploitation of marginal areas and less good agricultural land. During the fourth century BCE fewer rural sites appear, many in small clusters, and none are located more than 200 m above sea level (Gill, Foxhall, and Bowden 1997: 62–67). There are twenty-eight certain Hellenistic (323–100 BCE) sites, and fifty-four sites have a Hellenistic component. Of these, 40% lack a Classical component, suggesting some reorganization of settlement, perhaps in connection with the role of the peninsula as a Ptolemaic base. Overall, fewer Hellenistic than Classical sherds were identified. Most Hellenistic sites remain within 500 m of the sea, and as in the Classical period, they are concentrated on the western side of peninsula, where the polis site is located. However, there is also a significant concentration of sites at altitudes over 600 m above sea level. The main urban site (MS10)

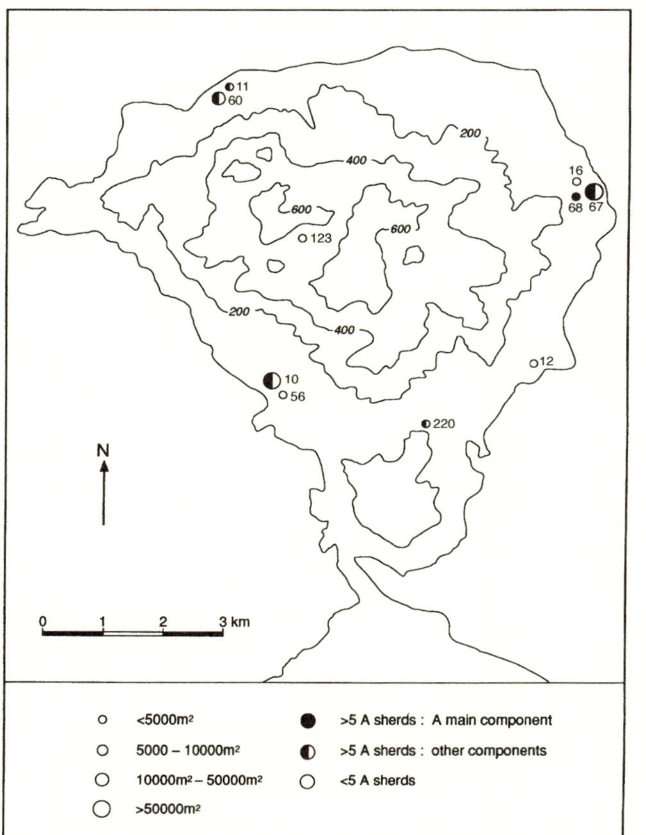

appears to shrink slightly while both village sites (MS67 and MS60) shrink dramatically (Gill, Foxhall, and Bowden 1997: 69–71).

Berbati-Limnes

The Berbati-Limnes Survey was carried out in the Berbati Valley, the fertile plain to the east of Mycenae, and the contrasting upland area around Limnes Village (Wells 1996). Only one possible Protogeometric sherd (tenth century?) was recovered, in addition to two excavated graves, one Early Geometric and the other Middle Geometric, already known from the area. Otherwise nothing was found dating to the period between the twelfth century BCE and the middle of the eighth century BCE (Wells 1996: 177). Geometric and Archaic material appears at twelve find spots; nine of these have material of the eighth century BCE, nine have material of the seventh and sixth

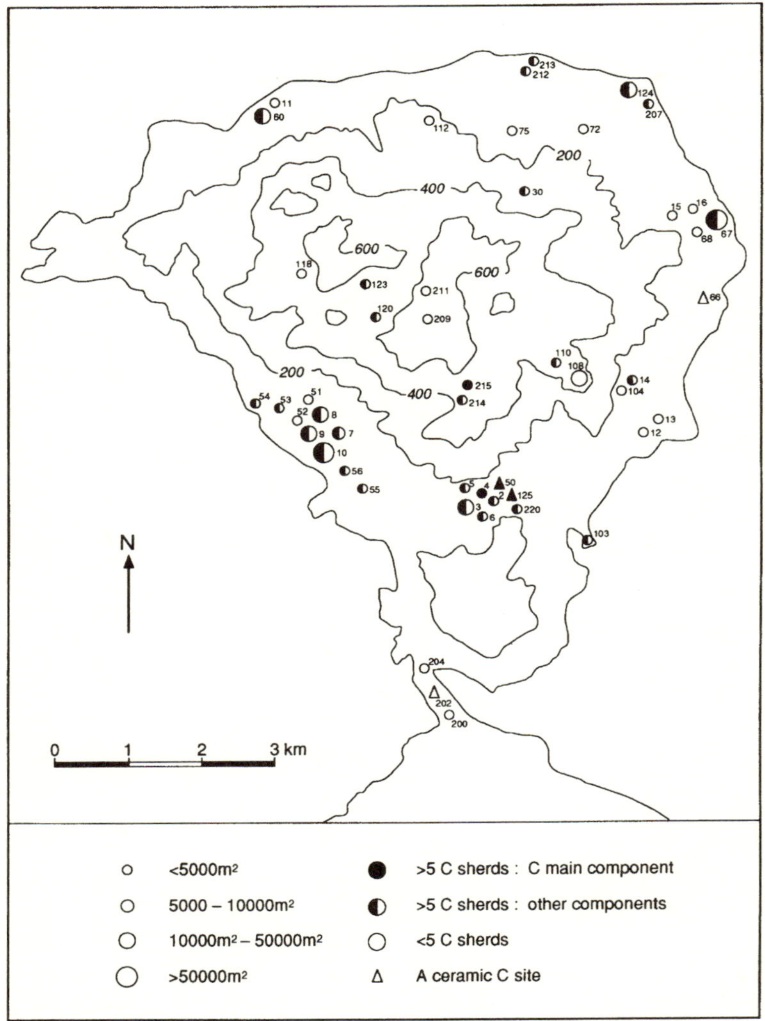

FIGURE 10-7. Methana, Classical sites (Gill, Foxhall, and Bowden 1997: 64, fig. 6.1).

centuries BCE, and four have material from all three centuries (Ekroth 1996: 214–15, figs. 33 and 34) (fig. 10-8). Find spots 20 and 24 form the core of the most important Geometric settlement in the Berbati Valley and contain the only definite Late Geometric I material; other find spots (7, 18) appear to be related to this settlement. In Late Geometric II, occupation spread from find spots 20–24 to two additional locations: the Phytesoumia spur with five find spots, and the area around the hill of Ag. Athenasios. All these areas continued to be inhabited into the seventh and sixth

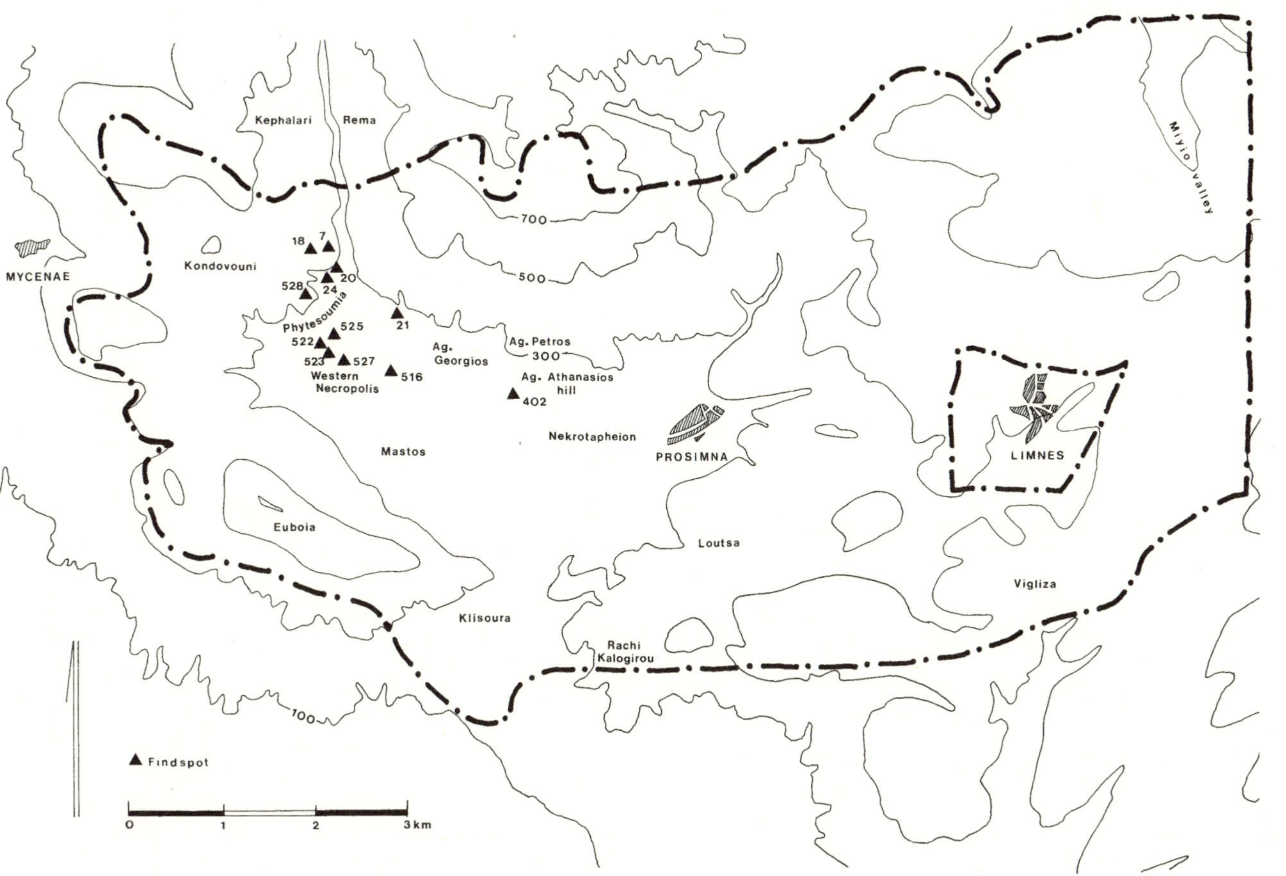

FIGURE 10-8. Berbati-Limnes Survey. Geometric-Archaic find spots (Wells 1996: 214, fig 13). Courtesy of the Swedish Institute at Athens.

centuries BCE. Late sixth- and early fifth-century BCE material is largely missing from the Berbati Valley assemblage, although occasional Late Archaic sherds appear at existing settlements (Ekroth 1996: 213). The mountainous Limnes area remained unoccupied during the Geometric–Archaic period, but there is some thin background sherd scatter, particularly along the ancient road (Ekroth 1996: 215).

Activity during the Classical and Hellenistic periods is documented at thirty find spots in Berbati, with an additional five in the rugged Limnes area (Penttinen 1996: 229) (fig. 10-9). There are thirteen definite fifth-century BCE sites, with some activity documented at another four. Most are located in the north-central part of the valley to the north of the main road between modern Nekrotapheion and the Roman bath. Find spot 426 in the far west of the survey area was occupied, and the slopes to the west of Kephalari remma appear to have been being visited at this time. The peak of settlement activity appears in the late fourth–early third centuries BCE, and a new pattern of settlement seems to emerge at this time. New sites increase the settlement density around Nekrotapheion. Sites on both sides of Kephalari remma at 300 m above sea level now begin to appear. Smaller clusters of sites appear to the west of Mastos, close to modern Panaghia. In the Limnes area the development of settlement is slightly different. Find spot 42 at Vigliza was probably permanently occupied, but find spots 309 and 307 appear on inaccessible mountain slopes. From the second century BCE there is a general decline in the number of sites (Penttinen 1996: 271 and 272, table 1).

Laconia

The area of the Laconia Survey covers the approximate center of the territory of ancient Sparta (Cavanagh et al. 2002: 1). The only evidence of activity during the Early Iron Age (1050–700 BCE) appears at the cult centers of Zeus Messapeus and the Menelaion, and is limited to the very end of the eighth century BCE. Nothing earlier appears in the rural territory (Catling 2002: 153), though there is material from Sparta itself. The Early Archaic period (700–600) remains a blank apart from the same two sanctuaries, and there is no indication of agricultural exploitation of anything except the best agricultural land on the plain (Catling 2002: 156).

The later Archaic and Early Classical period (600–450 BCE) sees a shift from nucleated settlement to widely dispersed small and medium-size rural sites. However, very little of the material recovered is earlier than the mid-sixth century BCE, and much dates from the second half of the sixth century (Catling 2002: 157). At least eighty-seven definite sites appear in this period, and nine new sanctuaries. Some evidence for later Archaic-Classical activity appears on seventy-two further sites (Catling 2002: 160–61). Almost all of these (74%) are small sites, but there is a small group of seventeen larger sites (19%), which could be high-status rural habitations or large farms, and six (19%), appear to be villages, small towns, and in one case a fortress (Catling 2002: 161–63). When the was area settled in the second half of the sixth century BCE, there was a discernible preference for occupation of the most fertile and easily worked soils (Catling 2002: 171–72), and avoidance of upland areas even in this peak period of rural occupation.

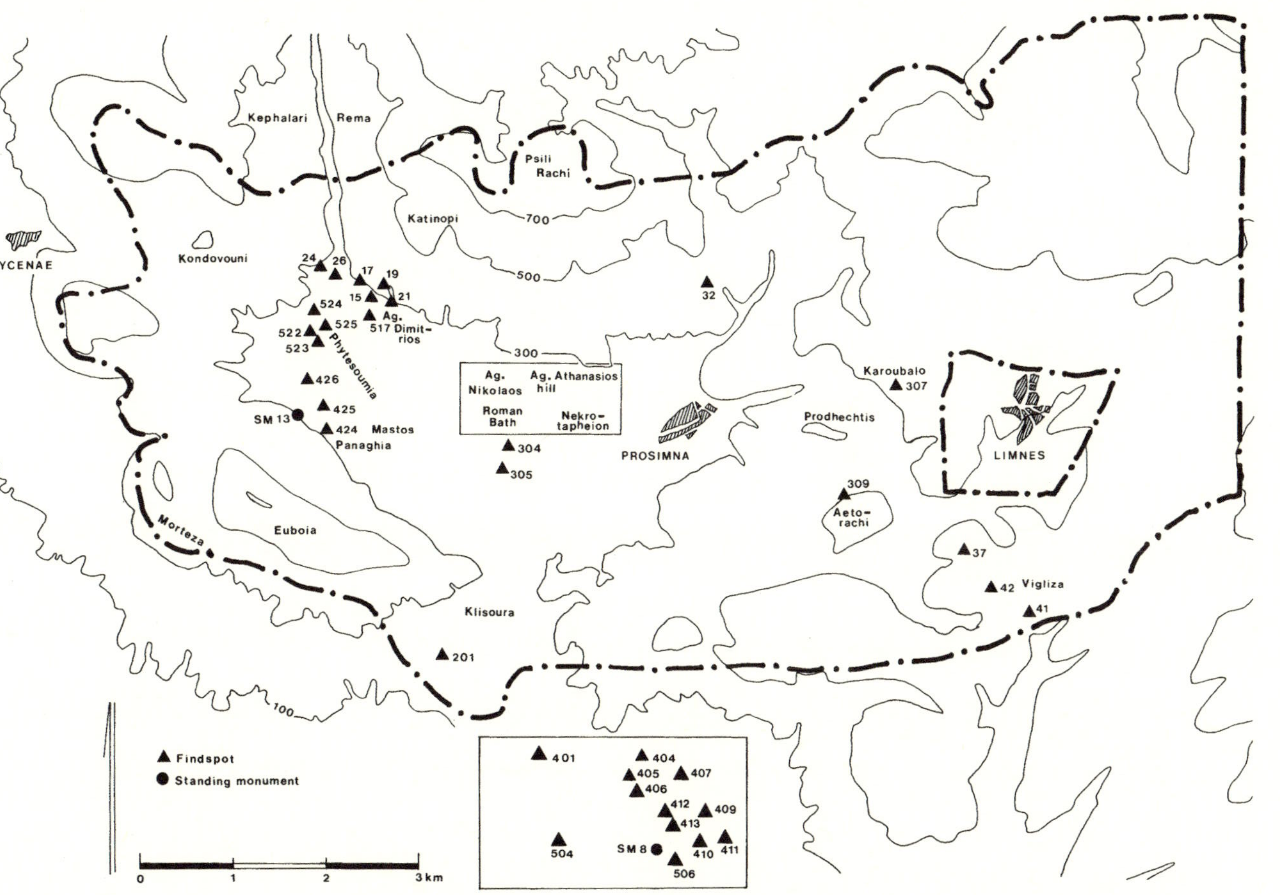

FIGURE 10-9. Berbati-Limnes Survey. Classical-Hellenistic find spots (Wells 1996: 274, fig 37). Courtesy of the Swedish Institute at Athens.

The Classical period (450–300 BCE) sees a sharp reduction in the total number of habitation sites, from about mid-fifth century BCE (Catling 2002: 184, 225). However, there is a concomitant trend toward increased site size, so this perhaps indicates a more nucleated phase. The eighty-seven habitation sites of Late Archaic times go down to forty-six over the Classical period; small farmsteads decline from sixty-four to twenty-seven (74% to 57%). Larger farms decline from seventeen to ten (20% to 23%); and there is a rise in village/hamlet sites from four to seven (5% to 16%), as well as two large sites (Catling 2002: 175–78). Sites continue to concentrate in the areas of the best soils (Catling 2002: 182–84). During the Hellenistic period (third–first centuries BCE) forty-eight definite and twenty-seven probable sites can be identified, although in this area the Hellenistic ceramic repertoire is less diagnostic than for the Archaic–Classical periods (Shipley 2002: 257, 260–61).

Pylos

The Pylos Survey was conceived in part as a "follow-on" from the Minnesota Messenia Expedition Survey (Alcock 2001: 190; Alcock et al. 2005). It was carried out by Jack Davis, Susan Alcock, and others in western Messenia, to the north and east of the Palace of Nestor at Pylos in 1991–95. Substantial reports have been published in *Hesperia* (Davis et al. 1997; Zangger et al. 1997; Alcock et al. 2005), and the project is also well published online at http://classics.uc.edu/prap/, including a full site gazetteer and pottery and small finds databases (though these are unedited and have not been updated since data entry in the field).

Very little material dating to the Submycenaean-Geometric range was discovered, and according to the published pottery report only three sites produced more than three certain sherds in the Geometric-Archaic range (Davis et al. 1997: 452–53). During the Archaic-Classical phase (seventh–fourth centuries BCE) there was a substantial increase in settlement and exploitation. But the investigators note the relative scarcity of Classical material, and the lack of evidence for small, dispersed rural farmsteads, suggesting that this might be a result of the Spartan domination on the region (Davis et al. 1997: 455–56; Alcock 2001: 195, fig. 13.2, 196–98; Alcock et al. 2005: 166–71). Indeed, the Archaic and Classical presence was substantially focused in one sector of the survey area (Area VI), which may well have been a sizable ancient village under the modern village of Romanou (Alcock 2001: 194–95 and fig. 13.3; Alcock et al. 2005: 163), and larger sites seem to have been the norm in this region (Alcock et al. 2005: 166–67). Not entirely surprisingly, the peak of occupation occurred in the Hellenistic period, after the liberation of Messenia (Davis et al. 1997: 456–57; Alcock 2001: 193). As in the case of the Boeotia Survey, it is possible to look directly at the raw ceramic data for activity/occupation in different periods (table 10-3, compiled using the unedited online pottery database, which may not be entirely accurate). It is clear from the sparse pottery finds that there is little evidence for substantial levels of settlement in the region before the seventh–sixth centuries BCE.

Kythera

The recent survey on the island of Kythera undertaken by Cyprian Broodbank and Evangelia Kyriatzi has not yet been fully published. The excellent project website

TABLE 10-3
Finds from the sites in the Pylos Regional Archaeological Project identified as Dark Age through Archaic based on the unedited online pottery database at http://classics.uc.edu/prap/

Site	Ceramic finds	Comments
E01 Romanou Glyfadaki	3 G-A; 15 A	Most material on the site is later Hellenistic and domestic in character.
I01 Koryfasio Beylerby	4 LH3-G; 9 Dark Age; 2 G; 10 G-A	
I04 Romanou Romanou	1 LPG-G; 2 Dark Age; 1 PG-G; 4 G; 9 G-A; 23 A; 2 A?	
M02 Gargliani Kalantina	6 G-A; 1 A?	

(http://www.ucl.ac.uk/kip/survey.php) clearly explains the sampling strategy and methodology, and presents preliminary results of data analysis. The project has discovered over two hundred sites. In the post–Bronze Age phases, Kythera shows a huge rise in site numbers during the Classical period, but only very small numbers of sites were occupied during the Archaic period. There is no evidence for Protogeometric or Geometric period occupation of rural sites (http://www.ucl.ac.uk/kip/sitedates.jpg).

Survey Data and the Development of the Polis Countryside

It is clear from the discussion of the survey data above that there are some common trends in the rural settlement record across Greece. Strikingly, the Iron Age through the Late Geometric period is a low point in the settlement record virtually everywhere in Greece. In many areas there is almost no record of any activity after the Bronze Age until the Late Geometric (c. 750–700 BCE) period, and even at that point the evidence is very thin in most places. Small nucleated settlements appear to be usual, generally located in proximity to the best agricultural land. Excavation evidence confirms this conclusion (e.g., Lathouriza: Lauter 1985, Mazarakis Ainian 1994; Zagora: Cambitoglou et al. 1971, 1988; Oropos: Mazarakis Ainian 1998). Certainly there is no evidence of substantial levels of dispersed rural settlement anywhere in Greece during the eighth century; indeed the Greek countryside appears to have been quite empty at this time. Another common trend is that movement onto "marginal" sloping land, whether for habitation or for agricultural exploitation, is relatively late everywhere, and generally coincides with settlement peaks occurring well after the Archaic period.

Beyond these basic common trends there is a considerable amount of regional variation in the development of different Greek countrysides in their specific polis settings, and even within the territory of any particular polis. These variations between poleis are clearly linked to different trajectories of historical development. The cases of Laconia (where rural settlement peaked early in the late sixth–early fifth centuries BCE), and Pylos (where dispersed rural settlement was largely absent before the

Hellenistic peak) make this particularly clear, intertwined as they both are with the very particular development of Sparta as a polis, and its distinctive mode of domination over the southern and southwestern Peloponnese.

In most (but not all) Greek countrysides, dispersed rural settlement, consisting of a range of different kinds of sites (including graves and small sanctuaries), becomes characteristic at some point between the second half of the sixth and the third centuries BCE, at periods when the urban centers themselves are also densely populated. However, as the Boeotian case of Thespiai shows, it would be simplistic to interpret all of these as small isolated farmsteads belonging to the same sociopolitical group within the polis. It is plain that a range of "farmsteads" at different scales is likely to be represented, and distinguishing a single large "farmstead" from a cluster of smaller "farmsteads" using surface survey techniques alone is often not possible. In addition, the "sites" recovered reveal only the headquarters of a "farm": it is likely in the majority of instances that the landholdings worked by the inhabitants would have included plots not directly adjacent to the structure itself (Osborne 198;, 2001; Foxhall 2001a, 2001b: 213). One of the things most difficult for archaeologists to judge is where the inhabitants of the sites revealed by surveys belong in the socioeconomic spectrum (Osborne 2004: 168–70). It may well be the case that even with the smallest sites we are not picking up the poorest farmers in the archaeological record at all, and that almost all of the "farmsteads" discovered belonged to relatively prosperous proprietors, with sufficient material goods to make an impact on disposal patterns. Slaves are certainly largely invisible, and even Morris and Pappadopoulos (2005) struggle to make a case for their presence on rural sites of the Classical period. On the other hand, wealth and poverty are relative, and some periods are clearly much wealthier overall in terms of the material goods, especially ceramics, that are available to a wide range of people, and which ultimately end up in the landscape.

That the peak of rural settlement varies so much in date from one area to another strongly suggests that dispersed habitation in the countryside may not have had much to do with widespread political changes or innovations in any one period, so establishing its link to a purported "hoplite revolution" across Greece is almost impossible. Rather, expansion (or decline) of dispersed rural settlement and changes in the exploitation of the countryside visible in the archaeological record are likely to be related to specific local factors. It is clear from the examples of Lakonia and Messenia that long-term political configurations may have had significant impact on the shaping of rural landscapes. However, it is probable that in most cases broadly socioeconomic factors and trends were most important (rather than overtly and narrowly political ones)—namely, those factors related most closely to the changing wealth and fortunes of the individual households that exploited the land. The patterns we see on the ground are likely to be the agglomeration of the activities and decisions of many different, individual households. Survey data generally provide no information about land tenure (Foxhall 2001b: 213–14), and a number of different land tenure arrangements could have produced the same archaeological patterns. Given the varied constitutions and political structures of the different poleis represented in the survey data, it may be remarkable that, beyond the differences in date, there is so much similarity in these patterns of dispersed rural settlement when they occur. The underlying causes, of course, need not be the same in every case. However, what this broad similarity might suggest is that the fundamental relationship of households with land held as private property was very deep-seated in Greek culture, documented in texts from as far back as Hesiod's *Works and Days*. In periods when investment in the countryside and pressure on land increased for whatever reasons (e.g., increased wealth, increasing population, additional sources of labor), individual households tried to make the most of the land to which they had access. Sometimes they might have carved out new cultivable lands where they had the means to invest in doing so. However, it is plain from the survey data discussed here that, except in periods when the best lands were densely settled, "marginal" hilly and mountainous lands and areas of poor soils were not intensively exploited or even occupied.

Conclusion

Where does this leave us with hoplites and the origin of the phalanx? For a start, the archaeological evidence strongly suggests that the Hanson hypothesis of an eighth-century move to dispersed agricultural settlement and the exploitation of "marginal" hillslopes and "*eschatiai*" is incorrect. The available archaeological data positively contradict this model. As van Wees (this volume) points out, practically all of the evidence that Hanson uses to support this view is derived from later periods, so that the picture he paints is anachronistic. Farmers in the eighth century appear to have lived in nucleated villages for the most part, using them as a base for cultivating the best agricultural land, generally located relatively close to these settlements. The evidence from archaeological surveys for this period is inadequate to produce even a very crude settlement hierarchy.

It is not until well into the sixth century in most parts of Greece that activity in the countryside becomes visible in any kind of meaningful way. However, even then, the extent of occupation and intensity of use is quite low in most places; Sparta seems to be somewhat exceptional in this regard. If we are looking for "the rise of the small independent farmer" (van Wees, this volume), we may not find him here either. There is no straightforward or easy way of mapping political structures such as the Solonian property classes, known from historical sources, onto the settlement hierarchies derived from archaeological data (although that has not stopped scholars from trying, e.g., Bintliff et al. 2007: 147–51). (And this is assuming that the production units associated with the Solonian property classes are correct—the "500 bushels" of the *pentakosiomedimnoi* is, of course, the only one that is absolutely certain because it is embedded in the name: Foxhall 1997.) Even in periods of intensive exploitation of the countryside from dispersed residential sites, as appears in many regions from the later sixth through third centuries BCE, we do not know for certain that we are seeing "the small independent farmer" on the ground. And this is a period when we know from written and iconographic sources that the citizen-hoplite was unquestionably well established in many places. Archaeologically documented "farmsteads" certainly vary in size and scale of production, and rural settlement is not uniform throughout the countryside. But could we tell whether these "farmsteads" were operated by small independent farmers? The example of the takeover of Thespian land by the Boeotians in the mid-fourth century, cited above, suggests that we cannot necessarily distinguish dependents from owner-occupiers in the archaeological record (Bintliff et al. 2007: 143).

I suggest that we are seeing different things in the archaeological and historical records. The written sources (and even the iconographic sources) primarily show us male individuals, often working together, but portrayed specifically as citizens, soldiers, and property owners. The archaeological data reveal households and their collective activities, not "homesteaders" or proprietors as individuals. The archaeological landscape that we see in the data is the aggregate pattern formed by the decisions and activities of many households. What it does show is a widespread engagement by the inhabitants of a polis with the agricultural landscape as property-*working* units (whether they were always property owners or not is another question) in, broadly speaking, later Archaic and Classical times. This creates an archaeological signature that is quite distinguishable from different ways of working the landscape visible in other periods (e.g., Roman and Late Roman phases; see Foxhall 2004). If this is correct, then it is hardly surprising that we cannot find individuals as "hoplite fighters," or even the origins of the phalanx, in the landscape data.

Bibliography

Alcock, S. 2001. A simple case of exploitation? The helots of Messenia. In P. Cartledge, E. Cohen, and L. Foxhall (eds.), *Money, Labour and Land: Approaches to the Economies of Ancient Greece*, 85–99. London: Routledge.

Alcock, S., A. Berlin, A. Harrison, S. Heath, N. Spencer, and D. Stone. 2005. Pylos Regional Archaeological Project, part VII: Historical Messenia, Geometric through Late Roman. *Hesperia* 74:147–209.

Alcock, S., and J. Cherry. 2004. Introduction. In S. Alcock and J. Cherry (eds.), *Side by Side Survey: Comparative Regional Studies in the Mediterranean World*, 1–9. Oxford: Oxbow.

Binford, L., S. Binford, W. Whallon, and M. Hardin. 1970. Archaeology at Hatchery West. *Memoirs of the Society for American Archaeology* 24:i–vii, 1–91.

Bintliff, J. 1999. Pattern and process in the city landscapes of Boeotia from Geometric to late Roman times. In M. Brunet (ed.), *Territoire des cités grecques*, 15–33. *BCH* suppl. 34. Paris: École française d'Athènes.

Bintliff, J., E. Farinetti, P. Howard, K. Sarri, and K. Sbonias. 2002. Classical farms, hidden prehistoric landscapes and Greek rural survey: A response and an update. *Journal of Mediterranean Archaeology* 15:259–65.

Bintliff, J., P. Howard, and A. Snodgrass. 1999. The hidden landscapes of prehistoric Greece. *Journal of Mediterranean Archaeology* 12:139–68.

Bintliff, J., P. Howard, and A. Snodgrass. 2007. *Testing the Hinterland: The Work of the Boeotia Survey (1989–1991) in the Southern Approaches to the City of Thespiai*. Cambridge: McDonald Institute.

Cambitoglou, A., A. Birchall, J. Coulton, and J. Green. 1988. *Zagora 2: Excavation of a Geometric Town on the Island of Andros*. Athens: Athens Archaeological Society.

Cambitoglou, A., J. Coulton, A. Birmingham, and J. Green. 1971. *Zagora 1*. Sydney: Sydney University Press.

Caraher, W., D. Nakassis, and D. Pettegrew. 2006. Siteless survey and intensive data collection in an artifact-rich environment: Case studies from the Eastern Corinthia, Greece. *Journal of Mediterranean Archaeology* 19:7–43.

Catling, R. 2002. The survey area from the Early Iron Age to the Classical period (c. 1050–c. 300 BC). In W. Cavanagh, J. Crouwel, R. Catling, and G. Shipley (eds.), *The Laconia Survey I: Methodology and Interpretations*, 151–256. London: British School at Athens.

Cherry, J. F., J. L. Davis, and E. Mantzourani. 1991. *Landscape Archaeology as Long-Term History: Northern Keos in the Cycladic Islands*. Los Angeles: University of California Press.

Davis, J. 2004. Are the landscapes of Greek prehistory hidden? In S. Alcock and J. Cherry (eds.), *Side by Side Survey: Comparative Regional Studies in the Mediterranean World*, 22–35. Oxford: Oxbow.

Davis, J., S. Alcock, J. Bennet, Y. Lolos, and C. Shelmerdine. 1997. The Pylos Regional Archaeological Project, part I: Overview and the archaeological survey. *Hesperia* 66: 391–494.

Dunnell, R. 1992. The notion "site." In J. Rossignol and L. Wandsnider (eds.), *Space, Time and Archaeological Landscapes*, 21–41. New York: Plenum Press.

Ekroth, G. 1996. The Late Geometric and Archaic periods. In B. Wells (ed.), *The Berbati-Limnes Archaeological Survey, 1988–1990*, 179–228. Stockholm: Swedish Institute at Athens.

Foxhall, L. 1997. A view from the top: Evaluating the Solonian property classes. In L. Mitchell and P. Rhodes (eds.), *The Development of the Polis in Archaic Greece*, 113–36. London: Routledge.

Foxhall, L. 2000. The running sands of time: Archaeology and short-term timescales. *World Archaeology* 31:484–98.

Foxhall, L. 2001a. Colouring in the countryside. *Journal of Mediterranean Archaeology* 14:216–22.

Foxhall, L. 2001b. Access to resources in classical Greece: The egalitarianism of the polis in practice. In P. Cartledge, E. Cohen, and L. Foxhall (eds.), *Money, Labour and Land: Approaches to the Economies of Ancient Greece*, 209–20. London: Routledge.

Foxhall, L. 2004. Small, rural farmstead sites in ancient Greece: A material cultural analysis. In F. Kolb (ed.), *Chora und Polis: Methoden und Ergebnisse der historische Landeskunde*, 249–70. Munich: Oldenbourg.

Gill, D., and L. Foxhall. 1997. Early Iron Age and Archaic Methana. In C. Mee and H. Forbes (eds.), *A Rough and Rocky Place: The Landscape and Settlement History of the Methana Peninsula, Greece*, 57–61. Liverpool: Liverpool University Press.

Gill, D., L. Foxhall, and H. Bowden. 1997. Classical and Hellenistic Methana. In C. Mee and H. Forbes (eds.). *A Rough and Rocky Place: The Landscape and Settlement History of the Methana Peninsula, Greece*, 62–76. Liverpool: Liverpool University Press.

Gillings, M. 2000. The utility of the GIS approach in the collection, management, storage and analysis of surface survey data. In J. Bintliff, M. Kuna, and N. Venclová (eds.), *The Future of Surface Artefact Survey in Europe*, 105–20. Sheffield: Sheffield Academic Press.

Giuliani, L. 2010. Myth as past? On the temporal aspect of Greek depiction of legend. In L. Foxhall, H.-J.Gehrke, and N. Luraghi (eds.), *Intentional History: Spinning Time in Ancient Greece*, 35–55. Stuttgart: Franz Steiner.

Hanson, V. D. 1999. *The Other Greeks: The Family Farm and the Agrarian Roots of Western Civilization*, 2nd ed. Berkeley and London: University of California Press. Originally published 1995, New York: Free Press.

James, P., C. Mee, and G. Taylor. 1994. Soil erosion and the archaeological landscape of Methana. *Journal of Field Archaeology* 21:395–416.

Jameson, M., C. Runnels, and T. van Andel. 1994. *A Greek Countryside: The Southern Argolid from Prehistory to the Present Day*. Stanford: Stanford University Press.

Laüter, H. 1985. *Lathureza. Beiträge zur Architektur und Siedlungsgeschichte in spätgeometrische Zeit*. AF2. Mainz am Rhein.

Lolos, Y., B. Gourley, and D. Stewart. 2007. The Sikyon Survey Project: A blueprint for urban survey? *Journal of Mediterranean Archaeology* 20:267–96.

MacDonald, W., and G. Rapp. 1972. *The Minnesota Messenia Expedition: Reconstructing a Bronze Age Regional Environment*. Minneapolis: University of Minnesota Press.

Mazarakis Ainian, A. 1994. Lathouriza. Mia agrotiki egkatastasi ton proimon istorikon chronon sti Vari Attikis. In P. Doukellis and L. Mendoni (eds.), *Structures rurales et sociéties antiques. Actes du colloque du Corfu 14–16 mai 1992*, 65–80. Paris: Les Belles Lettres.

Mazarakis Ainian, A. 1998. Oropos in the Early Iron Age. In M. Bats and B. d'Agostino (eds.), *Euboica. L'Eubea e la presenza euboica in Calcidica e in Occidente*, 179–215. Naples: Centre Jean Berard.

Mee, C., and H. Forbes (eds.). 1997. *A Rough and Rocky Place. The Landscape and Settlement History of the Methana Peninsula, Greece*. Liverpool: Liverpool University Press.

Morris, S., and J. Papadopoulos. 2005. Greek towers and slaves: An archaeology of exploitation. *American Journal of Archaeology* 109:155–225.

Mueller, J. 1974. The use of sampling in archaeological survey. *Memoirs of the Society for American Archaeology* 28:i–ix, 1–91.

Osborne, R. 1985. Buildings and residence on the land in Classical and Hellenistic Greece: The contribution of epigraphy. *Annual of the British School at Athens* 80:119–28.

Osborne, R. 2001. Counting the cost. *Journal of Mediterranean Archaeology* 14:212–16.

Osborne, R. 2004. Demography and survey. In S. Alcock and J. Cherry (eds.), *Side by Side Survey: Comparative Regional Studies in the Mediterranean World*, 163–72. Oxford: Oxbow.

Penttinen, A. 1996. The Classical and Hellenistic periods. In B. Wells (ed.), *The Berbati-Limnes Archaeological Survey, 1988–1990*, 229–84. Stockholm: Swedish Institute at Athens.

Pettegrew, D. 2001. Chasing the classical farmstead: Assessing the formation and signature of rural settlement in Greek landscape archaeology. *Journal of Mediterranean Archaeology* 14:189–209.

Renfrew, C., and M. Wagstaff. 1982. *An Island Polity: The Archaeology of Exploitation in Melos*. Cambridge: Cambridge University Press.

Shipley, G. 2002. The survey area in the Hellenistic and Roman periods. In W. Cavanagh, J. Crouwel, R. Catling, and G. Shipley (eds.), *The Laconia Survey I: Methodology and Interpretations*, 257–337. London: British School at Athens.

Sullivan, A., P. Mink, and P. Uphus. 2007. Archaeological survey design, units of observation, and the characterization of regional variability. *American Antiquity* 72:322–33.

Tartaron, T., T. Gregory, D. Pullen, J. Noller, R. Rothaus, J. Rife, L. Tzortzopoulou-Gregory, R. Schon, W. Caraher, D. Pettegrew, and D. Nakassis. 2006. The Eastern Korinthia Archaeological Survey: Integrated methods for a dynamic landscape. *Hesperia* 75:453–523.

Tuplin, C. J. 1986. The fate of Thespiae during the Theban hegemony. *Athenaeum* 64:321–41.

Van Wees, H. 2001. The myth of the middle-class army: Military and social status in ancient Athens. In T. Bekker-Nielsen and L. Hannestad (eds.), *War as a Cultural and Social Force: Essays on Warfare in Antiquity*, 45–71. Copenhagen: Royal Danish Academy of Sciences and Letters.

Van Wees, H. 2005. *Greek Warfare: Myths and Realities*. London: Duckworth.

Van Wees, H. 2007. War and society. In P. Sabin, H. van Wees, and M. Whitby (eds.), *The Cambridge History of Greek and Roman Warfare*, 1:273–99. Cambridge: Cambridge University Press.

Wells, B. (ed.). 1996. *The Berbati-Limnes Archaeological Survey, 1988–1990*. Stockholm: Swedish Institute at Athens.

Zangger, E., M. Timpson, S. Yazvenko, F. Kuhnke, and J. Knauss. 1997. The Pylos Regional Archaeological Project, part II: Landscape evolution and site preservation. *Hesperia* 66:549–642.

CHAPTER 11

Farmers and Hoplites: Models of Historical Development

HANS VAN WEES

Insofar as modern histories of ancient Greece have a grand narrative at all, it is almost always the story of the rise of democracy—too selective and limited even as an account of Athenian history, never mind the history of the Greek world at large. A rare exception is Victor Davis Hanson's *The Other Greeks* (1995), which writes the economic, social, political, and military history of Greece as the story of the rise and fall of the independent "yeoman" or "middling" farmer and his culture of "agrarianism." This is an admirable attempt to construct a more comprehensive model of historical development insofar as it offers an internally coherent explanation for a wide range of fundamental historical developments over a period of more than four centuries. In doing so, and in making social and economic change the primary driver of political and military change, rather than the other way round, Hanson points the way to just the sort of master narrative that Greek history needs.

But although *The Other Greeks* provides an account of the right kind, it seems to me that its story is in important respects wrong. I shall argue that something much like the rise of the small independent "middling" farmer posited by Hanson did occur, but only around 550/500 BC, two centuries later than he suggests, and only in some parts of Greece. The period 750–550/500, which for Hanson marks the rise and dominance of a class of small farmers and their characteristic military and political systems, was an era in fact dominated by gentlemen farmers, leisured landowners.[1] They established the first republics, which were oligarchic in nature, and the first heavy infantry militias, which were small and irregular. The period 550–300 BC, which for Hanson marks the slow demise of the small independent working farmer, in fact saw first the rise and then the decline of this social and economic class, along with political and military changes. But even when and where working farmers did become a significant force, they rarely dominated politics or warfare. Leisured landowners usually retained political power and continued to claim dominance in war, while in cities that developed more democratic forms of government working farmers were only one element among a coalition of forces opposing the landed elite.

The Republic of Yeomen: Hanson's Model

Center stage in *The Other Greeks* stands the "yeoman" or "family farmer," variously described as a "small" or "middling" landowner. One of the virtues of Hanson's account is that these terms, which other scholars tend to use quite vaguely, are precisely defined:

- The yeoman farmer owned about 10 acres (4 ha) of land, which was enough for him and his family to earn an independent livelihood.[2]
- A yeoman farmer's labor force consisted of his family and "one or two" slaves.[3]
- Yeomen farmers constituted nearly half, and no less than a third, of the population of most archaic and classical Greek cities.[4]

These small family farmers typically lived on the land, outside the city walls, and rarely went into town—"mostly just to vote and go home, disgusted at the noise, the squalor, and the endless race for pelf and power."[5] They emerged as a class circa 750–700 BC and became the dominant political and military force in Greek cities until 500/490 at least.[6]

The rise of the yeoman farmer, Hanson argues, was the result of an economic transformation set off by population growth in the late eighth century: a predominantly pastoral economy was replaced by a regime dominated by the cultivation of cereals, olives, and vines. In the process, many families carved out a new, independent living for themselves, in particular by occupying small plots of uncultivated land on the margins of the territory and making these new farms viable by means of intensive cultivation. Apart from the families who benefited from such "internal colonisation," there were also those who took part in external colonization, establishing themselves in new settlements abroad, and those who leased land from their richer neighbors.[7]

Their new prosperity and independence enabled yeomen farmers to acquire for themselves better arms and armor, specifically a large round shield and a bronze panoply of armor, which turned them into heavy infantry, and enabled them to fight hand-to-hand in a distinctive close-order formation: thus the hoplite phalanx emerged. This new military force was so successful that it drove other kinds of troops (horsemen, light-armed) out of business and reshaped warfare to fit its own interests, developing a set of "agonal" conventions that were closely tailored to the needs of a militia of small farmers.[8] At the same time, yeoman farmer-soldiers started to assert themselves in politics, and managed to impose their egalitarian ideals on the whole community, creating republics governed by "broad-based timocracies" in which all adult men of yeoman status, and the small elite above them, shared equal rights. This political transformation was usually a peaceful process, though in a few cases where change did not come quickly enough yeoman farmer-soldiers supported a coup d'état by a "tyrant" to expedite the process.[9]

From about 500 BC onward, and especially after the Persian Wars of 480–479, Greek cities faced new military demands that traditional yeoman militias could no longer meet: first the threat of Persian invasion itself, and then the endless wars for hegemony among the Greeks that followed, required the use of navies, cavalry forces, and various types of light-armed as well as hoplites, and often required full-time soldiers rather than farmer-militias. The military role of the yeoman-hoplite shrank. Further economic developments—the development of trade, craft production, and other nonagricultural sources of income—meant that other social groups gained political influence and rights, and the yeomen lost their dominance here, too. Finally, a trend toward concentration of landownership in the hands of a few threatened the very existence of small independent farmers. After 300 BC, the yeoman farmer-soldier was no longer a significant force.[10]

For all the merits of this account, at least one problem stands out immediately: among the Greek states that do not fit the model are Sparta and the cities of Crete, which is particularly troubling since the Spartans were the soldier-citizen ideal incarnate, while Crete provides us with the earliest evidence for the emergence of republican institutions. Yet in neither case were the soldier-citizens also yeomen. Instead, they were landowners who prided themselves on not tilling the soil but having serfs labor for them. Hanson does acknowledge these anomalies, calling them "strange," "a bizarre mutation," and even "outside the culture of the Greek polis," but offers no explanation.[11] The greatest problem with the model of *The Other Greeks*, however, is that all the evidence in support of it dates from the classical period, as we shall see. In archaic sources before the late sixth century, by contrast, there is nothing to indicate the rise of the yeoman farmer as an economic, military, or political force, and much to indicate the contrary.

Archaic Landowners and Cultivators: The Evidence

There is no doubt that small family farmers with ten-acre plots were a significant group in late classical Greece: ownership of a farm of this size was a threshold for citizenship in the fourth-century Crimea and Thessaly, as well as in Athens after the abolition of full democracy in 322 BC. It seems very likely that this was the minimum property level at which one could afford to serve as a hoplite in the militia.[12] The question is, however, whether there is any evidence for the existence of a significant social and economic class of this type of farmer in the early archaic period.

Homer's *Odyssey*

The first yeoman farm in the Greek literary record, as Hanson reads it, is the estate of Laertes described at the end of Homer's *Odyssey*. Here, old Laertes works with his own hands, cultivating vines, olives, and fruit trees on a plot that he himself has carved out on marginal land.[13] Hanson is well aware, of course, that Laertes is the father of Odysseus and a former ruler of Ithaca and so hardly an ordinary yeoman, but he argues that Homer nevertheless portrays the farm as small (1995, 48, 87), cultivated by a resident owner (51, 65) with the help of only "a few slaves" who are "close, intimate, fellow manual labourers" rather than deemed far below their owner (66; cf.

48), and he concludes that Laertes serves as "a representation of an entire class of new farmers" (49).

This is not a tenable interpretation of the evidence. First of all, the labor force on the farm does not consist of "a few" slaves, but of two large groups. Inside the farmhouse itself live Dolios, a slave who joined Laertes' household as part of his daughter-in-law's dowry and now "keeps" the farm (4.735–37), "an old Sicilian woman," evidently a bought slave (1.190–93, 24.211, 366), and their six sons (24.387–89, 497). Yet another son of this couple works as a goatherd (17.212–13), while a daughter is employed as a maidservant in town (18.321–23). Separate from this slave family (24.222–23) are an unspecified number of "coerced slaves" (*dmoes anankaioi*), who are numerous enough to be housed in a "shelter [*klision*] which ran all round the house" (24.208–10). The situation seems clear: Dolios' long service has been rewarded with "a house, a plot of land and a much-courted wife, the kind of thing which a well-disposed master will give to a slave who has worked hard for him" (14.62–65). The property is his master's, not his own, but he has the privilege of living in the house and having his own family, while ordinary slaves stay single and sleep in barracks. Since eight slaves live in the house, at least as many must surely live in the large outdoor "shelter," and we must infer the presence of a labor force of at least fifteen to twenty men.

Relatively egalitarian relations may exist between the privileged slave family and their master, but ordinary "coerced" slaves are excluded from the story: they do not get to greet their master on his return, let alone support him against his enemies, as Dolios and his sons do. And although Dolios' family share a meal with their owners, distinctions are observed: the slaves sit on low stools while Laertes and his family sit on chairs.[14]

Finally, the presence of the owner on this farm, and his active participation in manual labor, are due to exceptional circumstances. We are told that "Laertes himself acquired [the farm] once upon a time after he took very great trouble over it," and that he took his son Odysseus to visit when the latter was still a small child (*Od.* 24.205–12, 336–44). Homer must surely have imagined that Laertes was at the time still living in his house in town and taking an active part in public life, since he was, after all, "ruler over the Kephallenians" (24.378). The implication is that originally Laertes had left the running of this remote farm to Dolios and his wife, as a slave bailiff in charge of a slave workforce. Only in old age, in mourning for his missing son, did Laertes retire to this farm and express his grief by dressing and behaving like a poor farmer.[15] Even then he did not mingle with the rest of the workforce, but planted vines near the house while the rest went off farther afield performing heavy labor, gathering stones to build a wall (24.222–25).

In short, Laertes' farm is a large estate, cultivated by a large number of slaves, which under normal circumstances would be run by a slave manager on behalf of an absentee owner who lived in town and played only a supervisory role in its cultivation. We hear of only one other farm on Ithaca, which is again on marginal land, and this is owned by the second-richest family on Ithaca, who employ hired labor. Also to be found in the more remote parts of Ithacan territory are twelve herds of goats and a troop of about one thousand pigs, owned by Laertes' family, all managed by slaves.[16]

So far as one can tell from Homer, then, marginal land and indeed the countryside at large is occupied, not by small independent farmers, but by the estates, herds, slaves, and hired laborers of the very rich.

Hesiod's *Works and Days*

Hesiod at first sight seems to offer much more support for the idea that the yeoman farmer was a rising force around 700 BC, the probable date of his *Works and Days*. This poem exhorts the farmer to work hard so as to avoid "hunger," "debt," and "poverty," which sounds like—and has generally been taken as—advice addressed to farmers struggling to make a living and maintain their independence by the labor of their own hands. Hanson accordingly interprets Hesiod as representing the "small agriculturalist" (1995, 97), though he allows this "middling" yeoman a somewhat larger farm and labor force than normal: up to 15 acres (6 ha) rather than 10, and "two or more male slaves" plus a hired female servant, rather than one or two (107).

This higher number of slaves means that the dependent labor force on such a farm would be about as large as the labor force provided by the family itself, and the question arises whether one can still reasonably call this a "family" farm. By the standards of modern agribusiness, it is of course a tiny enterprise, but by the standards of the ancient Mediterranean world there would have been a significant gap in social and economic status between a family farm in the proper sense—cultivated by the labor of the family alone, except for short-term additional labor in peak seasons—and a farm with a permanent workforce of at least three servants. The question becomes all the more acute because Hanson in fact underestimates the size of Hesiod's farm and its labor force.

Hesiod's advice assumes the presence of at least four slaves, and at least two full-time hired laborers. A man starting up a farm needs "first of all a house and a woman and a plough ox—a woman bought, not married, who could also follow the cattle" (*W&D* 405–6). It has been plausibly argued that this is an adaptation of a proverbial line "a house and a woman and a plough ox" in which the woman is understood as the farmer's wife. If so, it is all the more striking that the poet decided to turn the proverb into advice to the farmer to buy a slave housekeeper even before he marries, and to employ this slave woman also in agricultural work, if necessary, to help out in plowing or in taking cattle to pasture.[17] Normally, the sowing and plowing will be done neither by the housekeeper nor by the farmer himself but by two other men, ideally forty-year-olds, who are regarded as the most reliable workers (*W&D* 441–47): they, too, are slaves (459). A third slave follows behind the plowman and sower to cover over the seeds with a mattock (469–71).

These are all the slaves individually identified, but there may be more: Hesiod always speaks of "slaves" in the plural, and if we take literally the implication that the farmer has a range of slaves of various ages from among whom he can pick his plowman and sower, and that younger slaves waste too much time "gawping after their peers," that is, yet more slaves (444, 447), we must infer quite a large staff. So four slaves, three male and one female, are the *minimum* servile workforce assumed by Hesiod.[18]

In addition, he recommends hiring male and female laborers at the end of the agricultural year: "when you have stored all supplies indoors, I urge you to appoint a hired man without a household [*theta t' aoikon poieisthai*] and seek a maidservant [*erithos*] without a child."[19] The timing makes sense only if they are hired for the duration of the next agricultural cycle, that is, on a full-time rather than seasonal contract. The purpose of hiring a mere two full-time laborers to complement a slave force of at least four is not obvious, and the point of the advice is probably not that one should hire one man and one woman but that, however many men and women one hires, they should have no landholdings or children to distract them from complete commitment to their paid work. In short, Hesiod's total full-time workforce, not counting family members, is at least six—four male agricultural laborers and two female domestic servants—and may be larger.

This is clearly no longer a "family farm" in any meaningful sense. To employ and feed so many, a 10- or 15-acre farm will not suffice. A family of four, plus six laborers, requires at the very least 20 acres (8 ha).[20] Another sign that Hesiod is not imagining a small farm is his assumption that land will be left fallow (*W&D* 462–64), presumably on a biennial rotation, as was normal Greek practice: leaving half the land uncultivated is something only a well-off farmer could afford to do.[21] Hesiod also assumes that the farmer owns a seaworthy ship, big enough to transport a substantial part of his harvest,[22] and that he keeps a range of livestock. The livestock are easily overlooked because Hesiod's account of the agricultural year features almost no animals, but the closing section on auspicious days includes good days for shearing sheep (775), building sheep pens (787), gelding goats, rams, boars, bulls, and mules (786, 790–91), taming sheep, oxen, dogs, and mules (795–97), and putting a yoke on oxen, mules, and horses (815–16). A man would yoke horses only if he owned a chariot, the Greek world's supreme symbol of wealth.

Given these indications of wealth, it is not surprising to find Hesiod's farmer playing a supervisory role. "You must show an inclination to *arrange* [*kosmein*] work in due measure," he is told (*W&D* 306–7, emphasis added). His job is to "tell the slaves in summer to build their winter shelters" (502–3), and in the harvest season, the busiest time of the year, he must "wake up the slaves; avoid shady benches and sleeping until dawn" (573–77). If these exhortations do not exclude the farmer working alongside his slaves, the arrangements for the summer do: the master sits in the shade, drinking imported wine, eating milk bread, beef, and lamb, while he "tells the slaves" to thresh and store the grain.[23]

Even more telling are the opening lines of the almanac of auspicious days: "You must announce to your slaves the days given by Zeus, observing them duly; the thirtieth of the month is the best to supervise work [*erga epopteuein*] and to distribute rations, when people judge truly in celebrating it" (765–67). The rest of the days then follow in more or less chronological order, starting with the first. The poet here evidently envisages a situation in which the farmer visits his land only once a month, to deliver provisions for his slaves and issue instructions about what work is to be done on which days. Even if the last day of the month was merely the "best," not the only, day on which to visit the farm, the fact remains that advice about good moments for supervision only makes sense for a farmer who is not permanently present on the farm.

Passages that urge the farmer to work hard must be seen in this light. Hesiod may say that "your slaves and you yourself alike" (*W&D* 459) should plow, and that the farmer should pray to Zeus "when you put your hand on the end of the plough-handle and apply the goad to the backs of the oxen" (465–69), but the verses that immediately precede and follow explicitly describe a team of three slaves doing all the work. There is nothing left to do for the farmer himself, except supervise and lend a hand occasionally. When Hesiod tells the farmer what to do "after you have stored all your food supplies inside the house," it is clear the storage of this grain in jars has been the work of slaves, and slaves alone; the farmer's role is to organize the storage (597–601). Even the most emphatic exhortations to "toil at toil after toil," to sow, plough and harvest "naked" (458–63), must therefore surely be taken as rhetorical: "toil" here means active, hands-on management of the farm, not physical labor—just as in Xenophon's picture of a large classical estate, the landowner's "toil" consists of walking, running, and riding from town house to farm and back again after supervising the slave workforce for a while.[24]

Hesiod's apparent worries about poverty, debt, and hunger thus take on a different complexion. The need to avoid "poverty" (*penia*) and have a "sufficient" (*arkios*) livelihood is frequently stressed, and modern readers tend to assume that "sufficient" means "enough to survive" while "poverty" means falling below subsistence level. But the classical Greek definition of "poverty" was "having to work for a living," as opposed to living off the labor of others, and there is no reason to think that Hesiod used the word differently.[25] To escape "poverty" and acquire a "sufficient" livelihood, then, was to have a farm large enough to support a workforce of slaves and hired workers as well as a family of leisured owners. As for hunger and debt,[26] I would argue that Hesiod's farmers are too well-off to be seriously at risk, and that the poet evokes the worst-case scenario as the ultimate justification for his ethical advice, to which we shall return in a moment.

It should in any case be noted that warnings of poverty, debt, and hunger are only part of the picture, and are balanced by equally many references to farmers aiming for wealth, and the "excellence" and "glory" that comes with it. Hanson himself rightly makes the point, missed by many other scholars, that Hesiod's farmer is unlike small farmers and peasants in so many other cultures, whose ambitions stop at subsistence and a fair share of what they regard as strictly limited resources. In Hesiod, the farmer aims for "untold prosperity" (376–80). He may trade his produce overseas to maximize his income ("the larger the cargo, the larger will be the profit upon profit," 643–45), and use this to increase his landholdings ("you may buy the estate of other men," 335–41) or his herds.[27] Hesiod's famous opening analysis of the nature of "competition" (*eris*) stresses that to strive to become richer than one's neighbor is a good thing, so long as the competition relies on productive work and does not spill over into deceit, perjury, and violence (11–26).

Indeed, the whole of the *Works and Days* is an extended exhortation to engage in "good" and steer clear of "bad" competition. For Hesiod, the crucial problem in contemporary society is that wealthy landowners adopt a leisured lifestyle and spend little time managing their estates, frittering away their property, while competing for greater wealth by illegitimate means—fraudulent litigation, theft, and force. His remedy is to tell these landowners that there is only one way to get rich legitimately and with lasting success: close and constant supervision of farmwork with a view to getting the most out of one's land and laborers. It is precisely because the poem is addressed to wealthy farmers who can in principle afford to leave the cultivation of their land to their slaves and hired men that Hesiod finds it necessary to stress the benefits of "toil," which hardly needed to be rehearsed at length for poorer farmers. Hesiod justifies his advice on religious grounds by telling stories about Prometheus and Pandora, and the five races of mankind (42–201), both of which serve to show that it is the gods' will that all men, not just the poor, should toil for a living, and that even the rich should not simply live off the labor of others:

> Gods and men are filled with indignation at one who would live without working, his disposition like that of stingless drones who devour what the bees have toiled for, eating without working. . . . Whatever your fortune [*daimon*], it is better to work (*W&D* 303–7, 314).

Hesiod's conjuring up of the specter of hunger and debt serves a similar purpose: it adds an economic justification for his moral advice. In practice, for the wealthy farmers whom he addresses, the threat of hunger may have been no more acute than the danger that the gods' "indignation" would somehow actually put an end to their dronelike existence, but the vulnerability of agriculture to natural disaster means that no farmer is completely safe from hunger and debt. This allowed Hesiod to remind them of the worst that could happen and to argue that the best way to prevent this was dedication to farm management.[28]

So the *Works and Days*, like the *Odyssey*, reveals the existence only of gentlemen farmers, employing slaves and hired laborers, and competing for wealth by fair means and foul. Within this group, there is a distinct ruling elite, the "lords" (*basileis*), who according to Hesiod's *Theogony* owe their status to their special eloquence and ability to settle disputes within the community. In *Works and Days*, however, these lords are sharply addressed as among the worst offenders in getting rich through deceit and violence.[29]

Solon's *Zeugitai*

The laws and poems of Solon, and above all the system of property classes that he instituted or adapted in 594 BC as the basis of Athens' political organization, constitute the most important archaic evidence for the distribution of landownership and its relation to politics and warfare. For Hanson, the third of Solon's property classes, the *zeugitai*, represents the "yeoman" family farmer and hoplite, given new political rights under Solon's reforms.[30] Since the *zeugitai* rank below the evidently wealthy "horsemen" (*hippeis*) and five-hundred-bushel-men (*pentakosiomedminoi*), but above the evidently poor "hired men" (*thetes*), it seems at first glance fair enough to assume that they are a "middling" group of small farmers. This assumption, however, is incorrect, as Lin Foxhall demonstrated in a paper published a couple of years after *The*

Other Greeks. She pointed out that the actual property qualification associated with the *zeugitai*, an annual harvest of at least "200 measures," shows them to be very much wealthier than yeomen farmers.[31]

There are several ways of calculating the economic level implied by an income of "200 measures" of agricultural produce. A simple indication is how many people it could feed. A standard daily ration for an adult male was one *choinix* of barley or wheat and one *kotyle* of wine; 365 *choinikes* amounted to 7.6 measures (*medimnoi*) of grain, and 365 *kotylai* to 2.5 measures (*metretai*) of wine.[32] One person therefore needed about 10 measures of grain and wine—which together formed the bulk of his diet—a year, and the minimum harvest of a *zeugites* could in principle sustain twenty adult men, though in practice we need to deduct up to a quarter of the grain harvest as seed corn for next year, and the actual number of men who could live off this income is about fifteen. Allowing for a small amount of other food and other expenses, this must still be approximately three times as much as the subsistence minimum for a family of four.

Alternatively, one can estimate what the sale value of such quantities of produce was. Although the evidence for prices is limited, the average price of barley in the late fifth and fourth century BC was 3 or 4 drachmas per *medimnos*, wheat 5 or 6 drachmas per *medimnos*, and wine probably 12 drachmas per *metretes*. After deducting seed corn, therefore, a *zeugites* might in principle sell 150 measures of barley or wheat for 450–600 dr or 750–900 dr, respectively, and his 200 measures of wine could be worth 2,400 dr. Yet at the time the minimum annual cost of feeding a family was a mere 3 obols a day, or about 180 dr a year. Even a crop of 200 measures of nothing but barley, the cheapest staple, was therefore worth at least two-and-a-half times as much as a family needed.[33]

Extrapolating the size of the farm from the size of the harvest is somewhat more speculative, but it can be done with a fair degree of precision by using comparative evidence for grain harvests in early twentieth-century Attica. A *medimnos* of barley or wheat weighed 27.5 and 33 kilograms, respectively; a *metretes* of wine or oil contained 38.88 liters.[34] A harvest of 200 measures of barley, Attica's main crop, thus amounted to 5,500 kg, and since modern records suggest that a yield of 800 kg per hectare was the maximum that could have been achieved in ancient Attica, this requires a minimum of 6.9 hectares, or 17.25 acres, under cultivation. We must double that amount to allow for biennial fallow, so that the minimum size of the *zeugites*' farm was 13.8 ha or 34.5 acres.

For wheat, a rather greater weight, 6,600 kg, and a lower maximum yield, 630 kg/ha, mean that we require a minimum 10.5 ha or 26.25 acres of cultivated land, plus fallow, that is, a minimum farm size of 21 ha or 52.5 acres.[35] For olive oil, the result is similar: to produce 7,775 liters at a maximum yield of 360 liters per hectare, the farmer needed 21.6 ha or 54 acres. Only wine could have been produced in sufficient quantities on the 10-acre farm envisaged by Hanson: 7,775 liters at a maximum yield of 2,500 liters per ha would have required only 3.1 ha or 7.8 acres.[36] But wine could never have been the major crop of Attica, since it formed a relatively small part of the diet, and there is no sign that Athens ever exported wine in any quantity. The main agricultural export was olive oil—already exempted from export restrictions by a law of Solon's—which required the most land of all.[37] Again, we must conclude that the farm of a *zeugites* was at least three times as large as the subsistence minimum of 10 acres.

Finally, we can calculate the approximate monetary value of these farms on the basis that the minimum price of agricultural land in the late fourth century BC was 50 drachmas per *plethron* and that one acre is 4.4 *plethra*.[38] Ten acres of land were thus worth at least 2,200 drachmas; 30 acres, the *zeugites*' minimum, cost at least 6,600. Even a modest house and furnishings, a few slaves, and some livestock would bring the total value of such a property quite easily up to 8,000 drachmas. By implication, the next-highest property class, the *hippeis*, who produced 300 measures, must have owned properties worth at least 12,000 dr (2 talents), and the highest class, the *pentakosiomedimnoi*, producing 500 measures or more, had estates worth 20,000 dr (3.3 tal.) or more. To put this in perspective, in the late fourth century the estimated level of wealth of the so-called liturgical class, the top 5 percent of rich Athenian families, was 3 talents or more, which coincides with Solon's highest property class. A citizen property census of 2,000 drachmas, very close to the 10-acre minimum, was set after the abolition of democracy in 322 BC and in all probability represented the smallest viable family farm for a yeoman citizen-soldier. *Zeugitai*, then, were three times as rich as these yeomen, and not much less than half as rich as the wealthiest-class men in Athens. Significantly, they owned properties just above 1 talent (6,000 dr), which is the estimated level above which one was rich enough to belong to the leisure class, exempt from the need to work for a living.[39]

The last calculations allow us to form some idea of the absolute and relative numbers of families belonging to each property class. In 322 BC, only 9,000 households owned properties worth 2,000 dr or more, and among them approximately 1,200 households fell in the liturgical class with estimated minimum properties of 18,000 dr. If the remaining 7,800 families were equally distributed over the property range from 2,000 to 18,000 dr, the minimum census for *zeugitai*, which we estimated at 8,000 dr, would have been met by about 6,000 families. In practice, such a perfectly equal distribution is unlikely, and more properties will have fallen at the lower end of the range, so that we may reckon with about 5,000 families in the top three property classes, or only just over half of all families at yeoman level or above. The total citizen population of Athens in 322 BC was about 30,000, so the richest 5,000 constituted about 17 percent of citizens.[40] And this was when public pay for jury and military service, and later also for attending assemblies and festivals, had done much to ensure a relatively even distribution of wealth. Under Solon, the proportion of citizens in the top three property classes must, if anything, have been smaller, and is unlikely to have been higher than 15 percent.

In short, Solon's *zeugitai* belong to the same group as the farmers in Homer and Hesiod: landowners who can afford to live off the labor of their workers and whose role on the farm is essentially supervisory. It was this class of gentlemen farmers, not yeomen, who received new political rights under Solon. His property class system was designed to break up attempts to monopolize power by an even narrower elite within the class of leisured landowners, the Eupatridae, whose name implies that they claimed hereditary privileges: Solon ensured that the entire leisure class—that is, all those rich enough to be able to hold office without pay—had access to at least the lower ranks of political office.[41]

Solon's *Thetes*

Homer and Hesiod tell us about gentlemen farmers and their slaves without revealing social and economic conditions at other levels of society, so although they do not mention the yeoman farmer, they do not positively exclude the possibility that he existed. Solon's property classes and the fragments of his laws and poetry, by contrast, do paint a picture of the condition of the nonleisured classes—and the yeoman has no place in it.

In Solon's scheme, the property class below the *zeugitai,* which embraces at least 85 percent of the population, is called *thetes*, "hired laborers." They are, in other words, people who do not have enough land to make an independent living and therefore need to hire themselves out as laborers to those who have land in abundance. Between these free laborers and the leisured elite no other group—no body of yeomen family farmers—is given a recognized status. If a sizable group of yeomen did exist, they were ignored, insultingly lumped together with the poorest, and granted no political role beyond attending assemblies, a privilege shared by all adult males. Alternatively, landownership may have been so uneven and polarized that there really were virtually no small independent farmers at all, just a yawning socioeconomic gap between the estate-owning elite and the mass of wage laborers with little or no land.

What we can gather from the fragments of Solon's poetry supports the second scenario. After his reforms, he prided himself on having resisted calls for the redistribution of land (fr. 34.7–9), but it is revealing that such calls were issued at all: only when wealth is very unevenly distributed and a large proportion of people simply do not have enough income to survive will such radical measures be demanded. Although stopping short of a full-scale redistribution, Solon did "liberate the earth" by "removing boundary markers planted everywhere," which in my view means that he restored illegally occupied or confiscated land to its rightful owners or to common use (fr. 36.3–7).[42] The other major demand, to which Solon did accede, was for a cancellation of debts, since indebtedness had got to the point where "the poor" (*penichroi*) were sold abroad into slavery by their creditors, or else left the country in order to avoid slavery. Others remained in Attica, "trembling at their masters' whims," evidently in a highly vulnerable position (frs. 4.23–25; 36.8–15). Solon stressed that it was only thanks to his reforms that the crisis did not escalate into bloodshed, for which both the rich and poor were fully prepared (fr. 36.20–25), and that "the people" had wanted him to go much further than reform: they expected him to seize sole power in Athens and force through more radical changes (frs. 32, 33, 34, 37).

Solon may have overstated his case, but his poems nevertheless offer clear evidence that Athens' *thetes* were being viciously exploited in the years around 600 BC and were on the brink of mounting a violent rebellion against the exploitative landed and leisured elite—including the *zeugitai*.[43] Classical evidence further fleshes out the picture with the information that many of the poor were *pelatai*, "clients" and dependants, of the rich, and worked on the land of the rich as *hektemoroi*, "sixth parters," which Hanson rightly understands as sharecroppers who were rewarded with only one-sixth of the harvest—a highly exploitative form of sharecropping, given that the most common sharecropping contracts divide the harvest fifty-fifty between cultivator and landowner.[44] *Thetes* would hardly have tolerated such conditions unless there was no other way to gain access to land because "all the land was in the hands of few" ([Arist.] *Ath. Pol.* 2.1, 4.1). Everything thus points to a situation in which the top three property classes monopolized most of the land, while the bulk of the population made do with tiny plots or no land at all. If everyone below the leisure class was labeled a "hired laborer," it was because there were indeed no independent yeomen farmers to speak of.[45] It is no coincidence that when Solon mentions farming in a poem counting the ways in which people try to make a living, his agricultural worker is not a small struggling landowner, but a hired laborer on an annual contract.[46]

Much like Hesiod, Solon acknowledges in his poetry that no amount of wealth is ever enough, since even the very rich want to be richer still, and that it is perfectly acceptable to "yearn for wealth," so long as one acquires it by legitimate means only. It is because the elite of Athens knew no such restraint but indulged in greed and *hybris*, arrogant aggression, according to Solon, that they had reduced the rest of the community to actual or virtual slavery and brought Athens to the brink of civil war.[47] He therefore helped the *thetes* by imposing limits on existing forms of exploitation, creating new kinds of legal protection, restoring usurped land to private and public ownership, and reducing incentives to compete for wealth by enacting sumptuary laws and a ban on most agricultural exports. The elite could console themselves with their new access to political office, in compensation for these economic and legal restrictions.[48]

A similar situation prevailed at Sparta a little before Solon's time. A line of an archaic poem that became proverbial warns that "love of wealth" might destroy Sparta, and a poem by Tyrtaeus alludes to calls for the redistribution of land in the late seventh century. In Sparta, too, large numbers of people were evidently falling below the subsistence minimum while others accumulated great wealth. Elsewhere, poets throughout the archaic period express concern about the consequences of competition for wealth, and we find stories in classical and later sources about civil conflicts that opposed landowners against dependent rural laborers, not independent smallholders. Debtors and clients rioted in Megara, circa 600; a bloody civil war between the rich and their agricultural laborers nearly ruined Miletus, probably in the late seventh century.[49]

Theognis' Rustics and Phocylides' Middling Men

Three snippets of verse dating to about 540 BC are Hanson's only other archaic evidence for the rise of the yeoman farmer. The first is a lament by Theognis of Megara (53–58):

> Cyrnus, this city is still a city but its people now are other men, who previously knew no courts or laws, but wore threadbare goatskins on their backs and grazed like deer outside this city. And now, son of Polypaos, they are good men, and those who used to be fine men are now worthless. Who could bear to see such things?

Hanson interprets this as a reference to "agrarians [who] had so . . . completely replaced birth by material success . . . that . . . now they wandered outside the walls of the *polis* with pretensions to actually being *agathoi*," that is, members of the elite (1995, 109–10); they are "new farmers who . . . rarely come into town, but "pasture like deer" on their isolated farms" (120), and have changed the social order by means of "not wealth, but work" (121).

This is a very strained reading of the passage. Clearly, those who used to live outside the town, according to Theognis, are no longer in the countryside but have moved into the city, and do not merely have a high opinion of themselves but have replaced the old elite. The claim that new men have gained dominance is repeated later, with the addition that their rise involved them marrying into the old elite on the strength of wealth, not work:

> Cyrnus, the good men of the past are now bad men, and those who used to be bad men are now good men. Who could bear to see such things: the good men less respected, worse men treated with respect? And the fine man courts the offspring of the bad one (1109–12). A fine man does not mind marrying a bad woman [born] of a bad man so long as [this man] gives him much wealth, nor does a woman refuse to be the wife of a wealthy bad man, but she wants riches instead of a good man. They respect wealth. (185–89).

There is no question here of a new agrarian middle class, but of high upward social mobility that turned poor country dwellers into rich city dwellers. Perhaps such high mobility really did occur or else Theognis merely slandered his rivals by claiming that they belonged to families of very low status. Either way, his underlying image is of a society divided between an urban elite and a group of rural poor who are so far removed from the trappings of civilization that they are more like animals than like humans: from his point of view, at any rate, this is still a polarized society without a middle class.[50]

Whatever Theognis thought of country dwellers, his verses show that a rural population did exist. But it does not follow that these were yeomen farmers, let alone that they were numerous. When Homer mentions "rustics" (*agroiotai*), they are always herdsmen, not farmers, and, if identified further, specifically herdsmen in the service of a rich owner.[51] Two fragments of Sappho, circa 600 BC, which gently mock an uncouth "country girl" and a rural wedding probably suggest farmers, but we cannot tell whether these are independent family farmers or dependent peasants. Theognis' reference to "grazing" suggests that, like Homer, he was primarily thinking of herdsmen as a group of particularly low status.[52]

The other two snippets of archaic poetry adduced by Hanson are couplets by Phocylides of Miletus. "If you seek wealth, take care of a fertile farm, for a farm, as they say, is a horn of plenty" (fr. 7) according to Hanson (1995, 111) refers to "homestead agriculture," but it is simply a very concise version of Hesiod's advice (as is fr. 9) and does not imply a small farm any more than *Works and Days* does. More interesting is the second couplet: "Those in the middle have many great assets; in the middle of the city I wish to be" (fr. 12). For Hanson, this is an expression of a long-lived "middling" ideal, established by yeomen farmers in the eighth century and still shared in the fourth century, most notably by Aristotle, who is cited at length (1995, 110, 114–19). Other scholars have adduced further evidence for this ideal, which advocated moderation and approved of those who were content to remain in the middle of the social hierarchy. Aristotle in particular argued that "middle people" (*mesoi*) provided balance and stability to communities that were in danger of being torn apart by the struggle between the rich and poor.[53]

Whereas the classical evidence is quite abundant and clear, however, an archaic concept of a "middling" lifestyle, let alone a "middling" social class, proves almost nonexistent. Some poets, like Hesiod and Solon, urged "moderation" in the pursuit of wealth, but this was not conceived of as a "middle" way. The closest Solon comes to using the concept of the middle is when he says that he "stood like a boundary marker in the space between the lines of battle" in a looming civil war (37.8–9). The image evokes political neutrality at a time of conflict, as do a few lines of Theognis that explicitly speak of staying "in the middle" (219–20, 331–32). Only once in Theognis is "the middle way" (*mesa*) used to mean "moderation" (335–36)—a significant conceptual innovation, but without any implication that such moderation was characteristic of a broader "middle" group. No such group appears anywhere else in Theognis, who, like Solon, sees the world strictly in polarized terms of upper-class "good men" (*agathoi*) and lower-class "bad men" (*kakoi*).[54]

Phocylides' couplet is in fact the sole archaic text that speaks of "those in the middle" as a group, and as a permanent element of the city as a whole. Who form this "middle class" is far from obvious: they may be a new class of yeomen farmers, or they may be the lower strata of the landed elite redefining themselves as a "moderate" middle class at a time when the very rich raised conspicuous consumption to new levels of extravagance. Hanson cites Aristotle's occasional association of the "middle" with a class of working farmers, but one cannot simply project classical idea(l)s onto Phocylides, and even less onto other archaic poetry. Even if one did, one would have to remember that Aristotle did not associate the "middle" with working farmers alone but was quite happy stretching the middle so wide that it could include, for instance, the lawgiver Lycurgus on the basis that he was regent of Sparta, not king. Moreover, Aristotle also conceded that almost nowhere in the Greek world had there ever been a middle class large enough to balance the forces of rich and poor.[55] So we cannot safely infer that a sizable yeoman class existed by the time of Phocylides. His concept of a middle class, and Theognis' concept of a middle way, are nevertheless significant: they show the emergence, circa 540 BC, of a conceptual space, as it were, that independent working farmers could in principle fill.

The Archaeologists' Empty Countryside

Material evidence for agriculture plays only a small role in Hanson's argument, but he does cite instances where field divisions indicate farm sizes. The only place where 10-acre farms emerge as the norm is the Crimea, where in the fifth century BC a general redistribution of land produced many plots of 11–12 acres. All the other instances are also of classical date, and reveal only a few more farms of about 10 acres, while the vast majority range from just over 20 acres to 100 acres. One estimate for early fifth-century

Metapontum suggests that only 8 percent of farms were 11 acres in size, 27 percent were 22 acres, and 63 percent covered between 33 and 88 acres. Hanson makes the fair point that evidently even the rich in Greece were not very much richer than the yeomen (although he concedes that the wealthiest may have owned more than one farm: 1995, 187; 195), but the fact remains that 10-acre farms are rare even in the classical material record, which does reveal estates large enough to enable a leisure-class existence.[56]

Elsewhere, a variety of archaeological survey projects has now revealed that the Greek countryside was largely "empty" until the late sixth century. The evidence is discussed more fully elsewhere in this volume, but one example may illustrate the point. The Laconia Survey, which covered a large area from the immediate northeast of Sparta itself to the border of Laconia, found no signs of habitation between 700 and 550 BC, only a few dedications at two sanctuary sites. At some point between 550 and 450, however, the landscape filled up dramatically, with dozens of farms, several hamlets, and even a small town. These remarkable findings are mirrored elsewhere, including Metapontum.[57] The material evidence is open to interpretation, of course, but it seems clear that it is incompatible with the notion of a sizable class of yeomen living on their farmsteads outside town before 550 BC. The emptiness of the landscape strongly suggests that landowners lived in town, and that cultivators lived there, too, or else lived on the land under such simple conditions that they left no trace in the archaeological record.

Conversely, the filling-in of the Greek countryside after circa 550 BC suggests a new pattern of landownership or agricultural exploitation. What exactly happened in Sparta remains unclear, since the regimented Spartan lifestyle kept citizens closely tied to the city, and they were unlikely to have begun to settle in the countryside. But elsewhere in Greece, the emergence of country-dwelling small farmers may explain the spread of rural settlement, and this may be our earliest evidence, perhaps along with Phocylides' praise of "middling men," for the rise of the yeoman farmer—from the mid-sixth century onward.[58]

The Republic of Gentlemen: Another Model

At the center of ancient Greek history stands a protagonist much less sympathetic than the hardworking independent farming family of *The Other Greeks*. This is the gentleman farmer, whom on the basis of the evidence discussed above we may define as follows:

- A gentleman farmer owned at least 30 acres (12 ha) of land, which was enough in principle for him and his family to afford a life of leisure in town, even if in practice many may have been actively involved in the management of their farms.
- A gentleman farmer's labor force consisted of at least four agricultural workers and two domestic servants, hired or slave.
- Gentlemen farmers constituted probably no more than 10–15 percent of citizens in most archaic Greek cities.[59]

In writing the history of Greece, we must take as our starting point that for almost the whole of the archaic age, leisured landowners and their laborers—sharecroppers, hired men, with or without a tiny plot of land of their own, slaves, and serfs—are the only significant social classes attested. Not until later did independent yeomen farmers emerge as a class in some parts of the Greek world, including Athens—and this development must have had a fundamental impact on the history of the classical period. This chapter cannot, of course, present a full-dress revised history of ancient Greece to rival *The Other Greeks*, but I will try to sketch what such a history might look like, even if this means making bold claims without being able to offer the further substantiation that they sorely need.

Land, Labor, and Rivalry for Wealth and Honor

The striking developments of the eighth century, especially from 750 BC onward, reflect the emergence of an elite of gentlemen farmers. Population growth at the time does not now seem as drastic as was once argued, and the evidence for a shift from pastoral to agricultural economies is very limited, so for an explanation we may look instead to the sort of fierce competition for wealth, both land and livestock, on which Hesiod comments. This presumably had been a feature of Greek life for centuries and may have ultimately produced a separation between landed elite and dependent labor by 750 BC. It was this new elite that displayed its wealth and consolidated its dominant position by settling together in larger nucleated settlements, building sanctuaries and filling them with dedications, as well as constructing fortifications, more complex houses, and more visible grave monuments. The relative egalitarianism that one can often observe in the material record from this time onward reflects an egalitarian culture *within* the landed elite. It did not extend to yeomen farmers, if there were any, let alone to dependent farmers or laborers, who remain essentially invisible in the archaeological record.[60]

Much of archaic history can be understood as the product of two basic dynamics: tension between egalitarianism and competitiveness within the class of gentlemen farmers; and tension between the landed elite and the rest of the population. Competition for honor (*time*), in the form of status and power, meant that every individual and family aimed to raise their own standing while not allowing their peers to advance themselves. Often an informal group of ruling families, such as the *basileis* of Hesiod's world, the Bacchiads of Corinth, or the Eupatridae of Athens, established itself within the landed elite, but their dominance was always resented and challenged by the other gentlemen farmers.[61] In order to end or prevent violent conflict between sections of the landed elite, Greek cities generally developed, in the course of the seventh and early sixth centuries, republican systems of government with clear rules for power sharing among all leisured landowners. Solon's property classes are an example of such timocratic republican institutions, which are far less "broad-based" than those envisaged by Hanson. Rivalry for status was meant to take place within this republican framework, but leading men were often not content to compete within the rules and instead established themselves as monarchs, "tyrants." This met fierce resistance, and a republic of gentlemen was usually soon restored.

Competition for wealth also led to conflict within the elite as well as to increasing exploitation of the labor force, debtors, and dependants. One response was to counter the ethos of conspicuous leisure and consumption with the ideology of "toil" that we find in Hesiod, according to which the only legitimate way to gain wealth was through active farm management, close supervision of the labor force, profitable sale of surplus, and a relatively austere lifestyle. Another response was to compete by seizing wealth from new sources, through the internal "colonization" of marginal land, by raiding or settling overseas, or even by means of the conquest of neighboring territory.

Homer and archaeology suggest that marginal land was not occupied by independent small farmers but by large estates and herds; presumably the landed elite used force and intimidation to prevent their poorer neighbors from carving out their own small farms here. New settlements abroad often seem to have started out on an egalitarian basis, but even if some or most of the colonists had been poor men at home, the communities they established abroad adopted the egalitarianism of a leisure class rather than of a community of working farmers. The model is Syracuse, where the Greek settlers subjected the local population and ruled as *gamoroi*, landowners, over native serfs.[62] Raiding overseas was widespread, and slaves must have been the raiders' main spoils, so that these expeditions not only alleviated the poverty of the ships' crews but also increased the wealth of the captains and created a supply of chattel slaves for their labor force. As for the conquest of neighboring territory, the reduction of the Messenians to a serf population feeding a leisured Spartan elite is usually regarded as unique, but there is evidence that it was by no means unusual in the archaic period.[63]

Despite the availability of external sources of land and labor and the preaching against violent greed by the likes of Hesiod and Solon, intense rivalry for wealth also led the gentleman-farmer elite to usurp the use of common and private land, exploit their workforce, enslave their debtors, and abuse legal process. This sparked widespread social crises from 650/600 BC onward, including radical calls for the redistribution of land in Sparta and Athens. Such social unrest could be tapped by ambitious members of the elite in their competition for status, enabling them to mobilize not only factional support within the elite but also broad popular backing for seizing monarchical power. Solon's pride in not having imposed himself as tyrant on Athens despite having the enthusiastic support of the masses shows how well established this pattern was by 600 BC.[64]

In many Greek cities, such crises were never more than temporarily resolved and continued to erupt over the following centuries. But some places did achieve greater stability in the second half of the sixth century. Athens and Sparta provide us with two models that were probably mirrored in other cities.

In Athens, the position of the poor working masses was gradually improved by means of internal reform that imposed restrictions on exploitation and offered better legal protection. According to later tradition the tyrant Peisistratus even provided direct material support for farmers in need of plow oxen or seed corn. Conquest of some overseas territory in Salamis, Sigeum, the Chersonese, and Chalcis also helped. The result was the emergence, finally, of a class of independent working farmers. In 322 BC, as we saw, Athens had about 5,000 leisure-class citizens, 4,000 independent working-class citizens, no doubt still mainly farmers, and another 20,000 or so citizens who labored for others. Note that yeomen "middling" farmers, although now a significant class, were the smallest social group, forming at most 13 percent of the citizen population. The proportions may have been similar by about 500 BC. This new social class remained *thetes* under the terms of the Athenian property-class system, however, and acquired no new formal political rights beyond their roles in popular assemblies and courts, unless perhaps they were entitled to serve on the reformed council instituted by Cleisthenes in 508 BC, which is not clear.

In Sparta, stability was achieved in the first instance by conquest of large tracts of land in Laconia and Messenia and the subjection of their inhabitants, which enabled large numbers of Spartiates to become gentlemen farmers, and staved off demands for a redistribution of land. This strategy continued after the completion of the conquest of Messenia, circa 600 BC, with attempts to seize land and labor also in neighboring Arcadia and Cynouria until circa 550 BC. After that, expeditions of conquest gave way to wars of hegemony, in which defeated enemies became subject allies rather than serfs. At about the same time, the famously "austere" and egalitarian material culture of classical Sparta emerged. It was thus probably in the late sixth century, when further conquests failed, that Sparta turned to a different way of avoiding internal conflict by creating a rigid distinction between leisure-class landowning citizens and a subject labor force, and inhibiting competition for wealth by imposing on all citizens a strictly egalitarian material culture while channeling rivalry for honor into highly regulated forms of competition.[65]

Far from being a "bizarre mutation" or Dark Age relic, the social and economic structure that we encounter in classical Sparta and the similar systems found in the towns of Crete and Thessaly were thus created in the late archaic period in response to the same pressures that affected Athens, Megara, Miletus, and other cities. The Spartan solution was to make as many citizens as possible gentlemen farmers at the expense of outsiders and to resort to extreme self-regulation of the leisure class. The Athenian model involved less self-regulation by the gentleman-farmer elite, and fewer conquests, but more protection of the working classes, which allowed a yeoman class to establish itself and play some part in political life even if its formal rights remained confined to voting in assemblies and juries.

Despite the reformers' best efforts, competition for wealth and status did not stop, and in many places ultimately proved more powerful than the laws and political structures that were set up to rein it in. Already by the late fifth century, there were signs of renewed concentration of land in the hands of a few, and a shrinking of the yeoman class and ultimately even of the gentleman farmer class. Renewed exploitation of credit and labor caused new social crises; timocratic regimes became narrower and often turned into oligarchies. Even the heavily regulated elite of landowning citizens in Sparta shrank at an alarming rate, from a possible 9,000 at the time of the sixth-century reform to a mere 1,100 on the eve of the battle of Leuctra in 371 BC. Most of the losses must be due to a concentration of wealth in the hands of fewer citizens, which caused the others to fall below the property requirement and become "inferiors."[66]

Only where the rise of the yeoman class was accompanied by other major economic and social developments was it possible for broader timocracies and even democracies to establish and maintain themselves. From the mid-sixth century onward, the scale of Greek overseas trade increased dramatically, as the appearance of specialized merchant ships suggests, and this allowed substantial groups of traders and craftsmen to develop in cities such as Athens. The rise of professional traders may indeed have been another factor that helped working farmers to gain their independence, insofar as they were able and willing to produce for the market, rather than for home consumption, and improve their profit margins.[67] The late sixth century also saw the first wars for naval hegemony and the adoption of the trireme as the dominant warship, which provided seasonal employment for increasingly large numbers of men, and made many of the poor and landless gradually less dependent on their wealthy neighbors for pay.[68] In fifth-century Athens, commercial and naval success were reinforced by imperial and other public revenues to create levels of prosperity that allowed not only yeomen farmers but also the rest of the working classes to assert themselves in politics. As a result, legal restrictions on office holding that still existed in name were no longer upheld after circa 450 BC, and, crucially, the introduction of pay for office enabled even working men to serve as councillors and magistrates.[69] Yeomen farmers played their role in such developments here and elsewhere, but it is telling that Aristotle regarded farmers as least likely of all working-class men to exercise their political rights, and that a coup d'état in Athens in 411 BC restored rule by the leisure class while cutting out yeomen farmers along with the rest of the "mob."[70]

The ultimate fate of the broad timocratic and democratic regimes that did take hold in Greece is a matter of controversy, but it seems likely that in the Hellenistic period, and under the Roman Empire, the trend was a return to de facto rule by rather narrow timocracies, even if the forms of democracy were commonly retained.[71]

The Development of the Hoplite Phalanx

If this sketch of the changing social and economic structures of the Greek world is along the right lines, then for most of the archaic age only the top 10–15 percent of the population, the gentlemen farmers, could afford to equip themselves with a hoplite panoply. The other 85–90 percent of the community were too poor to afford much armor, and if they fought at all, it must have been mainly with missiles. In other words, even a large archaic city with 10,000 adult males had a hoplite militia of only 1,000–1,500 men, while in many towns hoplites numbered in the hundreds. Not until the rise of yeomen farmers and other independent working families from the mid-sixth century onward could hoplite armies include up to 40 percent of the population and thus have significantly larger absolute numbers.

Our very limited evidence for hoplite numbers in the archaic age does not contradict this conclusion. The sole contemporary source is an inscription of unknown but surely archaic date reported by Strabo (10.1.10) that recorded a festival parade at Eretria in which 60 chariots, 600 horsemen, and 3,000 hoplites took part, presumably the whole of Eretria's forces. This may sound like a large number but it must be remembered that Eretria, a leading city in archaic Greece, controlled one of the largest territories held by any city-state: in the sixth century, it occupied about 900–1,000 km^2. If these troops amounted to 40–50 percent of the population, population density would have been extremely low. Corinth, with a territory of about the same size, raised a field army of 5,000 hoplites in 479 BC, which implies a total hoplite militia of at least 7,500, twice as large as Eretria's. And according to Herodotus, Naxos, with a territory about half as large, had a total of 8,000 hoplites in 500 BC. This suggests that the Eretrian forces listed in the archaic inscription represented a much smaller proportion of the citizen population.[72]

Our only other archaic figures are not contemporary: they derive from stories reported by Plutarch, who says that Solon conquered Salamis with a force of only 500 men, and that a catastrophic defeat around 600 BC left 1,000 Samians dead on the battlefield. Since Samos was at least as prominent a power as Naxos and had a slightly larger territory, one would have expected it to be able to raise 8,000 hoplites or more, and this massacre would not have been far above the average of 14 percent casualties for the loser in a hoplite battle. For the loss of 1,000 men to count as a historic catastrophe, the Samian militia must have been much smaller.[73]

The first indications of much larger numbers of hoplites come from 500 BC onward, beginning with the figure for Naxos already cited, followed by the figure of 6,000 Argive soldiers massacred by Sparta in the battle of Sepeia, circa 494 BC, and the figures for the Greek field armies in the Persian Wars, including Corinth's 5,000, Athens' 9,000, and the 3,000 each of Megara and Sicyon, all probably representing at most two-thirds of the total available number of hoplites.[74] Herodotus says that at Plataea the proportion of hoplites to light-armed was roughly fifty-fifty. Only Sparta still fielded an archaic-style leisure-class hoplite militia, making up a mere 12.5 percent of its forces.[75]

For a century and a half since the introduction of the hoplite shield and body armor, circa 700 BC, hoplite militias therefore consisted of leisure-class landowners. Working yeomen farmers began to join their ranks only from 550 BC onward. This chronology happens to fit well with Aristotle's famous account of the rise of the hoplite phalanx, which is commonly misused as evidence for the rise of a hoplite middle class in the seventh century:

> The first political system among the Greeks also emerged from the warriors, after the kingships: the very first form emerged from the horsemen—because strength and superiority in war lay with these horsemen, since hoplite forces are useless without organisation [*suntaxis*] and among the ancients there was no experience or order [*taxis*] in such matters, so that strength lay with the horsemen—but when the cities grew and those with hoplite equipment grew stronger, more people became part of the political system. . . . The ancient political systems were oligarchic and royal for good reason, because they did not have a large middle class on account of their small populations, so that the multitude, being few, was more ready to endure being ruled even when they *were* organized [*kai kata tên suntaxin*]. (*Pol.* 1297b16–28)

The idea here is not, as some modern scholars argue, that the introduction of hoplite equipment transformed warfare and politics at a stroke, but that there were two phases of development. Once upon a time, hoplite forces existed but oligarchies of horsemen still ruled because hoplites were too disorganized to play a significant military role and too few in number to assert themselves in politics. Later, however, hoplite numbers increased, their military efficiency improved, and their political power grew. Aristotle had already indicated in an earlier passage when, to his mind, this second phase began:

> In ancient times there were oligarchies in all cities whose power was based on their horses, for they used horses in their wars against neighbours, as did, for example, the Eretrians and Chalcidians and the Magnesians on the Maeander, and many of the others in Asia. (*Pol.* 1289b30–40)

The dates of the regimes "in Asia" are difficult to establish, but Aristotle knew that in Eretria the oligarchy of *Hippeis* was not overthrown until sometime after 546 BC, and that in Chalcis a similar oligarchy of *Hippobotai* was overthrown only in 506 BC. It seems to me that Aristotle here does little more than project his political philosophy into the past, and that his account is of almost no historical value. But if one does regard it as useful evidence, as Hanson and others do, then Aristotle supports the view that the rise of the hoplite phalanx was a two-stage process, which had political consequences only in the second stage, with the rise of the "middle-class" hoplite in the late sixth century.[76]

The strict separation between warriors and cultivators imposed in classical Sparta, Crete, and Thessaly was thus, again, no relic from the Dark Age, but a formalization of the norm established in the archaic age, when hoplites were leisured landowners, living off the labor of slaves and dependants. Even in late fifth-century Athens a formal obligation to serve in the hoplite militia was still confined to the *zeugitai* and the two richer property classes, that is, the leisured elite. The *thetes*, now including large numbers of yeomen farmers, were merely under a moral obligation to contribute to the defense of the city and to join in general mobilizations for short campaigns. The limited legal liability for hoplite service is why Athenian hoplite forces picked from "the list" (*katalogos*) were rarely larger than 1,000 or 2,000 men; why every man in such forces could afford to bring along a slave attendant; and why, according to Aristotle, it was "the rich," not the middle classes or the poor, who suffered the greatest casualties in the Peloponnesian War. The distinction between leisure-class and working-class hoplites faded in Athens only in the fourth century, when expeditionary forces were no longer handpicked from "the list," but mobilized by age group; it disappeared completely in 336 BC, when the state began to pay for the basic equipment and training of every hoplite in the reformed *ephebeia*.[77]

Few Greek states can have matched fifth-century Athens in the egalitarianism of its political climate or the sheer number of its yeomen hoplites. If the distinction between leisure-class and working-class hoplites was nevertheless preserved in military organization at least until the time of the Sicilian expedition, when Athenian democracy was at its peak, the distinction surely also continued to exist elsewhere in fifth-century Greece. Indeed, the creation of a leisure-class hoplite army remained the ideal of Greek intellectuals. Hippodamus of Miletus, Plato, and Aristotle built their ideal states on the premise that the citizens who ruled these states should be soldiers and leave the farming to others. In *Ways and Means*, the pragmatic Xenophon proposed fund-raising schemes designed to exempt all Athenian citizens from the need to work by providing them with a subsistence minimum at public expense. Greek thinkers did speak of farmers as good hoplites, made strong and tough by their toil, and determined to resist any invasion on account of their attachment to the land (Hanson 1995, 221–23, 242–43). But even if farmers made better soldiers than craftsmen or traders, they were still only second-best to rich landowning hoplites whose physical and mental fitness derived from elite leisure pursuits: wrestling, running, and other athletic exercises as well as hunting. In Hanson's terms, the "ugly muscle" of farmers may have been appreciated, but "elegant muscle" always continued to be rated most highly.[78]

The predominance of the leisure-class hoplite in the archaic age undermines Hanson's idea that the conventions of hoplite warfare, and indeed hoplite arms and armor as such, were shaped by the needs of yeomen farmers, who needed a kind of warfare that caused minimal disruption to their farming duties and was effectively confined to instantly decisive battles fought in close combat, "afternoon wars" in the summer season.[79] Since leisured gentlemen landowners were not subject to the same constraints on their time, this explanation will not work. It is in any case highly questionable whether archaic warfare was ever restricted to pitched hoplite battles, and not at all certain that archaic infantry battles were fought in the same way as classical hoplite battles. If, instead of relying on classical caricatures of what warfare was like "in the old days," one considers what little evidence we have for actual archaic wars, it quickly becomes obvious that sieges, ambushes, and raids were at least as common as pitched battle, and that the rules of engagement spanned the range from restricted "agonal" combat to the mobilization of all resources to inflict the greatest possible damage. Insofar as archaic warfare did have its limitations, these were not imposed by the interests of small farmers, but by the limited military manpower, military organization, and above all public finances of archaic cities.[80]

How one assesses the impact of the rise of the yeoman farmer in the late sixth century depends to a large extent on one's views on the nature of hoplite equipment. If, with Hanson and Cartledge, one believes that the hoplite's double-grip shield, restrictive Corinthian helmet, and heavy body armor are compatible only with fighting in a close-order formation, then the phalanx must have taken its classical form already in 700 BC, and the subsequent rise of the yeoman would have doubled the size of the phalanx without fundamentally changing anything else. If, however, with Snodgrass and Krentz, one believes that the shield and armor were designed simply to give added protection and could equally have been used in an open and fluid style of fighting, then the rise of the yeoman may have been the factor that transformed this earlier style of fighting and created the phalanx in its classical form. On the latter scenario, it is possible that archaic leisure-class hoplites were accompanied into battle by small groups of personal friends and dependants, some of them hoplites, others light-armed, like the heroes of Homer and their "retainers" (*therapontes*). The support and protection of these followers enabled them to carry relatively heavy and constricting armor, but made it impossible to form closed ranks of hoplites. With the rise of the independent working farmer, however, the pool of dependants was reduced while the proportion of poorer hoplites without followers of their own increased greatly. This may have tilted the balance toward relegating the remaining light-armed to the rear or flanks while forming the hoplites, at last, into an exclusive heavy infantry formation.[81]

It is notable that the heaviest panoplies, with bronze arm and thigh guards, disappear in the late sixth century, as do images in art of mounted hoplites, while the Corinthian helmet was abandoned in favor of more open-face types after 500 BC. Even more strikingly, as Peter Krentz has shown, two of the best-known "agonal" conventions for marking the end of hoplite battle, setting up a *tropaion* and concluding a truce for the retrieval of the dead, are first attested in the early fifth century BC. These changes suggest that the phalanx did indeed change in nature when the yeoman class emerged. Because personal followers were no longer on hand to assist their masters, the most restrictive armor was abandoned; and because a close formation replaced a fluid order, mounted hoplites vanished. Since close-order battles were decided at the moment either side broke and ran, without any prospect of rallying and resuming battle time and again in the Homeric manner, a *tropaion* marking the "turning point" now, for the first time, became a meaningful symbol, and immediate truces for the retrieval of the dead became viable and desirable.[82]

The rise of the classical phalanx and its conventions of battle may thus have begun only in the late sixth century, at the very same time that the scale of naval warfare increased exponentially with the introduction of the trireme, soon followed by notable developments in siege warfare and an increasing use of mercenaries. These developments undermined the military dominance of the leisure-class hoplite, but not of the hoplite as such or of pitched heavy-infantry battle: these continued to play as important a part as ever in the spectrum of military operations, and remained the most prestigious kind of soldier and form of combat throughout the classical period and beyond. The trend toward larger-scale warfare, however, meant that the numbers of citizen-hoplites were often too small to match a city's ambitions, a problem aggravated by shrinking numbers of hoplites as a result of the trend toward a renewed concentration of property. In the Hellenistic period, the result was generally a return to smaller, leisure-class militias, supplemented by mercenary forces.[83]

Whether the rise of the hoplite phalanx, as reinterpreted above, could still have inspired a "hoplite revolution" or "hoplite reform," as many have argued, is doubtful. With Hanson, I have argued that the fundamental changes were social and economic, and that changes in war and politics merely reflected these structural developments. This does not entirely rule out, however, the possibility that military changes in their own right did contribute to political change. After all, the most pervasive legitimation of political power in Greek thought was the idea that power was earned by playing a decisive role in war.[84] One could therefore still argue, in principle, that the adoption of hoplite armor around 700 BC was a factor in consolidating the power of an elite class of leisured landowners established about fifty years earlier, and that it contributed to creating an ethos of elite egalitarianism in these early republics of gentlemen. But there is no good evidence that the constitutional reforms and tyrannical coups of the seventh and early sixth centuries, which have traditionally been linked to the rise of the phalanx, were designed to give hoplites a share of political power; instead, as I have suggested, they seem concerned mainly to contain conflict within the hoplite elite and between this elite and its exploited labor force.[85]

If there ever was a hoplite revolution as conventionally envisaged, a military change that brought a share in power for up to half of adult male citizens, it would have taken place in the late sixth century. One might therefore look to tyrants like Polycrates and Peisistratus, or more promisingly to Cleisthenes and his reforms, as possible champions of the new class of yeomen hoplites—but again direct connections are hard to establish. If warfare did have an impact on politics, it would in any case have been the whole complex of late sixth-century military changes that did so, not just the further development of the hoplite phalanx. The rise of the yeoman hoplite went hand in hand with the rise of the trireme rower, and if they changed the face of Greek politics, they changed it together.

Notes

1. In response to comments by one of the anonymous referees for the press, I should clarify the term "leisured": perhaps somewhat provocatively, I use it to indicate landowners whose farms are cultivated by hired or coerced labor, i.e., those who can in principle afford to live in leisure. In practice, many members of this "leisure class" may well work quite hard in managing their farms, but they have at least the option of adopting a leisured lifestyle, unlike "working" yeoman farmers who rely largely on their own and their family's labor. I am grateful to both referees for their helpful comments and suggestions.

2. Hanson 1995, 5, 22, 193, 219, 359, 366, 368, 398. Ten to twenty acres is given as "'normative'" on p. 188, but a note here (478 n. 6) gives 8–10 acres as "typical" and 10 acres as "average."

3. Hanson 1995, 68, 70; and generally on pervasive use of slave labor by yeoman farmers: 50, 63–70, 127; cf. on Hesiod, below.

4. Hanson 1995, 105, 114, 207, 213, 374, 479 n. 6 (nearly half); 208, 406 (one-third to half). The statement that "one third to one half" of the population fell *below* yeoman status (411) is presumably a slip and should read "two thirds to one half."

5. Hanson 1995, 5–6; farmstead residence also, e.g., 22, 50–51, 65, 127.

6. Hanson 1995, 16 (economic changes from 750 onward); 202, 296, 328ff. (dominant 700–500 or 490); on p. 186, a line is drawn earlier, c. 550 BC, but it is also said that "widespread landed equality" continued until 400 BC.

7. Hanson 1995, 16, 32–33, 44 (agriculture v. pastoralism); 36–41 (population growth and consequences); 40 (leasing); 50–87 (intensive cultivation; esp. 79–85: marginal land).

8. Hanson 1995, 225–328.

9. Hanson 1995, esp. 202–19 (broad timocracies); cf. 202, 239, 471–72 n. 21 (tyranny).

10. Hanson 1995, 327–55, 369–75 (military developments); 359, 365–68, 375–79 (economic developments); 394–98 (rise of large estates, replacing family farms).

11. Sparta and Crete as anomalies: Hanson 1995, 105 (atypical, different development), 242 ("strange," "outside culture of polis"), 275, 293–94 ("special problems"), 333, 391–92 ("bizarre"), 484 n. 4; also 110 (Thessaly—lack of development from Dark Age).

12. Hanson 1995, 195 with 481 n. 12; cf. Burford 1993, 67–72, 113–16; Gallant 1991, 86–87. The property qualification of 2,000 dr. in Athens implies a 10-acre farm: see below.

13. *Od.* 24.205–12, 220–34, 244–57, 336–44, 361–411; cf. 1.189–93; 11.187–96.

14. *Od.* 24.384–85, 408–11; for the distinction, see van Wees 1995a, 151–53.

15. *Od.* 1.189–93 ("no longer" comes into town, and suffers "miseries" [*pemata*] on farm); 11.187–94 (wears "'bad clothes,'" does not sleep in a bed, but on the ground, "grieving, and sorrow waxes great in his heart"); 24.227–33 (poor, patched-up clothes express his grief).

16. Other marginal farm, hired labor: *Od.* 357–61 (owned by Eurymachus, the richest of Odysseus' rivals: 15.16–18). Herds: *Od.* 14.1–28, 103–5.

17. Adapted proverb: West 1978, 259–60. Aristotle cites only the "proverbial" verse (405) and omits the modification (406; *Pol.* 1252b11; *Oec.* 1343a21) because it suits his argument to treat the woman as the farmer's wife, and this does not prove that line 406 was a late insertion; no later than the third century BC it was widely known as a line of Hesiod's (Timaeus *FGrH* 566 F 157). The argument that 406 may not be original because Hesiod elsewhere does not show an interest in livestock (West 1978, 260) is not valid: see below. Hanson 1995, 107, 130–31, and, e.g., Edwards 2004, 83 n. 4, are therefore not justified in ignoring 406 and assuming that the woman is a wife.

18. Alternatively, the farmer had no real choice, and Hesiod described an ideal; cf. his recommendation of nine-year-old oxen for the plow (*W&D* 436–40): ideal, or ownership of numerous oxen? The possibility that the plowman and sower are hired laborers (West 1978, 270; Edwards 2004, 84) is ruled out by 459 (and made unlikely by 469–71).

19. *W&D* 600–608; for the meaning of the passage, see West 1978, 309–10. Alternatively, one could read "make a hired man homeless," i.e., dismiss him from your employment: either way, hired labor is used. Hanson 1995, 107, acknowledges the female laborer only.

20. See esp. Gallant 1991, 82–87; absolute minimum requirement is c. 2 acres per person.

21. Isager and Skydsgaard 1992, 108–14; Gallant 1982, 113–17; Jameson 1978, 125–30.

22. *W&D* 623–32, 689–91; there are auspicious days for a woodcutter to cut timber for houses and ships (807–8), to start building ships (809), to launch ships (817–18): these are the only nonagricultural activities (other than weaving) mentioned in the entire almanac.

23. Master: *W&D* 582–96; slaves: 597–600 (cf. 805–7: a good day for threshing, "while keeping a very close eye," i.e. ,supervising the threshing). The period during which the master sits in the shade starts "when the golden thistle flowers," which is around the summer solstice, i.e., 21 June (West 1978, 304 ad 582); the threshing begins at the rising of Orion, i.e., 20 June (West, 309 ad 598), so that the master's relaxation and the slaves' labor are simultaneous, as indeed the structure of Hesiod's account suggests. West 1978, 54 and 253, is therefore wrong to think that the master rests only after the threshing.

24. See Xenophon, *Oeconomicus* 11.12–18 (contra Hanson 1995, 65). Note the ambiguity about the role of the landowner's sons, if he has several: "more people, more care (*melete*), greater surplus" (*W&D* 380): more labor or more extensive supervision?

25. For the meaning of *penia*, see Hemelrijk 1925, 11–54; cf. van Wees 2004, 34–36; Finley 1973, 40–41. *Penia*: *W&D* 497, 638 (634–38: the "poor" man "is lacking a fine [*esthlos*] livelihood"), 717; *arkios bios*: 501, 577.

26. Hunger and debt: *W&D* 363–67, 394–404, 647; hunger: 298–302; debt: 477–78.

27. Hanson 1995, 98–102. Wealth as the goal in Hesiod: see also *W&D* 287–92, 312–13; expansion of herds is implied at *W&D* 308; cf. 102.

28. This analysis of *W&D* is developed further in van Wees 2009, 445–50.

29. *Theogony* 79–97; *W&D* 37–41, 202–11, 219–69.

30. Hanson 1995, 111–12; also, e.g., Murray 1993, 194 (*zeugitai* have "12+ acres").

31. Foxhall 1997, 129–32; see further van Wees 2001 and 2006a.

32. See Foxhall and Forbes 1982, 41–90.

33. Xenophon, *Poroi* 4.17 and 33, implies that 3 obols per day are a living wage for a family; see for prices and cost of living Markle 1985, 293–97; Loomis 1998, 220–31.

34. The weight of the *medimnos* is now known from the Grain-Tax Law of 374/3 BC (Rhodes-Osborne no. 26; Stroud 1998): 1 talent (27.5 kg) for barley; 1.2 talent (33 kg) for wheat. Previously, weights of respectively 33.55 and 40.28 kg had been widely accepted (after Foxhall and Forbes 1982) and were accordingly adopted in my own earlier calculations (van Wees 2001 and 2006a). Volume of *metretes*: Foxhall and Forbes 1982.

35. Maximum barley and wheat yields based on Gallant 1991, 77: statistics for average yields of Attica and Boeotia 1911–1950, inflated by chemical fertilizer from c. 1930 onward. See further van Wees 2001, 48–51; 2006a, 360–67.

36. Maximum oil and wine yields based on Amouretti and Brun (eds.), 1993, 554, 557–61.

37. Olive export: Plut. *Solon* 24.1; see further below, n. 48.

38. Minimum land prices: e.g., Lambert 1997, 229–33, 257–65; a higher price is also attested: Lysias 19.29, 42 (83 dr. per *plethron*).

39. On the 2,000 dr. census, see n. 40, and Hanson 1995, 296, 479, noted above. On liturgical and leisure-class censuses: Davies 1984, 28–29; Ober 1989, 128–29.

40. Diod. 18.18.4–5: 9,000 citizens owned 2,000 dr. or more; the vexed question of the total size of the citizen population implied by Diodorus, by Plutarch, Phocion 28.4, and by the census figures of Demetrius of Phaleron (Athenaeus 272c) is discussed in detail in van Wees 2011a, which ends up endorsing the common view that it was c. 30,000 in 322 BC. If only about 5,000 men belonged to the three highest property classes, one can see why after an earlier oligarchic coup in 411 BC citizen rights were restricted to the wealthiest 5,000 men, who at the time constituted rather less than half of those who served as hoplites in the Athenian army: see van Wees 2001, 56–59.

41. The only way to avoid this conclusion is to declare the Solonian property censuses a fiction (Ste. Croix 2004, 28–56; Valdéz Guía 2008, 70 n. 349), or to argue that they were originally much lower (Raaflaub 2006, 405–23; 2007, 128–32). In van Wees 2001, 54–56; 2006a, 362–67, I have tried to show that neither view is tenable.

42. See van Wees 1999a, 16–18.

43. On the threat of violent conflict, see also van Wees 2008a, 25–35.

44. Hanson 1995, 122; see further van Wees 1999a, 18–24.

45. See also Plutarch, *Solon* 13.1. Hanson regards the statements of pseudo-Aristotle and Plutarch about landownership as "somewhat of an exaggeration" and "an incorrect generalisation," on the grounds that by the late fifth century "at least two-thirds of Attica constituted small farmers" (1995, 122). My argument is that the rise of these small farmers occurred after, and partly as a result of, Solon's reforms. Hanson suggests that only a few small farmers whose enterprises failed resorted to extreme measures such as borrowing on the security of their own bodies, or accepting sixth-parter sharecropping contracts (122–24)—but failing farmers can spark a general crisis only if they fail in large numbers, and the question is what structural factors caused so many to fail (clearly not incompetence, as Hanson hints in suggesting that Solon's reforms rewarded "agricultural expertise," 125).

46. Fr. 13.47–48: "he labours for a year"; the verb *latreuein* implies a hired laborer.

47. Frs. 4, 4b, 4c, 11; see van Wees 1999a, 10–29; Fisher 1992, 69–75.

48. See van Wees 2006a, 376–81. Hanson 1995, 123–24, argues that Solon did nothing to help the *thetes*; on 122–23, he suggests that the export ban was an attempt to encourage yeomen farmers to cultivate "olives and vines" while restricting richer cereal farmers, but this cannot be right, because export of *all* produce other than olive oil was banned. The ban is also unlikely to be an attempt to convert farmers to olive cultivation. Rather, it deprived the richest farmers of the most profitable outlet for their surpluses and thereby removed an incentive to compete for more land; olive oil was exempted simply because it was already too important an export: van Wees 2009, 463; Stanley 1999, 229–34.

49. Sparta: Diodorus 7.12.6 ("love of silver"); Tyrtaeus fr. 2 West (redistribution of land), with van Wees 1999b, 2–6. Competition for wealth as a threat: Alcaeus fr. 360 L–P; Theognis, e.g. 227–32. Later evidence: Plutarch, *Mor.* 295cd, 304ef (Megara); Herodotus 5.28–29 (Miletus), as explained by van Wees 2008a, 29–31; contra Forsdyke 2005; and Hanson's view that such conflict was exceptional: 1995, 109, 119.

50. See van Wees 2000a, 57–63.

51. *Od.* 11.293 (herdsmen of Iphicles); 21.85 (herdsmen of Odysseus); *Il.* 11.676 (herdsmen of Itymoneus); *Il.* 11.548–55, 18.162 (herdsmen in similes); only at *Il.* 15.271–76 is the status of the *agroiotai* hunting in the mountains not clear.

52. "Rustics": Sappho, frs. 57, 110; cf. Crielaard 2009, 358–59. Hanson suggests that Theognis' rustics are "dressed like Laertes and Hesiod," i.e., as farmers (1995, 120; cf. 106–7); however, the "threadbare goatskin" is closer to the "bald deerskin" of a beggar (*Od.* 13.434–38), not only because both are worn out, but also because both are worn *instead of* a woolen cloak, whereas Hesiod's farmer (in wet, cold weather, *W&D* 536–46) and the swineherd Eumaeus (at night, *Od.* 14.428–31) wear good-quality goatskin capes *on top of* a cloak and tunic; on Homeric and archaic dress, see van Wees 2005; 2006b.

53. See esp. Morris 2000, 114–19 (classical), 157–71 (archaic); also Kurke 1999; contra Kistler 2004; Hammer 2004. Despite saying at one point that "archaic poets imagined *hoi mesoi* as self-sufficient farmers" (2000, 161), Morris argues that to be "middling" is essentially a state of mind and cannot be identified with a particular social group.

54. For Theognis' image of society, see van Wees 2000a; for Solon's image, see Mitchell 1997. Note also Theognis' rejection of "poverty" (i.e., having to work for a living) as a fate worse than death: 173–78, 181–82, 267–68.

55. Hanson 1995, 109–17, claiming on p. 115 that Aristotle "implies that agrarians of the middle had been widespread throughout the early *polis* history of Greece," on the basis of Aristotle, *Pol.* 1292b25–35, 1305a18–20, 1318b7–15. Contrast *Pol.* 1295a23–26, 37–40 (middle class very rare), 1296a18–22 (Lycurgus middle class). On Aristotle's flaws as a historian of archaic Greece, see van Wees 2002, 72–77.

56. Evidence cited by Hanson 1995, 195, with nn. 11–12. Metapontum: Carter 1990, 429, table 2 (his alternative estimate is even less favorable to Hanson's view); on p. 423, average farm size c. 350–300 BC, when settlement density was highest, is given as 41.5 acres (16.6 ha). The evidence for Halieis, which Hanson cites, concerns city blocks, not farm plots (Boyd and Jameson 1981); his claim that "farms in Greek Italy, as at Halieis, were . . . from 16.3 to 32.6 acres in size" is not supported by any of the evidence adduced.

57. Laconia survey: Cavanagh et al. (eds.) 1996, 2002. Metapontum: Carter 1981, 170, 174 (founded c. 650, first evidence of settlers in the countryside "middle of the sixth century"). See also the summary of survey results from Kea, Methana, Argolid, and Attica in Foxhall 1997, 122–27, and Foxhall's chapter in the present volume.

58. See also Morris 1998, 78. For the sake of completeness, I note two pieces of classical evidence for archaic Athens cited by Hanson as evidence for the existence of three classes. He suggests that the factions of "Shore" and "Hill" represented poorer farmers on marginal land opposed to the rich landowners of the "Plain" (it is not clear to me how this distinction is resolved into "three, not two, social groups"; 1995, 113). We are here not dealing with classes at all, but with three elite factions, each with its center in a different region of Attica (as *Ath. Pol.* 13.4 explains). Hanson also equates the *eupatridai* with landed elite, the *georgoi* with the yeoman class, and the *demiourgoi* with the landless (1995, 111, 113), when it is clear from the fact that in 580 BC all three groups are said to have been granted eligibility for the archonship (*Ath. Pol.* 13.2), which until 457 BC was open to the richest two property classes only, that the first two

groups are rich landowners (the *eupatridai* with hereditary privileges, the others without) and the third consists of rich owners of workshops and other specialists.

59. Given that they amounted to no more than 17% of the citizen population of relatively egalitarian fourth-century Athens. Two important questions, rightly raised by the referees and by Hanson's paper in this volume, are whether a "leisure class" of this size is feasible, and how it compares with the size of elites in other historical societies. Usable comparative data are not easy to come by and will require further research, but one suggestive parallel I happen to have come across is the social structure of a farming region in Puerto Rico in the 1950s, where 16% of landowners had farms of 30 acres or more, cultivated by wage labor, while 28% had farms of 10–30 acres cultivated by family labor (Wolf 1956, 201–3). It may very well be that proportional sizes of "leisured" elites in history have usually been smaller than 10–15%, and if so, a relatively large "leisure class" may be key to the distinctive historical developments of archaic Greece—but it was nevertheless only one-third the size of the class to which Hanson attributes this key role, and in a fundamentally different economic position.

60. While I follow in outline Morris's account of the changing degrees of egalitarianism in the archaeological record, I reject his idea that even in the most unegalitarian phases a broad elite of 25–50% of the population is represented, while in the most egalitarian phases the bulk of the remaining population, "the *kakoi*," are also represented (esp. Morris 1987, 84). I suggest that the archaic material from c. 750 onward still represents only the leisured elite, and that lower-level groups enter the record only in the late sixth century (creating the false impression of a huge population increase; see Morris 1987, 73, fig. 22). In more recent work, Morris has emphasized the changing ideology reflected in the record, rather than visibility of a wider group: esp. 1998; 2000, 109–91.

61. In my view the *basileis* of Homer are also a ruling group within an elite of wealth, rather than a closed aristocracy of birth (e.g., Finley 1977, 53, 59–60) or a fluid elite of merit (e.g., Ulf 1990): see van Wees, forthcoming a.

62. See van Wees 2003, 45–47; cf. Purcell 2005, 117–18, who argues that colonial allotments were much larger than "a minimum for survival."

63. Native serf populations in territories conquered in archaic Crete, Thessaly, Argos, Sicyon, Corinth, Epidaurus, and Elis, as well as Sparta: van Wees 2003, 33–66.

64. See van Wees 2008a for "popular tyranny," contra Forsdyke 2005; Anderson 2005.

65. Sixth-century (as opposed to seventh-century) reform: e.g., Finley 1968 (1981), 24–40; Hodkinson 1997; and in detail van Wees, forthcoming b. Regulation of competition for wealth: Hodkinson 2000, 151–302. Regulated competition for status: Cartledge 1996.

66. Signs of concentration of wealth: e.g., Morris 1992, 145–55. Decline of Spartan citizen numbers and landownership: Hodkinson 2000, 65–112. The late sources that claim Lycurgus redistributed all land to 9,000 citizens are peddling a third-century myth (Hodkinson 2000, 68–81), but the figure 9,000 as such may derive from the number of Spartiates included in the public messes when these were instituted in the late sixth century: see van Wees, forthcoming b.

67. Rise of trade: e.g., van Wees 2009, 457–60; Hanson dates this after 480 BC (1995, 359, 365–68, 375–79), which is surely too late. That small farmers produced for the market, at least in classical Athens, is clear from the comment in pseudo-Aristotle, *Oeconomica* 1344b33–34, 1345a18–19, that "'he Attic system" is for small farmers not to store their produce but to sell everything and buy all their food and other supplies in the market.

68. For the late sixth-century rise of the trireme, public navies, and wars of hegemony, see van Wees 2008b; forthcoming c; Nagy 2009. Hanson subscribes to the more common view that these were fifth-century developments (1995, 316, 334–36).

69. In the absence of pay for office, positions of power would in practice necessarily have been restricted to the leisure classes, even if they were notionally open to all.

70. Aristotle, *Politics* 1318b7–15; for the philosopher, the working farmer's inability to spend time on politics makes a farming democracy the "best" (i.e., least bad) form of democracy; he also claims that this was the oldest form of democracy (cf. 1305a18–20), as stressed by Hanson 1995, 116–17, but as we have seen there is no evidence for this. For the leisure-class regime of 5,000 citizens in 411, see above, n. 40.

71. Grieb 2008 argues that democracy survived longer than traditionally believed.

72. Size of Eretrian territory: Hansen and Nielsen 2004, 72, 652 (1,500 km^2 in fourth century); Walker 2004, 15 (one-third less in archaic period). From an Eretrian roster of c. 290 BC, Hansen 2006, 61–88, reconstructs a population of c. 4,000 adult male citizens, and argues that this represents an oligarchic regime with a high property census; Knoepfler 2007, 679–81, argues for a full franchise, but reconstructs a population of "easily" 6,000 citizens. Corinth: Salmon 1984, 19 (c. 900 km^2); 5,000 hoplites in 479: Herodotus 9.28; this may represent a two-thirds mobilization, which was the norm later: Thuc. 2.10, 47.1. Naxos: Hdt. 5.30.4; territory 430 km^2: Hansen and Nielsen 2004, 760.

73. Plut. *Solon* 9.2 (Salamis); *Mor.* 296ab (Samian dead). Samian territory: 468 km^2 plus mainland possessions: Hansen and Nielsen 2004, 1094. Casualty rates: Krentz 1985a.

74. Sepeia: Hdt. 7.148. Athens: 9,000 at Marathon: Nepos, *Miltiades* 5.1; Plutarch, *Moralia* 305b; Pausanias 10.20.2; to Athens' 8,000 at Plataea (Hdt. 9.28.6) one must add perhaps 1,000 hoplites serving as marines in the navy at the same time. Megara and Sicyon: Herodotus 9.28. Two-thirds mobilization: see n. 72, above. In 431 BC, Athens' field army was just under half of all available hoplites and cavalry: Thuc. 2.13.6–7.

75. Proportions: Hdt. 9.29; Sparta: seven light-armed helots for every hoplite; cf. 9.10.

76. Eretria: *Ath. Pol.* 15.2; *Pol.* 1306a35–36. Chalcis: Herodotus 5.77. The other indication of time, "when cities were growing larger," is of no use: at 1305a8–13, 18–28, Aristotle claims that "the cities were not large" at the time of Theagenes (c. 630), Peisistratus (c. 550), and Dionysius (c. 400); at 1310b17–31, he claims that "the cities had already grown large" at the time of Cypselus (c. 650), Peisistratus, and Dionysius. Critical analysis of Aristotle, see van Wees 2002, 72–77; contra, e.g., Hanson 1995, 237.

77. Size of expeditionary forces: Krentz 2007, 149 (table 6.1); slave attendants: Hunt 1998, 166–68; hoplite casualties among the elite: Aristotle, *Pol.* 1303a8–10; *Ath. Pol.* 26.1. For later developments, see van Wees 2004, 93–95, 103–4.

78. "Ugly muscle": Hanson 1995, 265; see further van Wees 2004, 89–95; 2007, 273–81.

79. Hanson 1995, 221–44; "afternoon wars": 378; cf. 255.

80. See Krentz 2000, 2002, 2007; van Wees 2004, 115–50, 232–40; 2011b.

81. Hanson 1995, 230–33; 1991; Cartledge 2001, 153–66. Snodgrass 1965; Krentz 1985b; 1994. For the view that no closed phalanx developed until the end of the archaic age, see van Wees 2000b; 2004, 166–97; Rey 2008, 107–287; cf. Wheeler 2007, 192–202.

82. On *tropaion* and truces, see Krentz 2002. For late archaic changes in armor, see Snodgrass 1999, 90–95; Jarva 1995. Mounted hoplites: Greenhalgh 1973; Brouwers 2007 argues that they played a crucial role in the adoption of hoplite armor.

83. See Chaniotis 2005, 20–26; Ma 2000, 343–49.

84. See Ceccarelli 1993; van Wees 1995b.

85. Contra, e.g., Cartledge 2001, 153–66; Salmon 1977. Andrewes's widely accepted theory linking the tyranny of Pheidon of Argos with the creating of the hoplite phalanx (1956, 31–42) is pure speculation; cf. the critical comments of Hall 2007, 145–54.

Bibliography

Amouretti, M.-C., and J.-P. Brun (eds.). 1993. *La production du vin et de l'huile en Méditerranée* (*BCH Supplément* 26). Paris.

Anderson, G. 2005. "Before *turannoi* were tyrants." *Classical Antiquity* 24:173–222.

Andrewes, A. 1956. *The Greek Tyrants*. London.

Blok, J., and A. Lardinois (eds.). 2006. *Solon of Athens*. Leiden and Boston.

Boyd, T., and M. H. Jameson. 1981. "Urban and rural land division in ancient Greece." *Hesperia* 50:327–42.

Brouwers, J. J. 2007. "From horsemen to hoplites: Some remarks on archaic Greek warfare." *BABESCH* 82:305–19.

Burford, A. 1993. *Land and Labor in the Greek World*. Baltimore and London.

Carter, J. C. 1981. "Rural settlement at Metaponto." In G. Barker and R. Hodges (eds.), *Archaeology and Italian Society* (BAR Int. Series 102), 167–78. Oxford.

Carter, J. C. 1990. "Metapontum—land, wealth and population." In J.-P. Descoeudres (ed.), *Greek Colonists and Native Populations*, 405–41. Oxford.

Cartledge, P. A. 1996. "Comparatively equal." In J. Ober and C. Hedrick (eds.), *Demokratia*, 175–86. Princeton.

Cartledge, P. A. 2001. "The birth of the hoplite." In id., *Spartan Reflections*, 153–66. London; originally published as "La nascita degli opliti e l'organizzazione militare" in S. Settis (ed.), *I Greci*, vol. 2, 681–714 (Turin 1996).

Cavanagh, W., J. Crouwel, R.W.V. Catling, and G. Shipley. 1996. *Continuity and Change in a Greek Rural Landscape: The Laconia Survey*, vol. 2: *Archaeological Data*. London.

Cavanagh, W., J. Crouwel, R.W.V. Catling, and G. Shipley. 2002. *Continuity and Change in a Greek Rural Landscape: The Laconia Survey*, vol. 1: *Results and Interpretation*. London.

Ceccarelli, P. 1993. "Sans thalassocratie, pas de démocratie? Le rapport entre thalassocratie et démocratie à Athènes dans la discussion du Ve et IVe siècle av. J.C." *Historia* 42:444–70.

Chaniotis, A. 2005. *War in the Hellenistic World: A Social and Cultural History*. Malden.

Crielaard, J. P. 2009. "Cities." In K. Raaflaub and H. van Wees (eds.) 2009, 349–72.

Davies, J. K. 1984. *Wealth and the Power of Wealth in Classical Athens*. Salem, NH.

Edwards, A. 2004. *Hesiod's Ascra*. Berkeley.

Finley, M. I. 1968. "Sparta." In J. P. Vernant (ed.), *Problèmes de la guerre en Grèce ancienne*. Paris; repinted as "Sparta and Spartan society" in M. I. Finley, *Economy and Society in Ancient Greece*, 24–40 (Harmondsworth, 1981).

Finley, M. 1973. *The Ancient Economy*. London; revised ed. 1985.

Finley, M. 1977. *The World of Odysseus*, 2nd ed. London; 1st ed. 1954.

Fisher, N. 1992. *Hybris: A Study in the Values of Guilt and Shame in Ancient Greece*. Warminster.

Fisher, N., and H. van Wees (eds.). 1998. *Archaic Greece: New Approaches and New Evidence*. London and Swansea.

Forsdyke, S. 2005. *Exile, Ostracism and Democracy*. Ann Arbor.

Foxhall, L. 1997. "A view from the top: Evaluating the Solonian property classes." In L. Mitchell and P. Rhodes (eds.) 1997, 113–36.

Foxhall, L., and H. A. Forbes. 1982. "Sitometreia: The role of grain as a staple food in classical antiquity." *Chiron* 12:41–90.

Gallant, T. W. 1982. "Agricultural systems, land tenure, and the reforms of Solon." *ABSA* 77:111–24.

Gallant, T. W. 1991. *Risk and Survival in Ancient Greece: Reconstructing the Rural Domestic Economy*. Stanford, CA.

Greenhalgh, P. A. 1973. *Early Greek Warfare: Horsemen and Chariots in the Homeric and Archaic Ages*. Cambridge.

Grieb, V. 2008. *Hellenistische Demokratie. Historia Einzelschriften 199*. Stuttgart.

Hall, J. 2007. *History of the Archaic Greek World, ca 1200–479 BCE*. Malden).

Hammer, D. 2004. "Ideology, the symposium, and archaic politics." *AJP* 125:479–512.

Hansen, M. H. 2006. *The Shotgun Method: The Demography of the Ancient Greek City-State Culture*. Columbia and London.

Hansen, M. H., and T. H. Nielsen. 2004. *An Inventory of Archaic and Classical Poleis*. Oxford.

Hanson, V. D. 1995. *The Other Greeks: The Family Farm and the Agrarian Roots of Western Civilization*. New York.

Hemelrijk, J. 1925. *Penia en Ploutos*. Amsterdam; reprint New York, 1979.

Hodkinson, S. 1997. "The development of Spartan society and institutions in the archaic period." In L. Mitchell and P. Rhodes (eds.) 1997, 83–102.

Hodkinson, S. 2000. *Property and Wealth in Classical Sparta*. London/Swansea.

Hunt, P. 1998. *Slavery, Warfare and Ideology in the Greek Historians*. Cambridge.

Isager, I., and J. E. Skydsgaard. 1992. *Ancient Greek Agriculture: An Introduction*. London and New York.

Jameson, M. H. 1977–78. "Agriculture and slavery in classical Athens." *CJ* 73:122–45.

Jarva, E. 1995. *Archaiologia on Archaic Greek Body Armour*. Rovaniemi.

Kistler, E. 2004. "Kampf der Mentalitäten: Ian Morris' 'elitist' versus 'middling ideology'?" In R. Rollinger and C. Ulf (eds.), *Griechische Archaik. Interne Entwicklungen—Externe Impulse*, 145–76. Berlin.

Knoepfler, D. 2007. "Érétrie." *Bulletin Épigraphique*, no. 327 (*REG* 120 [2007]: 679–81).

Krentz, P. 1985a. "Casualties in hoplite battle." *GRBS* 26:13–21.

Krentz, P. 1985b. "The nature of hoplite battle." *ClAnt* 4:50–61.

Krentz, P. 1994. "Continuing the *othismos* on *othismos*." *AHB* 8:45–49.

Krentz, P. 2000. "Deception in archaic and classical Greek warfare." In H. van Wees (ed.) 2000, 167–200.

Krentz, P. 2002. "Fighting by the rules: The invention of the hoplite *agōn*." *Hesperia* 71:23–39.

Krentz, P. 2007. "Archaic and classical Greek war." In P. Sabin et al. (eds.) 2007, 147–85.

Kurke, L. 1999. *Coins, Bodies, Games, and Gold: The Politics of Meaning in Archaic Greece*. Princeton.

Lambert, S. D. 1997, *Rationes Centesimarum: Sales of Public Land in Lykourgan Athens*. Amsterdam.

Loomis, W. 1998. *Wages, Welfare Costs and Inflation in Classical Athens*. Ann Arbor.

Ma, J. 2000. "Fighting poleis of the hellenistic world." In H. van Wees (ed.) 2000, 337–76.

Markle, M. M. 1985. "Jury pay and asembly pay at Athens." In P. A. Cartledge and F .D. Harvey (eds.), *Crux: Essays Presented to G.E.M. de Ste. Croix on His 75th Birthday*, 265–97. Exeter.

Mitchell, L. 1997. "New wine in old wineskins: Solon, *arete* and the *agathos*." In L. Mitchell and P. Rhodes (eds.) 1997, 137–47.

Mitchell, L., and P. Rhodes (eds.). 1997. *The Development of the Polis in Archaic Greece*. London.

Morris, I. 1987. *Burial and Ancient Society: The Rise of the Greek City-State*. Cambridge.

Morris, I. 1992. *Death-Ritual and Social Structure in Classical Antiquity*. Cambridge.

Morris, I. 1998. "Archaeology and archaic Greek history." In N. Fisher and H. van Wees (eds.) 1998, 1–91.

Morris, I. 2000. *Archaeology as Cultural History: Words and Things in Iron Age Greece*. Malden.

Murray, O. 1993. *Early Greece*, 2nd ed. No place; first ed. 1980.

Nagy, G. 2009. *Homer the Preclassic*. Washington, DC.

Ober, J. 1989. *Mass and Elite in Democratic Athens: Rhetoric, Ideology and the Power of the People*. Princeton.

Purcell, N. 2005. "Colonization and Mediterranean history." In H. Hurst and S. Owen (eds.), *Ancient Colonizations: Analogy, Similarity, Difference*, 115–39. London.

Raaflaub, K. A. 2006. "Athenian and Spartan *eunomia*, or: What to do with Solon's timocracy?" In J. Blok and A. Lardinois (eds.) 2006, 390–428.

Raaflaub, K. A. 2007. "The breakthrough of *demokratia* in mid-fifth-century Athens." In K. Raaflaub, J. Ober, and R. Wallace, *Origins of Democracy in Ancient Greece*, 105–54. Berkeley.

Raaflaub, K. A., and H. van Wees (eds.). 2009. *A Companion to Archaic Greece*. London and New York.

Sabin, P., H. van Wees, and M. Whitby (eds.). 2007. *The Cambridge History of Greek and Roman Warfare*, vol. 1. Cambridge.

Salmon, J. 1977. "Political hoplites?" *JHS* 97:84–101.

Snodgrass, A. 1965. "The hoplite reform and history." *JHS* 85:110–22.

Snodgrass, A. 1999. *Arms and Armour of the Greeks*. Baltimore; first ed. 1967.

Stanley, P. 1999. *The Economic Reforms of Solon*. St. Katharinen.

Ste. Croix, G. de. 2004. *Athenian Democratic Origins and Other Essays*, ed. D. Harvey and R. Parker with the assistance of P. Thonemann. Oxford.

Stroud, R. 1998. *The Athenian Grain-Tax Law of 374/3 BC* (*Hesperia* suppl. 29). Princeton.

Ulf, C. 1990. "Die Abwehr von internem Streit als Teil des "politischen" Programms der homerischen Epen." *Grazer Beiträge* 17:1–25.

Van Wees, H. 1995a. "Princes at dinner: Social event and social structure in Homer." In J.-P. Crielaard (ed.), *Homeric Questions*, 147–82. Amsterdam.

Van Wees, H. 1995b. "Politics and the battlefield: Ideology in Greek warfare." In A. Powell (ed.), *The Greek World*, 153–78. London and New York.

Van Wees, H. 1999a. "The mafia of early Greece: Violent exploitation in the seventh and sixth centuries BC." In K. Hopwood (ed.), *Organized Crime in Antiquity*, 1–51. London.

Van Wees, H. 1999b. "Tyrtaeus" *Eunomia*: Nothing to do with the Great Rhetra." In S. Hodkinson and A. Powell (eds.), *Sparta: New Perspectives*, 1–41. London.

Van Wees, H. (ed.). 2000. *War and Violence in Ancient Greece*. London and Swansea.

Van Wees, H. 2000a. "Megara's mafiosi: Timocracy and violence in Theognis." In R. Brock and S. Hodkinson (eds.), *Alternatives to Athens*, 52–67. Oxford.

Van Wees, H. 2000b. "The development of the hoplite phalanx: Iconography and reality in the seventh century." In H. van Wees (ed.) 2000, 125–66.

Van Wees, H. 2001. "The myth of the middle-class army: Military and social status in ancient Athens." In L. Hannestad and T. Bekker-Nielsen (eds.), *War as a Cultural and Social Force*, 45–71. Copenhagen.

Van Wees, H. 2002. "Tyrants, oligarchs and citizen militias." In A. Chaniotis and P. Ducrey (eds.), *Army and Power in the Ancient World*, 61–82. Stuttgart.

Van Wees, H. 2003. "Conquerors and serfs: Wars of conquest and forced labour in archaic Greece." In N. Luraghi and S. Alcock (eds.), *Helots and Their Masters in Laconia and Messenia*, 33–80. Washington, DC.

Van Wees, H. 2004. *Greek Warfare: Myths and Realities*. London.

Van Wees, H. 2005. "Trailing tunics and sheepskin coats: Dress and status in early Greece." In L. Cleland, M. Harlow, and L. Llewellyn-Jones (eds.), *The Clothed Body in the Ancient World*, 44–51. Oxford.

Van Wees, H. 2006a. "Mass and elite in Solon"s Athens." In J. Blok and A. Lardinois (eds.) 2006, 351–89.

Van Wees, H. 2006b. "Clothes, class and gender in Homer." In D. Cairns (ed.), *Body Language in the Greek and Roman Worlds*, 1–36. Swansea.

Van Wees, H. 2007. "War and society." In P. Sabin et al. (eds.) 2007, 273–99.

Van Wees, H. 2008a. "'Stasis, destroyer of men': Mass, elite, political violence and security in archaic Greece." In C. Brélaz and P. Ducrey (eds.), *Sécurité collective et ordre public dans les sociétés anciennes*, 1–48. Vandoeuvres-Geneva.

Van Wees, H. 2008b. "'Diejenigen, die segeln, sollen Sold erhalten': Seekriegführung und—finanzierung im archaischen Eretria." In F. Burrer and H. Müller (eds.), *Kriegskosten und Kriegsfinanzierung in der Antike*, 128–50. Darmstadt; English version in G. Fagan and M. Trundle (eds.), *New Perspectives on Ancient Warfare* (Leiden and Boston 2010).

Van Wees, H. 2009. "The economy." In K. A Raaflaub and H. van Wees (eds.) 2009, 444–67.

Van Wees, H. 2011a. "Demetrius and Draco: Athens' property classes and population in and before 317 BC." *JHS* 131:95–114.

Van Wees, H. 2011b. "Defeat and destruction: The ethics of ancient Greek warfare." In M. Linder and S. Tausend (eds.), *"Böser Krieg": exzessive Gewalt in der antiken Kriegsführung und Strategien zu deren Vermeidung*, 69–110. Graz.

Van Wees, H. Forthcoming a. *The World of Achilles*. Cambridge.

Van Wees, H. Forthcoming b. "Luxury, austerity and equality" and "The common messes." In A. Powell (ed.), *A Companion to Sparta*. Malden.

Van Wees, H. Forthcoming c. "Athens in context" and "Institutions." In H. van Wees, P. J. Rhodes, et al., *Athenian Public Finance, 594–86 BC*. Oxford.

Walker, K. G. 2004. *Archaic Eretria: A Political and Social History from the Earliest Times to 490 BC*. London and New York.

West, M. L. 1978. *Hesiod: Works and Days*. Oxford.

Wheeler, E. L. 2007. "Land battles." In P. Sabin et al. (eds.) 2007, 186–223.

Wolf, E. R. 1956. "San José: Subcultures of a 'Traditional' Coffee Municipality." In J. H. Steward (ed.), *The People of Puerto Rico*, 171–264. Urbana, IL.

CHAPTER 12

The Hoplite Narrative

VICTOR DAVIS HANSON

Why Don't We Know More about Hoplites?

There are few controversies in Greek history as spirited as those over the origins and nature of hoplite battle. The dilemma arises because we have few prose accounts of set battles before Marathon (490 BC). Consequently, it is far easier to take exception to a particular element of a general reconstruction than it is to risk offering a likely comprehensive scenario of the nature of the hoplite phalanx from meager evidence.

Surviving battle descriptions in later historians are fragmentary, and dependent largely on a prior oral tradition. Battle references to hoplites and/or mass fighting in Homer's epics and the subsequent lyric poets remain subject to raging controversy. Poetical interpretations often require the sensitivity of a literary critic to distinguish realistic portrayal from expressions that are metaphorical, or predicated on the formulaic, metrical, and vocabulary rules of poetic expression. The net result is we know almost no details about either the strategy or the tactics involved in early battles from the eighth to early fifth centuries. The Lelantine Plain, the wars for Messenia, the battle of Hysiai, the so-called Battle of Champions, Sepeia, and a host of other engagements are now mostly mere names.[1]

Representation on vases and in stone often reflects the conventions of artistic genres. It is, after all, nearly impossible to portray a phalanx in its proper three-dimensional perspective in ceramic painting or even on temple friezes. Pots and sculpture are hard to date. The subject matter is far more often mythological in theme than historical.

Physical remains of arms and armor are invaluable sources of evidence. But after some 2,500 years, artifacts are often poorly preserved, especially those with leather and wood components. Their original weights and sizes remain inexact; and it is sometimes difficult to determine whether surviving specimens in dedicatory and ceremonial circumstances were typical or exceptional. Often given the scarcity of evidence, discussion of hoplite warfare is compressed over three centuries, inasmuch as we do know to what degree arms and tactics were roughly similar or at wide variance in the decades between, say, 700 and 350 BC. And when ancient military analysts talk in the abstract about the weapons, tactics, and problems of the phalanx, they usually do so in reference to the Macedonian-inspired formations of the late Hellenistic period—as the extant Roman-era works of tacticians such as Arrian, Asclepiodotus, and Onasander attest.[2]

Moreover, the nature of hoplite battle involves not merely a question of source materials and military history, but is deeply embedded in the central controversies of the rise of the polis itself: who were hoplites, and did they reflect or cause (or even, were they largely irrelevant to) the major social and economic changes of Greek history? Did hoplites and phalanxes prove central to the security of the small Greek city-states? Or, given the beauty of hoplite arms and the romance of phalanxes, has the later Western tradition exaggerated their importance, and forgotten the invaluable role of Greek horsemen, archers, and lightly armed troops? In short, major economic, political, social, and cultural interpretations of Greek history hinge on how we interpret often narrow controversies of hoplite fighting.[3]

The Emergence of a Grand Narrative

Despite scholarly disagreements about hoplites, there has emerged over the last two centuries of classical scholarship what I would call the "grand hoplite narrative." This general consensus, with occasional qualifications, has found its way into most histories of Greece and runs along something like the following lines.[4]

Sometime in the late eighth century BC elements of the hoplite panoply began appearing in plenitude in Greece—prominently perhaps in the Peloponnese, but within decades throughout much of the Greek-speaking world. The concave round wooden shield, heavy bronze breastplate, greaves, and crested helmet, along with a thrusting spear with butt spike and ancillary sword, reflected a preference for fighting en masse in the phalanx. While the ensemble was often worn piecemeal and developed slowly, and while initially all sorts of differently armed warriors fought alongside hoplites, such heavy, cumbersome arms and armor eventually proved not only best suited for phalanx warfare but also disadvantageous for purely soloist fighters. The so-called hoplite panoply either reflected a desire to improve existing mass formations or, by the exceptional characteristics of such arms, began to prompt many of the novel tactics of phalanx warfare itself.[5]

By the mid-seventh-century BC at least, many Greek city-states fielded small armies of hoplite phalanxes that perhaps brought a stature to infantry warfare not enjoyed by either the wealthier and less numerous horsemen—or the more numerous and less wealthy lightly armed soldiers. Accordingly, the Greeks felt there were certain desirable conventions to hoplite battle, concerning its conduct and duration, that tended to mitigate the destructive nature of frequent warring among small city-states—even as they allowed that on occasion such moral protocols of heavy infantry combat were ignored or abbreviated in the heat of battle, or over the course of longer wars simply superseded by other strategies and tactics.[6]

Early hoplite battle, then, was conducted by infantrymen in cumbersome armor. Hoplites massed in columns several shields deep and collided with their opponents in some sort of shock battle, and perhaps after the fifth century, when equipment grew somewhat lighter, often at a trot or double-time. While there was chaotic and often vicious individual spear fighting along the front ranks, armies ideally tried to use their superior mass, solidarity, and cohesion to break apart the ranks of their opponents.

The round, double-gripped shield could provide its wearer only partial protection. Each hoplite found the right half of his body—especially his spear arm and shoulder—protected by the shield of the hoplite to his right. In some sense, the entire battle line was composed of fighters who simultaneously were both providing partial protection to, and receiving it from, their fellow hoplites at their sides. The greater depth of a phalanx was felt to provide commensurate increased—and desirable—thrust, even at the cost of taking more spearmen out of the initial collision and fighting in the killing zone. Accordingly, a hoplite ethos emerged stressing group solidarity and the need, as far as possible, to stay in one's assigned rank, as the cumbersome panoply made solo fighting riskier to both self and comrade—and skirmishing clearly negated the advantages of heavy armor, the large shield, and long spear. Phalanxes, accordingly, were calibrated by the depth of "shields" rather than of "spears"—again a reflection of the emphasis on collective protective solidarity rather than individual battle prowess.

In the battle zones at the front of the two armies, spears often were broken, while the middle and rear ranks soon sought to force and push the frontline hoplites on through the enemy's lines of shields. Elements of the phalanx usually advanced as a unit or collapsed together, often along tribal or regional contingents. Pursuit of the defeated was limited by both the weight of the panoply and the apparent reluctance to define victory by absolute annihilation of the enemy rather than the collapse of enemy advance and solidarity. Acknowledgment of the verdict of the battle was reinforced through a variety of rituals.[7]

The Greek islands, the horse-raising plains in Thessaly and Macedon, and tribal frontiers such as the mountainous regions of western Greece were, in terms of geography alone, less conducive to battle by hoplite phalanxes. But elsewhere on the small plains of the mainland the rise of hoplites is often associated with the simultaneous fruition of the Greek polis, especially the prominence of a broadening property-owning class, positioned somewhere in between the landless poor and the mounted wealthy.[8]

The prominence of hoplites in classical literature and art reflected both their utility on the battlefield—and a certain growing chauvinism of the middling warrior-citizen. There was certainly something visually arresting about the hoplite protective ensemble, from horsehair crest down to bronze greaves and even toe guards, enhanced when thousands of such armed warriors were arrayed in serried ranks—at least as we can tell from ancient literary descriptions and surviving vase paintings. And while the obvious combat limitations of heavily armed phalanxes were apparent to the Greeks as early as the Persian War, and all too real by the Peloponnesian War, city-states continued to invest in hoplite armies and often sought to defend or attack other city-states through decisive engagements, as the prominent hoplite battles of the fourth century attest.

Apart from reasons of military conservatism, and the general reverence for the autonomous property-owning heavy infantrymen, hoplite battle of some sort persisted for centuries from Archaic to Hellenistic times, quite apart from the social, political, and economical landscape of its origins. Few forms of warfare, after all, could concentrate so many fighters in such a small space to fight in such a decisive and public manner.[9]

The general notion that Greek warfare was both frequent and yet not genocidal; that there was ideally a preference for decisive infantry battle rather than extended skirmishing and inconclusive raiding; and that the Greeks accepted war as inevitable and a tragic element of the human experience was predicated at least in part on the ethos of hoplite fighting that usually offered clear-cut results, involved many of the voting citizenry, and did not result in a degree of casualties that would have ruined the city-state.

Currently, however, much of the above traditional hoplite narrative has been questioned. In what follows, rather than concentrate in depth on the myriad of individual controversies that have arisen recently, I briefly summarize some of the more contentious points of dispute, and hope to show that the traditional narrative best reflects our existing evidence as well as offering the most logical hypothesis about the nature of hoplite battle.[10]

Rich, Poor, Middle-Class—or Mixed Up—Hoplites?

Some critics have suggested that the notion of classical Greek hoplites as a distinct middling class—known in our sources often as *hoi mesoi*—is mostly a myth. Hoplite warfare, then, was supposedly instead mostly the domain of the upper classes that alone could afford armor; and fighting in mass formation is no reflection of an emergence of a new sort of Greek citizen.[11]

Yet the fact that the later Greeks themselves did not always recognize such a middle group in modernist terms as a clearly conceptualized "class"—or that the qualifications of *mesoi* at times were loose and fluid—does not negate its existence. Sometimes the argument for and against the presence of middling hoplites hinges on interpretation of Aristotle's famous description in his *Politics* about the rise of the city-state and its connection with its hoplite citizenry (4.1297b16–24):

> Indeed the earliest form of government among the Greeks after monarchy was composed of those who actually fought. In the beginning that meant cavalry, since without cohesive arrangement (*aneu suntaxeôs*), heavy armament (*to hoplitikon*) is useless; and experience and tactical knowledge of such hoplite systems (*tôn toioutôn empeiriai kai taxies*) did not exist in ancient times, and so power again lay with mounted horsemen. But once the poleis grew and those with hoplite armor became stronger (*tôn en tois hoplois ischusantôn*), more people shared in government (*pleious meteichon tês politeias*).

Note here Aristotle's impression that the city-states were at first dominated by horsemen, since hoplites were in small numbers and did not fully employ the tactics of the phalanx ("cohesive arrangement"). But as population grew, and once heavy equipment and those who used it found their optimum expression on the battlefield, then government reacted accordingly to incorporate this new group ("more people") of citizen-soldiers.

Aristotle's sociology elsewhere in the *Politics* about classes is not systematic or even consistent. He often is imprecise (as are we moderns who naturally prefer a simplistic rich/poor political dichotomy in casual political discourse even as we privilege the all-American "middle class") about the rich, poor, and middle classes. Nevertheless, Aristotle is also often unambiguous elsewhere in the *Politics* when talking about the relationships of hoplites to those who farm and own property (e.g., 4.1291a31–33), a common enough connection that echoes throughout Greek literature in diverse authors, in both implicit references and constant metaphors and similes.[12]

Equally importantly, middleness itself is reflected as a ubiquitous sociological ideal in Greek literature (e.g., cf. Phocylides: "Much good is there to the middle-ones; I wish to be midmost [*mesos*] in a city" [fr. 7.1–2]; cf. Euripides *Suppliants*, "the ones in the middle" [*hoi mesoi*"] are the "salvation of the city" [238–42]). Such generic idealization of the in-between is often naturally connected to the hoplite ranks that on the battlefield are framed at both ends by the mounted wealthy and the poorer lightly armed troops. In the rural sociology of the polis, they remain distinct from both the wealthy horse owners and the landless poor.[13]

Farmland is sometimes in Greek literature assessed by its potential to produce hoplites, emphasizing the natural generalized connection between those citizens who farm their own plots and those who fight in the phalanx. A variety of passages in classical authors equate farmers with hoplites and define them as the true measure of the city-states, as well as the generally held notion that the catalysts for most wars were disputes over borderlands among rival property-holding citizenries. The Spartan exception of having helots do much of their agricultural labor emphasizes the normal Greek belief that elsewhere farmers and hoplites were nearly synonymous: "Not by caring for our fields," the singular Spartans brag, "but rather by caring for ourselves did we acquire those fields (Plut. *Mor.* 214a72).[14]

There is also the more practical argument of demography and landscape. Take Athens—generally not associated as a major hoplite power—where rough estimates of the citizen population, average farm size, and total arable land make it likely that there were nearly twenty thousand middling farm owners, about the accustomed number of the hoplite class. That hoplites may have been a minority of the resident citizens within the city-state does not negate either the fact that they formed a middling group, or that Greek city-states could field hoplite armies in the many thousands.

In contrast, if we were to believe that "the model hoplite was not the working man whose fitness for war derived from hard labor, but the man of leisure who owed his fitness to dedicated physical and mental training," then we would have to assume that rather sizable numbers of the Greek citizenry—compare the some forty thousand hoplites who fought together at battles like Nemea—had enough capital not to work physically and the leisure to train for battle. Likewise there would be no reason for the constant references in (elite) classical literature to the connection between hard physical work on the farm or in the countryside and the readiness to fight.[15]

Was Greek Warfare Rare?

The common assumption of the hoplite narrative that Greek warfare was a relatively common event has been challenged recently on the odd basis that it is supposedly a fallacy hinging on a misreading of a single, though famous, passage in Plato's *Laws* to the effect that all Greeks are engaged in continuous war against those of other city-states.[16] At one point in Plato's dialogue, Cleinias, a Cretan, quotes an anonymous Cretan lawgiver: "What most people call 'peace' is nothing but a word, and in fact every city-state is at all times, by nature in a condition of undeclared war (*akêrutos polemos*) with every other city-state" (*Laws* 626a).

The orthodox interpretation usually cites the passage as further evidence of the Greeks' philosophical acceptance that periodic outbreaks of hostility were more to be expected than long periods of peace. Here the Athenian stranger and Cleinias are discussing the Cretan constitution—specifically, why the custom arose for group messes and the need for constant preparedness, given the perception of near-constant war. The explanation of a condition of undeclared war is not, as revisionists sometimes argue, followed by a sneer against the masses that are unaware of it, or an implication that ceaseless fighting was only a rarified theory. Instead the thought serves as a necessary explanation of why the anonymous Cretan lawgiver—as an authority responsible for the safety of the Cretan community—"established every one of our institutions, both in the public sphere and private, with an eye on war."[17]

But more importantly, there are plenty of other abstract observations, across a wide chronological spectrum, that reflect a similar Hellenic view of war as a near-constant and natural state of affairs. Most famously, Heraclitus remarked: "War is both father and king of all, some he has shown forth as gods and others as men. Some he has made slaves and others free." And in another—less often quoted—fragment, he reiterated that view of war as a natural state of affairs: "It should be understood that war is the common condition (*xunon*), that strife is justice, and that all things come to pass through the compulsion of strife" (frgs. 53, 80). It would be hard to imagine philosophers referring to war as "common" if it were felt to be a somewhat rare occurrence.

The point of these observations, which, again, cover a large chronological continuum, is that generic conflict is seen by abstract Greek thinkers as almost natural—a ceaseless, omnipresent state that at any time can alter even the very status of the citizen and slave. In Xenophon's *Hellenica* (6.3.15), for example, the Athenian envoy, Callistratus, matter-of-factly remarks in candid terms to his Spartan audience, "Moreover, we all know that wars are forever breaking out and being concluded, and that we—if not now, still at some future time—shall desire peace again."

Given that there were probably over a thousand city-states without a unified federal state, but with poorly demarcated borderlands, and plenty of contentious landowners who could both vote and bear arms, the observations of Heraclitus, Plato, and Xenophon seem quite natural.

The Tragic Acceptance of War

There is a certain Hellenic resignation—perhaps even cynicism—that the state of war among the city-states is something commonplace and that men should accept it as inevitable. The particular allegiances between the city-states that for a time might deter a war pale in comparison to the larger bellicosity of the poleis, and indeed of human nature itself, that ensure wars of some sort are near constant. War was seen either as Xenophon's natural state, or Plato's undeclared reality, or Heraclitus's king and father—or, in Thucydides's words, a "violent teacher" (5.82), or in Pindar's (fr. 15) formulation "a thing of fear."

Again, these reflections seem natural given the absence of a Panhellenic federal state, the sheer number of rival city-states, the limited amount of arable land in Greece, and the geography of small habitable enclaves set off from one another by hills and mountains that form convenient borders—and given especially a pretechnological age among a relatively small population in which wars of massive annihilation were largely unknown. To take a modern example, while warfare between the three North American nations—Canada, Mexico, and the United States—broke out in the last two centuries on only two or three occasions, one might imagine a very different, European-like scenario had there been fifty different contiguous American sovereign countries, rather than unified states of a single nation.

While it is easy to suggest the classical Athenian experience of near-constant warring is either atypical of its own history or that of other poleis, it is nonetheless probably true that Athens warred three out of four years in the fifth century, and perhaps two out of three over a longer continuum. Likewise, the fourth-century Spartan state suffered severe social dislocations, given its almost nonstop deployment of its officers abroad in the aftermath of the Peloponnesian War. The ubiquity of martial scenes in ceramic art and on temple friezes and pediments emphasizes the general Greek sense that war was a near-natural state of affairs—born out in literary genres from Homeric epic to the Greek historians that are devoted to an explication of war.[18]

The Greeks accepted the tragic notion that while war was impossible to legislate away, outlaw, or prevent from ever again breaking out, there were nonetheless ways to prevent individual wars and to mitigate their severity—through deterrence, a balance of power, the creation of coalitions, constant preparedness, eternal vigilance, and, when fighting broke out, acknowledgment of certain limitations on hoplite combat. This acceptance of inherent bellicosity is well illustrated in the Theban general Pagondas's speech before the hoplite battle of Delium (Thuc. 4.92) in which he outlined the need for constant vigilance against his Athenian neighbors, who were likely to be aggressive when they sensed weakness: "As between neighbors generally, freedom means simply a determination to hold one's own," and further: "People who, like the Athenians in the present instance, are tempted by pride of strength to attack their neighbors, usually march most confidently against those who keep still, and only defend themselves in their own country, but think twice before they grapple with those who meet them outside their frontier and strike the first blow if opportunity offers."[19]

Again, this tragic acceptance of armed conflict is not an endorsement of war's utility; nevertheless, it is antithetical to the modernist notion that human nature can be altered sufficiently—through greater education, training, and freedom from want—to ensure that war might be outlawed or eliminated entirely.

Fluid Fighting?

Some have advanced a different scenario of battle in which hoplites along the battle line fought at some distance from each other, in more fluid fashion, and in formations in which there was neither an initial collision nor a subsequent pushing to achieve a breakthrough.[20]

But once again there are general reasons to doubt this revisionism of the hoplite narrative, even as we concede that individual prowess in arms and bodily strength were highly desirable, and that matchups along the front ranks were frequent as both sides sought to fight their way into and break apart enemy formations. Being pushed often into an enemy line, while keeping the shield chest high to protect both oneself and the man on the left, does not preclude individual battle skill in stabbing the enemy, keeping one's balance, and avoiding incoming blows. In collisions of massed ranks, inevitably hoplites often fought individual hoplites.

That said, there is a rich Greek vocabulary for a "breaking" of the ranks, a "storm" of spears, and a literal "push"—images of collective efforts used to describe hoplite battles in a wide variety of authors. It is hard to accept that the repeated references to the *ôthismos* (the "push"), or its more frequent verbal forms (*ôtheô*), are merely figurative. Often supplementary vocabulary stresses the value of "density" and "depth," which is logical when both sides seek to use their mass to force an opponent off the battlefield. Emphasis is often placed on muscular strength and the superior physicality of one side over the other; likewise the Boeotian armies are distinguished both by their tendencies to stack unusually deep and by the logical corollary of the superior physicality of their hoplites.[21]

In a war of shock and pushing, one would expect hoplite battles to involve an initial advance by running, or at least by advancing in double-time, and a subsequent frequent breaking of spears—and that is often just what we read in our extant descriptions. Indeed, at most major classical battles, hoplites are specifically mentioned as approaching at some sort of double-time or trot—often in contrast to the Spartans, who were singled out as unique in marching in step to battle to the sound of pipes. In general, the need to keep close in rank and protect the man to the left is likewise emphasized and alone rewarded with formal commemoration. The shield is frequently praised as a defensive weapon, one used in unison with those along the battle line, and as the most common measurement of phalanx depth. Flinging down the spear or sword is rarely seen as proof of cowardice; abandoning the shield always is—presumably because it imperils the integrity of the entire line of hoplites.[22]

If phalanx warfare were not a matter of shock and pushing, why then in a Mediterranean climate would skirmishing hoplites carry spears and large shields, and wear such heavy bronze armor—an ensemble not particularly suitable for more fluid individual combat—and not to my knowledge replicated with skirmishers in similar climates? And why, time after time, would Greek authors warn that such heavily armed soldiers could not fight well on rough terrain—given that gaps would appear in the ranks and files as infantrymen stumbled or tried to avoid obstacles on the battlefield? Would not gaps be natural and expected if battles involved little more than individual skirmishing?

If density of rank, shock of collision, and pushing were not critical to hoplite battle, would not hills and broken ground be welcomed as places where a less compact phalanx with its fluid-fighting men in armor might ambush and waylay others—or might not such terrain at least be considered largely irrelevant to the outcome? Thucydides's famous statement of the night fighting above Syracuse, that even in daylight "each man hardly knows anything except what is occurring to himself" (7.44.1) better fits the notion of heavily armored men in mass rather than fluid skirmishers.[23]

Note as well that commemoration for bravery and excellence in battle usually is awarded on the basis of group cohesion, and maintaining order. Prizes and awards are not accorded—as was true in more fluid fighting scenarios in regions such as Iberia, Scythia, or Thrace—to the number or nature of kills that individual warriors can tally. The impression we receive is that in hoplite battle it is either difficult or less important to record "kills," but essential to preserve the integrity of the formation. That again is a reality hard to reconcile with the notion of armies grinding to a halt as they approached each other to allow individual warriors to battle and duel with an enemy of like kind.[24]

Analogies to either Macedonian phalangites or Roman soldiers or contemporary tribesmen who mass in formation only to advance in smaller groups and in greater fluidity are not convincing: Hellenistic phalangites, with much smaller shields on their neck or arms, used both hands to carry long pikes; Roman legionaries relied on throwing the *pilum* and the short *gladius* and employed single-grip shields.

Modern tribesmen with long spears who fought in fluid fashion usually did so in near-naked fashion. In contrast, I would imagine if anthropologists had discovered indigenous tribes in warm climates with odd Hellenic-like full suits of bronze armor, large, round, and concave willow shields, and thrusting spears, then they likewise would have recorded shock tactics similar to those of hoplite warfare. But such is not the case with modern lightly clad tribesmen who used spears.[25]

In addition, often battle narratives in Thucydides and Xenophon concentrate on entire contingents that advance or retreat collectively, and likewise either are annihilated or escape casualties as a whole. At Delium the Thespians are encircled and nearly wiped out in toto (Thuc. 4.96). At Nemea they meet the men from Pellene and both sides die in their places, suggesting a sort of death struggle between two mass contingents of colliding hoplites. At the same battle, the Spartans let entire contingents of the Athenians go by and then struck the unprotected sides of the retreating Argives (Xen. *Hell.* 4.2.16–23). Indeed, at Nemea, Xenophon talks of Athenian, Argive, Corinthian, Spartan, and Theban fighters who suffered collective fates—either near annihilation or almost no damage at all. At Coronea the Argives en masse run away, and the Thebans and Spartans hit each other as two identifiable contingents (e.g., Xen. *Hell.* 4.3.17). At Tegyra, the Spartans let the Thebans under Pelopidas come through an open lane, who then in turn collectively are broken apart. (Plut. *Pel.* 17.5). In the so-called Tearless Battle, entire formations of Arcadians collapse in unison from the panic of facing the Spartans (Xen. *Hell.* 7.1.28–32)—a sometimes frequent occurrence in hoplite battle that suggests a herd or group-like mentality of soldiers tightly massed, who may have decreased perception and are subject to rumor or blind fears of collapse—without ever seeing clearly the enemy himself.

The sense in many of these battles is not one of fluid stages involving small groups and pockets of individual duelers, where fatalities are roughly divided among warriors on both sides, but rather of collisions, collective retreats, and synchronized advances, in which entire columns of men attempt to keep close rank throughout the battle and thus seem to suffer terribly or escape losses altogether. Many hoplite battles have lopsided casualty figures that suggest not long episodes of individual combat, contingent on personal weapons prowess, but the sudden disintegration of units en masse, or in turn the near invulnerability of entire phalanxes whose enemies either flee or are caught unawares.

Was Hoplite Armor Heavy?

Key to the hoplite narrative is the notion that hoplite armor was heavy and cumbersome. What a hoplite soldier lacked in mobility, flexibility, vision, and comfort was more than offset by the protection offered by his panoply. Such metal, leather, and fabric protection, when used in proper concert with other similarly armed men, was felt to offer an ancient hoplite a reasonable chance of surviving spear, sword, and occasional missile attacks—and to ensure that the community usually did not lose large percentages of its male population in frequent hoplite fighting.

Recently that truism too has come under question, most notably by Peter Krentz, who reexamines the ancient evidence in concert with various calculations and modern conjectures to reduce the average classical panoply to less than 50 pounds.[26] The Greeks, of course, themselves commented often on the weight, discomfort, and clumsiness of their hoplite armor—a ubiquitous theme throughout Greek literature (see Ar. *Nub.* 988–89; Eur. *HF* 190; Xen. *Mem.* 3.10.9–14). Elements of the panoply such as the double-grip and concave shield seem designed to lessen the burdensome weight of the shield on the wearer. Arm, thigh, and other peripheral items over time appear to be discarded rather than to be continually added to the panoply. Breastplates become lighter, not heavier.

We can only offer informed guesses about the exact weights of the ancient panoply, in part because it is almost impossible to calibrate at which stage of its evolution were particular hoplite battles conducted. Bronze thigh, shoulder, foot, and hand protection would add weight; composite corselets composed of linen in lieu of the bell cuirass would lessen it. Early Corinthian helmets seem heavier than the later *pilos*; metal shield veneers and blazons, along with padding, grips, and straps, would add to the weight of shield. There are few extant breastplates and only one known wooden shield, and the size and tastes of individual ensembles under combat conditions perhaps varied widely. Surviving samples have weathered and corroded over centuries, and we are not sure exactly the types and treatment of woods typically used for shields and spears. Modern replication of ancient Greek arms is indeed helpful, but there remain variances between contemporary and ancient modes of fabrication and metal use.[27]

That said, the current controversy over the precise weight of the panoply is not about whether we moderns regard hoplite panoplies to have been heavy—that seems to have been a given—but rather whether the ensemble is to be regarded as *extremely* heavy. If earlier estimates of 70 pounds prove to have been excessive, or wrongly predicated on exclusively bronze corselets and full three-foot-diameter shields of hardwoods rather than smaller sizes and lighter woods, it is still not altogether clear how an ancient hoplite of 120–150 pounds, with even nearly 50 pounds of offensive and defensive gear, could have fought deftly out of formation.

A Late Phalanx?

The grand hoplite narrative allowed that the phalanx evolved in a complex fashion from the seventh century to the fourth, in the same manner that the Corinthian helmet and the solid bronze breastplate gave way to lighter models, as the Greeks increasingly encountered a wide array of challenges abroad, and at home innovative commanders over the centuries experimented with both armament and tactics.

Current revisionism that the phalanx was a more recent phenomenon of the fifth century seems likewise mistaken. Of course, greater population, more state control, and accumulated battle experience made "classical" phalanxes larger and more sophisticated—along with a synergy of specialized light and mounted troops, and more elaborate tactics of advance and concentration of force.[28]

Still, there is no reason to think the classical phalanx was all that much different from its archaic antecedents, much less that it had become something altogether novel, rather than a logical outgrowth of what we would expect would have been the natural evolution from its archaic forebearers.

There are a number of pragmatic considerations that explain perceived differences in early and late formations. First, archaic hoplites at war are largely known from vase painting and poetry; their classical counterparts in contrast are described in prose accounts in Herodotus, Thucydides, Xenophon, and the later historians and biographers. The latter offer more opportunity for detail, both of battle and tactics, in a way impossible in earlier epic and lyric poetry and vase painting. Nevertheless, it is remarkable that both the poet Tyrtaios and historian Xenophon, composing three centuries apart, alike speak of some sort of *ôthismos*. The scene of a line of hoplites portrayed on the Protocorinthian Chigi vase, dated around 650 BC, seems not that much different from a similar battle line sculpted on the Nereid monument in stone at Xanthos around 400 BC. On occasion it seems natural that hoplites can raid sanctuaries to employ arms for contemporary battle that must have been decades old, and should have been rendered obsolete, had phalanx fighting little pedigree and been a late development.[29]

Second, the logical connection between the known evolution in hoplite weaponry and the proposed idea of the phalanx proper first appearing in the fifth century is problematic. The traditional narrative often postulated that the introduction of heavy weaponry refined and improved earlier, less organized fighting in dense mass. As the polis grew larger and richer, phalanxes incorporated more hoplites, and warfare became more complex with greater maneuver and motion. In turn, armament in response gradually grew somewhat lighter and perhaps therein cheaper as well, often produced in "factories" by the state.[30]

But if instead phalanx warfare—that is, fighting in close formation—was a phenomenon mostly of the fifth century, followed by even more compact formations of the Macedonians, then are we to believe that earlier archaic hoplites with cumbersome arm and thigh guards, wearing the obtrusive Corinthian helmet and bronze bell corselet, fought as skirmishers in more or less fluid fashion, while their more mobile and lighter-clad successors belatedly discovered the advantages of fighting in solidarity and through shock? It would seem that the opposite sequence would be more credible—that as the phalanx suddenly coalesced and grew denser, began to rely on shock, and saw less fluidity, the crowded hoplites in the ranks would adopt more protective, not lighter arms and armor.

Finally, why would eighth- and seventh-century Greek warriors, fighting in loose formation and skirmishing, suddenly begin to fabricate heavy infantry arms and armor—only to discover their optimum usage over two centuries later? The hoplite panoply was not quite like any other set of arms and armament seen before or since. The notion that citizens would craft such armor only to fathom its ideal application three centuries after its creation is as unconvincing as it is unsupported by literary descriptions and artistic renditions. A modern analogy would be that in loosely organized games of traditional touch football where contact is forbidden and injuries are rare, a few players for some reason began appearing in heavy pads, helmet with face guard, and full body protection that hampered the very mobility that was vital to such a fluid sport. Then, after decades or even centuries of slogging about, they discovered that, while such cumbersome, hot, expensive, and heavy equipment kept putting them at a disadvantage in status quo light football, in time it could nevertheless prove especially apt for a new variation of brutal tackle football—though one unknown at the time they capriciously donned their original ensembles.

Deconstruction of Hoplite Battle

There is no typical hoplite battle, given regional variations, the nearly four centuries of development, and the leadership of later innovative commanders such as Pagondas, Brasidas, and Epaminondas. Nevertheless here are a few random observations on some well-recorded fourth-century hoplite battles that seem to confirm most of the elements of the traditional narrative—the attack on the run, the collision of mass formations, the frequent breaking of spears, and the subsequent role of mass and density of formations in deciding the battle.

The exceptionalism of the battle of Coronea was not, as often argued, just a result of an anomalous crash between Thebans and Spartans. Indeed, the mechanics of that horrific encounter were similar to the collisions found at other fourth-century battles. Otherwise, are we to assume that Agesilaus expected his hoplites in a split second to adopt a manner of fighting with which they had absolutely no prior experience?

Instead, what made Xenophon remark that Coronea "was like no other" battle of his time was the odd fact that the superior Spartan right wing, by its own volition, chose an optional, second-stage head-on collision against a similarly victorious Theban right wing—in a manner of sorts foreshadowing the right wing/left wing showdown of the best units at Leuctra (Xen. *Hell.* 4.3.16). Xenophon gives a brutal description of "shield to shield" fighting between Spartans and Thebans (Xen. *Hell.* 4.3.19), not because such crashes of arms per se were necessarily singular, but because, between two such evenly matched and lethal contingents, the accustomed impact of forces would, in this unique case, not so quickly result in the collapse of either side, but rather ensure a sort of mutual destruction. (And if fluidity were the norm, it would seem impossible that both mobile Spartans and Thebans could redirect, and retain rank and formation, to restart the battle ab initio.)[31]

At Nemea (394 BC) we hear of the advantage of weight that accrues to the Thebans in massing beyond even the agreed-on sixteen shields depth (Xen. *Hell.* 4.2.18). On the Boiotians' right side, the Thespians and the men of Pellene hit each other head-on and are nearly obliterated (4.2.20). The victorious Spartans across the way are ready to strike the retreating Argives front-to-front (4.2.22). But instead they allow the enemies to go on by and then engage them on their unshielded right sides. Here again, note the sense of the collective, since the assumption is that all the retreating Argives have remained in rank and thus will suffer from a commensurately collective strike from the intact formation of Spartans.

At Leuctra there is the usual run of the non-Spartan side (*dromô*), and the subsequent hand-to-hand fighting (*eis cheiras*), before the superior density (*puknotêta*) and weight (*baros/bareis*) of the Thebans bring advantage (Diod. 15.55.2–4).

The phalanxes of the Boeotians and the Lacedaemonians at Mantinea (362 BC) hit each other head-on, and, owing to the density of the blows, both sides break a great deal of their spears (*dia tên puknotêta tôn plegôn ta pleista suntripsantes*; Diod 15.86.2). Their bodies almost become intertwined (*sumplekomenoi de tois sômasi*; Diod. 15.86.3). Progress for the Thebans follows the successful entry of Epaminondas's Thebans, who charge in a tight mass (*meta toutôn sumphraxas, eisebalen eis mesous tous polemous*; Diod. 15.86.4). The army then seems to close to hand-to-hand fighting (*tôn allôn eis cheiras erchomenôn*; Diod. 15.86.4). Indeed the Boeotians use their density and depth to break through the ranks of the Lacedaemonians, like a trireme (*ôsper trirêrê prosege, nomizôn opoi embalôn diakopseie* (Xen. *Hell.* 23). Some of the enemy then panic as the Boeotians break through their phalanx (*diekopse tên phalanga tôn polemiôn*) as the "weight" of their formation seems to play the decisive role (*to baros*; Diod. 15.86.5). The battle then ends indecisively because, with the wounding of Epaminondas, the Thebans check their pursuit of the receding Lacedaemonians and each side claims a victory on one of the two wings.[32]

A Century-Long Orthodoxy

Finally, recent questions about hoplite war are too often framed as a revisionist questioning of an orthodoxy that grew up in the last twenty years among a "face-of-battle" group of scholars influenced by John Keegan and others.[33] In fact, the orthodoxy of late eighth- to early fourth-century hoplites of a middling group of citizens, neither rich nor poor, colliding with like kind in heavy armor, finally pushing en masse in efforts to break apart the cohesion of an enemy phalanx, in frequent wars over borderlands, was established, in varying degrees, over a centuries-long tradition in scholarship by historians as diverse as F. E. Adcock, J. K. Anderson, H. Delbrück, Y. Garlan, A. W. Gomme, G. B. Grundy, J. Kromayer, W. K. Pritchett, A. Snodgrass, and dozens of others who had no allegiance to any particular ideology, approach, or politics, but rather drew conclusions from their own close reading of Greek texts, inscriptions, and representations on vase paintings and stone.

One of the oddest elements of the present controversy over the grand narrative is the explaining away of what Greek authors themselves thought in the abstract about hoplite battle—in a variety of genres and over hundreds of years.

To discredit the narrative, one must assume that Aristotle was wrong when he said that once early hoplite soldiers gained knowledge of orderly formation and deployment, and their numbers increased, they naturally began to take a greater share in the consensual government of the polis, and that hoplites were useless without cohesive arrangement (*Pol.* 4.1297b16–24); that Herodotus was in error when he made the Persian Mardonius ridicule Greek hoplite battle as "silly" (*môria*) for its emphasis on fighting openly on "the most level ground," where both sides settled the issue by convention and mutual agreement (7.9.2); that Demosthenes was confused when he complained that the warfare of his own mid-fourth century did not resemble prior generations of hoplite armies that fought mostly seasonally, and did not count on the advantages of money, but followed customs and protocols (*Third Philippic* 48–52); that Polybius (13.3–6) was rhetorical when he complained that his ancestors avoided fraud, fought openly, accepted conventions, and settled their contests not with missiles but at close quarters, hand-to-hand—and that phalanxes have only one set time and place to fight, on clear and level ground (18.31.2–7).

The hoplite narrative has a long scholarly pedigree because it best accommodates both the extant literary and archaeological evidence about phalanx fighting and the larger social, economic, and political role of the hoplite. The narrative likewise makes logical sense about how most soldiers in unusually full armor might fight, both individually and collectively, and so it has withstood most revisionism. And while it is salutary always to reexamine the narrative's components—the precise weight of the hoplite ensemble, the exact status and class of the combatants, the degree to which other nonhoplitic forces were employed, and the Greeks' own views on hoplite battle—the main scholarly consensus of the last two centuries about hoplite battle is not likely to change.

Notes

1. For brief discussions about the difficulty of reconstructing early hoplite battle, see Connor 3–29; Frost 183–86; Hanson 2000a: 40–45; Wheeler 125–26; and most recently, Whitby 53–84. For most of the mid-twentieth century there had been a reaction against the *Sachkritik* of Hans Delbrück (cf. 33–52) and other German scholars, who on occasion rejected ancient literary accounts if they were deemed at odds with what they felt were the logical parameters of battle as seen from contemporary military thinking. Yet more recently theorists in general have once again returned to frequent skepticism of ancient authenticity; cf. Hornblower 22–53.

2. The problem of artistic representation of hoplites is often remarked upon; e.g., cf. Ahlberg 49–51; Cartledge 21; Pritchett 4.41; Salmon 91. There is still no consensus about how phalanxes might have been properly represented in cramped two-dimensional scenes on Greek black-figure vases. Early bronze sculptures of hoplites inform only about solitary figures; even temple friezes show largely only one side of warriors in linear battle. Scholars often fault the lack of clear-cut artistic expressions, but if they were themselves asked to paint a phalanx on a curved pot, or sculpt a row of fighting hoplites on a flat stone surface, the results of the more gifted might not be all that much different from what we often see in seventh- and sixth-century representations.

3. Early hoplite battle, for example, has variously been explained as a populist assault of tyrannies that overthrew mounted aristocrats; as aristocratic infighting among a rather small elite; as the rise of a broader base of middling agrarians; or simply as militarily efficacious fighting without much class significance and carried on at times by various social groups. It is certainly true that the Greeks often exaggerated the actual strategic importance of hoplites, and considered their losses far more grievous to the commonwealth than the deaths of other warriors: cf., e.g., Thuc. 6.17.5, 6.72.5, where Alcibiades inflates the importance of hoplite armies; and for hoplite chauvinism, see Arist. *Pol.* 8.1326a; Thuc. 3.98.4.

4. See most recently the grand narrative in Hunt 108–46. Cf. more of the standard view in Osborne 170–76. Perhaps the most traditional picture of heavily armed soldiers fighting en masse and pushing—as a reflection of a new agrarian class (e.g., "peasant-farmers") with a novel social and economic agenda—is elaborated upon by Murray 159–80.

5. On technology reflecting a preexisting tactical need versus the less plausible idea of it emerging ex nihilo to create new tactical possibilities, see Hanson 1991: 75–78.

6. On hoplite rituals, see Connor 3–29, and Ober 53–71. I do not think that the acknowledgment of such ritual components to hoplite fighting negates the obvious fact that at all times and places people sometimes refuse to follow rules and protocols. That ancient Greeks early on in the sixth and fifth centuries often resorted to ambushes, missile weapons, night attacks, raiding, and skirmishing does not nullify the simultaneous hoplite ideal that looked down on such "alternative" weapons and tactics.

7. The emphasis of ancient authors on the moral role of the hoplite shield—not as a tool of the individual fighter, but as central to the protection of both the man at the side and the integrity of the entire line of battle—is quite striking. Cf. Plut. *Mor.* 220a; Thuc. 5.71; cf. Plut

Pel. 1.5 (a valuable reminder why states did not punish those who abandoned offensive weapons like the spear or sword); Eur. *HF* 190ff.

8. For the role of geography in defining the parameters of the spread and commonality of hoplite warfare, see Hanson 2000b: 207–11. For those who believe that fluidity was central to hoplite battle, it would then be harder to see how geography would play much of a role in determining which areas were more likely prone to go hoplite. Indeed, the proverbial notions that hoplites were confined to particularly level and clear terrain, that their ranks and files reflected singular solidarity and interconnectability, that they did not undergo or need a great deal of weapons training, and that they had limited sensory perception—all make little sense if armored men dueled out of formation against like individuals. Fluid fighters might instead fight on far more rugged terrain.

9. For a review of earlier scholarship that made the connection between the rise of hoplite warfare and an emerging farming class and/or middle class, see Hanson 1999: 476 n. 4; cf. 463 n. 21. This idea of middling farmer hoplites goes back to the nineteenth century, and was embraced by a host of prominent scholars; see the survey of such prior arguments in Hanson 1996: 308 n. 4.

10. For some examples of prominent recent critics of the grand narrative, cf. van Wees 2004: 1–2; and, in general, Krentz 2002.

11. See most prominently van Wees 2004: 47, where his chapter subsection is titled "The Myth of the Middle Class Hoplite," and argues mostly from the idea of supposedly common misinterpretations of Aristotle's notion of the *mesoi*, centering on the above-mentioned passage in the *Politics*. (But see also van Wees 2004 elsewhere at p. 55: "The typical working-class hoplite was probably a small but independent farmer who owned about 10–15 acres of land (4–6 ha), worth 2,000 to 3,000 drachmas, and who could just about afford a hoplite panoply.") For a good example of the standard middling agrarian hoplite view, see Raaflaub 1997: 57, "The land-owning farmers, from the very beginning formed an integral element, both military and politically, in the evolving *polis*. Owing to this triple role of landowners, soldiers, and assemblymen, they naturally became *the* essential part of the citizen body."

12. On the natural, moral connection between farming and fighting, and the borrowing of war metaphors from farming, see Xen. *Oec.* 5.7, 14; Arist. [*Oec.*] 1.1342b5–7. Cf. Tyrt. 19.16; Xen. *Hell.* 4.4.12; Aesch. *Pers.* 818 (*thines nekrôn de kai tritospórôi*). The reformist Plato's call for more formal training (e.g., *Resp.* 2.374c), to his chagrin, assumes citizens normally were too busy to train extensively for phalanx battle. Van Wees 2004: 37, cites both philosophical calls for a break between agrarianism and hoplite service, and such realities in Sparta, Crete, and Thessaly—but that exceptionalism is more an argument *against*, not for, a widespread presence of a leisured or professional class of nonfarming hoplites in most of the city-states.

13. There is a vast modern literature on "middleness" and plenty of ancient referents. See Rahe 42; Spahn 7–15, 174–82; the corpus of notable ancient examples on *mesoi* is collated in Hanson 2000b: 112–21.

14. Farmland calibrated by its ability to raise hoplites: Arist. *Pol.* 2.1270a16; Plut. *Mor.* 414a; Theopompus *FGrH 115* fr. 225; Dem. 23.199. Combined hoplite and agrarian chauvinism: Pl. *Leg.* 4.707c; Thuc. 3.98.4. 4.126. 6.17.5; Hdt. 5.97. Borderlands as the catalysts for hoplite battle: Hdt 5.49; Plut. *Mor.* 213e3; cf. Hanson 2000b: 214–18.

15. The quote is from van Wees 2004: 55. On estimates of Attic acreage accounting for a large body of middle hoplite agrarians, see, in general, Jameson 1996.

16. E.g., cf. the classic synopsis of Arnaldo Momigliano, "War was an ever present reality in Greek life. . . . War was the centre of Greek life. . . . The Greeks came to accept war as a natural fact like birth and death about which nothing could be done" (120).

17. Cf. Pl. *Leg.* 626a. For the revisionist view, see, again, van Wees 2004: 3.

18. For the proverbial frequency of war making by the fifth-century Athenians, see Chamoux 162; de Romilly 1968; Zimmern 354; and for reasons why democracies are so prone to make war so often, see Hanson 2001: 17–26. For the toll taken on early fourth-century Sparta by constant military service, cf. Hodkinson, especially 153–57. Kyra Orgill in an unpublished 2005 MA thesis at California State University, Fresno, attempted to quantify the years Athens was at war in the fifth century and confirmed the traditional view of a near-constant bellicosity. (cf. the abstract at http://www.csufresno.edu/gradstudies/thesis/Spring2005pdfs/ABSTRACTKOrgill.pdf).

19. Note also that Pagondas gives here a defense of the doctrine of preemption and assumes that city-states would naturally attack others considered weak; and likewise, a state always must consider hitting a presumed enemy first, before it has a chance to attack with greater lethality. For some ancient examples of preemption, or, in addition, more general preventative war, see the Spartans' thinking that led them to invade Attica (Thuc. 1.118.2. 4.92.5), and Alcibiades's call to hit Sicily before it attacked Athens (6.18.3)—and the Syracusan democratic leader Athenagoras's recommendation for the Syracusans themselves to preempt: "It is necessary to punish an enemy not only for what he does, but also beforehand for what he intends to do, if the first to relax precaution would not also be the first to suffer." (Crawley translation, 6.39.5). The common thinking is that even when war is not actually breaking out, there is a constant tension between states that requires eternal vigilance.

20. The most prominent advocate of the "nonpushing" school is Krentz (see his essay and references in this volume), who emphasizes both the fluidity of hoplite battle, and the ubiquity of trickery and ambush in Greek warfare. But the dispute over the phalanx scrum is a long one, with a vast bibliography; see, for example, the review of the ancient and modern literature in Goldsworthy 1997; Krentz 2002; Luginbill 1994.

21. On these terms of mass shoving, breaking a line, and the use of the mass in Greek, see Pritchett 4.65–74. I do not know why some see much significance in an ancient author's choice of either the verb (*ôtheô*) or the synonymous abstract noun (*ôthismos*). For superior body strength and its role in battle, cf. Diod. 12.70.3, 15.39.1, 15.87.1; Plut *Mor.* 639e; cf. Theban depth: Thuc. 4.93.4; Xen. *Hell.* 3.2.13, 18; 6.4.12. On the need for hoplites to keep in rank and maintain order, cf. Lazenby 94–96.

22. For battles where hoplites are said to have run toward the enemy, cf. passages collected at Hanson 2000a: 135–51. There is an entire corpus of moral literature surrounding the shield that emphasizes that it is the one weapon of the panoply necessary for the entire line (see note 7). In addition, cf. the more generic references to the need to fight together that assume some sort of cohesiveness on the battlefield that is hard to reconcile with individual dueling and fluidity (e.g., cf. the idea that without cohesive formation hoplites "are useless" [Arist. *Pol.* 4.1297b20; Xen. *Oec.* 8.4]). There are a surprising number of references to broken spears in literature (and in scenes in Greek art; cf., e.g., Hanson 1999: 244; Hanson 2000a 87–88; 164; 245n).

23. In addition, there are the famous passages attesting to the unsuitability of the heavily armed hoplite fighting either in solo combat (Eur. *HF* 190ff; and cf. the ease of hitting someone while in rank: Xen. *Cyr.* 2.1.16–18) or on rough terrain that could break ranks and leave fully equipped soldiers at the mercy of lighter-armed and mounted troops (and, in contrast, the suitability of flat land for hoplite collisions): Hdt. 7.92; Polyb. 18.31.2–7; cf. 11.15.7–17; Arist. *Pol.* 5.1303b12. In recent years a number of groups and individuals have reconstructed hoplite shields, and remarked on the disadvantages of such equipment in staged fluid fighting, especially the double-gripped shield in comparison to more easily maneuverable center-grip shields: http://www.lloydianaspects.co.uk/armour/hoplite/hoplshld.html. Note that on occasion, at battles like Delium and Nemea, it is remarked that atypically rough terrain (the ravines at

Delium; the underbrush at Nemea) tends to bother hoplites and leads to unexpected and unwelcome surprises.

24. For the nature of the *aristeion*, see Pritchett 2.276–90. Why arises the moral disdain for shield tossers—and those who leave the line of battle (cf. Hdt. 7.1.104.4), or those whose cowardice endangers the line (Eur. *HF* 191–92)—in the collective martial ethos, if battles were determined by the preeminence of soloists? Cf. Aristotle (*Pol.* 7.1324b10–24) on the difference between nonpoleis societies who reward or emphasize individual kills—which de facto seems to me to suggest a contrast with phalanx warfare, where heavier armor, reduced vision, massed attack, and the need to keep formation would both make it harder to distinguish individual kills, and deprecate such knowledge in comparison with keeping the battle line unbroken and hoplites in rank protecting those at their right.

25. Cf. the plates (XIV–XVII) in van Wees 2004 of near-naked tribesmen with long spears advancing to battle in fluid fashion—as if such unprotected warriors in any way shed light on early hoplite spearmen sheathed in bronze, linen, and wood. Would we expect New Guinea highlanders to do the same if encumbered with the hoplite panoply?

26. See Krentz's essay in this volume, where he comprehensively reviews various methods for adjudicating weights of the panoply.

27. See again the arguments of Krentz, who would downgrade previous estimates of the hoplite panoply from about 32 kg (ca. 70 lbs.) to a high of 22 kg (ca. 48 lbs.). I do not know why Krentz believes that hoplite shields were rarely faced with bronze blazons, which in various manifestations appear ubiquitously in ancient literary accounts and in vase paintings.

28. E.g., "There are in fact good reasons why the classical phalanx could only have emerged in the classical period" (van Wees 2004: 196). Note the key phrase "classical phalanx" in contrast to just "phalanx." Yet, the "archaic" phalanx no doubt emerged in the archaic period, and the Hellenistic phalanx emerged in the Hellenistic period as well.

29. Some examples of the longevity of hoplite weapons: Paus. 4.16.7, 8.21.1; Diod. 17.18; Plut. *Pel.* 12; *Mor.* 241F17; Xen. *Hell.* 5.4.8.

30. There are a number of examples that refer to workshops that turn out arms and armor (Lys. 12.19; Diod. 14.43; Plut. *Mor.* 835B–C; Ar. *Av.* 491; *Pax* 1210ff; Dem. 36.11), and to the state or general in the field supplying weapons to hoplites (Diod 12.68.5, 14.43.2–3, 15.13.2; Thuc. 6.72.4, 8.25.6; Xen. *Hell.* 4.4.10; Aen. Tact. 10.7).

31. On the notion that Coronea was unique and not representative of the collisions of other battles, see, for example, van Wees 2004: 188. When Wheeler (209) says that Xenophon disapproved of the crash at the second stage of Coronea and that such a collision made the battle unusual, he misses entirely the point of the passage. Again, what was exceptional about Coronea was that (a) Agesilaus chose, unlike at the second stage at Nemea when such a gambit was shunned, to hit an opposing contingent head-on when he had perhaps the safer option of striking it, as it passed by, in the flank; (b) the battle ended up pitting the best troops, formerly stationed on the right wing of each respective army, in a direct collision, ensuring not the flight of a weaker contingent, but unusually savage fighting not characteristic of the usual formula (outside of Leuctra) of the strong wing hitting the enemy's weak counterpart. If we were to believe van Wees and Wheeler, Agesilaus chose suddenly to employ his phalanx in a manner in which his own hoplites would have had little, if any, prior experience.

32. Van Wees 2004: 188–91 envisions a quite different scenario. Running is simply to curb exposure to missiles, and prompted mostly by psychological considerations that bring no real physical advantages: hoplites "must have slowed down in the last few seconds and ground to a halt within 'spear-thrust.'" Frequent references to hoplite weight and pressure are "figurative."

And common examples of pushing, and the advantage that accrues from greater weight of the phalanx, refer to "psychological pressure."

33. So I do not understand what Wheeler (187) quite means by the rhetorical "This chapter's assessment of archaic and classical Greek land combat will not assume the correctness of the 'face-of-battle' approach"—a term he never explicitly defines.

Bibliography

Ahlberg, G. 1957. *Fighting on Land and Sea in Greek Geometric Art*. Stockholm: Svenska Institutet i Athen.

Cartledge. P. 1977. "Hoplites and Heroes: Sparta's Contribution to the Technique of Ancient Warfare." *Journal of Hellenic Studies* 97:11–27.

Cawkwell, G. L. 1989. "Orthodoxy and Hoplites." *Classical Quarterly* n.s. 39:375–89.

Chamoux, F. 1965. *The Civilization of Greece*. New York: Simon and Schulster.

Connor, R. 1988. "Early Greek Warfare as Symbolic Expression." *Past and Present* 119:3–29.

Delbrück, Hans. 1975. *History of the Art of War*, vol. 1: *Antiquity*. Trans. W. J. Renfroe. Lincoln: Greenwood.

Frost, F. 1984. "The Athenian Military before Cleisthenes." *Historia* 33:283–99.

Goldsworthy, A. K. 1997. "The *Othismos*, Myths and Heresies: The Nature of Hoplite Battle." *War in History* 4.1: 1–26.

Hanson, V. D., ed. 1991. *Hoplites: The Classical Greek Battle Experience*. London: Routledge.

———. 1996. "Hoplites into Democrats: The Changing Ideology of Athenian Infantry." In *Dêmokratia: A Conversation on Democracies, Ancient and Modern*, ed. J. Ober and C. Hedrick, 289–312. Princeton: Princeton University Press.

———. 1999. *The Other Greeks: The Family Farm and the Agrarian Roots of Western Civilization*. Berkeley and Los Angeles: University of California Press.

———. 2000a. *The Western Way of War*. Berkeley and Los Angeles: University of California Press.

———. 2000b. "Hoplite Battle as Ancient Greek Warfare: When, Where, and Why?" In Van Wees 2000: 201–32.

———. 2001. "Democratic Warfare, Ancient and Modern." In *War and Democracy: A Comparative Study of the Korean War and the Peloponnesian War*, ed. D. McCann and B. Strauss, 3–33. Armonk, NY: M. E. Sharpe.

Hodkinson, S. 1993. "Warfare, Wealth, and the Crisis of Spartiate Society." In Rich and Shipley 1993: 146–76.

Hornblower, S. 2007. "Warfare in Ancient Literature: The Paradox of War." In *The Cambridge History of Greek and Roman Warfare*, ed. Philip Sabin, Hans van Wees, and Michael Whitby, 1:22–53. Cambridge: Cambridge University Press.

Hunt, P. 2007. "Military Forces." In *The Cambridge History of Greek and Roman Warfare*, ed. Philip Sabin, Hans van Wees, and Michael Whitby, 1:108–46. Cambridge: Cambridge University Press.

Jameson, M. H. 1994. "Class in the Ancient Greek Countryside" In *Structures Rurales et Sociétés Antiques*, ed. P. N. Doukellis and L. G. Mendoni, 55–63. Paris: Les Belles Lettres.

Krentz, Peter. 2002. "Fighting by the Rules: The Invention of the Hoplite *Agôn*." *Hesperia* 71:23–39; reprinted in E. Wheeler, ed., *The Armies of Classical Greece*, 111–127 (Burlington: Ashgate, 2007).

Lazenby, J. 1991. "The Killing Zone." In Hanson 1991: 87–109.

Luginbill, R. D. 1994. "Othismos: The Importance of the Mass-Shove in Hoplite Warfare." *Phoenix* 48.1: 51–61.

Momiliagno, A. 1966. "Some Observations on Causes of War in Ancient Historiography." In *Studies in Historiography*. New York: Harper Torchbooks.

Murray, O. 1993. *Early Greece*, 2nd ed. Cambridge, MA: Harvard University Press.

Ober, J. 1998. *The Athenian Revolution: Essays on Ancient Greek Democracy and Political Theory*. Princeton: Princeton University Press.

Osborne, R. 1996. *Greece in the Making, 1200–479 B.C.* London: Routledge.

Pritchett, W. K. 1971–91. *The Greek State at War*, vols. 1–5. Berkeley and Los Angeles: University of California Press.

Raaflaub, K. 1979. "Soldiers, Citizens, and the Evolution of the Early Greek Polis." In *The Development of the Polis in Archaic Greece*, ed. L. Mitchell and P. J. Rhodes, 49–59. London: Routledge.

Raahe, P. 1993. *Republics, Ancient and Modern*. Chapel Hill: University of North Carolina Press.

Rich, J., and G. Shipley. 1993. *War and Society in the Greek World*. London: Routledge.

Romilly, J. de. 1968. "Guerre et paix entre cites." In *Probèmes de la guerre en Grèce ancienne*, 215–225. La Haye: Mouton & Co.

Salmon, J. 1977. "Political Hoplites?" *Journal of Hellenic Studies* 97:84–101.

Spahn P. 1978. *Mittelschicht und Polisbildung*. Frankfurt, Berne, and Las Vegas: P. Lang.

Van Wees, Hans., ed. 2000. *War and Violence in Ancient Greece*. London: Duckworth.

———. 2004. *Greek Warfare: Myths and Realities*. London. Duckworth.

Wheeler, E. 1991. "The General as Hoplite." In Hanson 1991: 121–72.

Whitby, M. 2007. "Reconstructing Ancient Warfare." In *The Cambridge History of Greek and Roman Warfare*, ed. Philip Sabin, Hans van Wees, and Michael Whitby, 1:54–84. Cambridge: Cambridge University Press.

Zimmern, A. 1931. *The Greek Commonwealth*. Oxford: Oxford University Press.

CONTRIBUTORS

Paul Cartledge is the inaugural A. G. Leventis Professor of Greek Culture, Faculty of Classics, University of Cambridge, and President of the Fellowship, Clare College. He is the author, coauthor, editor, or coeditor of more than twenty books and two monograph series. He holds the Gold Cross of the Order of Honour, Hellenic Republic, and is an Honorary Citizen of Sparti, Greece.

Lin Foxhall is Professor of Greek Archaeology and History at the University of Leicester, and has held posts at St. Hilda's College, Oxford, and University College London. She studied at Bryn Mawr College, the University of Pennsylvania, and the University of Liverpool. In 2005–6 she held a Humboldt Research Prize at Freiburg University and was Visiting Professor at the University of Aarhus in 2010. She has worked on archaeological projects in Greece and Southern Italy and currently codirects a field project in Calabria. She has written extensively on agriculture, land use, and gender in classical antiquity. Her publications include *Studying Gender in Classical Antiquity* (Cambridge University Press, 2013), *Olive Cultivation in Ancient Greece: Seeking the Ancient Economy* (Oxford University Press, 2007), as well as *Money, Land and Labour in Ancient Greece* (Routledge, 2002) with Paul Cartledge and Edward Cohen, and *Intentional History: Spinning Time* (Stuttgart: F. Steiner-Verlag, 2010) with Hans-Joachim Gehrke and Nino Luraghi. She lives in rural Leicestershire with her family and many fruit trees.

John R. Hale is a classical and underwater archaeologist at the University of Louisville. Since earning his BA degree at Yale and his PhD at Cambridge, he has conducted fieldwork in Scandinavia on the ancestors of Viking longships, in Portugal on ancient harbors, and in Greek and Israeli waters in a search of shipwrecks from the time of the Persian Wars. A rower himself, Hale takes particular interest in the role of oared galleys in ancient sea battles and the quest for maritime supremacy. In his book *Lords of the Sea* (Viking Penguin, 2009), Hale presents a new reconstruction of the Greek trireme, as well as a new interpretation of Athenian history that integrates the naval enterprises of Athens into the political and cultural life of the city. Hale has also investigated Delphi and other Greek oracle sites. His research has been published in

Antiquity, *Scientific American*, and *The Journal of Roman Archaeology*, among other publications. At the University of Louisville, Hale is an Adjunct Professor of Anthropology and Director of Liberal Studies.

Victor Davis Hanson received his PhD in Classics from Stanford University in 1980. He is Professor of Classics Emeritus at California State University, Fresno, and currently the Martin and Illie Anderson Senior Fellow in Classics and Military History at the Hoover Institution, Stanford University. Hanson is a weekly syndicated columnist for Tribune Media Services and the author or editor of twenty-one books, among them *The Western Way of War*, *The Other Greeks*, *Carnage and Culture*, and *A War Like No Other*. He is a recipient of the National Humanities Medal (2008), the Bradley Prize (2009), the Eric Breindel Award (2002), and the American Philological Association Award for Distinguished Undergraduate Teaching (1992). He lives on his farm in Selma, California, where he was born in 1953.

Donald Kagan is Sterling Professor of Classics and History at Yale University. His most recent books are *The Peloponnesian War* and *Thucydides: The Reinvention of History*.

Peter Krentz received his PhD in history from Yale University in 1979 and has since taught Greek and Roman history at Davidson College, where he is now the W. R. Grey Professor of Classics and History. He has written a series of articles about Greek warfare, leading up to *The Battle of Marathon* (Yale University Press, 2010).

Kurt A. Raaflaub is David Herlihy Professor of Classics and History emeritus at Brown University. His research interests cover archaic and classical Greek as well as Roman republican political, social, and intellectual history, and the comparative history of ancient civilizations. His books include *The Discovery of Freedom in Ancient Greece* (2004), *War and Society in the Ancient and Medieval Worlds* (coed., 1999), and *War and Peace in the Ancient World* (ed., 2007).

Adam Schwartz is a postdoctoral fellow at the Section for Greek and Latin, University of Copenhagen. He is the author of *Reinstating the Hoplite: Arms, Armour and Phalanx Fighting in Archaic and Classical Greece* (2009) and has published studies on Aristotle's *Politics*, Greek interstate alliances, and Homeric society. He currently does research on early Greek literacy.

Anthony Snodgrass served as Laurence Professor of Classical Archaeology at the University of Cambridge (UK) from 1976 to 2001. His first field of research was in Greek military equipment, later extended into the broader study of the archaeology of Early Iron Age and Archaic Greece as a whole.

Hans van Wees is Grote Professor of Ancient History at University College London. He is the author of *Greek Warfare: Myths and Realities* (2004), editor of *War and Violence in Ancient Greece* (2010), and coeditor of *The Cambridge History of Greek and Roman Warfare* (2007).

Gregory F. Viggiano received his PhD in classics from Yale University. He is assistant professor of history at Sacred Heart University in Fairfield, Connecticut. He and Kagan are the authors of *Problems in the History of Ancient Greece*.

INDEX

Abu Simbel, mercenaries' names inscribed at, 184
Achaean League, 92
Adcock, F. E., 16–18, 21, 28, 52n.73, 269
Aeschylus, 98–99
Agis, 9
agriculture: the emergence of hoplites and, xvi, 28–35, 97, 122–23, 176–77, 194–95, 217, 260–61; farmer-citizen-soldiers, 9–10, 17–18, 22–23, 34, 113, 271n.9; the gentleman farmer, definition of, 236; the Greek countryside/landscape, archaeological data regarding (*see* archaeological data); harvests and farms, estimating size and value of, 230–31; land ownership and the economic circumstances of farmers (*see* historical development); production for the market in classical Athens, 249n.67; soldiers of fortune escaping from farmwork, 182; the yeoman farmer, definition of, 223
Alcaeus, 97, 185–86, 188
Alcibiades, 272n.19
Alcock, Susan, 214
Alexander the Great, 11
Amathus bowl, 182–84
Anderson, J. K., 142, 269
Ando, Hiroshe, 79
Andrewes, Anthony, xiv, 16, 18–20, 138
Angel, John Lawrence, 166
Antimenidas, 185–86
archaeological data: Berbati-Limnes Survey, 209–13; Boeotia Survey, 198–99, 202–5; historical data and, 195, 217–18; the hoplite question, contributions to, xiii; intensive surveys: method, strengths, and limits of, 196–99; Keos Survey, 198, 202–6; Kythera Survey, 214–15; Laconia Survey, 212, 214, 236; Methana Survey, 207–10; Pylos Survey, 214–15; rural settlement, 215–17, 235–36; Southern Argolid Survey, 205–7; summary of survey projects, 200–201. *See also* data
Archidamus, 8
Archilochus of Paros, 97, 179, 190–91
Aristagoras, 7
Aristophanes, 137
Aristotle: agriculture, importance in Attica of, 172–73n.55; farmers, limited enthusiasm for, 240, 242; the grand hoplite narrative and, 269; hoplite phalanx, rise of, 241–42; the "middle" class, 235; middling farmers and government, relationship of, 33, 113, 260; political and military development, connection of, xiv, 1, 19, 75–76, 79–80, 259–60; size of cities, 250n.76
armor: of the classical period, 62–63; Corinthian helmet, 24–25, 51n.36, 60–61, 72n.7, 99–100, 117; corselet, 61–62; dedications of in sanctuaries, 87–88; disadvantages of hoplite, 24; evolution of hoplite, 35–38, 88, 99–100, 168–69; greaves, 62; the hoplite shield (*see* hoplite shield); introduction of hoplite, 14–16, 62; lightened form of the hoplite panoply, 62–63, 88; physiology of wearers, 165–68; representations of, 58, 61–69; shields (*see* shields); thigh and arm guards, 62; weight of, 8, 51n.36, 127–28n.28, 168, 265–66 (*see also* hoplite shield: weight of). *See also* equipment
Arrian of Nicomedia, 25, 159
art. *See* iconography
Asklepiodotos, 26, 140
Athenaeus, 179
Athenagoras, 272n.19
Athens: egalitarianism and number of yeomen hoplites in fifth-century, 242–43; hoplites in, 20, 125–26; leisure class, size of, 249n.59; political evolution in, 6; political stability of, conditions for the poor working masses and, 238–40;

Athens (*continued*)
population in 322 BC, 231, 247n.40; production for the market in classical, 249n.67; Solon's property classes and the distribution of wealth in, 229–33 (*see also* Solon)

Babylon, Greek mercenaries employed by rulers of, 185
battle formations: Etruscan adoption of hoplite, 88; hoplite equipment and close-order, 243–44; the hoplite shield and, 57–59, 91–92, 116–19, 139–40, 169 (*see also* hoplite shield); the phalanx (*see* phalanx, the); the rugby model, 8, 128n.41, 146
battle tactics: the charge, 140–42; the collision, 17, 25–26, 117–18, 128–29n.41, 142–43; flanks, concerns regarding, 9; flexibility of, 43–44; in fourth-century battles, 267–69; geography and, 271n.8; Grundy's description of, 7–12; massed fighting into phalanx fighting, question of how/why this development occurred, 75, 78; Near Eastern and Greek, comparison of, 100–101; pushing/shoving, 26–27, 59, 143–48, 263–64; revisionist view of, 115, 263–65; revolution in, the phalanx as, 12, 14–16 (*see also* phalanx, hoplite); Western way of war, uniqueness of, 22–23
Berbati-Limnes Survey, 209–13
Berve, H., 112
Blyth, P. H., 136, 159–61, 172n.38
Boardman, John, 136
Boeotian shield, 136–37
Boeotia Survey, 198–99, 202–5
Bol, Peter, 148
Bomarzo shield, 157–58, 160–61, 170n.5, 170n.12, 172n.38
Briant, Pierre, 98, 104n.14
Broodbank, Cyprian, 214

Cahn, David, 161
Cartledge, Paul: defend crops, readiness of wealthy nonaristocrats to, 55n.161; Homer, interpretation of, 45–46, 87; hoplite equipment and close-order battle formations, relationship of, 91, 138, 243; rugby analogy for fighting between phalanges, 143; sudden-change theory, nuances added to, xiv, 38–39
Cawkwell, G. L., xv, 41, 43–44, 81
Cherry, J. F., 198
Chigi vase: battle depicted on, 59, 142; dating of hoplite tactics using, xiii, 12, 15–16, 19, 160n.24; gradualist interpretation of, 68; Helbig as first to analyze, 12; hoplite phalanx, first undeniable depiction of, 67; piper depicted on, 15, 138; questions raised by, 67–68
chronology: approaches to dating emergence of the phalanx, 88–91; dedications of armor in sanctuaries as evidence regarding, 87–88; difficulties in dating emergence of the phalanx, 12–13; disappearance of the hoplite system, 92–93; early and lengthy evolution of the phalanx, arguments for, 101–3, 266–67; emergence of the phalanx, varying positions regarding, 137–38; gradualism, limited consensus regarding, 91; Hanson vs. van Wees on, 194–95; Homer and emergence of the phalanx, issues regarding, 85–87; the hoplite orthodoxy regarding, xii–xiv; hoplites, emergence of, 176 (*see also* soldiers of fortune); late development of the phalanx, arguments for, 42–43, 137, 244; "mature" phase of heavily armed hoplites, beginning and end of, 88; representations of hoplites on vases and, 63–70. *See also* grand hoplite narrative; historical development
city-state. *See* polis
civic ideology/mentality, hoplites and, 176–78, 180
colonization, 28, 31–32, 124
Cook, Erwin, 97
Corinthian helmet, 24–25, 51n.36, 60–61, 72n.7, 99–100, 117
Croce, Benedetto, 74
Cypselus of Corinth, 16, 19–20, 124–25

data: archaeological (*see* archaeological data); archeological *vs.* historical sources of, 194–95, 217–18. *See also* scholarship; sources
Davis, Jack, 214
Delbrück, Hans, 23, 135, 138–40, 144, 269, 270n.1
Demosthenes, 10, 269
Detienne, Marcel, 138
Diodorus, 163
Donlan, Walter, 166
Droysen, Johann Gustav, 23

economic class: commercial class in the eighth century, 54n.125; the gentleman farmer and the competition for wealth, 236–40; of hoplites, xii, 176–80, 194–95, 259–61; of landowners, models of historical development based on (*see* historical development); leisure class, size of in Athens, 249n.59; slave and master, relations between, 225; Solon's system of property classes, 229–33 (*see also* Solon); tensions between rich and poor in Athens and Sparta, 232–33
Edwards, A., 246n.17
Egypt, Greek mercenaries employed by rulers of, 184–85
Ehrenberg, Victor, 112–13

Epaminondas, 9
Eph'al, Israel, 100
equipment: armor (*see* armor); Etruscan adoption of hoplite, 88; nature of hoplite, impact of the yeoman farmer and, 243–44; Near Eastern influence on Greek military, 99–100; weapons (*see* weapons); weight of, 8, 127–28n.28, 135, 150n.6, 265–66
Euripides, 137, 168–69
evolutionary model for the Homeric texts, 89–90

Fagan, Garrett, 152n.73
feasting halls, 187–89
Ferrill, Arther, 100, 102
Finley, Moses I., 45, 56n.200, 77, 80, 85
Forbes, Hamish, 166, 172n.48
Forrest, W. G., 20, 28, 54n.125
Forsdyke, S., 122, 130n.78, 130n.82
Foxhall, Lin, xvi–xvii, 122, 166, 172n.48, 229–30
Fraser, A. D., 145–46, 152n.63

Garlan, Yvon, 23, 74, 269
Garnsey, P., 130n.78, 172n.42, 172n.48
Gawantka, Wilfried, 126n.6
Gerber, Douglas, 191n.21
Goldsworthy, Adrian, 143
Gomme, A. W., 145, 269
grand hoplite narrative, 257–59; bellicosity of the poleis and human nature, 262–63; economic class of hoplites, question of, 259–61 (*see also* economic class); fluid fighting described by revisionists, questions regarding, 263–65; fourth-century battles that confirm the, 267–69; long scholarly pedigree of, xii, 269–70; phalanx warfare, late development vs. lengthy evolution of, 266–67; warfare as a nearly constant and natural state, 261–62; weight of hoplite armor, controversy over, 265–66. *See also* historical development; hoplite orthodoxy; phalanx, hoplite
Greenhalgh, P.A.L., 23, 38, 117
Griffith, G. T., 23
Grote, George: on the evolution of military practice and political organization, 149; historical sense, passage to, 50n.14; Homeric society, argument for ninth-century, 49n.9; Homeric warfare, view of, 44–45; hoplite orthodoxy, contribution to, xii–xiii, 2–7, 12, 19; on military practice, 137; the phalanx, Tyrtaeus and dating of, 51n.55; Pheidon of Argos, dating of, 50n.20; political submission, Aristotle's inability to explain his ancestors', 50n.15
Grundy, G. B.: Corinthian helmet, weight of, 51n.36; hoplite orthodoxy, contribution to, 7–12, 17–19, 21, 28, 269; rugby analogy, use of, 144–45, 151–52n.58

Hale, John, 148
Hanson, Victor Davis: age of men in the phalanxes, 168; agrarian basis of hoplite development, 28–35, 79, 122, 176–77, 194–95, 217 (*see also* historical development); Aristotle on the hoplite phalanx, use of, 242; arms and armor, weight of hoplite, 135; collision of hoplites in battle, 118, 142–43; data sources used by, 195; frequency of Greek warfare, 178; Hesiod, the yeoman farmer thesis and, 226–29; hoplite equipment and the phalanx, 100, 243; hoplite orthodoxy, contribution to, xii, xv–xxvi, xx–xxi, 21–28, 134–35; hoplite shield, distinctive characteristics of, 91; hoplite shield and massed combat, view of, 58–59; Laertes as example of yeoman farmer, 224–26; material evidence of agricultural activity, the yeoman farmer thesis and, 235–36; medieval warfare, the phalanx and, 53n.112; pushing of hoplites in battle, 143; Solon's system of property classes, the yeoman farmer thesis and, 229–33; spears, use of, 142; Theognis and Phocylides, the yeoman farmer thesis and, 233–35; Thucydides' picture of the Spartan army, suspicions regarding, 141; "ugly muscle" of farmers not rated as highly as "elegant muscle" of landowners, 243; warships owned by city-states, 187; yeoman farmer, model of historical development based on, 222–24; yeoman/middling farmer, model of historical development based on (*see also* historical development)
Hector, 120–21
Helbig, Wolfgang, xiii, 12, 138
Henneberg, Macicj, 166–67
Henneberg, Renata, 166–67
Heraclitus, 261–62
Herodotus: Carians as inventors of military paraphernalia, 99, 184; division of forces by weapons, 149; the grand hoplite narrative and, 269; Greek mercenaries in Egypt, 184; Homer, dating of, 3; hoplite battles, characterization of, 178; hoplites in Naxos, number of, 241; "hoplite," usage of, 137; hoplite warfare, description of, 7; hoplite warfare in terrain commonly found in Greece, absurdity of, 78–79; Lykurgos, representation of, 77; Persian military practices, 98–99; "phalanx," usage of, 137; proportion of hoplites to light-armed soldiers at Plataea, 241; pushing and shoving of hoplites, 143–44, 146; on the shield of Sophanes in battle, 136; "stand at ease" command recorded by, 168

Hesiod: competition for wealth, 237; on farmers, 226–29, 234; households and land, documenting of relationship between, 217; moderation in pursuit of wealth urged by, 235; noble halls, despising of men in, 189; toil, ideology of, 238; war ignored when talking of farmers, 97
hetairoi, 188–89
Hippodamus of Miletus, 242
historical approach, 89–90
historical development: archaeological data and the yeoman farmer thesis, 235–36; archaic history, basic dynamics of, 237; the double-handled shield as tipping point in change of fighting styles, 78; evidence of the yeoman farmer in archaic Greece, 224–36; the gentleman farmer and the competition for wealth, 237–40; Hanson's yeoman farmer model of, 223–24; Hesiod as support for yeoman farmer thesis, 226–29; the hoplite phalanx and changing social/economic structures, 240–45; Laertes as faulty example of yeoman farmer, 224–26; of the polis, seventh-century agrarian and military revolutions underlying, 123–26; population growth and, 122, 223; Solon's property classes and the yeoman farmer thesis, 229–33; Theognis and Phocylides, the yeoman farmer thesis and, 233–35; van Wees's gentleman farmer model of, 236–37; yeoman/middling *vs.* gentlemen farmers as drivers of political and military change, 222, 243. *See also* grand hoplite narrative
Homer: agrarian property, military leadership and, 97; dates of completion of the *Iliad* and *Odyssey,* 89–90, 129n.55; evolutionary model of, 89–90; Greek voyages to the Near East, impact of, 181; heroic contrasted with hoplite fighting style, 2; history, precariousness of reading as, 78, 129n.54; the hoplite orthodoxy and, xi–xiii; hoplite style of fighting, rival interpretations of, 85–87; iconographic images and, 63; Laertes as faulty example of yeoman farmer, 224–26; marginal land, ownership of, 238; mass fighting in, 119; mode of combat described in, 101–2, 114–15, 119, 129n.56, 130n.64, 137; "phalanx" used by, 137; pushing by hoplites, 146–47; "rustics" as herdsmen, not farmers, 234; scholarly approaches to the interpretation of, 88–91; seafaring expeditions of aristocrats and followers, praise for, 188–89; value of, Grote's position regarding, 4; warfare in, 44–47; wine as loot, Odysseus' division of, 179
Homeric Question, 3, 7
Hoplite Association, 136, 171n.35
hoplite orthodoxy: Adcock's contribution to, 16–18; agricultural revolution, Hanson's account of, 28–35; Andrewes' contribution to, 18–20; battle, Hanson's account of, 21–28; brief overview of, 1; Cartledge's revision of, 38–39; Cawkwell's critique of, 43–44; challenges to, 35–44; gradualism, differences over degree of, 91; the gradualist attack on, xiv–xvii, 114; Grote's contribution to, xii–xiii, 2–7; Grundy's contribution to, 7–12; Hanson's reassertion of, xv–xvi, xx–xxi; the hoplite revolution, 119–20; Krentz's gradualist critique of, 41–42, 117–18; the long scholarly pedigree of support for, 269–70; Lorimer's contribution to, 14–16; Nilsson's contribution to, 12–14; revisionism, place of, 81n.7; Salmon's gradualist critique of, 39–41; Snodgrass's gradualist critique of, 35–38; van Wees's critique of, 41, 244–45; Viggiano's reassertion of, 113–26. *See also* grand hoplite narrative
hoplites and the hoplite tradition: conventions for marking the end of battle, 244; disappearance of, 92–93 (*see also* chronology); emergence of (*see* chronology); existence of before the phalanx, 148; as farmer-citizen-soldiers, 9–10, 17–18, 22–23, 34, 113, 271n.9; ideology of, 75, 79; knowledge about, consensus drawn from (*see* grand hoplite narrative); knowledge about, impediments to, 256–57 (*see also* data; sources); necessity of each city-state to field, 7–8; numbers of in the archaic age, 240–41; the phalanx (*see* phalanx, hoplite); physiology of compared to modern men, 167–68; the polis and, relationship of, xii–xiv, 3–7, 13–14, 176–80, 194–95; social and economic milieu of, xii, 176–80, 194–95; as soldiers of fortune (*see* soldiers of fortune)
hoplite shield: adoption of, 148–49; Assyrian infantry shield and, 99, 180; battle formations, implications for, 57–59, 91–92, 113–14, 116–19, 138–40, 169; as the decisive hoplite innovation, 77–78, 113–14; depictions of, 57–58; disadvantages of, 24–25, 116–17, 162–64; as Greek invention, 99; implications of adopting, xiii, 14–15, 18, 38; moral role of, 270n.7, 272n.22; physical characteristics of, 157–61, 170n.3; use of, 60–61, 161–64; weight of, 138, 161–62, 169; YouTube video showing use of, 139. *See also* shields
Hornblower, Simon, 82n.19, 147, 178
Hunt, Peter, 79, 82n.19
Hybrias the Cretan, 136, 179

iconography: artistic representation of hoplites, difficulty of, 270n.2; battle, representations of, 44, 63–70, 266–67; the Chigi vase (*see* Chigi vase); hoplite equipment, depiction of, 62, 88; the hoplite orthodoxy and, xiii–xiv, 12, 15–16,

35–36; hoplite phalanx, depiction of, 138; shields, depiction of, 44, 57–58, 60–61, 136–37, 157–58, 163; soldiers of fortune depicted in, 182–84; spears, depiction of use of, 142
ideology of hoplites, 75, 79
Iphicrates/Iphikrates, 11, 189

Jameson, Michael, 140–41

Kagan, Donald, 81, 143
Keegan, John, 23–25, 128–29n.41, 142, 148, 269
Keos Survey, 198, 202–6
Köchly, H., 23, 135, 138
Koroneia, battle of, 142–43
Krentz, Peter: collision of hoplite forces, disbelief in, 128n.41; distance between hoplites in the phalanx, 128n.37; end of hoplite battle, "agonal" conventions marking, 244; Greek terminology, changing meanings over time in, 88; hoplite equipment, weight of, 127–28n.28, 265, 273n.27; hoplite equipment and open, fluid style of fighting, compatibility of, 243, 272n.20; knowledge of Greek warfare in practice, our limited, 76; orthodox position, criticism of, xv, 41–42, 117–18; political change in Archaic Greece, hoplites and, 79; pushing forward in battle formations, view of, 59
Kromayer, Johannes, 23, 145, 269
Kunze, Emil, 87–88, 159
Kyriatzi, Evangelia, 214
Kythera Survey, 214–15

Lachmann, Karl, 3
Laconia Survey, 212, 214
Laertes, 194
Latacz, Joachim, 45–47, 78, 85–87, 89, 91, 114
Lawrence, T. E., 185
Lazenby, J. F., 142
Leimbach, Rüdiger, 86
Liddell, Henry George, 144
life expectancy, 173n.57
Liston, Maria, 172n.44
Lord, Albert, 45
Lorimer, H. L.: heroic tactics and contemporary arms and armor, images depicting, 57; Homeric warfare, view of, 44–45, 87; hoplite orthodoxy, contribution to, xiii–xiv, 14–16, 19, 35, 37, 138; iconographic commentary of, 64–67
Luginbill, Robert, 146
Luraghi, Nino, 180–83
Lykurgos/Lykurgus and the Lykurgean system, 6, 77

Ma, John, 92–93
Macan, R. W., 144

Mardonius, 7
Matthew, Christopher, 140, 142
mercenaries. *See* soldiers of fortune
Methana Survey, 207–10
military practices: cavalry, Greek use of, 11; composition of armies, comparison of Greek and Near Eastern, 97–99; dancing as part of hoplite training, 43; equipment, comparison of Greek and Near Eastern, 99–100; fighting tactics, comparison of Greek and Near Eastern, 100–103; the hoplite revolution in, xi–xiv; interactive evolution of the polis, political thought, and, 95–96, 103; length of citizen military service obligation, 167–68; lightly armed troops, Greek use of, 10–11; tactics (*see* battle tactics). *See also* warfare
Miltiades, 98, 149
Mimnermos/Mimnernus, 150n.14, 189–90
Minnesota Messenia Expedition, 196, 214
Mitford, William, 151–52n.58
Momigliano, Arnaldo, 271n.16
Morris, I., 126n.6, 127n.9, 131n.87, 248n.53, 249n.60
Morris, Sarah, 97, 216
Mumford, Lewis, 1

Nagy, Gregory, 89, 129n.55
Near East: Greek soldiers of fortune in, 180–84; "orientalizing" influence on Greek military practices, 96–102
Nebuchadnezzar II (king of Babylon), 185
Necho (king of Egypt), 185
Nicias, 9
Nierhaus, R., 35–36
Nilsson, Martin, xiii–xiv, 12–14, 51–52n.61, 51n.54, 150n.24

Olsen, Claus, 164
Oman, Charles, 53n.112
Orgill, Kyra, 272n.18
Orthagoras of Sicyon, 20
Osborne, R., 115, 127n.24, 130n.83

paeans, 141
Pagondas, 262–63, 272n.19
panoply. *See* armor
Pappadopoulos, J., 216
Papua New Guinea Highlanders, 70–72
Parke, H. W., 182
Parry, Milman, 45, 56n.200
Pausanias, 92, 137, 161
Peisistratus, 3–4, 238
Pericles, 8, 121, 130n.68
Petersen, Wolfgang, 143

phalanx, hoplite: Aristotle on the rise of, 241–42; centrality of for the Greek polis, 13–14; changing social/economic structures and development of, 240–45; depth of, 8–9; emergence of (*see* chronology); forming in the sea, 189; Homer and, 44–47, 85–87; hoplite armor and, relationship of, 35–38, 243 (*see also* armor); in the hoplite orthodoxy, xii; hoplite shield and, 57–59, 113–14, 116–19, 138–40 (*see also* hoplite shield); the nature of, 137–40; Near Eastern influence on development of, 96–97, 100–103; origin of, 29, 42–43, 49, 137, 194–95 (*see also* chronology); representations of, 63–70; second transitional stage after the invention of, 40–41; spacing of men in, 8, 42, 128n.37, 139–40; supremacy of in Greek warfare, 11. *See also* grand hoplite narrative
Pheidon of Argos, 41, 50n.20, 124–25
Philip of Macedon, 11
philological approach, 88–89
Philopoemen, 93
Phocylides of Miletus, 234–36
physiology of modern men compared to Greeks of antiquity, 165–68
Pindar, 1, 262
Pittman, Allen, 139–40, 142, 150n.8, 150n.30
Plato, 1, 43–44, 78, 242, 261–62, 271n.12
Pliny the Elder, 136, 158
Plutarch, 92, 141, 161, 241
police, shields used in riot control by, 139, 164–65
polis, the: conflict based on economic class, prevalence of, 237–40; development of, van Wees *vs.* Hanson on (*see* historical development); farmer-citizen-soldiers, armies consisting of, 9–10, 17–18, 22–23, 34; formation of, warfare-politics connection and, 75; "going hoplite": utilitarian *vs.* ideological reasons for, 75, 78–79; the hoplite revolution and, 120–26; hoplites and, relationship of, xii–xiv, 3–7, 13–14, 20–21, 40–41, 176–80, 194–95; interactive evolution of political thought, military practices, and, 95–96, 103; orthodox view and major challengers on the rise of, 112–16; "polis," usage of the term, 126n.6; rise of, Grote's interpretation of, 4–5; rural settlement and development of, 215–17; transformation of, seventh-century agrarian and military revolutions underlying, 123–26; warships owned by, lack of, 187
political thought, interactive evolution of the polis, military practices, and, 95–96, 103
Polyainos, 92, 137
Polybius, 27, 42, 101, 140–41, 269
population growth, 122–23, 223
Powell, J. E., 144
Pressfield, Steven, 134
Pritchett, W. Kendrick: Greek warfare, contribution to understanding, 134; Hanson's praise for, 23; hoplite orthodoxy, contribution to, 269; the hoplite phalanx in Homer, 114; hoplite warfare in Archaic Greece, 82n.19; Latacz's reading of Homer, historical implications of, 86; the rugby model, support for, 146; spacing between hoplites in the phalanx, 139; "Stele of the Vultures," reference to, 100
Psammetichus I (king of Egypt), 184
Pylos Survey, 214–15

Qurdi-Ashur-lamur, 181

Raaflaub, Kurt: aristocrats in pre-phalanx mass warfare, 129n.56; evolution rather than revolution, hoplite, 114–15, 120; the hoplite shield and phalanx, relationship of, 78; land-owning farmers as hoplites, role in the polis of, 271n.11; Latacz's close formations and the hoplite phalanx, 91; uniqueness of Greek political thought, 131n.101; uniqueness of Greek shield and hoplite arms, 128n.35
Rawlinson, George, 144
Renfrew, C., 196
Rieth, Adolf, 158–59, 161
Runciman, W. G., 79
Rüstow, W., 23, 135, 138
Rutherford, Ian, 141, 151n.39

Salmon, John, 39–42
Sappho, 234
Sargon II (king of Assyria), 98, 181
Scheidel, W., 123
Schleif, Hans, 159
scholarship: the historical approach to, 89–90; the iconographical approach to, 90; the philological approach to, 88–89. *See also* sources
Schwartz, Adam, 90, 116, 128n.28, 139, 146
Schwertfeger, T., 171n.27
Scott, Robert, 144
Sennacherib (king of Assyria), 181
shields: Assyrian, 180; Boeotian, 136–37, 148; circular used by seafaring soldiers, 189; of Dark Age warriors, 114; hoplite (*see* hoplite shield); materials and designs for, 135–37, 157–61; police use of, 139, 164–65; reenactors use of, 139; single-grip, advantages of, 116–17, 163
ships. *See* warships

Sidebottom, Harry, 54n.124
Sitch, Craig, 136
Snodgrass, Anthony: Carian claim to military inventions, denial of, 184; Cartledge's commendation for, 74; Corinthian helmet's craftsmanship, significance of, 72n.7; gradualist critique of the hoplite orthodoxy, xiv, 35–40, 42, 114; Greek warfare, contribution to understanding, 134; Homeric poems as source on warfare, 45, 129n.55; hoplite equipment, weight of, 127–28n.28; hoplite equipment in open and fluid style of fighting, 243; hoplite orthodoxy, contribution to, 269; iconographic commentary of, 67–69; mercenary tradition, mercantile nature of, 186; Near Eastern influences on Greek military development, 96, 99–100, 102, 180; the panoply, 87, 99–100; physical evidence, starting from, 119, 148; population growth in Athens, 131n.87
Snyder, Zack, 134
soldiers of fortune: artwork, depicted in, 182–84; in Egypt and Babylon, 184–86; Greek *vs.* Greek conflicts and, 185–86; hoplites as, 88, 179–80, 190–91; mercantile nature of, impact on Greek economy and, 186–87; in the Near East, 180–84; seaborne expeditions and raiding, 187–90; use of mercenaries by Greek city-states, 9–10
Solon: agrarian reforms and resistance to the redistribution of land, 232; aristocrats and oligarchy, reform of, 6; the hoplite revolution in Athens and, 125–26; moderation in pursuit of wealth urged by, 235; Nilsson's use of, 13; property classes, system of, 20, 229–33, 229–37; the *thetes* class (hired laborers), exploitation of and the uneven distribution of wealth, 232–33; tyrant, pride in not imposing himself as, 238; the *zeugitai* class as yeoman farmers, 229–32
Sophanes, 136
sources: Aristotle as, 79–80; the double-handed hoplite shield, peculiarity of, 77–78; military transformation in Sparta prior to 500, limited knowledge of, 77; problems of, 75–76, 256–57; Tyrtaeus/Tyrtaios, challenge of interpreting, 12–13, 51n.54–55, 76. *See also* data
Southern Argolid Survey, 205–7
Sparta: as a conquest-state, 77; disciplinary punishment, 161–62; distribution of land and wealth, concerns regarding, 233; emergence of hoplites in, 20; the hoplite revolution in, 125; major military transformation prior to 500, limited knowledge of, 77; membership in the polis and military service in, 97; political stability, strategies for achieving, 239; soldier-citizens of, landowners as, 224; transition to oligarchy in, 6
Starr, C. G., 130–31n.85
Strabo, 240

Tarn, W. W., 23
Themistocles, 21
Theognis of Megara, 233–35
Thompson, James, 166
Thucydides: battle formations and procedure, 8–9, 42–44, 53n.114, 117–18, 138, 140–41, 145; battle narratives of, collective action recorded in, 264; "hoplite," usage of, 137; *ōthismós* in, 144; phalanx in battle of Mantinea, description of, 3; "phalanx," usage of, 137; pipers, use of, 65, 138; "stand at ease" command recorded by, 168; Syracuse, battle of, 137; on war, 1; war as a violent teacher, 262
Tiglath-pileser III (king of Assyria), 98, 180–81
Troy (Petersen), 143
Trundle, Matthew, 182
Tullius, Servius, 40
Tuplin, C. J., 198–99
tyrants, 18–20, 28–29, 114
Tyrtaeus/Tyrtaois: difficulties of interpreting, 12–13, 51n.54–55, 76; fighting tactics described by, 42, 47–49, 138, 150n.14; hoplite ethos advanced by, 121, 177, 179; Lykurgos, no mention of, 77; phalanx, references to, 118–19; redistribution of land in Sparta, 233

van Wees, Hans: agrarianism and hoplite service, break between, 271n.12; battle formation, spacing of men in, 140; critique of the hoplite orthodoxy, xv–xvii; data sources used by, 195; evidence used by Hanson, challenge to, 217; fighting in the Highlands of Papua New Guinea, 70; fighting styles and equipment, fluidity of, 46–47, 70, 115; the gentleman farmer model and the competition for wealth, 236–40 (*see also* historical development); gradualism of, 91, 95; Hanson's yeoman farmer model, critique of (*see* historical development); Homer, interpretation of, 46–47, 86, 91, 101; hoplite shield and massed combat, view of, 58–59, 78, 91–92, 116–17; iconographic commentary of, 65–66, 68, 70; Near Eastern influence on Greek military practices, ignoring of, 96; phalanx, timing of development of, 49, 152n.74; propertied leisure class, hoplites as product of, 177, 195; soldiers of fortune, Greeks as, 179–80; soldiers of fortune and of Greek city-states, relationship of, 186; Tyrtaeus,

van Wees, Hans (*continued*)
interpretation of, 47–49; working-class hoplite, characteristics of typical, 271n.11
Veith, Georg, 23, 145
Viggiano, Greg, 91
Vikings, 186–87, 189

Wagstaff, M., 196
warfare: change in Greek after Persian invasions of the fifth century, 23; connection to politics, formation of the polis and, 75; division of forces by weapons, 97–99, 102–3, 149; economy of hoplite, 17–18, 23; formations (*see* battle formations; phalanx, the); frequency of, 74, 178–79, 261–62; Hanson's interpretation of hoplite, 21–28, 134–35; Homer as source on, 44–47; the hoplite revolution in, xi–xiv; length of Archaic wars, 135; paradoxes in Greek, 7–8; tactics (*see* battle tactics). *See also* military practices
warships: aristocratic ownership of, 187–90; seaborne expeditions of soldiers of fortune, 187–90; wars for naval hegemony and adoption of the trireme, 240
weapons: spears, 141–42, 150n.8. *See also* equipment
West, M. L., 246n.23
Wheeler, Everett, 96, 143, 273n.31, 274n.33
Wilamowitz-Moellendorff, Ulrich von, 12
Wolf, Friedrich August, 3
Woodhouse, W. J., 145
Woodward, A. M., 12–13

Xenophon: battle narratives of, 264–65, 268; battle tactics, discussion of, 43; citizen *vs.* mercenary armies, 173n.60; exemption of Athenian citizens from work, schemes for, 242–43; as Greek commander, 162; the Greek mercenary tradition and, 182; Koroneia, on the battle of, 53n.116, 142–43; landowners "toil" on large classical estates, 228; the prebattle paean, 141; pushing and shoving of hoplites, 144, 147; Spartan disciplinary punishment, holding the shield as, 161–62; spears, hoplite use of, 141; "stand at ease" command recorded by, 168; warfare as a nearly constant state, 261–62

Yadin, Yigael, 100
yeoman or middling farmers. *See* historical development